IN THIS SERIES

Socio-Economic Surveys of Three Villages in Andhra Pradesh:
A Study of Agrarian Relations
Edited by V. K. Ramachandran, Vikas Rawal, Madhura Swaminathan

Socio-Economic Surveys of Two Villages in Rajasthan:
A Study of Agrarian Relations
Edited by Madhura Swaminathan and Vikas Rawal

Socio-Economic Surveys of Three Villages in Karnataka:
A Study of Agrarian Relations
Edited by Madhura Swaminathan and Arindam Das

Socio-Economic Surveys of Three Villages in Tripura:
A Study of Agrarian Relations
Edited by Madhura Swaminathan and Ranjini Basu

SOCIO-ECONOMIC SURVEYS OF
Three Villages in Tripura

A STUDY OF AGRARIAN RELATIONS

Edited by

Madhura Swaminathan and Ranjini Basu

Foundation for
Agrarian
Studies

Tulika Books

Published by

Tulika Books

www.tulikabooks.in

in association with

Foundation for Agrarian Studies

www.agrarianstudies.org

© Foundation for Agrarian Studies 2019

First published in India 2019

ISBN: 978-81-937329-4-6

Printed at Chaman Enterprises, Delhi 110 002

Foreword

The fourth book in the Socio-Economic Survey series of the Foundation for Agrarian Studies is on Tripura, a State that has been relatively neglected in economic development research on India.

The book draws on primary data collected in Tripura as part of the Foundation's Project on Agrarian Relations in India (PARI). PARI, which began in 2005–06, is a project to study villages over a wide range of different agro-ecological regions in India. The major objectives of PARI are

- to analyse village-level production, production systems, and livelihoods, and the socio-economic characteristics of different strata of the rural population;
- to conduct specific studies of sectional deprivation in rural India, particularly with regard to the Dalit and Scheduled Tribe populations, women, specific minorities, and the income-poor; and
- to report on the state of basic village amenities and the access of the rural people to the facilities of modern life.

The project now covers 27 villages in 12 States of the country.

In the Tripura Round of PARI, household-level surveys were conducted in 2016 in three villages: Khakchang in Dasda block of North Tripura district, Mainama in Manu block of Dhalai district, and Muhuripur in Jolaibari block of South Tripura district. These villages were first surveyed in 2005 by a team from the Foundation for Agrarian Studies for a background study for the first *Tripura Human Development Report, 2007* (the lead author of the *Report*, Madhura Swaminathan, is the lead editor of this volume). The three villages represent three distinct agrarian and farming systems in the State. Khakchang in North district is a resettled forest village, once characterised by *jhum* (swidden or slash-and-burn) cultivation, with a small sector of lowland agriculture. Mainama village in Dhalai district has lowland and *tila* or upland cultivation. Muhuripur in South district is dominated by the lowland agriculture that is characteristic of the southern plains. Each village is distinct with respect to its tribe and caste structure.

The three villages have been surveyed in detail, by means of household- and village-level questionnaires, and a rich database has been brought to bear on the study of a hitherto much understudied State. A feature of the book is that the authors of each chapter were involved in the entire process of research – participating in fieldwork, data entry, and analysis, and writing chapters.

The book is based on fieldwork conducted in 2016 and 2005, and, as such, deals with the period when the Left Front in Tripura was in government. One contribution, however, is more contemporary, and places development in longer perspective. The interview with former Chief Minister Manik Sarkar reviews social and economic development in Tripura after 1978, and also covers events after 2018.

V. K. RAMACHANDRAN
Series Editor
August 1, 2019

Preface

This book is an outcome of the Tripura Round of the Project on Agrarian Relations in India (PARI) conducted by the Foundation for Agrarian Studies. It is based mainly on primary data collected in three villages of Tripura.

The first section of the book deals with the development trajectory of Tripura since 1978, and introduces the three study villages. Each of the villages has a distinct agro-ecological and social structure. Section II is on agrarian structure, production conditions, and agrarian relations in the three villages. Section III deals with the level and distribution of household incomes. It also deals with two distinctive features of the rural economy of Tripura, the role of homestead cultivation and rubber plantations in rural incomes. Section IV is on aspects of the standard of living. It includes chapters on household ownership of assets, household amenities, and housing. It also covers issues of schooling and education in the village. The fifth section of the book provides a summary of agrarian relations in the three villages. The last chapter brings together evidence from our village surveys on public support to rural households.

We are grateful to the many persons who contributed to the making of this book. Manik Sarkar followed and facilitated our research from 2005, when he helped us select the three study villages, to 2019, when he gave the interview that provides a framework for understanding agriculture and rural development issues in Tripura after 1978.

The fieldwork team was led by Shamsher Singh, Arindam Das, and Tapas Singh Modak. The team comprised authors of this book associated with the Foundation for Agrarian Studies as well as eleven investigators from Tripura, Anurani Debbarma, Birulal Debbarma, Hirak Debbarma, Jharna Debbarma, Pramod Debbarma, Prasanna Debbarma, Pritam Debbarma,

Shibani Debbarma, Lison Marak, Daya Mohan Tripura, and Jiban Tripura. Kalyan Das translated all relevant material and participated in the surveys as well. Arindam Das, Tapas Singh Modak, and T. Sivamurugan supervised data entry and processing.

Efforts of officers of the Government of Tripura, and particularly officials from the Planning (P&C) Department and the Rural Development (Panchayat) Department, were invaluable in helping with the logistics of fieldwork and different stages of this project. Anindya Kumar Bhattacharya of the Government of Tripura coordinated these efforts.

Preliminary findings from the survey were presented at a consultation meeting held at Agartala on March 18–19, 2017. Participants from the All India Kisan Sabha, Ganamukti Parishad, All India Democratic Women's Association, All India Agricultural Workers Union, and the Department of Agriculture and Horticulture, Government of Tripura gave us detailed comments on our presentations. Our special thanks to Narayan Kar, Ratan Das, Matilal Sarkar, Pranab Debbarma, and Haradhan Debnath. Biplab Sarkar and Niladri Dharmade presentations at the consultation and commented on draft chapters. Venkatesh Athreya, Aparajita Bakshi, Kaushik Bora, and Shamsher Singh provided inputs for individual chapters.Pushpita Dhar, Subhajit Patra, and Divya Devadiga assisted us in preparing the manuscript for publication. Bipin Chandran assisted V. K. Ramachandran with the interview with Manik Sarkar. Sandipan Baksi coordinated and oversaw the entire project.

The Rosa Luxemburg Stiftung (RLS) supported the Foundation for Agrarian Studies at various stages of this book project: during the village surveys in 2016, the follow-up case studies in 2017, the workshop at Agartala, and, finally, the writing of this book. The Editor of *The Hindu* permitted us to republish the article titled "The Tripura Model."

Parvathi Menon gave editorial advice on every chapter, giving detailed comments on content and style. The current text owes much to her efforts. Indira Chandrasekhar and her team at Tulika Books gave the book its final shape. M. V. Bhaskar of TNQ Books designed the cover.

MADHURA SWAMINATHAN
RANJINI BASU
July 2019

Contents

Tables, Maps, and Figures

CHAPTER 7: Agrarian Structure, Production, and Agrarian Relations in Mainama

CHAPTER 8: Agrarian Structure, Production,
and Agrarian Relations in Muhuripur

Chapter 9: Employment and Wages of Manual Workers

CHAPTER 10: Status and Determinants of Banking in the North-Eastern Region: The Case of Tripura

CHAPTER 11: Income Levels and Variations in Three Villages of Tripura

CHAPTER 12: Homestead Economy of Tripura

CHAPTER 13: Natural Rubber in Tripura

CHAPTER 16: Literacy and Schooling in Three Villages of Tripura

CHAPTER 18: Public Support for Rural Households

SECTION I

The Context

1

Tripura's Development Journey

Interview with Manik Sarkar

V. K. Ramachandran

The Left Front led by the Communist Party of India (Marxist) won the elections to the Tripura Legislative Assembly and formed the government in the State from 1978 to 1988, and again from 1993 to March 2018, 35 years in all.

In 1978, more than three decades after Independence and after three decades of Congress rule, Tripura was severely underdeveloped and lacking in democratic institutions and practice. The modernisation of Tripura's economy and society, the transformation of its democratic institutions, and the recognition in practice of tribal administrative and cultural rights, were all achievements of the Left Front government. In its very first year, the Left Front began the implementation of land reform, established a two-tier system of local government, established the Tripura Tribal Areas Autonomous District Council (TTAADC), and recognised Kokborok as an official language of the State. Tripura's progress from then through 2018, years in which the State saw broad progress in school education, road connectivity, electricity generation, agricultural development, new incomes from the formal sector, the establishment of peace, and the strict implementation of reservations for people of the Scheduled Tribes and Scheduled Castes, was a historic development journey.

No person is more qualified to speak of and analyse Tripura's development journey than **Manik Sarkar**, Chief Minister of Tripura from 1998 to 2018 and Polit Bureau Member of the Communist Party of India (Marxist). Manik Sarkar joined the Left movement in Tripura during the struggles around the demand for food in 1967, and first entered the Legislative Assembly in 1980.

In this interview with **V. K. Ramachandran**, conducted in Agartala on June 13 and 14, 2019, he reviews the achievements of Left Front governments in Tripura, and briefly discusses the situation after 2018 and the rise of one-Party authoritarianism in the State.

V. K. Ramachandran: Let us begin by discussing the transformative impact of the Left movement and Left Front government on society, economy, and government in Tripura.

Manik Sarkar: Tripura was for long a princely State. It merged with the Indian Union in 1949. Tripura was ruled by a feudal princely family, and the economy of the State was dependent completely on agriculture. It had a very backward agriculture; at that point, it was hard even to imagine modern agriculture in the State.

When the Communist Party-led government came to office in Tripura, the Congress had been in power at the Centre since Independence and in the State for almost three decades. This was a period of no perceptible development in fields such as agriculture, education, health care, electricity, or road and other connectivity. The question of industrial progress did not even arise. For the people at large in the State, it was not on the agenda at all.

Starting from "below zero"
With regard to infrastructure, the government did not start from point zero but from something negative. There were many parts of the State with no roads, hospitals, schools, safe drinking water, electricity. We had only two or three colleges. Rail connectivity was still a dream, quite unthinkable at that time. Air connectivity meant one aircraft a day, with no certain time of arrival or departure. You went to the airport in the morning, and by evening you had a chance of getting on the plane to Kolkata.

Beginnings of democratic change
The first Left Front government was formed in January 1978. Before tackling economic issues – education, agriculture, and other aspects of development, for instance – the first Left Front government took some very important steps towards democratic change. These were reforms for which the Communists and the Left had organised struggles during the period of princely rule and Congress rule.

Among these changes was the recognition of the main language of the Scheduled Tribes, Kokborok, a policy without which mass education or educational development in general could not be thought of. Another such change was the reservation of seats in educational institutions and in government employment for people from the Scheduled Castes and Tribes. This had been policy earlier, but the Left Front government was the first to implement it, and it did so very strictly.

The government began to restore tribal land that had illegally been transferred to non-tribal people to people of the Scheduled Tribes. It began the task of implementing radical land reform.

A further reform was the establishment of the Tripura Tribal Areas Autonomous District Council (TTAADC), initially under the provisions of the Seventh Schedule of the Constitution of India and subsequently under the provisions of the Sixth Schedule of the Constitution.

The government held democratic elections to panchayats. Although an Act existed during the Congress regime, I for one had never seen a democratic election to a panchayat. During my years in university, I learned that in some villages, village leaders, men with landed property (called *sardar*), would call people together and they would choose people to be chiefs or *pradhans* of village panchayats. The *sardar* would call for a show of hands and the members of the gathering would have to comply (any person who did not do so would not receive employment the next day on the farm of the *sardar*).

That was the system – a mockery of panchayat elections! When elections by secret ballot for the formation of panchayat bodies were introduced by the Left Front government, people were unbelieving: "Secret ballot for Parliament and Assembly elections, yes – but for panchayats too?" And when they came to vote, they did so in very festive mood.

With regard to urban bodies, there was a municipality in Agartala from the Maharaja's time. During the Congress regime, there were no elections for almost 30 years – it was always an administrator. The Left Front government organised elections in Agartala and began subsequently to form urban bodies in sub-divisional headquarters. These were initially nominated bodies, though elections by secret ballot were held within a year or year-and-a-half of their formation.

School education in Tripura
The Left Front government paid the utmost attention to school education. Where education had been free at the primary level, the Left Front now introduced free education until class 10. It also introduced free education for girls at the undergraduate level, a very important measure, and one that helped the people a great deal.

The government provided, particularly in primary classes, bananas and biscuits for children at school (Tripura was perhaps the first State after Tamil Nadu to provide food to children in schools). That one move, I can tell you, galvanised the people. That children would be given free food, bananas and biscuits, when they went to school could hardly be imagined.

As a matter of fact, we in the student movement had raised this demand in previous years. In those days, when school pupils who had participated in our programmes returned to school, teachers would admonish them and twist their ears for imagining that it was possible to receive free food in school. "These Communist boys and girls are creating trouble for us all," they said, "and destroying your good sense." It was the same teachers ("*didimoni*") who later served children the bananas and biscuits that came as a part of the new education policy.

The first Left Front government implemented the food-for-work programme, which helped the poorest of the poor, particularly the rural poor, very much. During the Congress regime, there was periodic starvation accompanied by starvation deaths. Parents were forced to sell their children, men came down from their villages and went in search of work to other States and to Bangladesh. Agriculture, such as it was, did not generate much employment. Among the tribal population, *jhum* (shifting or slash-and-burn) cultivation was widespread. By its very nature, *jhum* cultivation did not create work on any significant scale in the countryside.

In these circumstances, food-for-work brought real economic help to the people and was a very important programme.

Impediments to social progress
I have spoken of these achievements, but taking up these issues and implementing them one by one was no smooth sailing!

When land that had illegally been transferred from the tribal people was restored to them, our opponents created much confusion. When the TTAADC (Tripura Tribal Areas Autonomous District Council) was about to be constituted, reactionary forces under the leadership of the Congress again tried to create trouble and unrest. In 1980, even communal conflict was created.

These conflicts were overcome by the government because of the help and cooperation of the people of our State. The people of Tripura wanted peace, and they wanted to remain united. That general sentiment actually helped a lot, as did the confidence of the people in the Left Front, and the conviction that the Left Front government would never do anything to harm the common people of our State.

The Left Front government of 1993

The first Left Front government thus laid the foundation for future development. In my understanding, the achievements of subsequent Left Front governments were made possible by the policy initiatives of the first Left Front government.

The Congress–TUJS government, which used the support of the extremist forces, was the outcome of a conspiracy hatched by the Congress at the Centre when Rajiv Gandhi was Prime Minister.

In 1993, Dasarath Deb became Chief Minister of the third Left Front government. He had been Minister in charge of tribal welfare and education, and subsequently Deputy Chief Minister, in the first phase of the Left Front government. The Congress–TUJS government sought to destroy many of the achievements of the Left Front, so we had to clear the ashes and start afresh. Once again, we had to overcome political obstacles, including the onslaught of extremism. Many extremists did of course surrender, but new groups were formed as well.

A new approach to development planning

The fourth Left Front government took office in 1998. It took a completely new approach to development planning in the State.

The first main area of concentration was agriculture, and the major slogan in this regard was "attain self-sufficiency in the production of foodgrain." Before 1998 Tripura was dependent on imports of foodgrain for survival. While peasants remained poor, large sums of money were spent on bringing food from outside. The dependence on imports distorted economic growth, and restricted the growth of a modern workforce and industry in the State.

In this effort to attain self-sufficiency, the government turned to the agricultural scientists of Tripura and organised a discussion with them. We asked: why is Tripura dependent on the import of foodgrain? Why can we not stand on our own feet in this regard? You are scientists in the field, most of you are from Tripura – can you help overcome this problem? We assured them of any kind of help they needed from the government. The scientists told us that it was the first time such a question or task had been asked of them. They said that if the government was to "trust us, lead us, and help us," they would be able to change agriculture in the State. Our development efforts and the ten-year perspective plan for agriculture followed.

In order to put the government's vision for agriculture into practice, certain specific tasks had to be completed. First, 60 per cent of the area of Tripura is hill or forest. Since arable land is limited, we had to set targets for double and triple cropping. Secondly, the area under irrigation had to be expanded. Thirdly, with regard to other inputs, the government had to ensure the supply of quality seeds and fertilizers to farmers at subsidised rates. Fourthly, farmers needed credit. We organised meetings of bankers and urged them to advance credit to farmers. Kisan credit cards were issued. Next, the government began to develop marketing infrastructure, without which there could be no forward linkages from agriculture.

Our effort was first with respect to rice cultivation, after which we began to diversify. We conducted a survey to understand internal demand, and from rice, we moved to mustard, potato, and horticultural crops. We also began to produce seeds locally.

We then shifted towards inland fisheries, and meat, poultry, and milk production. Average per capita annual consumption of fish and meat crossed the all-India average, and per capita consumption of eggs was also in the region of the national average. Poultry and egg production suffered on account of regular culling of birds during episodes of bird flu (the virus spread from Bangladesh, to which we are adjacent). Although we wanted to improve milk production, this was an area in which we were below the national average with regard to annual per capita consumption. We mentioned this matter in the Assembly and outside, and noted that it would take time and effort to reach the national level.

Infrastructural development
Agriculture thus contributed to employment and the development of the labour force. So did employment under the Mahatma Gandhi National Rural Employment Guarantee Act (MGNREGA). We need MGNREGA not as a mere earth-cutting scheme, but to develop roads and water bodies.

Road connectivity in the State developed. In many places, our rural roads were in better condition than the National Highway! We created multiple access roads to different locations; it reached a point where panchayat chairpersons would stay awake at night thinking of routes along which to build new roads.

Where we were once an electricity-deficient State, we are now surplus with regard to power generation. We needed the help of Bangladesh to complete and commission the Palatana Power Plant in the Udaipur sub-division, in return for which we were required to sell them electricity.

The Congress government was very hesitant to approve the proposal and to share electricity. Finance Minister P. Chidambaram opposed the gas-based power project at Monarchak in the Sonamura sub-division, West Tripura, on the grounds that Tripura was a small State that did not need to generate so much power. Manmohan Singh finally accepted the proposal for Monarchak and to share electricity from the Palatana project with Bangladesh. Palatana now supplies power to different parts of the State and other parts of North Eastern India.

In doing all of these, the State created scope for industries and industrialisation. In order to build industry, road connectivity, power, the purchasing power of the people at large, and peace and tranquility are all very important. Investors would be attracted not by the size of our market, which is very small, but by the amenities and incentives that we offered. At that time the North Eastern States were competing with each other for attracting industrial investment. Not many investors came to Tripura from outside the State, but small and medium investors from within the State did respond to our incentives. Although we cannot claim a big change in respect of industrialisation, there was definite progress. No doubt about that.

This development of agriculture and rural purchasing power, and the consequent development of trade and commerce, industry, and the market in general, created a new labour force in a significant way. Without such development, the government would not have been able to address the problem of employment even to the extent that it did. We know, however, that no government in our country can address this problem by creating employment only in the government sector. Unemployment continues to be a burning problem in the country as a whole and in Tripura.

Peace played an important part in development in the years after the formation of the fourth Left Front government.

In the initial stages the situation was such that we could not go out into the field and implement the plans we had chalked out. Implementing officers – engineers, agricultural scientists, doctors, teachers – could not work freely or fearlessly because of the extremist onslaught.

Two or three extremist outfits were at work. They had camps across the border, which was very porous. ULFA (United Liberation Front of Assam), NSCN(IM) (National Socialist Council of Nagaland [Isak-Muivah]), NSCN(K) (National Socialist Council of Nagaland [Khaplang]), and Tripura outfits functioned across the border. They had the blessings and support of the ISI (Inter-Services Intelligence).

There was also a political aspect to this. Extremist groups understood that if the Left Front governments were able to implement their programme, the extremists and their political masters and guides would be squeezed out of their political space. It was their slogan that they would not lay down arms until the Left Front was removed from government.

Thus, at one point, the main task of the Left Front government was to bring peace to the State, a task that would not be achieved without combating extremism. But the policy that we worked out was unique. We analysed their demands; we saw that hardly any development had occurred in the tribal areas and that there were genuine grounds for their grievances. The first three Left Front governments tried their best to address these questions.

When one outfit surrendered, another appeared. Our approach at first was to ask them to put forward their demands in concrete terms. We explained that the demand for an independent Tripura was unacceptable; other than that, we asked them to put forward their social and economic demands. We explained that they could speak to us or to representatives of the Central government, that we would not obstruct talks.

We asked them, in essence, to give peace a chance. We said: Tripura has been ruled by the maharajas and by the Congress; the problems of tribal people were created by the erstwhile rulers. We asked the people to give time to the Left Front government to implement its programme. The Left Front government is not taking away the rights of the people; on the contrary, it is returning rights to the tribal people – rights, for example, to their own language, to education and job security, and to land.

We went to the family members of the young men and women who had joined the extremists and asked them to pursue and bring back their young people to normal life, and persuade them to shun the path of violence and join the democratic stream.

We also asked them to support our basic peace and development approach: that development required peace and that peace would be sustainable only if there was development.

At the same time, the security forces were allowed to deal with and combat extremists, but were told to function carefully. They were not to be trigger-happy. Firepower was not to be used without judging a situation and unless the security forces were compelled to do so. If people not connected with extremists were hit, the extremists would gain ground.

I had asked you in 2016 about the Left Front government's strategy for peace. You said it had three component parts.

Yes. First, an inclusive political campaign drawing on all sections of the people for peace; secondly, the implementation of development programmes focussing on the tribal population; and thirdly, security measures.

For proper development of the State, the tribal areas had to be developed. We declared on the floor of the Assembly that of every 100 rupees spent on development, 60 to 70 rupees would be spent on development of the tribal areas. We were able to build a common platform on this matter: there was no negativity or questioning with regard to this decision.

How would you fix the dates on this change? By which year was peace achieved?

At no point did we claim that the problem of extremism had completely been overcome. The continued existence of NLFT outfits and the Tiger Force and their camps was known to us and the Government of India. When you came back from your field studies in 2016 and you said that the situation had changed completely, I told you that although we had the upper hand, the problem was not entirely over. These organisations had the backing and support of other extremist organisations in the North Eastern region. They were fostered and nurtured indirectly by the CIA and ISI. They did not like to see peace in India and in the North East.

Nevertheless, if we are to go by the annual reports on internal security sent by the Police department to the Home Ministry, reports that provide data on extremist-related incidents (including, for example, data on the number of attacks, the number of killings, and the number of abductions), for five to six years prior to the end of our government in February 2018, the curve had declined with regard to these parameters. The number of occurrences in respect of some of the parameters was down to zero in the years preceding 2018. The curve had started declining seven to eight years prior to February 2018. Without that happening, our development work would not have been possible.

Let us now turn to the role of women in Tripura's development transformation under the Left.

The part played by women in the development of the democratic movement and overall development was brilliant.

During the period of the Left Front government, in agitational programmes and in political campaigns, women contributed the lion's share. In many places and on many occasions, the number of women participants exceeded the number of men in these movements. This was a legacy of the Ganamukti Parishad days, when Dasarath Deb led the movement and special attention was paid to organise tribal women.

We must recognise the very important role of women in the development of the democratic left movement in Tripura.

In the local bodies, where 50 per cent of seats are reserved for women, office-bearers laboured hard and sincerely – they did not know how to hide the truth – and those who worked under women's leadership could not undermine the efforts of women leaders to develop the State.

With regard to work under the Mahatma Gandhi National Rural Employment Guarantee Scheme, about 65 per cent of the workers were women. Once again, the serious and sincere work by women, who did their best to create assets through their work, must be properly appreciated.

On women entering new spheres of economic and social activity when the Left Front government was in office

We paid particular attention to including women in government work and activity, including field-level work. We recruited more women in the police, and women became a presence in traffic management and in police station management. We made an effort to provide space for women in the posts of Block Development Officers, Sub-Divisional Magistrates, and District Magistrates.

Women were important in the creation of work through self-employment and incomes through self-help groups. Women began to invest in small enterprises, and tribal and non-tribal women entered rural markets as shop owners, as they had not done in earlier years.

What were the broad changes in the socio-economic characteristics of different classes in Tripura society over this period?

That question cannot be answered easily, and not without proper study and analysis.

Nevertheless, I can say from my limited experience that a middle class has been growing very fast in our society. This is a section that was able to utilise the new economic, educational, and other opportunities that have been created. Their purchasing power has increased. This middle class is different from the middle class as it existed and as we understood earlier: the middle class that has emerged today cannot be equated with the middle class of the past. Among them is a section that is not against neo-liberalism; indeed, who believe that neoliberal economic policy is good for them. There are other sections that have been working in the banking and insurance sectors and public sector undertakings, persons with relatively high incomes and with many modern facilities available to them. Many of them are not inimical to neoliberal policies. They influence society in different, subtle ways. Their sons and daughters have been groomed in a new atmosphere; they have regular discussions on lifestyle and on the standard of living that they enjoy.

These new influences are reflected in the sphere of politics. This section is not interested in what we are saying about changing the socio-political system and creating a classless, exploitation-free society. Most of them cannot actually grasp these ideas or understanding.

In this respect, the conditions that prevailed during my school-going and university days do not prevail now. New problems confront the development of a real democratic movement and Left movement.

In the countryside, some households began to earn new incomes from salaries and new incomes from commercial agriculture.

There were also absentee landowners. In dealing with their land, they had new ideas on mechanisation, new systems of cultivation and multi-cropping, and forward linkages. Of course, capitalism in agriculture is not as developed in Tripura as in many parts of the rest of India. Those who we call the "new rich" are rich in relation to this State and its economy.

This group arose among people of the Scheduled Tribes and non-Scheduled Tribes. The changes that occurred in their lives between our surveys of 2005 and 2016, for example, were phenomenal.

Just phenomenal. It is likely that this section generally voted against us in the most recent Assembly elections.

Did you see their hostility coming?

Yes, to some extent. Our approach is class struggle, and their understanding is that the way the Communists want to change society and the country is not going to help them. Between our understanding and the ideology of the new rich is a contradiction, one that cannot be underestimated.

Their new economic status is, in fact, a result of the development policies of the Left.

Exactly. The development that has taken place in Tripura over this period is because of our policies.

One incontestable fact emerges from the data and from all you have said in this interview: decades of Left rule brought immense change for the poor in Tripura. So why did the Left lose so badly in the election?

The most important reason is that power in the hands of a State government is very very limited. As a result of our policies, people's expectations grew. In order to meet them, we needed finances, and the Central government, Congress and BJP, did not help us in that respect. They knew that if they met our demands for increased funds, our popularity among the people would grow even more. It was a deliberate political measure to prevent us from meeting the expectations of the people, particularly with regard to employment.

Before the Assembly election, the BJP raised the slogan, "Give us a missed call today, and we will give you a job when we win the election." They announced that there were 52,000 State government posts lying vacant. This was a false figure; the number was far less than 25,000, since it was our practice regularly to fill vacant posts in the State government (there were, however, vacancies in Central government posts). The BJP campaign was that all 52,000 posts would be filled in the first year of a BJP government being voted to power.

The BJP distributed lakhs of leaflets among the people which said that if voted to power, they would implement the recommendations of the Seventh Central Pay Commission *in toto*. They said that those who now earn salaries of 20,000 rupees a month would earn 40,000 rupees, those who earn 40,000 rupees would earn 80,000 rupees, and those who earn 65,000 to 70,000 rupees would earn more than a lakh.

With regard to the MGNREGA, we demanded that it be expanded, while the Central government cut back on allocations to the scheme. During the election campaign, however, the BJP said that if they won the election, they would increase the number of guaranteed days of employment under the scheme from 100 days to 200 days, and the minimum daily wages from 170 rupees to 340 rupees.

With regard to social pensions, our government gave pensions of 700 rupees to 1,100 rupees per person per month. It was no small achievement to have ensured pension coverage for more than 4,00,000 people in a State such as Tripura. The BJP promised that they would raise the amount to 2,000 rupees if voted to government.

The campaign also won tribal support.

Since its inception, the Left Front government worked for the tribal people – in the spheres of health, education, culture, income enhancement, and employment, and for their rightful share in government.

In recent years, however, the new rich and developing middle class, students, and youth – some even from traditional CPI(M) families – began to imagine a separate tribal State, created by means of bifurcation of the State of Tripura. In a fully tribal State, they thought, all jobs, contracts, appointments, admissions would go 100 per cent to tribal people. The Left Front government implemented 31 per cent reservation strictly; but in a separate tribal State, there would be 100 per cent provision for Scheduled Tribe people.

In an earlier phase, extremist organisations had called for an independent Tripura (*swadhin* Tripura). While independence had been rejected as a wrong slogan, the creation of a new State by bifurcating the old one had occurred in other parts of the country and appeared possible to them here as well. From the Central government, none other than the Prime Minister's Office encouraged this idea.

We cannot ignore the fact that a section of our traditional supporters, that is, people who had a role in bringing the Left Front to office and sustaining it, were misled by this propaganda. They thought: we have seen more than 25 years of Left Front governments, now let us see if the BJP can deliver on their promises. It may be possible, they thought, because the BJP is managing the show from Delhi, and the Prime Minister, and Finance and Home Ministers themselves have made the promises. The propaganda of the BJP actually created that level of illusion among the people, who began to think: if we push the button for them, we may benefit.

So last year, at the time of the Assembly election, did you see it coming?

No.

We countered their propaganda with evidence. We showed that these promises had not been implemented in the BJP-ruled States. We said that when we raised these issues, the Centre did not concede our demands. (And now that they have won the elections, they have not implemented what they promised.)

We did our best to make people understand, but this very slogan, "Let us change," had effect; in this system, the desire for change is inevitable and not that wrong. It is not like Kerala, where governments have changed every five years. People had seen this government for more than 25 years and they thought: "Let us see. If the BJP implements these policies, good; if not, we shall oust them after five years." In Sikkim, too, a long-standing government was voted out.

Your view is that the Assembly election reflected new demands and aspirations, rather than alienation from or hostility to the Left.

Yes, this is the basic ground reality.

In the last Autonomous District Council (ADC) elections, our share of total votes came down by eight or nine percentage points. We tried to identify the causes, and respond with ideological, political, and organisational measures.

At the time of the formation of ADC village committees (which correspond somewhat to gram panchayats), we saw improvements, although we did not fully cover the damage that had been done. We won the panchayat elections, we won elections to the ADC and to ADC village committees. In the Assembly election, we believed that although the Left Front would lose some seats, it would form the government.

When you are in government for more than 25 years, then new and fresh people, who have no experience of class struggle, or mass struggle and repression, become members of panchayats, Members of the Legislative Assembly, and of the Autonomous District Council, and possess different positions. They cannot be blamed for this. Yet I would say that the direct link between our organisations and the mass of common people was weakened to a certain extent. It is undoubtedly an organisational weakness. In addition, the level of political consciousness and ideological understanding of the general membership of our class and mass organisations was not adequate to meet the challenge we faced.

Another factor was that, at the grassroots level, I would not say that there was corruption but that favouritism was developing. In many areas, this alienated a section of the people from us, people who thought: let the

Left Front be voted out of government, and if the new government fails, then they too can be changed and we shall oust them as well.

So there was no profound alienation of the masses from the Left?

No, I think not. The voting figures, too, do not indicate it.

What explains the further events – the inability to function, the further slipping in the recent election?

It is because they began the campaign of terror right from the start.

They were aware that this victory of theirs was not because of their policies, politics, or ideology, but was won by means of money power, use of the mass media, especially social media, and all the illusions they created.

On March 3, 2018, the results were known by noon, and the attacks began that afternoon. Their main target? Our middle-rank cadre, local committee members, and sub-divisional committee members. They targeted our mass organisations and our Party offices. That is how they began.

During the Congress–TUJS regime, the chosen method of repression was mainly individual annihilation. In the present regime, nine of our comrades have been killed. Their overall tactics, however, are not the same as during the Congress–TUJS period.

Today, they are subjecting our supporters to extreme psychological pressure, while at the same time attacking their means of livelihood. They do not allow our supporters to use their agricultural fields, water bodies, shops, or vehicles to earn a daily income and maintain their households.

Many households in Tripura have one or two government employees. Most households in the countryside receive employment through MGNREGA. In urban areas, most families have a member receiving employment through the Tripura Urban Employment Programme (TUEP). They told such people that they would lose their jobs if they continued with the Left. With regard to social pension schemes, they drew up a chart of 40,000 to 45,000 people whom they threatened to exclude from the list. They told people who were getting assistance through housing schemes that they would not receive the next tranche of government aid if they did not stop supporting the Left.

Where a man is a government employee and his wife a worker of the All-India Democratic Women's Association, the man is told that he will be transferred if his wife does not stop working for the organisation. They tell him: your daughter is in college; who can guarantee that she will come back safe in the evening? Your son is a graduate, and whether or not he gets a job depends on you. Do you want a family that can live in peace? If you do, then stop working with Left organisations. If you continue to do so, all will be shattered.

So they have killed people, maimed people (and have, in some cases, prevented injured people from going to hospital), and have attacked our offices and mass media sources.

The panchayat by-elections took place in this context. It was nothing but a mockery of elections; in 96 per cent of the seats, they did not allow the opposition to submit their nominations.

During the parliamentary election, they did not allow us to go to the people as we wanted, or even to distribute leaflets from house to house. In election meetings, the crowds varied, but in each meeting, hardly 50, 60, 100, or 200 were able to brave the odds and show their faces. Our candidate in Tripura West, Sankar Prasad Dutta, was attacked more than ten times; Jiten [Jitendra Chaudhury], who stood in Tripura East, was attacked more than three times. A section of our voters was prevented from coming to the polling booths; another section did not come.

It is difficult for someone on the outside to understand the terror campaign in Tripura, or for a person sitting in Agartala to understand the situation in the countryside.

What are the tasks ahead in rural Tripura?

As I have indicated over this long conversation, the years from 1978 to 2018 were years of momentous change for the people of rural Tripura, tribal and non-tribal. Nevertheless, there is still far to go – with respect to employment, human development, the growth of incomes, and the development of the productive forces in our society.

Today, there is a serious dearth of work for daily wage earners and, as a consequence, conditions of starvation and semi-starvation have been reported. We are also receiving reports of starvation deaths and the sale of children from some tribal areas. Workers of income-poor families have begun to migrate in search of work. My view is that, by and large, the economic situation in rural Tripura is in shambles.

A precondition for the development that we envisage is democratic political space, the freedom to function politically. This is absent today.

Tripura has been dragged to the path of one-party authoritarian rule, and subversion of democracy, flagrant encroachment on the right to franchise, and onslaughts on civil liberties and human rights in Tripura have become the order of day. The atmosphere of peace, amity, and solidarity that existed is in peril. Crimes against women and cases of homicide have increased. There have been brutal attacks on people of the religious minorities.

In the circumstances, our efforts and the efforts of all peace-loving and democratic-minded people in Tripura are concentrated on restoring democracy, peace, and the rule of law. In this effort, the people of Tripura seek and deserve unstinted support from secular, democratic people from all over the country.

2

An Introduction to the Three Villages

Arindam Das

.

The Foundation for Agrarian Studies (FAS) has conducted detailed village surveys in different agro-ecological zones as part of its Project on Agrarian Relations in India (PARI). The broad objectives of the PARI surveys are:

- To analyse village-level production, production systems and livelihoods, and the socio-economic characteristics of different strata of the rural population;
- To conduct specific studies of sectional deprivation in rural India, particularly with regard to the Dalit and Scheduled Tribe populations, women, specific minorities, and the income-poor; and
- To report on the state of basic village amenities and the access of the rural people to the facilities of modern life.

In 2006, Andhra Pradesh was the first State studied as part of PARI.[1] Tripura was the tenth State chosen for study, and household surveys were conducted in three villages: Mainama in Manu block of Dhalai district, Muhuripur in Jolaibari block of South district, and Khakchang in Dasda block of North district. Sample surveys were conducted in the three villages during May–June 2016.

The three villages – Mainama, Muhuripur, and Khakchang – were first surveyed in 2005 for the *Tripura Human Development Report, 2007.*[2] We reselected them for the PARI survey of 2016. The villages have distinct

---

[1] Our local investigators were Lison Marak, Jiban Tripura, Hirak Debbarma, Pramod Debbarma, Birulal Debbarma, Anurani Debbarma, Shibani Debbarma, Pritam Debbarma, Prasanna Debbarma, Jharna Debbarma, and Daya Mohan Tripura.

[2] See http://fas.org.in/tripura-human-development-report/

topologies, land use patterns, and crop systems. Muhuripur of South district represents settled agriculture that is characteristic of the plain regions. Khakchang from North district is a resettled forest village, characterised by slash-and-burn cultivation (*jhum*). The third village, Mainama of Dhalai district, represents settled plain and *tila* or cultivation on slopes.

Khakchang

Location

Khakchang village is in Dasda block of Anand Bazaar tehsil, North district. The village is located near the Jampuii Hills, the border between Tripura and Mizoram. The village is located 13 km from Dasda block and 26 km from Kanchanpur, the sub-divisional headquarters and nearest town. It has seven hamlets spread over 5,919 acres, some as far as 8 km from the village market and the Tripura Tribal Areas Autonomous District Council

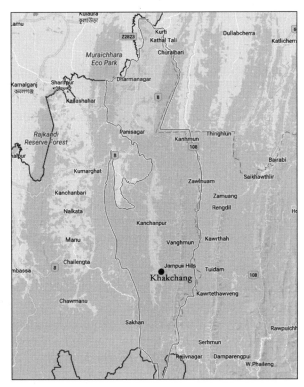

Map 1 *Location of Khakchang village, North district, Tripura*

(TTAADC) office. The hamlets are Ananda Bazar (East), Subhas Nagar, Braja Kumar Para, Ganchera Para, Horsing Para, Madhu Chandra Para, and Prem Chandra Para. The most isolated hamlet, Braja Kumar Para, is at a distance of 10 km from the village market.

Village Infrastructure

Khakchang village is connected to Kanchanpur by an all-weather road. Most of the hamlets, however, are connected to the village market and the main road by brick-and-mud roads that are traversable only by foot in the monsoon. Only one of the hamlets has a fully *pucca* all-weather road link. Of the seven hamlets, five have provisions for electricity and piped drinking water. In the electrified hamlets, almost 80 per cent of households have been given electricity connections and the others have been provided with highly subsidised solar panels. Piped water is supplied through public stand-posts. There is a post office, a branch of the State Bank of India, a ration shop, and two medical stores near the village Autonomous District Council (ADC) office. Khakchang has three primary schools, two middle schools, one secondary school, and one higher secondary school.

Population

There were 589 households resident in the village with a population of 2,884. Our sample survey covered 86 households. Khakchang is a resettled village, and 95 per cent of the households were Reangs while the remaining 5 per cent were Tripuris, both Scheduled Tribes (Table 1).

Land use and agriculture

Khakchang is characterised by different types of agricultural production and tenurial systems, ranging from slash-and-burn shifting cultivation, other more settled forms of *jhum* cultivation (where vegetation is burnt

Table 1 *Distribution of households and population by social group, Khakchang, 2016*

Social group	Number of households	% of total households	Females	Males	Persons	% of total population
Reang (ST)	559	95	1361	1364	2725	94.5
Tripuri (ST)	30	5	79	80	159	5.5
All	589	100	1440	1444	2884	100.0

Note: ST stands for Scheduled Tribe.
Source: PARI survey data (2016).

Map 2 *Location of the three study villages in Tripura*

every three years), to more settled forms of plantation agriculture, homestead cultivation, and lowland rice cultivation. Rice, vegetables, tubers, and tree crops are grown on *jhum* fields and homesteads, and mixed cropping often involves the cultivation of thirty or more varieties of plants. About 98 per cent of the lands are rainfed.

Mainama

Location

Mainama village is in Manu block, Chailengta tehsil of Dhalai district. Mainama is 3 km from Manu, the block headquarters and nearest town. The other nearby town is Chailengta, also 3 km away. The district headquarters is at Ambassa, at a distance of 31 km. The nearest railway station is at Manu.

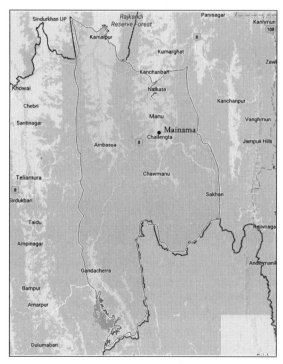

Map 3 *Location of Mainama village, Dhalai district, Tripura*

Mainama panchayat was divided into two in January 2015. Our sample survey of 271 households was conducted in the two adjacent village panchayats, Mainama and North Mainama. The villages are part of the TTAADC area. There were about 1,451 households resident in eleven hamlets (*para*) in the two villages. The hamlets are Areghore Para, Arjun Para, Hakrai Para, Brata Kumar Para, Lambabil Para, Bhuban Das Para, Duranta Para, Dayal Para, Bangali Para, Madhab Master Para, and Tilak Para. The sample of 271 households was drawn from all eleven hamlets.

Village Infrastructure

The village is connected to Manu by an all-weather road, but the hamlets are scattered and many are connected only by mud-and-brick roads, some of which are accessible only by foot during the monsoon. There is a bus stop in the village. Other means of transport are autorickshaws and jeeps. The village has a post office, a ration shop and a medical store, and two primary health centres. All the hamlets have been connected to the grid, although there still remain around 195 households without an electricity connection. The village has seven primary schools, four middle schools, a higher secondary school, and a degree college.

Population and Caste

In 2016, the population of the two village panchayats together was 6,693 in 1,451 households. According to the Ordinary Resident Register (ORR) database of 2014–15, there were 666 households in Mainama and 765 households in North Mainama, with corresponding populations of 2,872 and 3,291 respectively.

As per the Census of 2011, Mainama village had 1,232 resident households and a population of 5,586, of which 2,880 were males and 2,706 were females – that is, a sex ratio of 940 females per thousand males.

Mainama is a multi-caste, multi-religious, multi-tribe village with a significant population of Scheduled Tribes (STs). The main languages spoken here are Kak-Barak, Chakma, and Bengali. Chakmas (ST), Tripuris (ST) and Kapalis (Other Backward Class, OBC) constituted about 86 per cent of the village population. ST households constituted 67 per cent of all households in Mainama. The three main tribes were Chakma, Tripuri, and Mog, of whom the largest number were Tripuri (43 per cent of all households). OBCs constituted 26 per cent of households in the village. Other Caste Hindus constituted 4 per cent, Scheduled Castes (SCs) 1 per cent, and Muslims 2 per cent of all households.

Table 2 *Distribution of households and population by caste, Mainama, 2016*

Social group	Number of households	% of total households	Females	Males	Persons	% of total population
Tripuri (ST)	618	42.6	1388	1549	2937	43.88
Chakma (ST)	342	23.6	781	731	1512	22.59
Kapali (OBC)	310	21.4	673	809	1482	22.14
Rudra Pal (OBC)	43	3.0	117	73	191	2.85
Muslim	29	2.0	48	76	124	1.85
Kayastha (Caste Hindu)	24	1.7	67	67	134	2
Baishya (Caste Hindu)	19	1.3	38	38	76	1.14
Mali (SC)	9	0.7	10	19	29	0.43
Unspecified (SC)	9	0.7	10	14	24	0.36
Barna (ST)	5	0.3	14	19	33	0.49
Banik (Caste Hindu)	5	0.3	10	5	14	0.21
Brahmin (Caste Hindu)	5	0.3	5	14	19	0.28
Debroy (Caste Hindu)	5	0.3	5	10	14	0.21
Goala (OBC)	5	0.3	5	10	14	0.21
Karmakar (OBC)	4	0.3	5	14	19	0.28
Napit (OBC)	4	0.3	10	5	14	0.21
Unspecified (OBC)	5	0.3	5	19	24	0.36
Mog (ST)	5	0.3	10	10	19	0.28
Unspecified (Caste Hindu)	5	0.3	5	10	14	0.21
All	1451	100.0	3206	3492	6693	100.0

Note: ST stands for Scheduled Tribe, SC stands for Scheduled Caste, and OBC stands for Other Backward Class.
Source: PARI survey data, 2016.

Land Use, Irrigation and Cropping Pattern

Mainama has a mix of lowlands and sloping or *tila* lands. The Manu river forms one of the boundaries of the village. The lowlands are mostly under paddy cultivation. The slopes are used for rubber cultivation. About 55 per cent of the sown area of the village is under rubber. Extensive vegetable cultivation is done on the river banks. Homestead cultivation is a prominent feature of this village.

Muhuripur

Location

Muhuripur village is in Muhuripur tehsil of Jolaibari block, South district. Muhuripur is about 15 km from the district headquarters at Belonia, and 4 km from the block headquarters at Jolaibari. The nearest towns are Belonia and Santirbazar, 15 km from the village. The village is geographically divided into East Muhuripur and West Muhuripur. The residential area is constituted of eleven hamlets or *paras* that are spread over 551 hectares. Our sample household survey covered 214 households across the eleven hamlets. The hamlets are Banabihari Para, Majumder Para (West), Dharani Kanta Para, Janglia Para, Latuatila Para, Nath Para, Tanti Para, Majumder Para (East), Tilla Para (No. 1), Ramthakur Para, and South Muhuripur Para.

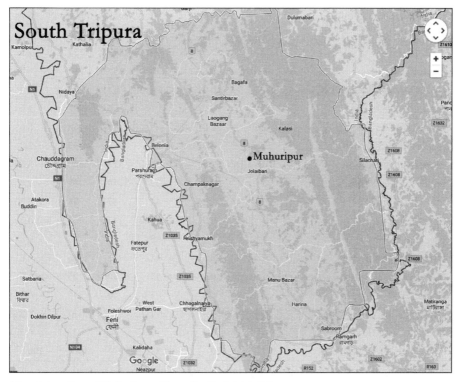

Map 4 *Location of Muhuripur village, South district, Tripura*

Village Infrastructure

The village is connected by an all-weather road. The normal means of transport used are bus, jeep, and autorickshaw. There is a post office, a branch of Tripura Gramin Bank, and a medical store in the village. The health centre is at distance of 1 km. The nearest sub-divisional hospital is at Belonia and the district hospital is at Santirbazar. The village has four primary schools, a secondary school, and a higher secondary school.

Population

There were 1,054 households and 4,404 persons resident in Muhuripur. Muhuripur is a multi-caste village. Of the 1,054 households, 627 households

Table 3 *Distribution of households and population by social group, Muhuripur, 2016*

Social group	Number of households	% of total households	Females	Males	Persons	% of total population
Kayastha (Caste Hindu)	491	46.6	998	1067	2064	46.9
Tanti (OBC)	137	13	243	322	564	12.8
Halladas (SC)	77	7.3	159	173	332	7.5
Napit (OBC)	68	6.5	126	155	281	6.4
Baishya (Caste Hindu)	65	6.0	88	131	219	5.0
Brahmin (Caste Hindu)	42	4.0	104	98	202	4.6
Goala (OBC)	32	3.0	79	79	158	3.6
Namasudra (SC)	32	3.0	53	42	95	2.2
Mahishyadas (SC)	26	2.5	83	73	156	3.5
Banik (Caste Hindu)	25	2.4	39	50	89	2.0
Sutradhar (OBC)	21	2.0	41	57	98	2.2
Mali (SC)	9	0.9	18	13	31	0.7
Nag (Caste Hindu)	5	0.5	5	10	15	0.3
Karmakar (OBC)	5	0.5	11	16	26	0.6
Rudra Pal (OBC)	5	0.5	15	10	25	0.6
Nama (SC)	5	0.5	5	10	15	0.3
Poddar (SC)	5	0.5	11	11	21	0.5
Baidya (Caste Hindu)	4	0.4	9	4	13	0.3
All	1054	100	2087	2321	4404	100

Note: SC stands for Scheduled Caste and OBC stands for Other Backward Class.
Source: PARI survey data (2016).

were Caste Hindu, 272 households were OBC, and 154 households were SC households. The main language spoken was Bengali. Caste Hindus constituted 55 per cent of all households and Dalit (SC) households constituted 15 per cent of all households. The major castes were Kayastha, Tanti, Napit, Goala, Halladas, and Mahisyadas with Kayastha households comprising 46 per cent of all households in the village. Halladas (SC) constituted 7 per cent of all households in the village.

Land Use, Irrigation and Cropping Pattern

Muhuripur is a lowland village, characterised by the cultivation of rice. The main source of irrigation in the village is river lift irrigation. A wide variety of vegetable crops, including winter potato, are cultivated on and near the river bed. Mulberry cultivation and sericulture are part of the contemporary village economy. There is also rubber cultivation on sloping land.

Sampling Procedure

The FAS survey of villages in Tripura was a stratified random sample survey. In each village, the strata were based on hamlets. This was done on the assumption that a hamlet is homogenous with respect to caste or tribe, landholding pattern, and occupation. In some cases of remote hamlets, a few of them were combined into one stratum.

The criterion for classifying a remote hamlet was its distance from the main village centre with the farthest hamlets being identified as remote. In two villages, Khakchang and Mainama, due to their spread-out nature and mixed topography, this classification became crucial. In Khakchang, five out of a total of seven hamlets, namely, Braja Kumar Para, Ganchera Para, Horsing Para, Madhu Chandra Para, and Prem Chandra Para, were the remote hamlets. In Mainama, eight out of the eleven hamlets, namely, Aghore Para, Arjun Para, Hakrai Para, Brata Kumar Para, Lambabil Para, Bhuban Das Para, Duranta Para, and Dayal Para, were the remote hamlets. There were no remote hamlets in Muhuripur. The common characteristics of these remote hamlets were their sloped terrain and inaccessibility, with connection often only by foot.

The list of hamlets and the number of households in each were obtained from the panchayat office, based on the Ordinary Resident Register household survey conducted in 2015. This list was used for stratification and sampling. After arranging the households in each stratum, we drew sub-samples from every hamlet with probability approximately proportional to the number of households in each hamlet.

Since non-uniform sampling proportions of strata were used in three villages, the multiplier or weight was used for each observation. The value of the multiplier was the ratio of the total number of households to the number of sample households in the stratum to which the household belonged. The sample size was 86 in Khakchang, 271 in Mainama, and 241 in Muhuripur.

The primary survey was carried out in May–June 2016 to capture the socio-economic characteristics of the preceding agriculture year (July 2015–June 2016). A detailed household questionnaire was used for the survey. The questionnaire was divided into the following major sections:

- Demographic data, including data on caste, religion, education, and occupations
- Ownership and operational landholdings of households in the agriculture year 2015–16
- Land sales and purchases
- Cropping pattern and crop production
- Homestead cultivation
- Input use for cultivation
- Animal resources
- Employment and income from agriculture and non-agriculture labouring out
- Salaries, artisan earnings, remittances, and incomes from business activities other than crop production
- Income from minor forest produce
- Housing and household electricity, sanitation, and water facilities
- Indebtedness
- Ownership of assets.

Besides the household questionnaire, general information about the village was collected from the village panchayat. Details of the questionnaire are available at www.fas.org.in.

Appendix Tables

Appendix Table 1 *Population and sample by hamlet, Khakchang, 2015–16*

Hamlet	Total population	Sample size
Ananda Bazar (East)	72	17
Subhas Nagar	152	25
Braja Kumar Para	71	4
Ganchera Para	81	7
Horsing Para	118	22
Madhu Chandra Para	69	8
Prem Chandra Para	26	3
All	589	86

Appendix Table 2 *Population and sample by hamlet, Mainama, 2015–16*

Hamlet	No. of households	No. of sample households
Aghore Para	71	25
Arjun Para	166	19
Hakrai Para	41	12
Brata Kumar Para	181	21
Lambabil Para	6	2
Bhuban Das Para	51	9
Duranta Para	70	15
Dayal Para	44	7
Bengali Para	380	92
Madhab Master Para	250	40
Tilak Para	191	29
All	1451	271

Appendix Table 3 *Population and sample by hamlet, Muhuripur, 2015–16*

Hamlet	No. of households	No. of sample households
Banabihari Para	109	19
Majumder Para (West)	94	22
Dharani Kanta Para	32	6
Janglia Para	76	15
Latuatila Para	101	21
Nath Para	75	14
Tanti Para	87	15
Majumder Para (East)	145	26
No-1 Tilla Para	49	13
Ramthakur Para	84	22
South Muhuripur Para	202	40
All	1054	213

3

An Introduction to the Agrarian Economy of Tripura

Sumedha Bajar
with a Note on "Land Reforms in Tripura" by Saqib Khan

Tripura, a former princely state ruled by maharajas of the Manikya dynasty, merged with the Indian Union in 1949, and was accorded the status of a 'C' category State in 1950. This status was changed to that of Union Territory in 1956. It was only on 21 January 1972, under the North-Eastern Areas (Reorganisation) Act, 1971, that Tripura attained full statehood.

Until recently, Tripura was divided into four districts – Dhalai, North Tripura, South Tripura, and West Tripura. However, with effect from 21 January 2012, four new districts – Khowai, Unakoti, Sipahijala, and Gomati – were created from the existing ones. North Tripura was divided to create the new district of Unakoti, West Tripura was divided to create the districts of Khowai and Sipahijala, and Gomati was carved out of South Tripura.

Tripura has witnessed a demographic transformation over time, primarily as a result of Bengali migration. This took place in three surges: the first was a result of India's Partition in 1947; the second influx of refugees occurred after the second India–Pakistan war in 1965; and the last took place after the liberation of East Pakistan and formation of Bangladesh in 1971 (De 2014). The arrival and eventual settlement of Bengalis brought about a significant change in the predominantly tribal agrarian structure of the State. Tribals practised shifting or *jhum* cultivation, while the migrants brought with them the practice of settled cultivation. In many parts of the State, private ownership replaced communal ownership of land. Enactment of the Tripura Land Revenue and Land Reforms Act (1960), with subsequent amendments, brought about major changes in the status of land ownership and land use.

In this chapter, we begin with a brief history of land reforms, which played an important role in achieving more equitable distribution of land in Tripura's rural countryside. We then provide details of Tripura's agricultural sector and the changes observed in recent years based on official statistics. We look at the land use pattern in Tripura in the four districts of Dhalai, North Tripura, South Tripura, and West Tripura. This is followed by a discussion on the shift in cropping patterns in the State, the pace and pattern of agricultural and horticultural growth, changes in yields of the major agricultural crops, and the status of irrigation in the State.

Land Reforms in Tripura

Saqib Khan

Tripura is one of the few States of the country that has had a successful land reforms programme.

The State has seen many waves of settlers. A gradual, economy-induced trend of immigration, largely of non-tribals (Bengalis), took place during the second half of the nineteenth and early decades of the twentieth century from the neighbouring districts of British Bengal and Assam, particularly the districts of Comilla (Tippera), Noakhali, and Sylhet (Ganguly 1983; Chakraborty 2004). The Partition of India in 1947 and the communal riots that followed in several areas of what was then East Pakistan (now Bangladesh) led to an unprecedented wave of migration of Bengali Hindu refugees into Tripura. This historic migration reversed the demographic balance of the State, resulting in a steady decline of the proportion of tribal people in the total population. The non-tribal population almost doubled in three decades, rising from 7.82 lakhs in 1961 to 11.05 lakhs in 1971 and 14.69 lakhs in 1981 (Chakraborty 2004). This impacted negatively on the lives of tribal people, especially in the loss of their land to the migrant settlers.

The struggle of the Ganamukti Parishad (GMP) against alienation of tribal land along with problems arising from refugee rehabilitation led to enactment of the Tripura Land Revenue and Land Reform Act (TLRLR) in 1960 by Parliament. The 1960 Act repealed all previous legislations on land enacted during the princely regime[1] and

[1] The Manikyas ruled over Tripura uninterrupted from the fifteenth century onwards

also abolished the old land tenures. The new, comprehensive Act simplified land tenure and conferred substantial rights on tillers of the soil. This included the abolition of intermediaries, tenancy reform and security of tenure for under-*raiyat*s (sharecroppers), imposition of a ceiling on landholdings, and prevention of fragmentation of holdings (Government of Tripura 1976; Datta 1980; Das 1990). With the abolition of intermediary rights on land, the actual tiller was brought in direct contact with the State (Chakraborty 2004). After a further period of struggle by the GMP, when the issue was raised in Parliament by the Communist Party of India (Marxist) leader and Member of Parliament Dasaratha Deb, the central government included Section 187 in the TLRLR. This prohibited transfer of tribal land to a non-tribal without previous permission of the District Collector in writing (Deb 1967, 1974; Basu 1996; Bareh 2001).

Though the 1960 Act was the first comprehensive legislation related to land reforms in Tripura and therefore important, it proved to be ineffective in many ways. It could not, for example, ensure fixity of tenure or freedom from eviction for tenants. Nor could it prevent exorbitant rents imposed by landlords (Datta 1987; Das 1990; Chakraborty 2004). Section 187 of the Act, which prohibits transfer of tribal land to non-tribal persons, proved to be inadequate to prevent such transfers. Its provisions were circumvented as unregistered transfers without the Collector's permission (Chanda 2006) became widespread, and non-tribal immigrants purchased lands from the tribals through *benami*[2] deeds. Also, the legislation was silent on penal action in case of breach of Section 187 and there was no provision for restoring illegally transferred land to the original tribal owner (Government of Tripura 1976).

As a result, Section 187 remained on paper and its violations continued unabated (Basu 1996). The State administrative machinery's indifference towards strict implementation of the 1960 Act led to indiscriminate transfer of land from tribals to non-tribals in contravention of legal provisions (Debbarma 2005; Saha 2009). For

---

till India's Independence. Some of the land legislations undertaken by the princely regime were the rules relating to land revenue enacted in 1880, and the Landlord and Tenant Act of 1886, both enacted by Birchandra Manikya (1862–1896).

[2] The term for land held by a person in another, often fictitious, name.

example, under the Congress-led Sachindralal Singha (1963–71) and Sukhomoy Sengupta (1972–77) governments, hundreds of acres of tribal land were directly or indirectly allowed to be handed over to non-tribal persons (Deb 1974, 1984; Datta 1987; K. Debbarma, undated).

Thus, the TLRLR Act had serious limitations and failed to safeguard the rights of tribals over their land (Khan 2018). Though the Second Amendment to the Act in 1974 brought in the provision of restoration of tribal land, changes in the cut-off date of this restoration diluted the spirit of the amendment.[3] Overall, land reforms were not implemented in true spirit in the 1960s and 1970s in Tripura.

It was with the CPI(M)-led Left Front government, which came to power in 1978, that attempts were made to implement land reforms in both letter and spirit. This was done in two phases: first, during the first two Left Front governments led by Nripen Chakraborty from 1978 to 1988; second, during the Left Front governments led by Dasaratha Deb in 1994–98 and Manik Sarkar in 1998–2018.

There are four areas of achievement in land reforms in Tripura.

1. *Illegal transfer of tribal lands stopped and land restored to original owners* Immediately after coming to power, the Left Front government arranged for the return of land from Bengalis (non-tribals) to their original owners (tribals). A statement made by Revenue Minister Biren Datta to the State Assembly on 5 January 1979 showed that in less than a year the government had returned 201.3 acres to 318 tribal families, and the work of returning 67.72 acres to another 54 families was underway (Biren Datta 1979). Till September 2005, almost 9,000 cases of restoration had been handled and 7,147 acres had been restored to tribal families (Government of Tripura 2007).

To further strengthen the provision for preventing illegal transfer of tribal land and to plug the loopholes in the TLRLR Act, a new Sixth Amendment of the Act was passed in 1994. This amendment incorporated the provision of preventing re-transfer of restored lands

---

[3] The Second Amendment of the TLRLR Act was enacted by the Congress government in 1974. Section 187 was a part of the original TLRLR Act, enacted in 1960. The Governor of Tripura promulgated the Second Amendment as an ordinance on 28 February 1974 and then a Bill was introduced in the Assembly on 15 March 1974. Despite vociferous protests by the Left, it was put to a voice vote and finally passed on 25 March 1974.

to non-tribals. In other words, further safeguards were put into the Act to protect the tribals. This was not an easy task as proper records of the original transfer did not exist. However, the Sixth Amendment made land restoration compulsory for all transfers made after 1969. Non-tribal people who possessed illegally transferred lands were issued notices and made to return the lands to the original tribal landowners (Kilikdar 2002).

With regard to land restoration, the Sixth Amendment inserted a new Section 187B(1) titled "Restoration of Land" into the Act whereby in case of any transfer of land belonging to a Scheduled Tribe (ST) person in contravention of Section 187 to a non-ST person, a Revenue Officer specially appointed for this purpose was to evict such a non-ST person by an order in writing and restore the possession of the land to the transferer.

Secondly, the amendment fixed the quantum of punishment for encroaching on tribal land. Any illegal occupation or possession of tribal land by a non-tribal person was made a cognisable and non-bailable offence with imprisonment for a term of up to two years plus a fine of up to Rs 3,000. Further, the burden of proof for the purpose of Section 187B, that the transfer of land was not made in contravention of Section 187(1), or that the occupation of land was not made without lawful authority, was put on the transferee or occupier.

Thirdly, in Section 187(1)(C), in contrast to previous provisions, it was ensured that regardless of where the tribal persons mortgaged their land – whether with a cooperative society or a bank, the Tripura Housing Board, the central or State government, or any other financial institution – the ownership of that mortgaged land remained with them and was not transferred to a non-tribal person.

Fourthly, it curtailed the jurisdiction of civil courts with a view to protect tribal lands. No transfer or instrument of transfer – including a decree or order passed by any court, tribunal or authority – made in contravention of Section 187(1) was to be registered or in any way recognised as valid in any court, tribunal or authority (K. Debbarma, undated).

The land restoration process initiated by the Left Front government was not without social and political complexities. The first issue was that there was a section of poor non-tribals who had occupied the lands of tribals or somehow purchased it from them, for whom these lands were the only means of livelihood. The Left Front government saw to it that poor non-tribals who were rendered landless by the process of restoration were financially compensated. It formulated a scheme for their resettlement (Biren Datta 1979). In this way, the tribal people were given back the land that had been illegally transferred from them, and, at the same time, the non-tribal people who had to give up their lands were compensated by the Left Front government.

Land reform gave rise to opposition from those whose lands were taken away. Amra Bangali (We Bengalis), an outfit created by Anand Marg, opposed the land policy. Extremist groups were formed clandestinely under the patronage of the Tripura Upajati Juba Samiti (TUJS), which was from its inception aligned politically with the Congress.

2. *Protecting the rights of the peasantry: the Fifth Amendment of the TLRLR Act, 1979*

The second feature of land reform was ensuring the rights of the peasantry. In this regard, the passing of the TLRLR (Fifth Amendment) Act on 23 March 1979 was an important step. Through this amendment, the rights of *bargadars* (sharecroppers) were added to the TLRLR Act 1960.

The Fifth Amendment mainly sought to protect the interests of sharecroppers and to restore land to such sharecroppers who had been unlawfully evicted from the land (Banik 2011). Now the sharecroppers were to get four-fifths of the agricultural produce, and one part was to go to the owner of the land.[4]

Protection of sharecroppers against eviction was an important feature of this amendment. Participating in the discussion on the Bill, Chief Minister Nripen Chakraborty highlighted this feature and the situation that had prevailed before the amendment in a speech to the Assembly. He said:

> It has been enshrined in the amendment that the *jotedar* would not

---

[4] Speech by Nripen Chakraborty, "Consideration and Passing of the Tripura Land Revenue and Land Reforms (Fifth Amendment) Bill, 1979," Tripura Legislative Assembly Proceedings, 23 March 1979.

be in a position to evict the sharecropper without going to the court of law. False cases were foisted by *jotedars* on sharecroppers so that they did not register their names and were compelled to leave the land. The *jotedars* used to harass and intimidate them with the help of police and other officials. Sharecroppers used to be evicted, but they did not have the courage or financial security to complain against *jotedars*. Such was the situation earlier that one might be allotted a plot of land one year and asked to give up that land the next year. In this way, land was transferred from one person to another. In many places, the *jotedars*, through forged documents, successfully used to prove that they were cultivating their land themselves and not the sharecroppers. Now the onus was put on *jotedars* to prove that they themselves cultivated that particular land and not the sharecroppers.[5]

Secondly, provision of special machinery for registering names of sharecroppers and revision of entries was made. Before this amendment, there was no clarity on the position of *bargadars*. They were not recorded as under-*raiyats* in the land records of the government, and were not allowed to acquire the rights of the *raiyats*.[6] By the Fifth Amendment in 1979, the *bargadars*' names were to be recorded in a separate register prepared under Section 46-A (Das 1990).

3. *Relief to the peasantry against indebtedness*
The third feature of land reform was provision of relief to the peasantry (both tribals and non-tribals) against indebtedness and usurious practices of moneylenders. This was done mainly through the passing of the Tripura Agricultural Indebtedness Relief Act, 1979. This Act replaced the Tripura Agricultural Debtors Relief Act, 1976 that had been passed by the Assembly with a view to provide relief to landless labourers, marginal farmers, rural artisans, sharecroppers,

---

[5] *Ibid.*

[6] Under-*raiyat* basically means a sharecropper. The TLRLR Act 1960, after the Fifth Amendment in March 1979, defines *raiyat* as "a person who owns land for purposes of agriculture paying land revenue to the government and includes the successors-in-interest of such person," and under-*raiyat* as "a person who cultivates or holds the land of a raiyat under an agreement, express or implied, on condition of paying therefore rent in cash or kind or delivering a share of the produce" (Kilikdar 2002: 34–35).

and small farmers who were indebted. The 1976 Act had remained mostly on paper in the absence of a proper enforcement procedure (Banik 2011).

The 1979 Act contained a new provision of debt waiver that was absent in the 1976 law. By this provision, all debts advanced by creditors before the commencement of the 1979 Act, including interest, of marginal cultivators, landless peasants, and skilled labourers whose annual income was not more than Rs 2,400 were to be waived. No such debt due from a debtor was to be recoverable from him, or from movable or immovable property belonging to him. Further, the creditor was liable to return all the mortgaged properties of the borrower.[7]

4. *Redistribution of land to the landless and poor peasants*

The fourth feature of land reform was redistribution of land to the landless and poor peasants, which included both tribals and non-tribals. This process included taking over of surplus ceiling land by the State government and its redistribution, along with government-owned or *khas* land, to the landless. After the Left Front government assumed office in January 1978, about 53,000 acres of land were distributed among almost 29,000 landless and homeless families between 1978 and 1981. Data from Legislative Assembly Proceedings show that between January 1978 and 31 December 1981, a total of 12,828 landless families were given 23,548.54 acres, and 4,612 homeless families were given 955.55 acres. Thus, a total of 12,036 landless and homeless families were given 27,901.01 acres of *khas* land.[8]

In the 1980s, the Left Front government adopted measures to implement the 20-point programme declared by Prime Minister Indira Gandhi, and acquired surplus and fallow land for redistribution among landless and poor families. The extent of implementation of the programme was, however, below expectations. This was because

---

[7] Copy of the Tripura Agricultural Indebtedness Relief Act, 1979, and speech by Biren Datta, "Consideration and Passing of the Tripura Agricultural Indebtedness Relief Bill, 1979," Tripura Legislative Assembly Proceedings, June 1979.

[8] See, "29,000 landless and homeless families given land in the last four years," *Daily Desher Katha* (Agartala), 18 February 1982.

the quantity of surplus land acquired was only about 2,000 acres (Ray 1991; Roy 2012). It has also been argued that there were very few large holdings in Tripura, and therefore the total amount of ceiling-surplus land in the State was limited (Deb Barma 1991). Still, a total area of 2,011.65 acres was declared surplus land throughout the State on the basis of a rough assessment in the 1980s. Out of this, the Tripura government took possession of over 1,916.2 acres. Around 1,518.5 acres were distributed among the SCs, STs, and others engaged in agriculture, while the rest of the surplus land, i.e. 95.4 acres, could not be taken possession of due to legal obstacles (Ray 1991).

Data from the Revenue Department on land redistribution and number of beneficiaries show that the greatest extent of land was redistributed and the number of recipients was the highest between 1978 and 1998. In this period, the Left Front was in government except for the years between February 1988 and February 1993, when the Congress–TUJS held power.

The *Tripura Human Development Report 2007* shows that between 1997–98 and 2004–05, a total of 34,598 acres of *khas* land were distributed to 37,349 families (Government of Tripura 2007, p. 64). Recent data from the State government's Revenue Department show that from 2012–13 to 2016–17, a total of 3,447.91 acres of *khas* land were allotted to a total of 25,426 landless and homeless families. Of these, 9,829 ST families received 1,599.09 acres – the highest among all social groups.[9]

Table 1 *Distribution of land under land reforms and number of beneficiaries, Tripura, 1972–2017*, in acres and number

Parameters	Till 1972	1972–78	Till 1998	Till 2011–12	2013–17
1 Amount of land distributed under land reforms	39,507.27	71,771.36	2,06,798.89	2,27,052.76	3,447.91
2 No. of recipients	42,461	44,892	1,62,593	1,86,538	25,426

Source: Revenue Department, Government of Tripura (2014, 2017).[10]

[9] "Category-wise allotment of land," Revenue Department, Government of Tripura, Agartala, 2017.

[10] "Tripura rajyor bhoomi sanskar ebong rajaswa prashashaner kajer agragati" (Progress of the work of land reforms and revenue in Tripura State), Revenue Department, Government of Tripura, Agartala, 2014.

Land Use Pattern and Land Distribution

Tripura's economy is predominantly agrarian in nature with more than 42 per cent of its population directly dependent on agriculture and allied activities. Until fairly recently, the State's economy was characterised by a high poverty rate, low per capita income, inadequate infrastructure, and low levels of industrialisation (Government of Tripura 2013). However, in recent years, there have been encouraging signs of economic growth. In 2014–15, the economy achieved an annual average growth rate of 9.2 per cent (with the new base of 2011–12), and the gross State domestic product (SDP) at constant prices increased from Rs 192,090 million in 2011–12 to Rs 250,860 million in 2014–15.

The contribution of agriculture and allied activities to gross SDP was around 33 per cent in 2014–15. According to the Census of 2011, around 42 per cent of total main workers in Tripura were engaged in agriculture, of which cultivators formed about 23 per cent and agricultural labourers about 19 per cent. The total cultivable area in 2012–13 was around 2.77 lakh hectares, or 26 per cent of the total geographical area of the State. The State has high population density (350 people per sq. km, according to Census 2011), and, because it is landlocked and hilly, has limited land available for agricultural activities and expansion. These features have created both challenges and opportunities for Tripura's agricultural sector.

The State imports large quantities of rice and other agricultural products to feed its populace. Chronic deficiencies in domestic production of foodgrain have long been a cause of concern, reflected in Tripura's Perspective Plan announced in 2000–01. The aim of the ten-year Perspective Plan on Agriculture was to make the State self-sufficient in most agricultural commodities through increased use of high-yielding varieties of seeds in production, expansion of the State's irrigation potential and cropping intensity, and by attracting investments in agriculture. Owing to the shortage of land available for cultivation of cereal crops, emphasis was given to maximising land utilisation by growing multiple crops, exploring horticultural development, and introducing plantation crops. There is great scope for improving the diversity of fruit and vegetables cultivated, given the fertile soil, abundant moisture, and sub-tropical climate that the State has to offer.

More than 60 per cent of the land area of Tripura is under forests and only 27 per cent is under agriculture – of the area under agriculture, 97 per

Table 2 *Land use classification, Tripura, 1960–2014, in '000 ha*

State/Union Territory/ Year	Geographical area	Forests	Not available for cultivation	Other uncultivated land excluding fallow land	Fallow land	Net area sown	Total cropped area	Agricultural land/cultivable land/cultivable land/arable land	Cultivated land
1960–61	1045	636	43	159	17	211	249	331	223
1970–71	1048	630	51	122	5	240	345	333	243
1980–81	1048	572	126	96	4	251	405	351	253
1990–91	1049	606	133	28	6	277	463	311	282
2000–01	1049	606	134	28	2	280	301	310	281
2005–06	1049	606	133	27	4	280	280	311	283
2006–07	1049	629	139	22	4	255	276	277	258
2007–08	1049	629	139	21	6	255	276	279	259
2008–09	1049	629	139	21	4	256	263	278	258
2009–10	1049	629	141	20	4	256	267	277	258
2010–11	1049	629	141	20	4	256	350	277	258
2011–12	1049	629	141	20	4	256	371	277	258
2012–13	1049	629	141	20	4	256	368	277	258
2013–14	1049	629	146	15	3	256	483	275	256

Source: Government of Tripura (2014).

cent is under the cultivation of food crops. Net sown area as a percentage of total geographical area increased from 20 per cent in 1960–61 to 24 per cent in 2012–13. Net sown area between 2000–01 and 2005–06 was constant at 2,80,000 hectares, but declined thereafter to 2,56,000 hectares, which was what it was in the 1980s (Table 2). At the same time, area sown more than once has seen a rise in recent years. Area unavailable for cultivation, i.e. land under non-agricultural use, and barren and uncultivable land, has been on the rise. In 2013–14 it stood at 1,46,000 hectares, or 13 per cent of the total geographical area of Tripura.

Due to its high population density and continuing fragmentation of landholdings, the average size of holding in the State, low to begin with, declined from 1.25 hectares in 1976–77 to 0.49 hectare in 2010–11. Table 3 gives the average size of operational holding for each size-class. The decline in size of holding was due to fragmentation of landholdings. Small and marginal farmers constituted 96 per cent of total cultivators in the State.

The size of operational holdings of marginal cultivators in Tripura fell from 0.31 hectare in 2000–01 to 0.28 hectare in 2010–11, whereas the all-India figure for 2010–11 was 0.39. This is significant, as we can see from Table 4: close to 50 per cent of the total area under operation was under marginal holdings, which accounted for 87 per cent of the total share of holdings. Marginal and small holdings together accounted for 96 per cent of the total number of holdings and 76 per cent of the total area under operation. On the other hand, medium and large holdings, which constituted less than 0.5 per cent of total holdings, made up 6 per cent of the total area under operation. Since 1995–96, the percentage of

Table 3 *Average size of holdings by size-class, Tripura and India, 2000–01, 2005–06, 2010–11, in hectares*

Size-class	Tripura			India
	2000–01	2005–06	2010–11	2010–11
Marginal	0.31	0.28	0.28.	0.39
Small	1.37	1.37	1.38	1.42
Semi-medium	2.55	2.51	2.52	2.71
Medium	5.12	5.29	5.06	5.76
Large	0	15.35	13.47	17.38
All	0.54	0.48	0.49	1.15

Source: Agricultural Census of India.

Table 4 *Distribution of number and area of holding for all size-classes, Tripura and India, 1995–96, 2000–01, 2010–11*, in percentages

Size-class	Tripura						India	
	1995–96		2000–01		2010–11		2010–11	
	Share of holding	Share of area	Share of holding	Share of area	Share of holding	Share of area	Share of holding	Share of area
Marginal	82.3	46.8	84.7	48.4	86.3	49.3	67.1	22.5
Small	13.3	32.3	11.4	28.7	9.5	26.7	17.9	22.1
Semi-Medium	3.9	17.4	3.5	16.6	3.7	18.8	10.04	23.6
Medium	0.33	3.0	0.4	3.3	0.46	4.7	4.25	21.2
Large	0.02	0.4	0.02	0	0.01	0.36	0.7	10.6

Source: Agricultural Census of India.

Table 5 *Distribution of average size of holding by size-group and social group, Tripura, 1995–96 to 2010–11*, in hectares

Social group	Year	Marginal	Small	Semi-Medium	Medium	Large	All
SCs	1995–96	0.27	1.35	2.50	5.54	13.57	0.40
	2000–01	0.28	1.32	2.55	4.95	0.00	0.41
	2010–11	0.25	1.37	2.51	4.81	0.00	0.36
STs	1995–96	0.45	1.41	2.49	5.41	15.44	0.87
	2000–01	0.39	1.39	2.53	5.14	12.71	0.75
	2010–11	0.35	1.39	2.50	5.05	13.75	0.76
Others	1995–96						
	2000–01	0.28	1.36	2.59	5.15	124.38	0.46
	2010–11	0.26	1.36	2.57	5.13	13.21	0.40
All	1995–96	0.33	1.38	2.50	5.31	76.89	0.60
	2000–01	0.31	1.37	2.55	5.16	78.77	0.56
	2010–11	0.28	1.38	2.52	5.07	14.29	0.49

Source: Agricultural Census of India.

area operated in the State has increased for marginal and medium-sized holdings, but has seen a decline for small holdings.

Till the early 1950s, the tribal population formed a majority within the overall population of Tripura. The Partition brought about a demographic change with non-tribals from across the border moving into the State. At present, the State's population comprises 31 per cent Scheduled Tribes (STs) and around 17 per cent Scheduled Castes (SCs). In terms of net area sown, STs cultivated around 43 per cent and SCs cultivated around 15 per cent of the 2,56,000 hectares of cultivated land in Tripura. The average size of landholdings of STs was around 0.76 hectare in 2010–11, which, although low, is higher than the average size of landholding of SCs (0.36 hectare). It can be seen clearly that for all social categories, the average size of holdings has been decreasing over time and the decline has been greater for STs. While there were no large farmers among SCs, the average landholding size of large farmers among STs was 13.75 hectares.

District-wise Estimates

Going by the original four-district division of Tripura, the average size of operational holdings showed a consistent decline in all four districts between 1995–96 and 2010–11. West Tripura and South Tripura appear to

Table 6 *Area under land use, average size of holding, and net sown area, by district, Tripura, 1995–2011*, in hectares

Year	District	Total holdings		Average size of holding	Net sown area
		Number	Area		
1995–96	Dhalai	23428	21306	0.91	17777
2000–01	Dhalai	66317	40714	0.61	36485
2005–06	Dhalai	71894	37747	0.53	34275
2010–11	Dhalai	73512	37442	0.51	34613
1995–96	North Tripura	66707	40331	0.60	35029
2000–01	North Tripura	87065	57446	0.66	49309
2005–06	North Tripura	84988	51908	0.61	45878
2010–11	North Tripura	86163	51122	0.59	44076
1995–96	South Tripura	79263	51353	0.65	44339
2000–01	South Tripura	139491	72745	0.52	64588
2005–06	South Tripura	177637	88019	0.50	78729
2010–11	South Tripura	183739	88434	0.48	79476
1995–96	West Tripura	131629	68231	0.52	56680
2000–01	West Tripura	186555	99079	0.53	83644
2005–06	West Tripura	230876	102760	0.45	90956
2010-11	West Tripura	235065	107947	0.46	97860

Source: Agricultural Census of India.

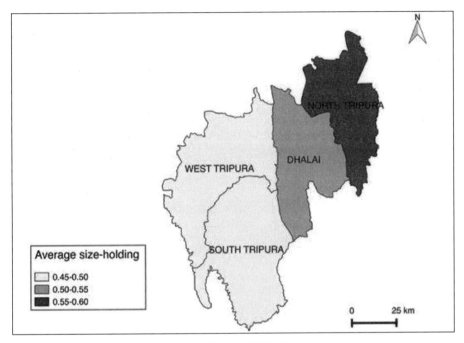

Map 1 *District-wise average size-holding, Tripura, 2010–11*, in hectares

Source: Based on Agricultural Census.

be under growing land pressure, which is reflected in their low average size of holding. From Table 6 (and Map 1) we can see that the average size of holdings was the highest in North Tripura (0.59 hectare), followed by Dhalai (0.51 hectare), South Tripura (0.48 hectare) and West Tripura (0.46 hecatre). West Tripura had the largest area under cultivation, followed by South Tripura, North Tripura, and Dhalai. In fact, 38 per cent (97,860 hectares) of total net sown area (2,56,000 hectares) in Tripura is located in West Tripura, followed by 31 per cent in South Tripura (79,476 hectares).

Distribution of Workers in Agriculture

According to Census 2011, of total workers (main and marginal)[11] in Tripura, 85 per cent lived in rural areas and 42 per cent were dependent on

---

[11] The census classifies workers into two groups: main workers, who worked for the major part of the reference period, i.e. six months or more; and marginal workers, who did not work for the major part of the reference period, i.e. less than six months.

agriculture for main work. The percentage distribution of main workers according to the economic classification for Census 2001 and Census 2011 is given in Table 7.

The proportion of both cultivators and agricultural labourers among main workers has been declining in Tripura. The share of cultivators declined from 38 per cent in 1991 to 23 per cent in 2011 and the proportion

Table 7 *Share of different types of workers to total main workers (rural and urban combined), Tripura, 1991, 2001, 2011,* in percentages

Type of worker	1991	2001	2011
Cultivator	38.09	26.88	22.90
Agricultural labourer	25.70	24.03	18.74
Manufacturing, processing, servicing, etc	1.42	2.90	1.79
Other workers	34.79	46.19	56.56

Source: Government of India (2001, 2011).

Table 8 *District-wise share of cultivators and agricultural labourers in main workers, Tripura, 2011,* in percentage

District	Share of cultivators in work force (%)		Share of agricultural labourers in work force (%)	
	2001	2011	2001	2011
Dhalai	35.6	33.9	24.9	19.3
North Tripura	29.5	23.0	11.5	14.2
South Tripura	35.9	28.0	24.4	25.7
West Tripura	21.1	18.1	16.5	16.8

Source: Government of India (2001, 2011).

Table 9 *District-wise ratio of cultivator (CL) to agricultural labourer (AL), Tripura, 2001, 2011*

District	CL/AL 2001	CL/AL 2011
Dhalai	1.446	1.782
North Tripura	2.567	1.624
South Tripura	1.475	1.105
West Tripura	1.283	1.093

Source: Government of India (2001, 2011).

of agricultural labourers declined from 26 per cent in 1991 to 19 per cent in 2011. There has been correspondingly a substantial increase in the share of workers included in the "other workers" category.

We found that at the district level (using the four-district division of Tripura), Dhalai and South Tripura had more than 50 per cent of main workers in agriculture either as cultivators or agricultural labourers (Table 8). This marks a decline from 2001, when more than 60 per cent of main workers were engaged in agriculture in these two districts. The proportion of agricultural labourers, however, declined only in Dhalai (from 25 to 20 per cent). In the three other districts, their numbers increased. South Tripura had the highest share of agricultural labourers in 2011.

In fact, the cultivator to agricultural labourer ratio increased in Dhalai between 2001 and 2011. This implies that there were more cultivators as compared to agricultural labourers, and this ratio increased in the ten-year period between 2001 and 2011.[12]

Cropping Pattern

The two major farming practices in Tripura are settled cultivation in the plains and shifting cultivation in the hills. About 98 per cent of the land area is still utilised for food crops and only 2 per cent is under non-food crops. The major crops are paddy, pulses, and oilseeds. In 2011–12, 56.3 per cent of the gross cropped area was under paddy. Pulses, oilseeds, maize, wheat, jute, cotton, and sugarcane together covered less than 5 per cent of gross cropped area. Tripura is the second largest producer of natural rubber after Kerala in the country, and this sector holds considerable scope for development as its productivity, at 1,200 kg/ha/year, is very high.

Foodgrain. The State is deficit in foodgrain production and has to import to meet demand. About 27 per cent of the land is available for cultivation and the bulk of the cultivated area is under rice, wheat, other cereals, and pulses (Table 10). Rice yield has risen from 2,010 kg/ha in 1995–96 to 2,800 kg/ha in 2013–14. This is mainly due to the initiatives taken under the State government's ten-year perspective plan that aims to achieve self-sufficiency in food production. Foodgrain production has increased from 5.13 lakh tons in 1999–2000 to 7.7 lakh tons in 2014–15, against a requirement of 8.79 lakh tons.

---

[12] For the other three districts the ratio has declined, and most substantially for North Tripura, where the ratio went down from 2.56 to 1.62.

While West Tripura had the largest area under rice cultivation and the highest production, South Tripura had a higher average yield. The South district also had the highest area, production, and yield of pulses. Table 12 presents district-level crop production in the State in 2013–14. In all the districts rice occupied the maximum cultivated area, and yields were highest in Sepahijala, Gomati, and South Tripura. Other important crops in terms of area under cultivation were maize, pulses, and oilseeds.

Farmers in North Tripura largely grew rice, maize, wheat, and pulses. However, across these crops, the yield was lowest in the North district. In South Tripura, rice, maize, pulses, rapeseed, and mustard were the important crops. Before getting divided, West Tripura had the largest area under rice cultivation of all four districts, and maize occupied the second largest area under cultivation. In Dhalai, rapeseed/mustard, oilseed, and potatoes occupied the largest area under cultivation after rice, followed by maize. This pattern saw a shift by 2013–14, when there were large areas under maize, pulses, and sesame. The area under pulses was higher in North Tripura, Unokoti, Dhalai, and Khowai, but the yield was higher in Sepahijala, Gomati, and South Tripura. Gomati district had the largest area under jute and *mesta* in 2013–14.

Cash crops. The State grows jute and *mesta,* sugarcane, cotton, and other fibres. Of these, jute and *mesta,* though important in the mid-1990s, has seen a steady decline in area even though yields have remained the same. A notable feature has been the shift from cash crops towards horticultural crops, plantation crops, and vegetables. This shift can be mainly attributed to poor market access and low profitability of cash crops.

Horticultural crops. Tripura's agroclimatic conditions – fertile soil with abundant rainfall – offer significant scope for the development of the horticulture sector. Horticultural crops, which include vegetables, flowers, fruit, plantations crops, and spices, account for 21 per cent of the State's gross cropped area. In 2013–14, about 89,000 hectares were under cultivation of fruit, plantation crops, and flowers. Tripura is the largest producer of "true potato seed" in the country, and the quality of pineapple grown here is highly acclaimed.

Rubber and tea. Tripura is the second largest producer of natural rubber after Kerala, with its productivity at around 1,200 kg/ha/year. In 2012–13 alone, Tripura produced 37,277 metric tons (MT) of rubber. This sector can

Table 10 *Share of different crops in total gross cropped area, Tripura, 2009–10, 2010–11, 2011–12,* in percentages

Crops	Percentage of total gross cropped area		
	2009–10	2010–11	2011–12
Paddy	54.5	55.8	56.3
Maize	0.4	0.7	0.8
Wheat	0.2	0.2	0.1
Pulses	1.4	1.6	1.8
Oil Seeds	0.8	0.9	1.0
Jute and *mesta*	0.3	0.3	0.3
Cotton	0.2	0.2	0.2
Sugarcane	0.2	0.2	0.2
Horticultural crops (including vegetables, flowers, fruits, plantations, and spices)	21.0	20.0	20.4
Tea	1.8	1.7	1.7
Rubber	10.1	10.1	11.2
Others (drug, narcotics, medicinal, and minor non-reporting crops)	9.2	8.3	6.0

Source: Government of Tripura (2013).

Table 11 *Area, production, and yield of major horticultural crops, Tripura, 2013–14,* in hectares and metric ton

	Crop	Area (hectares)	Production (metric tons)
1	Pineapple	11590	162260
2	Jackfruit	10120	302183
3	Banana	13644	134257
4	Orange	6302	33905
5	Coconut	6912	19483
6	Cashewnut	5368	4047
7	Summer vegetables	13869	166177
8	Winter vegetables including potato	18626	280741

Source: Government of Tripura (2014).

be expanded further, especially in the hilly rural areas of the State. There are around 55 tea gardens in Tripura, covering an area of 7,500 hectares.

Table 12 *Area, production, and yield of major crops at district level, Tripura, 2013–14,* in hectares, tonnes per bale, and kg per hectare

Crop	North Tripura	Unokoti	Dhalai	Khowai	West Tripura	Sepahijala	Gomati	South Tripura
Rice								
Area	32584	17245	32839	24338	24283	49364	31355	42246
Production	82938	47101	82847	69580	69932	145436	92293	121704
Yield	2545	2731	2523	2859	2880	2946	2943	2881
Maize								
Area	955	310	862	511	387	490	328	746
Production	1178	438	1141	613	521	617	426	929
Yield	1234	1413	1324	1200	1346	1259	1299	1245
Wheat								
Area	48	43	19	3	9	13	4	11
Production	92	95	37	6	18	24	8	20
Yield	1917	2209	1947	2000	2000	1846	2000	1818
Gram								
Area	52	0	0	43	0	0	0	30
Production	40	0	0	35	0	0	0	20
Yield	769	0	0	814	0	0	0	667
Other pulses								
Area	537	528	455	390	164	118	123	354
Production	399	401	349	381	124	93	82	229
Yield	743	759	767	977	756	788	667	647
Total pulses								
Area	2610	1162	2974	1437	756	658	521	2032
Production	1842	828	2032	1087	539	464	425	1479
Yield	706	713	683	756	713	705	816	728
Groundnut								
Area	33	33	221	54	104	4	23	141
Production	35	47	244	73	122	4	29	171
Yield	1061	1424	1104	1352	1173	1000	1261	1213
Sesame								
Area	280	195	916	280	150	245	248	510
Production	154	132	493	148	89	153	140	397
Yield	549	676	538	529	593	624	565	779
Rapeseed/ mustard								
Area	408	334	405	378	91	208	283	510
Production	313	259	348	317	64	177	250	431
Yield	767	775	859	839	703	851	883	845

(continued)

Table 12 (continued)

Crop	North Tripura	Unokoti	Dhalai	Khowai	West Tripura	Sepahijala	Gomati	South Tripura
Total oilseeds								
Area	721	562	1542	712	345	457	554	1161
Production	502	438	1085	538	275	334	419	999
Yield	696	779	704	756	797	731	756	861
Potato								
Area	NA	NA	1220	562	474	1110	NA	NA
Production	NA	NA	21497	10879	9088	21379	NA	NA
Yield	NA	NA	NA	NA	NA	NA	NA	NA
Chilies								
Area	333	NA	343	NA	1664	NA	NA	2102
Production	1358	NA	1393	NA	6520	NA	NA	8701
Yield	NA	NA	NA	NA	NA	NA	NA	NA
Turmeric (dry)								
Area	336	NA	770	NA	360	NA	NA	441
Production	2621	NA	6006	NA	2808	NA	NA	3440
Yield	NA	NA	NA	NA	NA	NA	NA	NA
Ginger								
Area	378	NA	51	NA	552	NA	NA	840
Production	3122	NA	421	NA	4560	NA	NA	6938
Yield	NA	NA	NA	NA	NA	NA	NA	NA
Sugar (cane)								
Area	180	103	111	48	34	74	64	350
Production	9581	5974	5496	2668	1576	4209	3162	16932
Yield	53228	58000	49514	55583	46353	56878	49406	48377
Jute production in bales of 180 kg								
Area	76	105	48	38	23	21	253	79
Production	625	848	391	322	176	178	2216	613
Yield	8.22	8.08	8.15	8.47	7.65	8.48	8.76	7.76
Mesta production in bales of 170 kg								
Area	63	87	283	53	15	8	197	148
Production	521	822	2362	417	119	66	1526	1170
Yield	8.27	9.45	8.35	7.87	7.93	8.25	7.75	7.91
Cotton								
Area	277	44	351	69	11	13	121	63
Production	353	65	587	103	16	20	165	86
Yield	1.27	1.48	1.67	1.49	1.46	1.51	1.36	1.37

Source: Government of Tripura (2014).

Irrigation

Even though Tripura receives high rainfall, development of its irrigation potential could help to further enhance the productivity of its agricultural sector. The area under irrigation increased from around 2,000 hectares in 1972 to 1,14,000 hectares by the end of March 2015. However, the percentage of irrigated area to gross cropped area remained almost constant, at around 10 per cent. There are no major irrigation projects in Tripura. The three medium-sized irrigation projects are those of the Gumti, Khowai, and Manu. The primary sources of irrigation are minor works, like lift irrigation, deep tubewells, diversion schemes, shallow tubewells, tanks, etc.

Tripura's irrigation status based on size-class of landholding (Table 13) shows that only 22 per cent of land under marginal cultivation received any kind of irrigation. Close to 60 per cent of marginal landholdings were wholly unirrigated, and it is to be noted that most landholdings in Tripura are marginal holdings. Only around a quarter of small landholdings received any kind of irrigation.

Table 14 presents the source of irrigation by different size-classes. It is interesting to note that around 80 per cent of Tripura's irrigation came from "other sources" followed by canals and tubewells. Marginal farmers had little access to canal irrigation, and they relied instead on tube-wells and tanks. However, with only 22 per cent of total area receiving any

Table 13 *Operational holdings by size-classes and irrigation status, Tripura, 2010–11,* in numbers and hectares

Size-class	Total holdings		Wholly irrigated holdings		Wholly unirrigated holdings		Partially irrigated holdings			Holdings receiving irrigation	
	No.	Area	No.	Area	No.	Area	No.	Total area	Irrigated area	No.	Net irrigated area
Marginal	499054	139700	10.7	9.0	72.2	59.2	17.1	20.9	13.2	27.8	22.2
Small	55043	75809	11.5	10.5	60.9	54.7	27.6	25.9	14.3	39.1	24.7
Semi-medium	21544	54265	6.3	5.3	7.0	62.4	23.5	22.5	11.0	29.8	16.2
Medium	2752	13942	8.1	6.8	53.5	47.0	38.4	34.9	1.4	46.5	18.2
Large	86	1229	10.5	6.7	45.3	43.4	44.2	44.0	15.6	54.7	22.3

Source: Agricultural Census of India.

Table 14 *Operational holdings by size-class and type of irrigation, Tripura, 2010–11, in numbers and hectares*

Size-class	Total holdings		Canals		Tanks		Wells		Tubewells		Other sources		Total net irrigated area
	No.	Area	No. of holdings irrigated	Area irrigated	No. of holdings irrigated	Area irrigated	No. of holdings irrigated	Area irrigated	No. of holdings irrigated	Area irrigated	No. of holdings irrigated	Area irrigated	
Marginal	499054	139700	6256	3.51	5524	3.44	4276	0.63	10700	6.08	122021	86.3	31036
Small	55043	75809	13400	12.69	1127	3.49	12963	3.30	14126	8.78	19019	71.7	18752
Semi-medium	21544	54265	4329	12.37	332	3.49	4272	4.93	4364	5.66	5901	73.5	8818
Medium	2752	13942	936	11.25	42	4.84	921	2.71	932	4.29	1207	76.9	2542
Large	86	1229	38	13.50	0	0.00	38	3.28	38	3.28	47	80.3	274
All classes	578479	284945	24959	7.95	7025	3.51	22470	2.16	30160	6.76	148195	79.6	61421

Source: Agricultural Census of India.

Table 15 *Irrigation status, district level, Tripura, 2010–11,* in percentages

District	Holdings receiving irrigation	
	Number of holdings as percentage of total holdings (%)	Net irrigated area (%)
Dhalai	10.0	7.9
North Tripura	27.6	12.8
South Tripura	24.3	23.2
West Tripura	39.3	29.0
All Districts	29.0	21.6

Source: Agricultural Census of India.

kind of irrigation, the scope for expansion is promising. With an area of around 1,78,000 ha under paddy and horticultural crops, the scale of irrigation requirement for the State can be estimated.

From Table 15, we can observe that in 2010–11, West Tripura had the highest percentage of net irrigated area (29 per cent) and the highest number of holdings receiving any form of irrigation (39.3 per cent). Dhalai has the least levels of irrigation with only 10 per cent of total holdings under irrigation and having only 7.9 per cent of net irrigated area.

Summary

The economy of Tripura has a substantial dependency on its agriculture sector. The dominant role played by agriculture is evident both from its share in net State domestic product, which is close to 30 per cent, as well as by the large proportion of workers employed by the sector (around 42 per cent of main workers are engaged in agriculture). The average size of landholding is less than 0.5 hectare, and the sector comprises largely small and marginal farmers. The main crops grown in the State include rice, which accounts for 57 per cent of gross cropped area, pulses and oilseeds. In recent years, there has been a movement away from cash crops to horticultural crops and vegetables. This has been attributed to the State's favourable agroclimatic conditions, fertile soils and abundance of rainfall. The State could, however, pay greater attention to the development of irrigation projects, and provide more access to modern inputs and markets for this sector to take off and be a source of reliable livelihood. An increased focus on horticulture would bring extra income for people who are otherwise deprived of employment opportunities outside agriculture.

References

Banik, Pankaj (2011), *Legislative Assembly of Tripura: A Survey*, Kolkata: Levant Books.

Bareh, Hamlet (2001), *Encyclopaedia of North-East India, Volume VIII: Tripura*. New Delhi: Mittal Publications.

Basu, Pradip Kumar (1996), *The Communist Movement in Tripura*, Calcutta: Progressive Publishers.

Chakraborty, Dipannita (2004) *Land Question in Tripura*, New Delhi: Akansha Publishing House.

Chanda, Saroj (2006), *Prekshapata Tripura* [Background of Tripura], Agartala: Tripura Darpan.

Das, Jitendra Nath (1990). *A Study of the Land System of Tripura*, Guwahati: Law Research Institute, Eastern Region.

Datta, Biren (1979), "Bhoomi sanskar sankrant nirbachani ghoshna o ek borshore baam front sarkarer kaaj" [Announcements made regarding land reforms during election and the work of Left Front government in one year], *Desher Katha* (Agartala), 5 January.

Datta, Jyotirmay (1987), "Land and Land Relations in Tripura," in B. B. Dutta and M. N. Karna (eds), *Land Relations in North East India*, New Delhi: People's Publishing House.

Datta, Narendra Chandra (1980), "Land Reforms," in Jagadis Gan-Chaudhuri (ed.), *Tripura: The Land and Its People*, Delhi: Leeladevi Publications.

De, Nilanjan (2014), *A Historical Analysis of Migration in Tripura: 1900–1971*, Delhi: Research India Publications.

Deb, Dasaratha (1967), *Protection of the Land of Tripura's Tribal People*, Agartala: Janasiksha Cooperative Limited.

—— (1974), *Tripura Land Revenue and Land Reforms (Second Amendment) Act, 1974: Another despicable step towards slaying of tribals*, Agartala: Janasiksha Cooperative Limited.

—— (1984), "Sastha tafshiler aandolan ekhano thambe na" [The struggle for Sixth Schedule won't stop even now], *Daily Desher Katha* (Agartala), 11 October.

Deb Barma, Aghore (1991), "Land Reforms in Tripura," in Malabika Das Gupta (ed.), *The Impact of Land Reforms in North East India*, Guwahati: Omsons Publication.

Debbarma, Khakchang (undated), *Politics of Land Alienation and Problem of its Restoration in Tripura*, available at http://dspace.nehu.ac.in/bitstream/1/8962/1/Politics%20%28K%20Debbarma%29.pdf, viewed on 20 March 2014.

Debbarma, Narendra Chandra (2005), *History of the Land System and Land Management in Tripura*, Agartala: Manjushree Publications.

Ganguly, J. B. (1983). *The Benign Hills: A Study in Tripura's Population Growth and Problems*, Agartala: Tripura Darpan Prakashani.

Government of Tripura (GoT) (1976), *A Decade of Development: Tripura*. Agartala: Directorate of Public Relations and Tourism, Government of Tripura.

―――― (2007), *Tripura Human Development Report 2007*, Agartala: Government of Tripura.

―――― (2013), *Economic Review of Tripura 2012–13*, Agartala: Directorate of Economics and Statistics Planning Department, Government of Tripura.

―――― (2014), *Statistical Abstract of Tripura 2014*, Agartala: Directorate of Economics and Statistics Planning Department, Government of Tripura.

Government of India (GoI) (2001), *Census of India 2001: Primary Census Abstract*, New Delhi: Registrar General and Census Commissioner of India, Ministry of Home Affairs, Government of India.

―――― (2011), *Census of India 2011: Primary Census Abstract*, New Delhi: Registrar General and Census Commissioner of India, Ministry of Home Affairs, Government of India.

Khan, Saqib (2018), "A reading without history: Questioning a flawed reading of Left politics in Tripura," *Economic and Political Weekly*, 53 (7), 17 February; available at https://www.epw.in/engage/article/reading-without-history-questioning-flawed-reading-left-politics-tripura, viewed on 17 February 2018.

Kilikdar, Bibhas Kanti (ed.) (2002), *Code of Tripura Enactments Volume I*, Agartala: Law Department, Government of Tripura.

Ray, Jagat Jyoti (1991), "Impact of Land Reforms in Tripura," in Malabika Das Gupta (ed.), *The Impact of Land Reforms in North East India*, Guwahati and New Delhi: Omsons Publications.

―――― (2012), *Bidroh bibartan o Tripura* [The Evolution of Revolts and Tripura], Agartala: Tripura Darpan.

Saha, Dinesh Chandra (2009), *Tripuray gana andolaner bichitra dhara* [Diverse streams of Tripura's mass movement], Agartala: Writers Publication.

4

The Tripura Model[1]

V. K. Ramachandran and Madhura Swaminathan

In the late 1990s and early 2000s, Tripura embarked on a unique path to peace, one that was not dependent solely on security measures but involved investment in human development and people's participation in the implementation of socio-political and economic policy as well. More than a decade later, the human development consequences of peace have been remarkable.

In 2005 and 2006, we spent some months in rural Tripura as part of work on the *Tripura Human Development Report* (the Government of Tripura and the United Nations Development Programme [UNDP] had commissioned the Foundation for Agrarian Studies [FAS] to write the report). The threat of violence was ever present, and elaborate arrangements had to be made to ensure the safety of the members of our team, mainly students and youth. Although insurgency was on the decline by the time the *Tripura Human Development Report 2007* was published, acts of insurgent violence still continued. Indeed, the idea that the people had to be free from threats to life and limb in order to achieve their full potential was an important part of the *Report*.

Tripura Chief Minister Manik Sarkar has often said that economic and social investments and people's involvement are essential components of the peace process in the State. The landmark repeal of the Armed Forces (Special Powers) Act, or AFSPA, in 2015 in the State was an outstanding symbol of the success of this policy.

We returned to Tripura in the summer of 2016 to resurvey three villages we had first surveyed in 2005. The principal change was a

[1] Op-ed in *The Hindu*, dated 15 November 2017.

palpable atmosphere of peace and personal safety in the State, even in its most remote reserved forest settlements. The progress achieved over the last ten years in several indicators of human development – especially in education, health, and employment – is the State's peace dividend, and is worthy of public attention.

Let us examine some of these achievements.

Growing Literacy

Literacy has been described as being "the basic personal skill that underlies the whole modernising sequence." Separatist militancy in Tripura was an obstacle to the spread of literacy and schooling. Progress in literacy has been particularly rapid in Tripura over two decades. According to the Census, the share of literate persons above the age of 7 years rose from 73 per cent to 87 per cent between 2001 and 2011. We now have data from surveys conducted in 2005 and 2016 in Khakchang, a fully Scheduled Tribe village in North district, Mainama, a village in Dhalai district whose population is 67 per cent Scheduled Tribe, and Muhuripur, a village in South district.

A measure of progress in schooling of the population in these villages is the number of years of completed schooling among women in the age-group 18 to 45 years. In Khakchang in 2005, more than 50 per cent of women in the age-group had not completed even a year of schooling. By 2016, the median number of completed years of schooling among women in the age-group was seven – outstanding progress for a decade. The corresponding figure for Mainama, also a Scheduled Tribe-dominated village, was six years in 2005 and nine years in 2016.

Data from the National Family Health Survey (NFHS) indicate that the infant mortality rate (IMR) in Tripura almost halved between 2005–06 and 2014–15, declining from 51 per thousand live births to 27 per thousand. According to data from the most recent Sample Registration Bulletin, IMR further declined to 20 per thousand in 2015.

Employment and Labour Force

Peace and security enable the expansion of employment and livelihoods.

The growth rate of per capita State domestic product (SDP) has been over 8 per cent per annum in eight out of the last ten years (2005–06 to 2014–15). In the last four years, when per capita net domestic product of

India was growing only at around 5 per cent per annum, per capita SDP in Tripura grew at 9 to 10 per cent a year.

For the last five to six years, Tripura has ranked first among the States of India with respect to implementation of the Mahatma Gandhi National Rural Employment Guarantee Act (MGNREGA). Over this period, the average number of days of employment obtained per household in India ranged between 40 and 50 days. In Tripura, from 2011–12 to 2014–15, the corresponding figure was about 80 days a year. In 2015–16, the number rose to 94 days. The unilateral decision of the Government of India to reduce the allocation of resources for the rural employment guarantee scheme has hit the State government hard. According to Gautam Das, editor of the Agartala-based daily *Desher Katha*, the present allocation will be adequate only to create 42 days of employment per household in the current year.

An important feature of Tripura's economy over the last decade has been a rise in labour force participation and work force participation, particularly among women. This is in marked contrast to India as a whole, where data show a decline in female labour force participation and work force participation over time. National Sample Survey (NSS) data show that in rural India, female labour force participation fell from 49 per cent in 2004–05 to 36 per cent in 2011–12. In Tripura, however, over the same period, female labour force participation rose from 17 per cent to 38 per cent (urban areas showed a slightly lower rate of growth than rural areas).

A labour force, by definition, includes those in work and those seeking work. The work participation rate (WPR) rose among men and women, rural and urban, over the seven-year period. According to NSS data, the female work participation rate in rural Tripura rose from 12 per cent in 2004–05 to 31 per cent in 2011–12. In rural India, it fell from 49 per cent to 35 per cent over the same period. In Tripura, work participation rates rose among males, urban and rural, and among urban females as well.

Looking Ahead

An important factor in the dramatic rise in work participation rates, especially among women, has been the improvement in the security environment, which encouraged women to enter the labour force in much larger numbers than before. The rise in work and labour force participation rates, particularly among women, is both a positive achievement and a challenge. The challenge is to generate adequate employment opportunities to absorb the increasing number of women who will join the work force. Tripura's path of development is one that respects administrative autonomy for regions where people of the Scheduled Tribes are predominant in the population and the principle of unity of its diverse people. An inclusive path of development, one that encompasses the poorest in the population and the most far-flung of forest-based human settlements, is a precious legacy. It would be great unwisdom to reverse or disrupt such a path.

SECTION II

Agrarian Structure, Production, and Agrarian Relations

5

Socio-Economic Classes in Three Villages of Tripura

Tapas Singh Modak and Madhura Swaminathan[1]

This book is based mainly on household-level data collected by the Project on Agrarian Relations in India (PARI) in three villages in Tripura: Khakhchang in North District, Mainama in Dhalai District and Muhuripur in South District. The data pertain to the agricultural year 2015–16.

One of the objectives of PARI is to identify and understand the nature of agrarian classes in the countryside. Households are classified on the basis of the means of production and other assets that they own, the labour power that they employ or sell in the course of work for others, the surpluses they produce, and the incomes that they earn. The specificities of each region are of special importance in the final identification of socio-economic classes in a given village.

In general, households in PARI villages are classified in the following way (Ramachandran 2011). *Landlords and big capitalist farmer households* own the most and best land in the villages. Members of these households do not participate in the major agricultural operations on the land. *Peasant households* constitute the sector of petty producers that lies between landlords and rich capitalist farmers on the one hand, and manual workers on the other. Members of peasant households work on all or some of the major manual operations on the land. The peasantry is not a single class but is stratified with respect to household income, labour use, and asset ownership. *Manual worker households* derive most of their incomes from and spend most of their working time on wage work, agricultural and non-agricultural. There are also classes and social strata in the village that

[1] We are grateful to T. Sivamurugan for being part of the data analysis and to V. K. Ramachandran for participation in the process of classification.

are not directly involved in crop or agricultural production. These include households dependent primarily on business activity or salaries or other sources of income.

The villages surveyed in Tripura, like villages elsewhere in India, presented us with their own distinct set of circumstances. First, there were no landlords or rich capitalist farmer households in any of the three villages. Secondly, the class of landless manual workers, that is, manual workers with no ownership or operational holdings of land, was relatively small. Most manual worker households were involved in some form of cultivation.

Three further features of cultivators and cultivation in the study villages are noteworthy. First, the scale and type of cultivation varied by type of land, and comprised the following distinct types of cultivation: lowland, upland or *tila*, *jhum* or slash-and-burn, and homestead. Since there are clear differences in terms of land quality, farming practices, and value of production as between lowland and upland, we have, in this book, assumed an equivalence between 1 acre of lowland and 1.5 acres of upland. A second feature of cultivator households in the villages is that the terms of possession of land take different forms: as fully private property, as land obtained under the provisions of the Forest Rights Act, and as upland common land that is assigned by custom to households for *jhum* cultivation. A third feature of note is the diversification of occupations and incomes among cultivator households. On account of these three features of cultivators and cultivation, we have used extent of operational holdings and type of cultivation as the main criteria for categorising cultivator households.

Khakchang Village, North Tripura District

In the village of Khakchang, there were no landlords or rich capitalist farmers. At the other end of the class hierarchy, there were households with no operational holdings of land. In this group, we identified two categories, based on the nature of income generation: manual workers dependent on wage labour and manual workers with diversified incomes. The two categories identified thus are:

Manual worker: No operated area and more than 50 per cent of household income from manual work; and

Manual worker with diversified income: No operated area and less than 50 per cent of household income from manual work.

Three types of cultivation other than homestead cultivation were prevalent in Khakchang: *jhum* cultivation, lowland cultivation, and non-*jhum* upland cultivation. *Jhum* cultivation is hilltop slash-and-burn cultivation, and is also sometimes shifting cultivation. Farming practices on *jhum* land were not intensive, they were low in input use, and dependent mainly on family and exchange labour. Non-*jhum* upland cultivation was on the slopes of nearby hills and involved some form of terracing, and was again dependent on family labour. Crops such as banana, pineapple, and rubber were grown on such uplands. In addition, there were pockets of lowland cultivation, mainly rice and vegetables, in Khakchang.

In Khakchang, each type of cultivation is distinct and associated with specific crops, levels of input use, and income levels. We classified cultivators on the basis of type of land and cultivation practices. The classification is as follows:

1. Cultivator: *jhum*
2. Cultivator: mixed (*jhum* and lowland cultivation)
3. Cultivator: lowland
4. Cultivator: non-*jhum* upland

Lastly, as in other villages, we have a non-agricultural or non-cultivator stratum comprising households dependent mainly on incomes from salaries or business or other sources (such as pensions and remittances).

The socio-economic classification of all households in Khakchang is given in Table 1.

Table 1 *Distribution of households by socio-economic category, Khakchang, 2016* in numbers and per cent

Type of cultivation	Number of households	Share in per cent
Cultivator: *jhum*	240	41
Cultivator: mixed	60	10
Cultivator: lowland	122	21
Cultivator: non-*jhum* upland	51	9
Manual worker	49	8
Manual worker with diversified income	53	9
Non-agricultural households: salaried, business and others	14	2
All	589	100

Source: Survey data.

Eighty per cent of households in Khakchang were cultivators, and *jhum* cultivators comprised around 41 per cent of all households – the largest single group of cultivators. Households that cultivated no land constituted 17 per cent of all households. All of them were either manual workers or manual workers with diversified sources of income. A very small section of the population was identified as non-agricultural.

To understand these socio-economic categories better, we computed annual household incomes and classified households into the following five income groups:

1. ≤Rs 50,000 per annum
2. >Rs 50,000 ≤100,000
3. >Rs 100,000 ≤Rs 200,000
4. >Rs 200,000 ≤Rs 300,000
5. >Rs 300,000

Tables 2a, 2b and 2c show that households dependent on *jhum* cultivation had relatively low incomes, with most of them earning less than Rs 100,000 a year. There were no *jhum* cultivators who earned incomes more than Rs 200,000. Cultivators with non-*jhum* upland crops, on the other hand, had relatively high incomes, all above Rs 100,000.[2] In

Table 2a *Distribution of households by socio-economic class and annual household income, Khakchang, 2015–16* in numbers

Socio-economic class	≤50 K	>50 K ≤1 lakh	>1 lakh ≤2 lakh	>2 lakh ≤3 lakh	>3 lakh	All
Cultivator: *jhum*	75	97	69			240
Cultivator: mixed	17	8	27	8		60
Cultivator: lowland	16	71	24	5	5	122
Cultivator: non-*jhum* upland			14	16	21	51
Manual worker	22	21	5			49
Manual worker with diversified income		16	21	11	5	53
Non-agricultural	8				5	14
Total	137	213	160	40	37	589

Source: Survey data.

---

[2] Members of the "cultivator: non-*jhum* upland" class had not yet received any plantation incomes because plantation production had not yet begun in the survey year, and government salaries and business incomes were still the main income sources of these households.

Table 2b *Distribution of households across socio-economic classes, by annual household income, Khakchang, 2015–16* in per cent

Socio-economic class	≤50 K	>50 K ≤1 lakh	>1 lakh ≤2 lakh	>2 lakh ≤ 3 lakh	>3 lakh	Total
Cultivator: *jhum*	31	40	29	0	0	100
Cultivator: mixed	28	13	45	13	0	100
Cultivator: lowland	13	58	20	4	4	100
Cultivator: non-*jhum* upland	0	0	27	31	41	100
Manual worker	45	43	10	0	0	100
Manual worker with diversified income	0	30	40	21	9	100
Non-agricultural	57	0	0	0	36	100

Source: Survey data.

Table 2c *Distribution of households according to annual household income, by socio-economic class, Khakchang, 2015–16* in per cent

Socio-economic class	≤50K	>50 K ≤1 lakh	>1 lakh ≤2 lakh	>2 lakh ≤ 3 lakh	>3 lakh
Cultivator: *jhum*	55	46	43	0	0
Cultivator: mixed	12	4	17	20	0
Cultivator: lowland	12	33	15	13	14
Cultivator:non-*jhum* upland	0	0	9	40	57
Manual worker	16	10	3	0	0
Manual worker with diversified income	0	8	13	28	14
Non-agricultural	6	0	0	0	14
Total	100	100	100	100	100

Source: Survey data.

terms of incomes, there appears to be a hierarchy corresponding to the four categories of cultivators. Among manual workers, the incomes of households with diversified incomes were higher than of those dependent on wage labour alone.

We also examined the area sown by different socio-economic classes during the reference year (Table 3). An interesting point that emerged from these data is that the share of land operated by cultivators with mixed cultivation was higher than their share in the population. The share of land operated by *jhum* cultivators was also greater than the share of *jhum* cultivators in the population.

Table 3 *Household sown area owned by each socio-economic class as proportion of all sown area in the village, Khakchang, 2016,* in numbers and per cent

Socio-economic class	Number of households	Percentage of total households	Extent of sown area in acre	Percentage of all sown area in per cent
Cultivator: *jhum*	240	40.7	321.3	45.8
Cultivator: mixed	60	10.2	143.9	20.5
Cultivator: lowland	122	20.7	138.3	19.7
Cultivator: non-*jhum* upland	51	8.7	97.6	13.9
Manual worker	49	8.3	0.0	0.0
Manual worker with diversified income	53	9.0	0.0	0.0
Non-agricultural	14	2.4	0.0	0.0
Total	589	100.0	701.1	100.0

Source: Survey data.

Mainama Village, Dhalai District

In Mainama village, there was no household that belonged to the traditional class of landlords. There were three major types of cultivation (in addition to homestead cultivation): upland cultivation, in which the crops grown were rubber, banana, and pineapple; orchards and plantations; and lowland rice and vegetable cultivation.

We defined four categories of cultivators based on the extent of operational holdings:

1. Cultivator sub-marginal: operational holding <1 acre
2. Cultivator marginal: operational holding ≥ 1 <2.5 acres
3. Cultivator small: operational holdings >2.5 acres <5 acres
4. Cultivator medium: operational holdings >5 acres.

Among households with zero operational holdings, we identified two groups:

Manual worker: zero operational holdings and more than 50 per cent of household income from manual work.

Manual worker with diversified income: zero operational holdings and less than 50 per cent of household income from manual work.

Lastly, we identified a separate stratum of non-agricultural households, that is, households dependent on incomes from salaries, business, and other sources.

Table 4 shows the distribution of households in Mainama by socio-economic category. Manual workers accounted for 21 per cent of all households, and non-agricultural households for another 12 per cent. The remaining 67 per cent of households were cultivator households. Among cultivators, those with sub-marginal (<1 acre) and marginal (>1≤2.5 acres) operational holdings constituted the majority, 52 per cent of all households in the village. Households whose operational holdings were more than 5 acres in extent constituted around 4 per cent of households.

Table 4 *Distribution of households by socio-economic category, Mainama, 2015–16, in numbers and per cent*

Socio-economic class	Number of households	Share in per cent
Manual worker	187	13
Manual worker with diversified income	110	8
Cultivator: sub-marginal	438	30
Cultivator: marginal	321	22
Cultivator: small	163	11
Cultivator: medium	63	4
Non-agricultural	169	12
All	1451	100

Source: Survey data.

Table 5a *Distribution of households by socio-economic class and household income, Mainama, 2015–16 in numbers*

Socio-economic class	≤50K	>50 K <1 lakh	>1 lakh <2 lakh	>2 lakh <5 lakh	>5 lakh <9 lakh	>9 lakh	Total
Manual worker	65	78	45				187
Manual worker with diversified income	19	10	56	25			110
Cultivator: sub-marginal	142	141	93	57	5		438
Cultivator: marginal	25	110	86	83	7	11	321
Cultivator: small	16	38	44	46	12	6	162
Cultivator: medium	5		10	43	6		63
Non-agricultural	25	20	24	59	30	10	169
Total	297	397	358	314	59	26	1451

Source: Survey data.

Table 5b *Distribution of households across socio-economic classes, by annual household income, Mainama, 2015–16 in per cent*

Socio-economic class	≤50K	>50 K ≤1 lakh	>1 lakh ≤2 lakh	>2 lakh ≤5 lakh	>5 lakh ≤9 lakh	>9 lakh	Total
Manual worker	35	42	24	0	0	0	100
Manual worker with diversified income	17	9	51	23	0	0	100
Cultivator: sub-marginal	32	32	21	13	1	0	100
Cultivator: marginal	8	34	27	26	2	3	100
Cultivator: small	10	23	27	28	7	4	100
Cultivator: medium	8	0	16	68	10	0	100
Non-agricultural	15	12	14	35	18	6	100

Source: Survey data.

Table 5c *Distribution of households according to annual household income, by socio-economic class, Mainama, 2015–16, in per cent*

Socio-economic class	≤50K	>50 K ≤1 lakh	>1 lakh ≤2 lakh	>2 lakh ≤5 lakh	>5 lakh ≤9 lakh	>9 lakh
Manual worker	22	20	13	0	0	0
Manual worker with diversified income	6	3	16	8	0	0
Cultivator: sub-marginal	48	36	26	18	8	0
Cultivator: marginal	8	28	24	26	12	42
Cultivator: small	5	10	12	15	20	23
Cultivator: medium	2	0	3	14	10	0
Salaried, business and others	8	5	7	19	51	38
Total	100	100	100	100	100	100

Source: Survey data.

To understand income differences across socio-economic classes, we grouped households into six categories of annual household income:

1. ≤Rs 50,000 per annum
2. > Rs 50,000 ≤100,000
3. >Rs 100,000 ≤Rs 200,000
4. >Rs 200,000 ≤Rs 500,000
5. >Rs 500,000 ≤Rs 900,000
6. > Rs 900,000

Table 6 *Distribution of operational holding by socio-economic class, Mainama, 2015–16* in numbers and per cent

Socio-economic class	Number of households	Percentage of total households	Extent of operational holding (in acres)	Percentage of all operational holding (in per cent)
Manual worker	187	13	0.0	0
Manual worker with diversified income	110	8	0.0	0
Cultivator: sub-marginal	438	30	259.9	11
Cultivator: marginal	321	22	663.1	28
Cultivator: small	163	11	705.8	29
Cultivator: medium	63	4	766.8	32
Salaried, business and others	169	12	0.0	0
All	1451	100	2395.6	100

Source: Survey data.

The cross-tabulation of household income groups and socio-economic classes in Tables 5a, 5b, and 5c shows clear patterns. Manual workers and sub-marginal cultivators were concentrated in the lower income groups. The incomes of 77 per cent of all manual worker households was less than Rs 100,000 a year. By contrast, 78 per cent of medium cultivator households had annual incomes of more than Rs 200,000 a year. Of all non-agricultural households in Mainama, 73 per cent had incomes that were higher than Rs 100,000 a year.

Lastly, we examined the extent of operational holding among different socio-economic classes (Table 6). Medium cultivator households accounted for 4 per cent of households and controlled 32 per cent of operational holdings.

Muhuripur Village, South District

In Muhuripur village too, there was no farmer who belonged to the traditional class of landlords.

There were three distinct types of cultivation in Muhuripur: lowland cultivation (rice and vegetables), upland cultivation, and homestead cultivation. Lowland cultivation was the most significant type of cultivation in the village.

As in Mainama, the final classification of cultivator households was based on the extent of land operated by households. Three categories were identified.

1. Cultivator sub-marginal: operational holdings <1 acre
2. Cultivator marginal: operational holdings >1 ≤2.5 acres
3. Cultivator small: operational holdings >2.5 acres

Two categories of manual workers were identified:
Manual worker: No operational holdings and more than 50 per cent of household income from manual work.
Manual worker with diversified income: No operational holdings and less than 50 per cent of household income from manual work.

There was also a non-agricultural stratum, households dependent on salaries, income from business and other sources.

Table 7 shows the distribution of households in Muhuripur village by the socio-economic classes we have proposed. Sub-marginal cultivators were the single biggest group in the village and constituted 44 per cent of all households

We grouped households by annual household incomes into the following categories:

1. ≤Rs 50,000 per annum
2. >Rs 50,000 ≤100,000
3. >Rs 100,000 ≤Rs 200,000
4. >Rs 200,000 ≤Rs 500,000
5. >Rs 500,000

Table 7 *Distribution of households by socio-economic category, Muhuripur, 2016,* in numbers and per cent

Socio-economic class	Number of households	Share of all households
Manual worker	108	10
Manual worker with diversified income	159	15
Cultivator: sub-marginal	469	44
Cultivator: marginal	182	17
Cultivator: small	49	5
Non-agricultural	87	8
Total	1054	100

Source: Survey data.

Table 8a *Distribution of households by socio-economic class and size-class of annual income, Muhuripur, 2015–16*, in numbers

Socio-economic class	<50K	>50 K <1	>1 lakh <2 lakh	>2 lakh <5 lakh	>5 lakh	Total
Manual worker	41	57	11	0	0	108
Manual worker with diversified income	15	70	63	10	0	159
Cultivator: sub-marginal	124	186	103	56	0	469
Cultivator: marginal	30	36	73	33	10	182
Cultivator: small	6	5	21	9	9	49
Non-agricultural	4	0	25	44	13	87
Total	220	354	294	152	33	1054

Source: Survey data.

Table 8b *Distribution of households across socio-economic classes, by annual household income, Muhuripur, 2015–16*, in per cent

Socio-economic class	≤50K	>50 K ≤1	>1 lakh ≤2 lakh	>2 lakh ≤5 lakh	>5 lakh	Total
Manual worker	38	53	10	0	0	100
Manual worker with diversified income	9	44	40	6	0	100
Cultivator: sub-marginal	26	40	22	12	0	100
Cultivator: marginal	16	20	40	18	5	100
Cultivator: small	12	10	43	18	18	100
Non-agricultural	5	0	29	51	15	100

Source: Survey data.

Table 8c *Distribution of households according to annual household income, by socio-economic class, Muhuripur, 2015–16*, in per cent

Socio-economic class	≤50K	>50 K ≤1	>1 lakh ≤2 lakh	>2 lakh ≤5 lakh	>5 lakh
Manual worker	19	16	4	0	0
Manual worker with diversified income	7	20	21	7	0
Cultivator: sub-marginal	56	53	35	37	0
Cultivator: marginal	14	10	25	22	30
Cultivator: small	3	1	7	6	27
Non-agricultural	2	0	9	29	39
Total	100	100	100	100	100

Source: Survey data.

Table 9 *Distribution of operational holding by socio-economic class, Muhuripur, 2015–16,* in numbers and per cent

Socio-economic class	Number of households	Share in total households	Extent of operational holding in acres	Percentage of all operational holdings
Manual worker	108	10	0.0	0
Manual worker with diversified income	159	15	0.0	0
Cultivator: sub-marginal	469	44	298.4	36
Cultivator: marginal	182	17	325.0	39
Cultivator: small	49	5	214.4	26
Non-agricultural	87	8	0.0	0
Total	1054	100	837.8	100

Source: Survey data.

Cross-tabulations of socio-economic class and household income are shown in Tables 8a, 8b, and 8c.

Most manual worker households earned less than Rs 100,000 a year, and most non-agricultural households earned more than Rs 100,000 a year. Among cultivator households, the distribution of households across income groups is broadly as expected, that is, the majority of sub-marginal cultivator households had incomes of less than Rs 100,000 a year, and the majority of small cultivator households had incomes of more than Rs 100,000 a year.

The distribution of households across income groups thus broadly corresponds to our socio-economic classification.

Table 9 shows the relative share of different classes in the population and the share of landholdings in the village operated by them. Cultivators with small holdings constituted 5 per cent of all households but operated 26 per cent of landholdings.

Summary

To sum up, our socio-economic classification of households is based on a study of production conditions actually prevalent in the region.

In terms of class structure, a notable feature of all three villages was the absence of a traditional class of landlords. Secondly, the class of manual workers, or those without any operational holding of land and dependent on wage labour, comprised 8 per cent of all households in Khakchang and

13 per cent of all households in Mainama – a smaller proportion than in other villages studied in the course of PARI. Thirdly, the stratum of non-agricultural households was relatively small in all three villages.

With regard to the peasantry, there was much variation across the three villages. Our classification in each village is based on different types of farming and on the extent of land cultivated by households. In Khakchang, a substantial section of cultivators were engaged in subsistence-like *jhum* cultivation. In Mainama, a substantial section of cultivators grew plantation crops commercially on upland. Muhuripur is mostly a lowland rice-growing village. The categories of cultivators in each of the three villages are perhaps not distinct classes but differ substantially in socio-economic terms (in terms of operational holdings of land and household income, for instance), and have thus been studied separately in this book.

Reference

Ramachandran, V. K., 2011, "The State of Agrarian Relations in India Today," *The Marxist*, vol. 27, nos. 1–2, January–June.

6

Agrarian Structure, Production, and Agrarian Relations in Khakchang

Ranjini Basu, Ritam Dutta, Subhajit Patra, and Arindam Das[1]

Khakchang is illustrative of the tribal-dominated forest villages of Tripura. It is located in Dasda block, in Ananda Bazaar tehsil of North Tripura district. It is at a distance of 13 km from Dasda block and 26 km from Kanchanpur, the sub-divisional headquarters and nearest town, and is connected to both by an all-weather road. It is close to the Jampui Hills, at the border of Tripura and Mizoram. The village is part of the Tripura Tribal Areas Autonomous District Council (TTAADC). It is a newly settled or regrouped village, formed in 2003. It has seven hamlets, spread across an area of 5,919 acres. Some of the hamlets are as far as 8 km from the village centre. In 2016, there were a total of 589 households in the village, with a population of 2,884. About 95 per cent of the households belonged to the Reang tribe and the rest to the Tripuri tribe.

This chapter discusses the agrarian structure, production, and agrarian relations in Khakchang village. The chapter is divided into six sections on: (i) land tenure structure and land use; (ii) irrigation; (iii) cropping pattern, crop yields, and incomes from crop production; (iv) machine use in agriculture; and (v) labour absorption in agriculture. The final section is a summary.

[1] Ritam Dutta authored the section on "Land Tenure and Land Use." Subhajit Patra and Arindam Das jointly wrote the section on "Labour Use in Crop Production." Ranjini Basu, with assistance from Tapas Singh Modak, wrote the sections on "Irrigation," "Cropping Pattern and Crop Incomes," and "Machine Use in Agriculture." Ranjini Basu was the lead author of the overall chapter. We are grateful to Shamsher Singh for his note on community cultivation practices in *jhum*.

Land Tenure and Land Use

The greater part of agricultural land in the village is of an undulating hilly nature. Of all the study villages in Tripura, Khakchang had the greatest extent of forest coverage. *Jhum* or swidden agriculture is practised on the slopes, and is wholly dependent on rainfall. Lowland agriculture is limited to small pockets of the village. In 2016, a team from the Foundation of Agrarian Studies (FAS), under its Project on Agrarian Relations in India (PARI), surveyed 86 households in Khakchang, which together possessed a total of 296 acres of agricultural land. The analysis in this chapter has been made using sample weights for overall village projections.

In this chapter, we refer to sloped land as upland, and to low-lying plains as lowland. Uplands accounted for 89 per cent of all agricultural land in the village, of which almost half was under forest cover. The remaining 11 per cent of agricultural land were lowlands, used primarily for paddy and vegetable cultivation.

Land Tenure

The agricultural land owned by households in the village could be classified into three categories: owned land, assigned land, and occupied or encroached land.

Owned land: Agricultural land over which the household has complete ownership rights, including the right to sale.

Assigned land: Land received by a household under title deeds or *pattas* from the government. The household has "use rights" over such land, but does not have the "right to sale." Assigned land transferred by inheritance to a household has been considered as its *patta* holding.

Occupied or encroached land: The National Sample Survey Organisation (NSSO) defines this type of land as "otherwise possessed land." This type of land comes under the possession of a household through encroachment. The household does not have any ownership or sale rights over this land.

Table 1 shows the distribution of land under possession of households in Khakchang village according to the type of tenure. Most of the agricultural land (81 per cent) was assigned to households that had user rights alone. The proportion of assigned land in Khakchang was the highest among the three study villages. Fifteen per cent of the total land was fully owned by households; that is, they held the rights of use as well as sale over this land. Around 3.9 per cent of all agricultural land was encroached or occupied.

Table 1 *Distribution of land under possession according to tenure, Khakchang, 2016,* in numbers, acres, and percentage

Type of tenure	Households		Extent		Average size in acres
	Number	Per cent	Acres	Per cent	
Assigned	448	76.1	1703.53	80.8	3.8
Occupied	85	14.4	81.48	3.9	0.96
Owned	245	41.6	323.84	15.4	1.32
All*	589	100	2108.85	100	3.6

Note: *Households possessed multiple plots across different types of tenure. Percentages have been calculated on total number of households in the village, and do not add up to 100. *Source:* Survey data.

Implementation of Forest Rights Act, 2006

Khakchang presents an example of successful implementation of the Forest Rights Act (FRA), 2006, in Tripura. The FRA was a major enabling factor in the government's ambitious programme of providing secure land rights to tribal families in Khakchang. Just over 80 per cent of the total land in the village was distributed among households through title deeds or *pattas*.

Khakchang started as a resettled village in 2003, where conflict-affected tribal households were relocated. A majority of these households were landless. The State government's policy thrust on implementation of the FRA ensured security of land rights to this vast section of marginalised households. Along with security of tenure, FRA beneficiary households were also given opportunities for employment and livelihood by linking them with various line departments of the government.

From Table 1 it can be seen that 76 per cent of all households in Khakchang were beneficiaries of the FRA. They were collectively assigned 81 per cent of the total land in the village. As a result of the effective implementation of FRA, clear title deeds were provided to the owners of over 96 per cent of all agricultural land in the village.

Land Use

Land use definitions are given in Appendix 1 of this chapter. The category of cultivated plain land was used for paddy and vegetable cultivation. Upland or sloped land was broadly classified into five categories: plantation, orchard, *jhum*, forest, and *tila*. As can be seen from Table 2, 41.8 per cent of the entire land area in Khakchang was under forest

Table 2 *Distribution of land according to land use, Khakchang, 2016,* in per cent

Type of land	Proportion
Cultivated plain land	11.2
Jhum land	13.3
Orchard land	1.4
Plantation land	6.3
Forest land	41.8
Tila land	21.7
Ponds	4.3
All lands	100

Source: Survey data.

cover and another 21.7 per cent was sloped *tila* land that was left fallow. This left only 36.5 per cent of land for agriculture. In agriculture, *jhum* (paddy and vegetables) and lowland cultivation were the two significant cropping typologies, covering 13.3 per cent and 11.2 per cent of all land respectively. Rubber plantations covered 6.3 per cent of agricultural land (the lowest coverage among the three study villages).

Size of Landholding and Landlessness

The average size of landholding possessed by a household in Khakchang was 3.6 acres, while the coefficient of variation was 0.84 (Table 3). The average size of operational holding in the village was 3.8 acres, a figure considerably higher than the national average of 1.57 acres as reported in the NSSO's 70th Round, 2013. Khakchang had the largest average size of landholding across the three study villages, due to its predominantly hilly and forested topography.

A Reang household residing in Ganchera Para, one of the remote hamlets of Khakchang, was the largest landowner in terms of possession and operational landholding, with 13.6 acres of uplands. In the survey

Table 3 *Descriptive statistics of possession and operational holdings, Khakchang, 2016,* in acres

Tenure	Average size	Largest landholding	Coefficient of variation
Possession	3.6	13.6	0.84
Operational	3.8	13.6	0.8

Source: Survey data.

Table 4 *Size-class distribution of operational holdings, Khakchang, 2016*, in per cent

Size-class	Proportion of households	Proportion of area
Landless (0 hectare)	8	0
Marginal (1 hectare)	37	14
Small (1 to 2 hectares)	22	20
Semi-medium (>2 to 4 hectares)	29	53
Medium (>4 to 10 hectares)	4	13
Large (>10 hectares)	0	0
All	100	100

Source: Survey data.

year, the household engaged in *jhum* cultivation on 1.6 acres while the rest remained fallow. They sold some portion of their *jhum* produce in the market. However, the main source of income for this household was from the head of household's pension and remittances sent by their grandson.

Table 4 provides the size-class distribution of operational holdings in Khakchang. The size-classes employed are broadly those used by the Indian Council of Agricultural Research (ICAR) as well as the National Sample Survey of Land and Livestock Holdings.[2] A majority of the households belonged to the marginal and small land-size category, i.e. those who operated less than 2 hectares of operational holdings. There were no households that operated more than 10 hectares of agricultural land.

Landlessness was low in Khakchang, with only 8 per cent of households reporting no land for cultivation. We must note here, however, that a majority of the landless households in the village were not dependent on agricultural work as their primary source of income. In our sample, two landless households relied on incomes from labouring out on agricultural tasks, while another two households reported government salaries as their primary source of income. Business, religious activities, and remittances were the other sources of income for the remaining landless households.

The low proportion of operationally landless households in Khakchang can be explained by three factors. First, the implementation of the Forest Rights Act. As mentioned above, it was the single most important policy in ensuring land rights to the majority of households in the village.

---

[2] The NSSO records up to three decimal points but we have considered only up to two decimal points. The landless size-class used here only includes households whose extent of operational holding is zero.

There were two other additional contract arrangements which made land available to Khakchang residents for undertaking jhum cultivation. These were the lottery system of land allocation among tribal families, and the contract leasing system in the Jampui Hills. Both these arrangements allowed households to engage in jhum cultivation in successive years. Jhum by nature cannot be performed on the same plot of land in consecutive years. The contract leasing system in the Jampui Hills existed even before the implementation of the Forest Rights Act, 2006. Therefore, it provided access to land for Khakchang residents who had not yet received security of tenure through the FRA. These arrangements present a combination of joint community land and labour practices, and are described in separate boxes below.

Box 1
Lottery System for Land Cultivation
Shamsher Singh

The different forms of farming practices found in Khakchang were *jhum* (slash-and-burn cultivation), terrace farming on uplands, lowland rice and vegetable cultivation, and homestead cultivation. Rice, vegetables, tubers, and tree crops were grown on *jhum* fields and homesteads, and mixed cropping often involved the cultivation of thirty or more varieties of plants. In three to four *paras*/hamlets of the village that were located far in the hills at a distance from the village centre, common or community *jhum* cultivation was in practice. Other *paras* also had *jhum* cultivation but on a smaller scale.

Allotment of forest land for cultivation takes place through a lottery system. Based on the number of households in a *para*, a committee is formed in the month of *Agrahan* (November) to carry out the lottery procedure for the winter season. All heads of households take part in a *para* meeting to form the committee. In Khakchang village, the size of these *para* committees varied from six to eleven members. The committee draws lots in the month of *Poush* (December–January). Members elected to the Autonomous District Council (ADC) from respective *paras* are also on the committee. A committee has a tenure of three years.

Before the lottery process takes place, the committee takes a decision on the location and overall size of the land that will be cultivated in the season. The hills are vast, and covered with forests and vegetation. The area to be prepared for cultivation in a particular season depends on the number of households participating in the lottery system, as once a patch is cultivated, it must remain fallow for the next three years. Ease of access to the cultivated area for all households of the hamlet is also taken into consideration.

Different Land-size Groups under the Lottery System

Lots are drawn for three land-size categories. Land here is measured according to its seed requirement. A tin (usually an empty oil container) is used for measurement. According to the local custom, one tin (usually containing 10 kg of paddy seed) is required for one kaani (approximately 1 acre).

In the lottery there were three land-size categories in Khakchang village:

1. Group A: 5–6 tins or *kaanis*
2. Group B: 3–4 tins or *kaanis*
3. Group C: 2 tins or *kaanis*.

The decision on the composition of the groups is taken by the *para* committee. Residents familiar with the process told us that two factors weigh with the committee in taking this decision. The first concerns the food security of the household, that is, the paddy requirement of the household based on the number of minors and adults.

The second is the availability of labour in the household. Even though cultivation and crop operations are carried out collectively by all households that participate in the lottery system, a household should be in a position to ensure adequate labour for the land it wishes to cultivate. According to key respondents in the village, the labour availability criterion is important to make common cultivation fair and just for all households.

Different groups are allocated land at different locations. These locations and plots are mapped and marked. What is important to note is that many of the participating households have *pattas* to plots of land. However, once they are part of the lottery process, there is no guarantee that they will get to cultivate the same plot. Households thus get different plots of land every season.

How Do Crop Operations Take Place in Common Cultivation Process?

The lottery system ensures that households under different groups work together on each other's land throughout the season and on all operations – from clearing the forest and preparing the land right up to post-harvest operations.

We were told by the participants and committee members that working members of all households participate in all operations on the whole *tila*. This practice ensures that no household lags behind in carrying out crop operations and the spirit of community is preserved by sharing land and labour.

As mentioned earlier, there are different land-size groups, and some households do cultivate more land than others. However, the labour component is also shared proportionately among these households.

Box 2
Contract Leasing System in Jampui Hills

Interview with Bindu Reang by Ritam Dutta

Bindu Rai Reang is a resident of Horsing 2 hamlet, and the son of the person after whom the hamlet was named. The household had 9.6 acres (5.6 acres in the name of Bindu Reang and 4 acres of *patta* in his son's name) of assigned forest land in their possession. The household had last carried out *jhum* cultivation on the Jampui Hills in 2015. Three members of the household including Bindu Reang participated in the *jhum* operations. Members of the Lushai community, who live in the Jampui Hills, formed a committee that used a lottery system to allocate land for *jhum* cultivation. The fixed cash rent for each of the allotted plots was Rs 500, irrespective of size and land quality. Residents of Horsing 1 and Horsing 2 hamlets of Khakchang, who belonged to the Reang tribe, participated in this specific leased form of *jhum* cultivation on the slope of the Jampui Hills. Before every *jhum* cycle a meeting took place to decide which households of these hamlets would enter into a lease contract for that particular year. However, the underlying factors that led the committee to reach the decision of choice of households were not clear. In 2015, twenty-five resident households of Khakchang had undertaken *jhum* cultivation under this specific contract in the Jampui Hills. There was no restriction on households entering this contract in successive years. Under a similar arrangement, however, land was leased out by residents of Khakchang (Horsing 1 and Horsing 2 hamlets) to the Lushais, but free of rent.

Jhum cycle

Under the contract leasing system of *jhum* cultivation, the process of land allocation takes place in the month of *Poush* (December–January). The slashing operation takes place in *Magh* (January–February), and the burning is over by mid-*Choitro* (April). Cleaning of the land is done towards the end of *Choitro*. Bindu Reang cultivated 4 *tin* of land in 2015, and used family and exchange labour for slashing, burning, and cleaning operations, which took a total of thirty days.[3] The sowing operation followed, and harvesting happened over a period of a couple of months. Harvesting and sale of vegetable produce is done once or twice every week from the later part of *Shrabon* (August) till *Ashwin–Kartik* (October).

[3] *Tin* is the local unit of land measurement in Khakchang. Each unit denotes the area that can be cultivated through broadcasting seeds contained in one tin. Tin in a metal container with an average volume of 10 kgs, traditionally used as a measure in *jhum* cultivation.

Homestead

Table 5 provides the distribution of homestead land according to type of tenure. Among the study villages, Khakchang had the greatest proportion of households residing in homesteads assigned to them by the government. Around 5.6 per cent of the households had assigned homesteads. However, the majority of the households, or 79.5 per cent, had full ownership rights over their house sites.

Cultivation on homestead land in Khakchang was at a scale that was much smaller than in other study villages. Homestead cultivation was primarily undertaken for household consumption with very few instances of produce being sold. At 0.71 acre, the average homestead size of Khakchang was higher than that in the other two study villages, mostly owing to its hilly and sloped terrain. The largest homestead holding was of 4 acres. Thirty-one out of 86 households that were surveyed performed homestead cultivation, and of these all but one household cultivated vegetables. However, a bigger homestead did not necessarily translate into larger homestead area under cultivation. The largest extent under cultivation for a single household was 0.4 acre, with a majority of the households cultivating on much smaller plots.

Table 5 *Distribution of homestead land according to tenure, Khakchang, 2016, in per cent*

Tenure	Number of households	Proportion of households
Assigned	33	5.6
Occupied	96	16.3
Owned	468	79.5
All*	589	100

Note: *Some households had multiple homestead plots across different types of tenure. Percentage has been calculated on total number of households in the village.
Source: Survey data.

Irrigation

In Khakchang, *jhum* cultivation was entirely dependent on rainwater for irrigation. The acreage under lowland rice and vegetable cultivation was limited, constituting only about 11 per cent of total land in the village. The lowlands were irrigated by rivulets coming down from the hills. Water had to be manually lifted – no mechanical pumps were in use for irrigation.

Cropping Pattern and Crop Incomes

The cropping pattern in Khakchang was marked by the dominance of *jhum* cultivation that is practised on hilly and forested terrain. Fifty two per cent of the gross cropped area was under *jhum*, on which multiple crops were grown including millets and paddy (Table 6). Next came paddy cultivation on the limited lowlands available in the village, which comprised 21 per cent of the gross cropped area. Orchards, mostly of banana and pineapple, covered another 11 per cent of the gross cropped area. Rubber, a relatively new presence in the cropping cycle of the village, was still in its growth stage in plantations spread over 8 per cent of the gross cropped area. Vegetable cultivation formed 4 per cent of the total cropped area of the village. The category "other" in Table 6 includes crops which could not be classified under any of the other crops.

The present cropping pattern in the village is an outcome of government policy directed at ensuring sustainable livelihoods for rural households. Due to the precarious nature of incomes from *jhum* cultivation (discussed in detail in the next section), the State government first attempted to shift households to tea and coffee plantations by providing financial assistance. This, however, was a failure owing to factors such as unsuitable soil quality, lack of technical know-how, and absence of post-production infrastructure. The focus then shifted to introducing rubber plantations, which were considered more suited to the natural conditions of Tripura (see chapter 13 in this volume). Khakchang presents a case of transition,

Table 6 *Proportion of different crops in gross cropped area, Khakchang, 2016, in acres and per cent*

Crops	Area (acres)	As proportion of gross copped area (%)
Jhum cultivation	382.3	52
Paddy (lowland)	155.2	21
Paddy (sloped land)	5.4	1
Orchard	79.1	11
Rubber	59.7	8
Vegetable (lowland)	31.6	4
Other	25.1	3
All	738.4	100

Source: Survey data.

providing a mix of *jhum* cultivation, a few remaining tea plantations, and an early stage of expanding rubber plantations.

One of the unique characteristics of Khakchang is the diversity of crops in its cropping cycle. A total of 63 varieties of crops were listed in the village, with a maximum of 42 crops being grown by a single household. (For a complete list of all the crops found in the village, see Appendix 2.) This can be attributed to *jhum* cultivation, which involves a process of mixed broadcasting of seeds, including different varieties of millets, paddy, maize, sesame, mustard, vegetables, and even cotton. Additionally, the village also had segments of land under plantation crops such as areca nut and rubber. There were a few tea plantations. Banana, pineapple, and melons were the most commonly grown fruits. Khakchang is therefore also a case study for biodiversity in Tripura.

In the next section, we discuss crop incomes from two of the most prominent types of cropping in the village – *jhum* and lowland paddy cultivation.

Cost of Cultivation and Farm Business Incomes

Unlike the other two survey villages, in Khakchang, we have only estimated cost A2 or paid-out costs, without the imputed cost of family labour. This is because of the unique community labour relations prevalent in the village. Fifty-six per cent of labour use came from family labour, while 29 per cent was exchange labour (see section on labour absorption below). Owing to the significant travel time taken to reach the fields in *jhum* cultivation and the communal nature of the work, it was difficult to disaggregate the labour time invested in *jhum*, or to make a clear distinction between family and exchange labour. We therefore considered paid-out costs only while estimating farm business incomes of households.

"Jhum" cultivation

Jhum cultivation was the most prominent cropping pattern in Khakchang, with 52 per cent of the gross cropped area under this form of cultivation in our survey year. Table 7 provides the average gross value of output, paid-out costs, and farm business income from *jhum* cultivation. We found that the average farm business income from *jhum* cultivation was Rs 29,327 per acre. This was mainly due to the high average gross value of output relative to the small amount of paid-out costs incurred by the households involved in *jhum* cultivation. However, the point to be noted is that *jhum* cultivation by nature cannot be performed on the same plot

Table 7 *Average gross value of output, paid-out cost, and farm business income, "jhum" cultivation, Khakchang, 2016,* in Rs per acre

	Rs per acre
Gross value of output (GVO)	32,573
Paid-out cost/cost A2	3,246
Farm business income	29,327

Source: Survey data.

Table 8 *Average expenditure on different cost items, "jhum" cultivation, Khakchang, 2016,* in Rs per acre and per cent

Cost items	Rs per acre	Per cent
Seed	1537	47.4
Manure	0	0
Fertilizer	6	0.2
Plant protection	2	0.1
Irrigation	0	0
Casual labour	1374	42.3
Animal labour	0	0
Machine labour	0	0
Rent	158	4.9
Other costs	169	5.2
Cost A2	3246	100.0

Source: Survey data

of land in successive years. Generally a gap of three years is maintained before undertaking *jhum* on the same plot of land. Thus, for all practical purposes, 1 acre under *jhum* is equivalent to 4 acres under any other annual crop. Therefore, while calculating the profits accruing from *jhum,* this period of non-utilisation of the land has to be factored in. Under these conditions, the actual profit from *jhum* for a household came to about Rs 7,332 per acre annually (calculated by taking three years as the period for land rejuvenation).

The low level of cost A2 in *jhum* cultivation can be explained by taking a closer look at the average expenditure on different cost items in Table 8. The only two significant costs were on seeds and on wage labour, comprising 47 per cent and 42 per cent of all paid-out costs respectively. Wage labour in *jhum* cultivation was minimal, as it largely involves family and exchange labour (see section on labour). There was no use of machine or animal labour, and all operations were done manually using hand implements. *Jhum* cultivation was entirely dependent on rainfall. A highly labour-intensive and communal form of farming without the use of any form of modern machinery, and with bare minimum use of fertilizers, made the traditional form of *jhum* cultivation appear cheap.

Lowland paddy

Lowland paddy was the next most prominent crop in Khakchang, comprising 21 per cent of the gross cropped area of the village. There was only one seasonal paddy crop, a kharif crop, in the village. Cost A2 has been calculated for paddy without the imputation of family labour, primarily because of the predominance of the communal form of farming practice in the village, which makes it difficult to segregate family and exchange labour.

Productivity

Table 9 provides the average yield of kharif paddy grown in the lowlands of Khakchang. It compares the village average with the average yield reported at the district and the State level. It was found that the average yield of paddy in Khakchang (1,168 kg per acre) was lower than the North Tripura district average (1,177 kg per acre), and lower even than the Tripura average (1,253 kg per acre). Khakchang had the lowest rate of paddy productivity among all the PARI study villages. As compared to other paddy-producing States, the village and State average in Tripura were found to be rather low.

Table 9 *Average yield of paddy, Khakchang, North Tripura district, Tripura, 2015–16 and 2014–15, in kg per acre*

Crop		Khakchang village	North Tripura district	Tripura State
Paddy (lowland)	Average	1168	1177	1253
	Minimum	500		
	Maximum	1800		

Source: Survey data. Figures on yield of *aman* (kharif) paddy for North Tripura district and Tripura state for 2014–15 are from Government of Tripura (2015).

Farm Business Income from Paddy Cultivation

Table 10 provides the average gross value of output, paid-out costs, and farm business incomes from cultivation of paddy in the lowlands of Khakchang. It was found that households that grew paddy received a profit of Rs 11,071 per acre. The low cost of cultivation of paddy was one of the factors for positive profits despite low yields. This has been explained below through an analysis of the expenditure on different cost items.

Expenditure on casual or wage labour (37 per cent), machine labour (23 per cent), and rent (29 per cent) comprised the major items in the overall cost of paddy cultivation in lowland Khakchang (Table 11). However,

Table 10 *Average gross value of output, paid-out cost, and farm business income, paddy (lowland), Khakchang, 2016, in Rs per acre*

	Rs per acre
Gross value of output (GVO)	18,988
Paid-out cost/cost A2	7,917
Farm business income	11,071

Source: Survey data.

Table 11 *Average expenditure on different cost items, paddy (lowland), Khakchang, 2016, in Rs per acre and per cent*

Cost items	Rs per acre	Per cent
Seed	577	7
Manure	41	1
Fertilizer	0	0
Plant protection	76	1
Irrigation	0	0
Casual labour	2938	37
Animal labour	0	0
Machine labour	1809	23
Rent	2325	29
Other costs	152	2
Cost A2	7917	100

Source: Survey data.

given the overall insignificant levels of wage labour in the village, the expenditure on casual labour was not too high in absolute terms. The cost of machine labour included the rented cost of power tillers used for ploughing operations, and was restricted to the lowlands of the village. A general absence of agricultural inputs like fertilizers and manure, and the absence of use of machinery in irrigation were striking features of agriculture. These factors together kept the cost of cultivation for paddy low in Khakchang.

Other cropping cycles were insignificant in the overall village cropping scheme. In our sample, we found only four households that were engaged in vegetable cultivation in the lowlands. There were nine households that owned rubber plantations, although there was no income from them as the trees had not yet attained maturity. Seven households had fruit orchards, primarily of banana and pineapple, although only four had realised income from them. Some of the pineapple orchards were financed by an Indo-German collaboration.

Farm Business Incomes for Households

Households were classified according to a combination of the two major crop cycles in the village: *jhum* and lowland cultivation (paddy and vegetables). We found that of the cultivating households, a majority (58 per cent) undertook only *jhum* cultivation. Next in significance were households that performed only lowland cultivation (28 per cent). Only 14 per cent of the cultivating households were involved in a combination of *jhum* and lowland cultivation in the survey year.

A look at the average incomes from crop production shows that those who performed only *jhum* cultivation received an income of Rs 33,602 (Table 12). However, these households formed the poorest sections of the village. Crop incomes formed the major share of their household incomes, while other cultivating households had more diversified income sources (see chapter 11 in this volume). The annual incomes from crop production of households that combined *jhum* and lowland cultivation, referred to as "cultivators: mixed" in the table, were the highest. The "cultivators: lowland" households had an average annual income of Rs 10,428. It is important to note here that lowland vegetable cultivation was done only by a few households (four in our sample), and all lowland cultivation was restricted to only one season (kharif). There is therefore scope for extending lowland cultivation in the rabi or winter season, thereby raising the crop incomes of households. This would only be possible with greater

Table 12 *Average annual income from crop production by socio-economic class, Khakchang, 2016, in numbers, per cent, and Rs per household*

Socio-economic class	Number of households	Mean income from crop production
Cultivator: *jhum*	240 (58)	33,602
Cultivator: mixed	60 (14)	50,331
Cultivator: lowland	117 (28)	10,428

Note: Figures in parentheses denote percentages.
Source: Survey data.

state support through extension services and the expansion of irrigation.

Once the rubber plantations mature, they will substantially raise the incomes of their owners, and also the overall share of crop incomes in Khakchang.

Use of Machinery in Agriculture

Jhum cultivation was not mechanised, and was done predominantly with the aid of traditional hand tools, such as the *dao* (a multipurpose heavy knife), spade, sickle, axe, hoe, etc. Machines were used only for ploughing and threshing operations in the lowland areas. In lowland paddy cultivation, about 62 per cent of the cropped land was ploughed using power tillers, and paddy from 58 per cent of the lowland was threshed by machines. In our sample survey, we found only one household that owned a power tiller. Use of machinery was largely dependent on the rental market. The cost for both ploughing and threshing operations was Rs 200 per hour.

Use of Labour in Crop Production

This section examines the use of labour in crop production in Khakchang. As was noted in the earlier sections, *jhum* cultivation was the mainstay of a large section of village residents, with a share of 52 per cent in the gross cropped area of the village. It is a traditional annual crop cycle, involving the use of only human labour. *Jhum* provided an inventory of multiple foodgrains and vegetables for the household that mostly utilised them for consumption through the year. Shifting cultivation was carried out predominantly by family and exchange labour in communal forms of farming. A household undertaking *jhum* engaged all able-bodied family members for about seven to eight months of the year. Crop operations included clearing and cleaning the field, digging pits, sowing, hand weeding and harvesting, transporting, threshing and winnowing. Table 13 presents the average number of labour-days spent on each of the *jhum* cultivation operations for an area measuring 1 *tin* (area covered by broadcasting 10–12 kg of mixed seeds), which approximates to 1 acre.

The cultivation process starts with the selection of plots, normally done in the month of January. In the month of February/March, land preparation is done – cleaning, slashing, and burning of wild foliage. The slashing operation requires on an average 20 days per *tin* (10 kg seed) area. This task is performed by family and exchange labour. The foliage is burnt after two months of the start of the slashing operation. Most crops in *jhum* are sown in the months of May–June, with some vegetables sown in July. This operation is entirely done by family labour. The participation of female family labourers is high, at 47 per cent of the total labour force. In *jhum* cultivation, weeding is a major operation, done three to four times during the entire crop cycle. Weeding absorbs the largest share of human labour, especially female labour. This operation too is conducted using family and exchange labour. The harvesting operation starts in the month of October and continues till December. Here too family labour

Table 13 *Operation-wise average number of days in "jhum" cultivation for 1 "tin" (10–12 kg mixed seed) area, Khakchang, 2016*, in number of days

Type	Operation	Month(s) of activity	Labour-days
Land preparation	Selection of plot	January	2
	Cutting vegetation	February–March	20
	Burning	April	1
	Clearing forest	April	5
Sowing	Mixing seed, digging pits, and sowing	May–June	6
Weeding	Hand weeding (three to four times)	August–September	50
Harvesting, post-harvesting	Paddy harvesting, transporting, threshing, winnowing	October–November	40
	Vegetable harvesting	October–December	20
All operations			150

Source: Survey data.

is mainly used for harvesting and post-harvesting operations. In the basket of mixed crops cultivated under *jhum*, paddy is the most important crop. It absorbs a total of forty labour-days in harvesting, transporting, threshing, and winnowing operations for an area of 1 *tin* (10 kg seed area). Other crops, including vegetables, are harvested as and when they mature between the months of October to December. *Jhum* cultivation is labour-intensive and requires about 150 days of employment on roughly 1 acre of cultivated land.

Composition of Labour Use

The composition of labour use in Khakchang showed that about 54 per cent of total labour was absorbed by *jhum* cultivation, whereas 39 per cent was absorbed by lowland cultivation (Table 14). Plantation crops, largely rubber, absorbed 7 per cent of the total labour use in the village.

In Khakchang, 80 per cent of the gross cropped area was cultivated in the summer season and accounted for 92 per cent of total labour use (Table 15). The reason for such a high volume of labour use was the extensive and intensive *jhum* cultivation, spread across the summer season. The labour absorption in annual plantation crops was only 8 per cent of total labour absorption.

Table 14 *Composition of labour use in Khakchang, 2016,* in per cent

Village	Plain land cultivation	*Jhum* cultivation	Plantation	Total
Khakchang	39	54	7	100

Source: Survey data.

Table 15 *Distribution of labour use across seasons in Khakchang, 2016,* in per cent

Village	Summer crop	Annual crop	Total
Khakchang	92	8	100

Source: Survey data.

Table 16 *Composition of total labour use in Khakchang, 2016,* in per cent

Village	Family labour	Hired labour	Exchange labour	Total
Khakchang	56	15	29	100

Source: Survey data.

Forms of Labour

Family labour was the main source of labour supply in Khakchang. The use of exchange labour along with family labour was an important characteristic of community *jhum* farming in the village. The proportion of family labour used in total cultivation ranged from 54 per cent to 73 per cent, based on the particular cropping pattern. Labour absorption in *jhum* cultivation comprised 63 per cent family labour, while in lowland paddy cultivation the proportion was 54 per cent. The share of exchange labour in total labour use stood at a significant 30 per cent.

Gender Composition

Human labour was the only form of labour involved in crop production in Khakchang. Table 17 shows the sex-wise distribution of family and hired labour. Crop production in the village was largely the domain of male workers. The contribution of female labour to total labour use in *jhum* cultivation was 30 per cent. Weeding, sowing, and harvesting operations saw the greatest participation of female labourers. All land preparation operations were exclusively done by male workers. In the case of lowland cultivation, female workers were primarily engaged in transplanting and weeding operations.

Table 17 *Distribution of family and exchange labour, by sex, in Khakchang, 2016,* in per cent

Village	Family labour: male	Family labour: female	Exchange labour: male	Exchange labour: female
Khakchang	86.3	13.7	73	27

Source: Survey data.

Table 18 *Distribution of family and exchange labour across crops, by sex, in Khakchang, 2016,* in per cent

Crop	Family labour: male	Family labour: female	Exchange labour: male	Exchange labour: female
Jhum	59.7	40.3	86.9	13.1
Paddy	61.1	38.9	65	35
Rubber	88.1	11.9	0	0
Other	54.1	45.9	0	0

Source: Survey data.

Table 19 *Distribution of labour-days in jhum cultivation, by sex, Khakchang, 2016,* in per cent

Operation	Male	Female	Total
Land preparation	92.4	7.6	100
Digging pits and sowing	54.3	45.7	100
Weeding	56.8	43.2	100
Inter-cultural operation	100.0	0.0	100
Harvesting and post-harvesting	60.1	39.9	100

Source: Survey data.

Female participation was higher in lowland paddy cultivation as compared to *jhum* cultivation (Table 18). In lowland paddy cultivation, 38.9 per cent of all family labour and 35 per cent of all exchange labour was performed by female workers. On the other hand, in *jhum* and rubber cultivation operations, male workers contributed the most labour – both family and exchange. The use of hired wage labour in Khakchang was the lowest among the three study villages in Tripura, at just 15 per cent of total labour use.

Summary

This chapter discussed agrarian production relations in Khakchang village, located in Dasda block of North Tripura district. A resettled village created in 2003, Khakchang consists of an entirely tribal population of Reang and Tripuri households. The village terrain is predominantly hilly, with 41.8 per cent of total land under forests and just 11 per cent comprising lowlands. In all its characteristics, it is illustrative of the many tribal-dominated forest villages of Tripura.

Implementation of the Forest Rights Act, 2006 brought tenurial security to a majority of the village residents. Khakchang had the highest number of FRA beneficiaries among the three study villages, with 76 per cent of all households in the village having received forest *patta*s. The lottery system of land allocation in the village and contractual lease system in the Jampui Hills were an important feature of Khakchang's agrarian economy. These community land arrangements allowed the village households to perform *jhum* cultivation using family and exchange labour. Landlessness in Khakchang was the lowest, at 8 per cent, among the three study villages.

The predominance of *jhum* cultivation in Khakchang showed interlinkages between land and labour relations through community arrangements. *Jhum* cultivation was practised on 52 per cent of gross cropped area. Lowland cultivation, including of paddy and vegetables, covered 25 per cent of the gross cropped area. Rubber plantations were not yet mature and had not started generating income.

Incomes from both *jhum* and lowland cultivation were low. Paddy productivity was the lowest in Khakchang among the three study villages. However, households managed to gain a profit due to the low costs of fertilizers and manure, the absence or minimal use of animal and machine labour, and heavy dependence on family and exchange labour in both forms of cultivation. *Jhum* provided a greater average crop income as compared to income from only lowland cultivation, although the overall household incomes of the *jhumias* were less diversified. In contrast, lowland cultivation was limited to only one season, and there is scope for expanding into other seasons with adequate state support.

Labour supply for agriculture in Khakchang was met predominantly by family and exchange forms of labour, with the share of hired labour at 15 per cent. *Jhum* cultivation accounted for 54 per cent of labour use, utilising family and exchange labour that spanned across eight to ten months of the year, and involved only intensive human labour. Lowland cultivation accounted for 39 per cent of labour, which was restricted to the kharif season. There was dominance of male labour in both family and exchange labour. However, female participation was high in lowland rice cultivation, especially in transplanting and weeding operations.

Appendix 1

Definition of Land Use Categories

- *Cultivated plain land.* Land used for cultivation of seasonal crops, like paddy and vegetables. This land is a distinct unit of cultivation, separate from the homestead, and therefore does not include kitchen garden cultivation practised on the homestead.
- *Plantation land.* Land devoted to cultivation of plantation crops, such as rubber, areca nut, pineaspple, and banana.
- *Orchard land.* Land under fruit trees and other trees not classified as plantation crops, such as bamboo, jackfruit, etc.
- *Jhum land.* Land used for shifting or *jhum* cultivation (slash-and-burn method). This land forms part of hill slopes or uplands.

- *Forest land.* All land area under forest cover, or land so classified under any legal enactment or administered as forest, whether state-owned or private. This was not under any cultivation.
- *Tila land.* Sloped land not included in any of the above classifications, and kept fallow.

APPENDIX 2
List of Crops, Khakchang, 2016

Ash gourd	Cotton	Lady's finger	Pineapple	Thaichumo*
Banana	Cucumber	Maikrok*	Potato	Tomato
Basil	Dormai*	Maize	Pumpkin	Turmeric
Beans	Elephant ear	Masinga*	Radish	Ushoi*
Bitter gourd	Elephant foot	Milok manda*	Ridge gourd	Watermelon
Bottle gourd	Faraksi*	Murma*	Rubber	Wild brinjal
Brinjal	Foxtail millet	Mushrui*	Sesame	Wild potato
Broad beans	Garlic	Mustard	Snake gourd	
Chian*	Ginger	Mustard greens	Spiny gourd	
Chikar*	Gourd	Muthai*	Sweet potato	
Chilli	Green pigeon peas	Onion	Sword bean	
Chinan*	Green stalks	Osundui*	Tapioca	
Cluster beans	Hamchang*	Paddy	Tarostolor*	
Coriander	Karmol*	Peas	Tea	

Note: *Names in local language.
Source: Survey data.

Reference

Government of Tripura (2015), *Basic Statistics: Area, Production and Yield*, Department of Agriculture and Farmers Welfare, Government of Tripura, available at http.// agri.tripura.gov.in/basic_statistics

7

Agrarian Structure, Production, and Agrarian Relations in Mainama

Ranjini Basu, Ritam Dutta, Tapas Singh Modak,
Subhajit Patra, and Arindam Das[1]

Mainama is located in the Manu block of Dhalai district, Tripura. It is at a distance of 3 km from Manu town, the block headquarters, and is connected by an all-weather road. The village is part of the Tripura Tribal Areas Autonomous District Council (TTAADC). In 2016, there were 1,451 households in the village, spread across eleven hamlets. The Scheduled Tribe (ST) population in Mainama constituted 66.2 per cent of all households. Tripuris (42.6 per cent) and Chakmas (23.6 per cent) were the two major social groups within STs. Twenty six per cent of the remaining households belonged to Other Backward Classes (OBCs), 4 per cent to the Caste Hindu social group, and 2 per cent were Muslims.

This chapter discusses features of the agrarian structure, production, and agrarian relations in Mainama village. The chapter is divided into six sections that discuss (i) the land tenure structure and land use in the village; (ii) irrigation systems and practices; (iii) cropping patterns, crop yields, and incomes; (iv) the extent of machine use in agriculture; and (v) the forms of labour absorption in agriculture found in the village. In the last section we summarise our findings.

---

[1] Ritam Dutta authored the section on "Land Tenure and Land Use;" Tapas Singh Modak wrote the sections on "Irrigation," "Cropping Pattern and Crop Incomes," and "Machine Use in Agriculture;" Subhajit Patra and Arindam Das jointly wrote the section on "Labour Use in Crop Production." Ranjini Basu is the lead author of the overall chapter.

Land Tenure and Land Use

Mainama has a mixed topography. One-third of the total land area is plain land and the rest is sloped. The river Manu forms one of the boundaries of the village with extensive vegetable cultivation on its river bed. It was the largest of the three survey villages, both in terms of acreage and number of households. In our sample survey, 271 households were surveyed. They collectively owned 450 acres of land. In this chapter, weighted results have been used to provide projections for the entire village.

We have classified plain land as lowland, and undulating or sloped land as upland. The topographical characteristics of land play an important role in characterising the agrarian structure and production relations in Mainama. About 33 per cent of total agricultural land in the village was lowland, and 67 per cent was sloped land. More than half the sloped land or upland was used to cultivate plantation crops. This was primarily rubber, along with a small proportion of areca nut, pineapple, and banana. The plain land was largely put to cultivation of paddy and vegetables.

Land Tenure

As in the other study villages, we classified land possessed by households in the village into three categories: owned land, assigned land, and occupied or encroached land.

Owned land: Land over which the household has complete ownership rights, including the right to sell.

Assigned land: Land received by a household under title deeds or *pattas* from the government. The household has "use rights" over the holding, but not "right of sale." Assigned land transferred by inheritance to a household has been considered as its *patta* holding.

Occupied or encroached land: The National Sample Survey Organisation (NSSO) defines this type of land as "otherwise possessed land." The land is under possession of the household through encroachment. The household does not have any ownership or sale rights over this land.

Table 1 shows the distribution of land under possession of households according to form of tenure. The majority of the land under possession of households (74.9 per cent) was under complete ownership rights of the households. About 13.5 per cent of the possessed land was assigned to households through formal *pattas*. Thus, households had formal rights over 88.4 per cent of all land under possession in Mainama. This is

Table 1 *Distribution of land under possession according to tenure, Mainama, 2016, in numbers, acres, and percentages*

Type of tenure	Households		Extent		Average size (acres)
	Number	Per cent	Acreage	Per cent	
Assigned	177	12.2	350.28	13.5	1.98
Occupied	124	8.5	302.47	11.6	2.44
Owned	876	60.4	1948.29	74.9	2.22
All*	1451	100	2601.04	100	1.72

Note: *Households owned multiple plots across different types of tenure. Percentages have been calculated on total number of households in the village, and do not add up to 100.
Source: Survey data.

important because having formal possession rights helped the households in gaining access to formal credit.

Implementation of Forest Rights Act, 2006

Implementation of the Forest Rights Act (FRA), 2006 contributed to more equality in the possession of land by households. It raised the number of households with formal rights over land in their possession. Twelve per cent of households in the village were beneficiaries of the FRA, under which they received formal *pattas* of forest land from the government (Table 1). Around 14 per cent of all agricultural land in Mainama was under these *pattas*. The average size of *pattas* distributed among beneficiaries was 1.98 acres. This was higher than the average size of land under possession (1.72 acres) and of operational holding (1.64 acres) of households in the village.

Land Use

Further, we classified land according to use. (Land use definitions are available in Appendix 1.) The category of cultivated plain land was used for paddy and vegetable cultivation. Upland or sloped land was broadly classified into five categories: plantations, orchards, *jhum* land, forests, and *tila* land. Table 2 gives the distribution of agricultural land according to land use. It shows that 40.1 per cent of the land in Mainama was under annual plantation crops. Next came lowlands, at 31 per cent, where paddy and vegetables were grown. Land under *jhum* or shifting cultivation was insignificant. About 18.8 per cent of the land, comprising stretches of forest land and fallow sloped or *tila* land, was not cultivated. The share of water bodies, mainly ponds, was 6.7 per cent of all agricultural land in Mainama.

Table 2 *Distribution of land according to land use, Mainama, 2016,* in per cent

Type of land	Proportion
Cultivated plain land	31
Plantation land	40.1
Orchard land	3
Jhum land	0.4
Forest land	6.2
Tila land	12.6
Water bodies	6.7
All	100

Size of Landholding and Landlessness

The average size of land in the possession of households in Mainama was 1.72 acres and the coefficient of variation (CV) was 2.04 (Table 3). The largest landholding measured 40.4 acres. This was owned by a salaried household, where both the head of the household and his wife were government employees. This household had leased out 24 acres of land on shared rent basis. If we omit this household, the average possession of land by households in the village falls to 1.56 acres, and the largest landholding size to 16.34 acres. When it came to operational landholdings, the average size in Mainama was 1.64 acres and the CV was 1.68 acres. The largest operational holding measured 18.6 acres. Operational holdings were more equally distributed than land under possession of households in the village. It is important to note that the average size of holding, both in terms of possession and operational holding, of a household in Mainama was higher than 1.57 acres, which was the national average size of ownership holding as reported in the NSSO's 70th Round, 2013.

Table 4 looks more closely at the size-class distribution of operational holdings in Mainama. The size-classes used by the National Sample Surveys of Land and Livestock Holdings have been used for the analysis.[2] It was seen that households that operated marginal holdings of less than

---

[2] The NSSO records up to three decimal points but we have considered only up to two decimal points. The landless size-class used here considers only households whose extent of operational holding is zero.

Table 3 *Descriptive statistics of possession and operational holdings, Mainama, 2016*, in acres

Tenure	Average size	Largest landholding	Coefficient of variation
Possession	1.72	40.4	2.04
Operational	1.64	18.6	1.68

Source: Survey data.

Table 4 *Size-class distribution of operational holding, Mainama, 2016*, in percentages

Size-class	Proportion of households	Proportion of area
Landless (0 hectare)	33	0
Marginal (<1 hectare)	46	27
Small (1 to 2 hectares)	14	29
Semi-medium (>2 to 4 hectares)	4	16
Medium (>4 to 10 hectares)	4	28
Large (>10 hectares)	0	0
All	100	100

Source: Survey data.

1 hectare of land constituted almost half (46 per cent) the population of the entire village. However, the proportion of acreage under marginal holdings was 27 per cent of all the agricultural land in the village. There were no large landholdings or holdings greater than 10 hectares in the village.

Landlessness in this village was significant, with 33 per cent of its households having no access to land for agricultural activities. However, this proportion was still lower than the figures projected by the NSSO in 2011–12 for both Tripura and India: 62.2 and 48.5 per cent, respectively (Rawal 2013).

Among the operationally landless households, the primary source of income of one-fourth was government salaries. For the rest of the landless population, earnings from agricultural and non-agricultural labouring-out activities constituted the primary source of income. Earnings from other sources, like pensions, remittances, business and trade, and animal resources, also provided income for some of the households. Interestingly, there were some non-cultivating households whose primary income was rent from land leased out.

Tenancy

The presence of an active tenancy market in Mainama ensured access to land for those who had no land or limited possession of agricultural land, largely with respect to lowlands. About 30 per cent of the entire operational land in the village was leased in under different arrangements. Table 5 shows the distribution of tenancy in the village. It was seen that 19.7 per cent of households had leased-in land, as compared to 11.2 per cent households who leased out land. However, the acreage leased out by households was greater than the area leased in by households. In other words, on an average, tenant households in Mainama leased in smaller plots (0.84 acre) as compared to the average size of plots leased out by landholders (1.67 acres).

Table 6 shows that the extent of land leased in was almost proportionately spread between fixed rent and sharecropping arrangements. In terms of number of households, 131 entered into fixed annual tenancies. Next in significance were 77 households that cultivated on seasonal crop shared rent tenancies. Of the households that leased in land on a fixed rent basis,

Table 5 *Distribution of tenancy, Mainama, 2016*, in acres, numbers, and percentages

Number of households that leased in land	285
Acreage of land leased in	238.7
Share in total operational area (%)	30
Number of households that leased out land	163
Acreage of land leased out	271.96
Share in total land under possession (%)	60.4

Source: Survey data.

Table 6 *Distribution of tenancy according to type of tenancy, Mainama, 2016*, in acres and percentages

	Fixed rent		Share rent	
	Acreage	Proportion	Acreage	Proportion
Leased-in land	129.45	54	109.25	46
Leased-out land	142.03	52	129.93	48

Source: Survey data.

74 households paid their rent in cash while 82 households paid in kind, primarily in the form of paddy. Sharecropping was prevalent as seasonal contracts, mainly for paddy cultivation. There were 113 households who paid the rent as part of their paddy produce, while 12 households had entered into sharecropping arrangements for vegetable cultivation. Paddy was grown on 75 per cent of the total leased-in land, with vegetables cultivated on 24 per cent. The remaining 1 per cent was under fodder grass.

The largest proportion of tenant households (125 out of 285) belonged to the socio-economic class of "cultivators: sub-marginal," operating on less than 1 acre of land (Table 7). This points to the fact that the tenancy market in Mainama helped the smallest cultivators gain agricultural land for operation. Tenant households belonging to the class of "cultivator: sub-marginal" leased in, on an average, 0.44 acre of agricultural land. The biggest proportion of lessor households (47 out of 163) were from the "salaried, business, and others" non-cultivating category. These households possessed land despite not being involved in the production process. In terms of acreage, this class of non-cultivators leased out the greatest amount of land in the village, 78.8 acres.

Due to geographical variation within Mainama, tenancies were more concentrated among central *para* households than among remote *para*s. This was because the central *para* residents had larger possession of lowland near where the tenancy market was functional. About 175 central *para* households had leased in 126.1 acres of agricultural land, while 110 remote *para* households had leased in 112.6 acres of land. This meant that through the tenancy market, remote *para* households were able to receive access to

Table 7 *Distribution of tenancy according to socio-economic classes, Mainama, 2016,* in acres and numbers

Socio-economic class	Extent leased in (number of lessee households)	Extent leased out (number of lessor households)
Manual worker	NA	27.7 (19)
Cultivator: sub-marginal	55.1 (125)	39.7 (38)
Cultivator: marginal	74.2 (83)	77.9(23)
Cultivator: small	90.4 (67)	38.7 (30)
Cultivator: medium	18.9 (11)	9.2 (7)
Salaried, business, and others	NA	78.8 (47)

Source: Survey data.

lowland, which was generally not available to them through possession. On the other hand, 124 central *para* households leased out 232.5 acres of lowland, while 40 remote households leased out 39.5 acres. This also shows the greater availability of lowland among the central *para* households.

Homestead

One of the chief features of cultivation in Mainama was the importance of homestead cultivation. The NSSO defines homestead as the dwelling of the household together with the courtyard, compound, garden, outhouse, place of worship, family graveyard, guest house, shop, workshop and offices for running household enterprises, tanks, wells, latrines, drains, and boundary walls annexed to the dwelling. A majority (92 per cent) of the households in Mainama village had full ownership rights over their homesteads. Table 8 provides the tenurial distribution of homestead land among the households. About 95 per cent of all households had legal rights over their homesteads, which includes 2.8 per cent households who received homestead *pattas*.

In our sample survey, 98 per cent of all households reported the extent of their homestead land. It was found that 141 of 271 households practised some form of cultivation on their homestead. Vegetable cultivation on homestead land was common practice among households in this village. Out of 141 households cultivating homestead land, 139 households carried out vegetable cultivation. (Homestead farming is discussed in greater detail in chapter 12 of this volume.) Access to homestead cultivation provides opportunities to supplement household nutritional needs and incomes. The average size of a homestead in Mainama was 0.41 acre, while the largest homestead holding was of 6 acres.

The nature of homesteads varied according to the location of the hamlet.

Table 8 *Distribution of homestead land according to tenure, Mainama, 2016,* in per cent

Tenure	Number of households	Proportion of households
Assigned	41	2.8
Occupied	75	5.2
Owned	1338	92.2
All*	1451	100

Note: *Households had multiple homestead plots across different types of tenure. Percentages have been calculated on total number of households in the village and do not add up to 100.
Source: Survey data.

The central *para*s were mainly lowland areas with greater population density as compared to the remote *para*s, which were mainly located on sloped land and spread out. As a result, the average homestead extent for households in the central *para*s was 0.35 acre, lower than in the remote *para*s where it was 0.52 acre.

The organisation of the homestead also differed between the central and remote *para*s. A typical homestead in a central *para* comprised the house, a small area for the courtyard, space for homestead cultivation, and some trees like areca nut, coconut, jackfruit, bamboo, and mango planted on the inner boundaries. Vegetable cultivation was practised in some of the central *para* households. On the other hand, a typical homestead in a remote *para* was larger in area and was usually situated on sloped terrain. Here the household would have a house, occasionally some open space with vegetable cultivation on a portion of the homestead, and a substantial extent of fallow land.

Case Study 1. This household is located in Tilak *para*, a central *para* of Mainama. This household was completely dependent on agricultural production for its livelihood. Besides crops, they also cultivated vegetables like potato, chilli, yam, ridge gourd, and brinjal, and raised areca nut saplings on 0.13 acre of homestead land. While most of the vegetables were for home consumption, potato and areca nut saplings were sold in the market. In fact, a major source of income for this household came from selling areca nut saplings.

Case Study 2. This household in Arjun *para*, a remote *para* of Mainama, comprised salaried members with the head of the household and his wife working for the central government. They practised homestead cultivation only for home consumption. Homestead cultivation was carried out on 0.6 acre of land, where they grew vegetables like ginger, yam, spiny gourd, ridge gourd, green peas, bottle gourd, pumpkin, and brinjal. Though not primarily a peasant household, its members still undertook homestead cultivation.

Irrigation

The Manu river flows next to Mainama, and is the main source of irrigation for the village. Topography however acts as a constraint on the spread of irrigation, which is restricted to the lowlands. Here too, only agricultural lands close to the river could access irrigation water. Table 9 shows that

Table 9 *Distribution of net sown area of crop by source of irrigation, Mainama, 2015–16,* in acres and per cent

Source of irrigation	Extent (acres)	Share (%)
River	276	38
River lift irrigation	32	4
Pond	49	6
Rainfed	391	52
Total	748	100

Note: Plantation and orchard lands are not included here.
Source: Survey data.

about 48 per cent of total net sown area in the village was irrigated, and the rest (52 per cent) was dependent on rainwater. Privately owned diesel and electric pumps were primarily used to draw water from the river for irrigation. There was an active water market in the village. The pump owners, after own use, sold water to other cultivators for paddy and vegetable cultivation. About 38 per cent of the net sown area was irrigated using private pumps. The pump owners sold water to irrigate a much larger area than their own acreage.

The State government built a river lift irrigation (RLI) scheme on the Manu river. However, its command area covered only three hamlets of the village, or just 4 per cent of the total net sown area. In addition, nearly 6 per cent of the cultivated land was irrigated by pond water. Several ponds were dug under the Mahatma Gandhi National Rural Employment Guarantee Scheme (MGNREGS).

Cropping Pattern and Crop Incomes

On account of the topography of Mainama, the agricultural pattern can broadly be divided into lowland cultivation and sloped land cultivation. The village largely comprised sloped land, primarily covered by rubber plantations. Rubber and other orchard crops (like banana and pineapple) constituted about 52 per cent of total gross cropped area in the village (Table 10). The remaining 48 per cent of total gross cropped area was mainly under seasonal crops. Paddy was the most important seasonal crop, sown on about 40.5 per cent of the gross cropped area. Paddy was grown in two seasons, pre-kharif (May–June to August–September) and kharif (August–September to November–December). It was followed by

Table 10 *Proportion of different crops in gross cropped area, Mainama, 2015–16,* in acres and per cent

Crop season	Crops	Area (acres)	As proportion of GCA (%)
Pre-kharif	Paddy	244	12.4
Kharif	Paddy	552	28.1
	Vegetables	24	1.2
Rabi	Vegetables	95	4.8
	Others	39	2.0
Annual	Rubber	999	50.8
	Other annual crops	13	0.7
All	Gross cropped area	1966	100.0

Source: Survey data.

vegetables in the kharif and rabi seasons (accounting for 6 per cent of the gross cropped area). Vegetables were grown specifically as intercrops on the river bed. The main vegetables were potato, chilly, spiny gourd, brinjal, pointed gourd, ridge gourd, and radish.

On sloped land, rubber was the most important annual crop in Mainama. Rubber trees have an eight-year gestation period and thereafter have a long productive life. In between rubber trees, banana, turmeric, and different kinds of spices were cultivated. The second most important crop cycle was paddy cultivation in the pre-kharif and kharif seasons. The third crop cycle was paddy cultivated in the pre-kharif or kharif season, and on land kept fallow in the rabi season. Vegetables were grown on tiny plots of land (mostly on the river bed) in the rabi season, or during both kharif and rabi seasons, depending on access to river water.

In the following section we examine the yield, cost of cultivation, and farm business income from major crops.

Cost of Cultivation and Farm Business Incomes

Productivity of paddy

Table 11 shows the average yield of paddy in the pre-kharif and kharif seasons in Mainama village, Dhalai district, and the State of Tripura as a whole. In both seasons, the average yield of paddy in Mainama was higher than the district and State average. Importantly, the average yield of paddy

Table 11 *Average yield of paddy, Mainama, Dhalai district, Tripura, 2015–16 and 2014–15,* in kg per acre

Crop	Mainama village	Dhalai district	Tripura State
Paddy (pre-kharif)	1459.2	1130	1064
Paddy (kharif)	1289.4	1224	1253

Source: Survey data. Figures on yield of pre-kharif and kharif paddy for Dhalai district and Tripura state for 2014–15 are from Government of Tripura (2015).

Table 12 *Average yield of paddy by location, Mainama, 2015–16,* in kg per acre

Crop	Central *para*	Remote *para*
Paddy (pre-kharif)	1569.1	1303.9
Paddy (kharif)	1358.5	1221.2

Source: Survey data.

during pre-kharif was much higher than during kharif season in Mainama in the survey year. However, in comparison to other paddy-growing States, Tripura lagged behind in terms of its average yield of paddy.

On account of different forms of farming practices and diversity in the operated crop land, a large variation was observed in paddy yield across the village. It ranged between 500 kg per acre and 2,500 kg per acre. Table 12 shows that cultivator households belonging to central hamlets attained higher paddy yields as compared to their counterparts in the remote *paras*.

The Tripura government had taken various measures to promote and spread the system of rice intensification (SRI) through the Block Agricultural Offices and *gram panchayats*. However, the survey data revealed that only a few cultivator households had adopted SRI techniques, but without a significant rise in production. From our interviews with households that had cultivated paddy using SRI technique in the survey year, we found cases where cultivators were unaware of certain basic principles of the technique in cultivation.[3] Take the example of Mr Tripura, a retired government employee and resident of Mainama village who cultivated paddy in the kharif season on 0.4 acre of land in 2015–16. He was part of the farmers' group that received training in SRI techniques from the Block Agricultural Office. Under the government scheme, he received 1 kg of paddy seed, 10 kg of urea, 5 kg of superphosphate, and a cash subsidy of Rs 2,100 from the Agriculture Department. The crop

[3] Case studies were conducted by Biplab Sarkar and Ranjini Basu in March 2017.

was damaged due to a pest attack during its flowering stage. He did not apply bio-fertilizer on his field as he was instructed to do during the SRI training, because he believed that his land was already fertile and did not need additional inputs. Controlling the moisture content of soil is a significant factor in ensuring the proper growth of seedlings. However, Mr Tripura's field did not fulfil this requirement. This resulted in very low production of only 450 kg per acre. His experience suggests that extension services and awareness programmes must improve to promote the SRI technique effectively.

Farm business income from paddy cultivation
Table 13 shows the estimated average gross value of output (GVO), paid-out cost and imputed value of family labour (A2+FL), and net farm business income (FBI) incurred from paddy cultivation. Paddy cultivation was non-remunerative for cultivators in Mainama village in the reference year. About 67 per cent of the total number of paddy cultivators incurred losses from paddy cultivation during the survey year. On account of higher productivity, during the pre-kharif season the losses from paddy were comparatively lower than in the kharif season. We see a similar pattern across the central and remote hamlets (Table 14). The cultivators

Table 13 *Average gross value of output (GVO), paid-out cost and imputed value of family labour (A2+FL), and farm business income (FBI) in paddy cultivation, by season, Mainama, 2015–16, in Rs per acre*

Crop season	Crop	GVO	A2+FL	FBI
Pre-kharif	Paddy	25141	26046	−905
Kharif	Paddy	22533	24446	−1913

Source: Survey data.

Table 14 *Average gross value of output (GVO), paid-out cost and imputed value of family labour (A2+FL), and farm business income (FBI) in paddy cultivation, by season, by hamlet, Mainama, 2015–16, in Rs per acre*

Hamlet	Pre-kharif			Kharif		
	GVO	A2+FL	FBI	GVO	A2+FL	FBI
Central	26720	25359	1360	23877	24146	−269
Remote	21808	26805	−4996	21276	24726	−3450

Source: Survey data.

Table 15 *Average gross value of output (GVO), paid-out cost plus imputed value of family labour (A2+FL), and farm business income (FBI), paddy, by socio-economic class, Mainama, 2015–16*, in Rs per acre

Socio-economic class	Pre-kharif			Kharif		
	GVO	A2+FL	FBI	GVO	A2+FL	FBI
Cultivator: sub-marginal	24714	29127	−4413	22366	26500	−4134
Cultivator: marginal	26739	23404	3335	23732	24999	−1267
Cultivator: small	23239	15753	7487	21381	20652	729
Cultivator: medium	23795	14444	9351	21997	18474	3524

Source: Survey data.

in remote hamlets incurred much higher losses as compared to those in central hamlets. This difference was mainly because of the higher productivity and gross value of output obtained by the cultivators of central hamlets. Central para households had greater access to irrigated lowland close to the river, which could have been one of the reasons for higher productivity.

Table 15 shows the average gross value of output (GVO), paid-out cost and imputed value of family labour (A2+FL), and net farm business income (FBI) from paddy cultivation for different socio-economic classes. A striking feature was that the "cultivator: sub-marginal" households (with operational holdings of >0<=1 acre) incurred negative incomes in both seasons. The two agrarian classes of "cultivator: small" and "cultivator: medium" incurred low levels of positive income from paddy cultivation. Interestingly, the two poorer agrarian classes of "cultivator: sub-marginal" and "cultivator: marginal" obtained higher productivity and gross value of output from paddy cultivation as compared to "cultivator: small" and "cultivator: medium" households (with operational holdings of >2.5<=5 and >5 acres). However, the difference in net farm incomes between the socio-economic classes was mainly because of the much higher cost of cultivation incurred by "cultivator: sub-marginal" and "cultivator: marginal" households. In the next section, we examine in detail the item-wise cost for paddy cultivation, in order to understand the difference in incomes across socio-economic classes.

Cost of production of paddy

The estimation of cost of cultivation for paddy showed that there were large differences across socio-economic classes (Table 16), as a result of the diversity of operated land in Mainama and the distribution of operational land size-classes in its many hamlets. It is clear from our survey data that the characteristics of operational holding-based socio-economic classes in the study villages of Tripura are unique among other villages surveyed under PARI in other parts of India. (See chapter 11 in this volume, on household incomes.)

Households in remote hamlets possessed sloped land in greater proportion than central hamlet households. Their average holding size was larger than those with lowland holdings. While households in remote hamlets were classified into the agrarian classes of "cultivator: small" and "cultivator: medium," with operational land of >2.5<=5 and >5 acres, the agricultural practices of these cultivators were generally characterised by low levels of input and machine use. The difference in the cost of cultivation among the various socio-economic classes can be explained on the following three counts.

First, as Tables 16 and 17 show, labour cost (both casual labour and imputed value of family labour) was the largest cost component for paddy cultivation. What is striking here is that labour use and subsequently the cost borne for it was much higher for "cultivator: sub-marginal" and "cultivator: marginal" classes (that is, households with operational holdings of >0<=1 acre and >1<=2.5 acres), in comparison to "cultivator: small" and "cultivator: medium" classes (that is, households with operational holdings of >2.5<=5 acres and >5 acres). This was because labour use was largely concentrated in the smaller holdings cultivating paddy (Table 24).

Secondly, households belonging to the "cultivator: sub-marginal" and "cultivator: marginal" classes incurred higher costs for machine labour. This can be explained in two ways. On the one hand, the use of machines, particularly power tillers for ploughing operations in remote hamlets, was restricted owing to the rugged terrain. On the other hand, "cultivator: sub-marginal" households of central hamlets were mainly dependent on machines hired on rent for land preparation operations.

Thirdly, the average per acre costs for seed, manure, fertilizer, plant protection and irrigation were low for all agrarian classes. This was because the cultivators received substantial assistance for input use from the different State government programmes. However, we observed from the survey that the use of fertilizers was much lower among cultivators in remote hamlets than those in central hamlets.

"Cultivator: sub-marginal" and "cultivator: marginal" households

Table 16 *Average expenditure on different cost items in paddy cultivation, in pre-kharif season, by socio-economic classes, Mainama, 2015–16*, in Rs per acre

Cost item	Cultivator: sub-marginal	Cultivator: marginal	Cultivator: small	Cultivator: medium
Seed	729	651	639	948
Manure	567	315	48	809
Fertilizer	729	630	0	0
Plant protection	170	132	133	126
Irrigation	294	129	0	570
Casual labour	6972	7528	4867	4918
Animal labour	726	403	407	249
Machine labour	3969	3465	1268	1080
Rent	1887	1924	0	0
Other costs	505	452	141	261
Cost A2	16548	15629	7502	8960
Imputed family labour (FL)	12579	7775	8251	5484
Cost A2+FL	29127	23404	15753	14444

Source: Survey data.

Table 17 *Average expenditure on different cost items in paddy cultivation, in kharif season, by operational landholding size classes, Mainama, 2015-16*, in Rs per acre

Cost items	Cultivator: sub-marginal	Cultivator: marginal	Cultivator: small	Cultivator: medium
Seed	670	441	556	784
Manure	387	325	246	454
Fertilizer	872	415	236	218
Plant protection	190	178	85	106
Irrigation	204	109	153	365
Casual labour	5667	6599	5707	3039
Animal labour	389	574	321	856
Machine labour	3502	3241	1823	574
Rent	2108	2723	1978	1783
Other costs	454	548	675	264
Cost A2	14444	15153	11780	8445
Imputed family labour (FL)	12056	9846	8872	10029
Cost A2+FL	26500	24999	20652	18474

Source: Survey data.

concentrated in central hamlets attained a higher yield of paddy than cultivators in remote hamlets. However, this yield gap was not sufficient to meet the higher paid-out costs borne by "cultivator: sub-marginal" and "cultivator: marginal" households. The latter cultivators used more inputs, employed greater machine and wage labour, as compared to cultivators belonging to the agrarian classes operating bigger farms in remote *paras*. This resulted in the "cultivator: sub-marginal" households incurring losses, while the cultivators operating larger land made comparatively higher but nevertheless low levels of income from paddy cultivation.

Rubber

Rubber plantations occupy a very important place in the economy of Mainama village. After years of insurgency, a large number of landless tribal households that had migrated from areas of violence were resettled in Mainama, and they were provided with rubber plantations under State government schemes. (The rubber economy is discussed in chapter 13 of this volume.) In the survey year, rubber plantations occupied about two-thirds of the total operated land in Mainama. About 40 per cent of total cultivator households owned rubber plantations. However, large areas under rubber had not yet begun to yield latex and were still in gestation. Hence, incomes from rubber plantation were very low in the overall village economy during the survey year. In the future, as the trees mature, earnings from rubber will contribute significantly to the household incomes of rubber cultivators in Mainama.

Vegetables

Vegetable cultivation was a highly commercialised activity in Mainama. Vegetables were mainly intercropped on the river bed during both kharif and rabi seasons. The yield of vegetables could not be estimated, as it was difficult to measure the extent of individual crops in the intercropped

Table 18 *Average gross value of output (GVO), paid-out cost and imputed value of family labour (A2+FL); and farm business income (FBI), in vegetable cultivation, Mainama, 2015–16, in Rs per acre*

Crop	Number of cultivators	GVO	Cost A2+FL	Farm business income
Vegetables	213	54725	53567	1159

Source: Survey data.

system. Of the total number of cultivator households in Mainama, 24 per cent (mostly residents of central hamlets) were involved in vegetable cultivation. The average extent of land under vegetable cultivation per household was extremely low, at just 0.2 acre. There was significant variation in incomes from vegetable cultivation among the cultivators, depending on the variety of vegetables grown. The average income from vegetables over the total paid-out cost and imputed value of family labour was low, at just Rs 1,159 per acre (Table 18).

Farm business incomes from net sown area
Table 19 shows the average gross value of output (GVO), cost A2, cost FL, combined cost A2+FL, and farm business income of net sown area across socio-economic classes, counting all crops together during the survey year. The rationale for taking net sown area instead of operational holding in the calculation was that a substantial extent of sloped agricultural lands lay fallow in the reference period. In addition, rubber plantations that had not yet begun to yield were not considered in our calculation. The average gross value of output per acre of net sown area, as discussed above, was much higher for households belonging to "cultivator: sub-marginal" and "cultivator: marginal" classes (with operational holdings of >0<=1 acre and >1<=2.5 acres), as compared to "cultivator: small" and "cultivator: medium" classes (with operational holding >2.5<=5 acres and >5 acres). However, households belonging to the "cultivator: sub-marginal" class incurred losses from crop production over cost A2 and FL. The imputed cost of family labour was the highest for the "cultivator: sub-marginal" class among all socio-economic classes, which points to their

Table 19 *Average gross value of output, paid-out cost and imputed value of family labour (A2+FL) and farm business income of net sown area, by socio-economic class, Mainama, 2015–16 in Rs per acre*

Socio-economic class	GVO	Cost A2	Cost FL	Cost A2+FL	FBI on cost A2+FL
Cultivator: sub-marginal	37119	23217	17755	40972	−3853
Cultivator: marginal	36563	18285	13240	31525	5038
Cultivator: small	31583	14009	9875	23884	7700
Cultivator: medium	27229	10912	9997	20909	6320
All	35551	19506	14783	34289	1262

Source: Survey data.

dependence on family labour for cultivation. Households belonging to the socio-economic classes of "cultivators: marginal," "cultivators: small," and "cultivators: medium" received positive levels of incomes from crop production.

Table 20 shows the proportions of different crops in total gross cropped area across different socio-economic classes. Importantly, households under "cultivator: medium" class, with operational holdings of over 5 acres, had 78 per cent of their agricultural land under rubber plantations; for households of "cultivator: marginal" and "cultivator: small" classes, it was about 50 per cent; and "cultivator: sub-marginal" households, with operational holdings of less than 1 acre, kept most of their land under paddy and vegetable cultivation. When their rubber trees attain maturity, earnings from rubber will significantly increase the crop incomes of rubber-cultivating households.

Table 21 shows income from crop production per household by socio-economic class in Mainama. It was highest for households in the

Table 20 *Proportion of different crops in total gross cropped area, by socio-economic class, Mainama, in 2015–16, in per cent*

Socio-economic class	Paddy	Rubber	Vegetables and other lowland crops	All
Cultivator: sub-marginal	73	14	13	100
Cultivator: marginal	40	51	9	100
Cultivator: small	46	48	6	100
Cultivator: medium	15	78	7	100

Source: Survey data.

Table 21 *Average annual incomes from crop production by socio-economic class, Mainama, 2015–16, in Rs per household*

Socio-economic class	Number of households	Average annual income from crop production (over the cost A2+FL)
Cultivator: sub-marginal	378	−394
Cultivator: marginal	249	8753
Cultivator: small	139	20078
Cultivator: medium	39	42570
All	805	8052

Source: Survey data.

"cultivator: medium" class with operational holding of over 5 acres (Rs 42,570), and this declined steeply for agrarian classes with smaller holdings. Households in the "cultivator: sub-marginal" class had negative income from crop production in the reference period. This income disparity will change once the plantations begin to yield, as noted earlier.

Use of Machinery in Agriculture

The extent of machine use in agriculture was generally low in Mainama, given its largely sloped terrain. Use of machinery was primarily limited to lowland paddy and vegetable cultivation. In remote hamlets, the rugged terrain prevented the expansion of machine use. For instance, most of the land preparation operations for paddy cultivation done by residents of remote hamlets used animal labour – even in the case of the larger landholding households. In rubber plantations, machines were not used for any operation. In contrast, ploughing operations in the lowlands were primarily done by hand-held power tillers. Tractors had not been introduced in the village till the survey year.

Machines were used for irrigation, plant protection, and threshing operations. There were a total of 84 power tillers, 11 thresher machines, 102 diesel pumps, and 53 electric pumps in 2015–16 among our sample households in Mainama village. Data on the purchase year of agricultural machinery show that a substantial proportion of agricultural machinery was purchased after 2010: 53 per cent of total diesel pumps, 79 per cent of total power tillers, 66 per cent of total sprayers, and all threshing machines.

Importantly, the survey data revealed that there was significant encouragement and assistance from the State government to increase the use of machines in agriculture. Cultivators received substantial subsidies to purchase agricultural machinery. There were also schemes for free disbursal of machines through the Block Agriculture Office. For instance, the power tiller owners reported that they received assistance up to Rs 75,000, while sprayers were distributed for free among cultivators. Table 22 shows that about 65 per cent of total diesel pumps, 40 per cent of total power tillers, and 59 per cent of total sprayers in the village were received either through subsidies or free of cost from the State government under different schemes. We also found that a high proportion of subsidised agricultural machinery was bought after 2010 in Mainama village.

Table 22 *Distribution of subsidised agricultural machinery, by year of purchasing, in Mainama, 2015–16*, in per cent

Year	Diesel pump	Power tiller	Sprayer
Before 2005	23	18	15
2005 to 2010	24	0	18
After 2010	53	82	67
Total	100	100	100
Proportion of subsidised machines in total machines	65	40	59

Source: Survey data.

It is noteworthy that the maximum use of machinery was in the form of hired machines. For example, in paddy cultivation, 85.6 per cent of the land was ploughed with hired power tillers, and threshing of 99.2 per cent of the output was done by hired machines. The rent contract for land preparation operations was time-rated, whereas threshing operations were both time-rated as well as based on acreage. The average rate for ploughing by a power tiller was Rs 250 per hour. For threshing operations, the rate ranged between Rs 200 and 250 per hour, or between Rs 1,000 and Rs 1,250 per acre, in our survey year.

Labour Absorption in Crop Production

There were three forms of labour in Mainama: family labour, hired or wage labour, and exchange labour. Long-term farm servants were not present in the village.

As pointed out earlier, paddy was the most important seasonal crop in the village, along with a small amount of vegetable cultivation, mainly on the river bed. Rubber was the most important annual crop. Transplanting, weeding, and harvesting operations in paddy and harvesting in vegetable cultivation saw the greatest absorption of hired labour and of female labour in particular.

General Features of Labour Use

Due to the seasonality of crop production, labour use was mostly concentrated in the kharif season. Production of kharif crop absorbed 41.5 per cent of total labour use. Pre-kharif crops absorbed about 24.6 per cent of total labour use. Only 10 per cent of total labour was used during the

Table 23 *Distribution of labour use across seasons in Mainama, 2015–16,* in per cent

Village	Pre-kharif	Kharif	Rabi	Annual	Total
Mainama	24.6	41.5	10.3	23.5	100

Source: Survey data.

Table 24 *Distribution of labour use across crops in Mainama, 2015–16,* in per cent

Village	Paddy	Vegetable	Rubber	Total
Mainama	61.9	16.2	21.9	100

Source: Survey data.

rabi season. The remaining 23.5 per cent of the entire labour use in the village was primarily absorbed by rubber plantations all through the year.

In terms of crops, most of the labour was absorbed by paddy as it was grown twice a year in the village (kharif and pre-kharif). Of total labour, 61.9 per cent was absorbed in paddy cultivation and only 16.2 per cent was engaged in vegetable cultivation in the rabi season (see Table 24).

Family Labour and Hired Labour

Cultivation using family labour was the norm for crop production in Mainama. The proportion of hired labour in total labour use was 41.7 per cent (Table 25). This indicated great dependence on family labour for crop operations. Exchange labour was not significant in this village, at about 1 per cent of the total labour demand. Family labour constituted 57.3 per cent of total labour use in the village. Family labour was used extensively for paddy, vegetable and rubber cultivation. However, in operations such as transplantation, weeding, harvesting of paddy and collecting latex from rubber trees, hired labour was used. Among the peasant classes, the use of family labour was uniform and comprised more than 50 per cent of total labour use. However, the "cultivator: sub-marginal" class (operating on less than one acre) utilised the highest proportion of family labour, 65.8 per cent of total labour use (Table 26).

Paddy cultivation was primarily performed by family labour. Sixty per cent of the total labour used in paddy cultivation was family labour, whereas 40 per cent was hired labour. Similarly, for vegetable cultivation, the share of family labour was higher than of hired labour. However, in rubber plantations the proportion of hired labour in total labour use was greater than the share of family labour.

Table 25 *Composition of total labour use in Mainama, 2015–16, in per cent*

Village	Family labour	Hired labour	Exchange labour	Total
Mainama	57.3	41.7	0.9	100

Source: Survey data.

Table 26 *Distribution of labour use by type across socio-economic classes, Mainama, 2015–16, in per cent*

Socio-economic classes	Family labour	Hired labour	Exchange labour	Total
Cultivator: sub-marginal	65.8	33.5	0.7	100
Cultivator: marginal	54.3	44.7	1.0	100
Cultivator: small	53.1	46.1	0.9	100
Cultivator: medium	58.0	40.4	1.6	100

Source: Survey data 2015–16.

Gender Composition of Total Labour Use

A striking feature of our data is the gender gap within family labour and hired labour in crop operations. Table 27 shows the sex-wise distribution of family and hired labour across cultivators. The sex composition of labour use shows that male workers were mainly engaged in family labour, whereas female participation in the hired labour market was high. Female labourers mostly participated in transplantation, weeding, and harvesting operations in paddy and vegetable cultivation, and in various operations in rubber plantations.

In Mainama, male workers contributed 67.4 per cent of total family labour use (Table 27). Across all socio-economic classes, more than 60 per cent of family labour was contributed by male workers. The proportion of female labour in crop production varied from 30 to 40 per cent of total family labour. Female participation in family labour gradually increased as landholding increased. In Mainama, the proportion of female family labour participation in raising plantation crops was greater than in paddy cultivation. This was because, as seen earlier, "cultivator: medium" households with larger landholdings tended to have more area under plantations. By contrast, "cultivator: sub-marginal" households cultivated a greater extent of paddy, and used more male than female family labour.

Table 27 shows that 55 per cent of the total daily-rated hired labour demand was met by male labourers. The class of "cultivator: sub-marginal"

Table 27 *Composition of family and hired labour use, by sex and socio-economic class, Mainama, 2015–16, in per cent*

Socio-economic class	Family labour		Hired labour	
	Male	Female	Male	Female
Cultivator: sub-marginal	70.1	29.9	40.3	59.7
Cultivator: marginal	69.7	30.3	52.8	47.2
Cultivator: small	63.6	36.4	68.7	31.3
Cultivator: medium	60.9	39.1	52.1	47.9
All	67.4	32.6	55.4	44.6

Source: Survey data.

absorbed the largest share of female hired labour for cultivation. This was because the share of female hired labour used in vegetable cultivation was higher than in paddy cultivation (Table 27).

Types of Wage Contracts

The two major types of wage contracts prevalent in Mainama were daily-rated and piece-rated contracts. Table 28 shows the total hired labour-days under different wage contracts. Most of the operations were done on the basis of time-rated contracts. Around 72 per cent of total hired labour-days were absorbed by daily-wage contracts and 28 per cent by piece-wage contracts. The most prevalent form of piece rates in the village was surface (area) piece rates.

Table 28 *Distribution of hired labour, Mainama, 2015–16, in per cent*

Village	Daily-rate labour	Piece-rate labour	Total
Mainama	71.7	28.3	100

Source: Survey data.

Table 29 *Composition of hired labour use in Mainama, crop-wise, 2015–16, in per cent*

Crop	Hired labour on daily wage contract	Hired labour on piece rated contract
Paddy	64	36
Rubber	82	18
Vegetable	88	12

Source: Survey data.

Crop-wise labour use shows that about 36 per cent of total labour used in paddy cultivation was employed on piece-rate contracts (Table 29). In paddy cultivation, piece-rated labour use was prevalent in transplanting, weeding, and harvesting operations. Rubber and vegetable cultivation was almost entirely done on daily-wage contracts. Of the total labour used in rubber plantations, 18 per cent was employed on piece-rated contracts, accounting for 17 per cent of the total labour hired for all crops on piece-rated contracts.

Summary

This chapter discusses the agrarian structure, production, and agrarian relations of Mainama village in Dhalai district of Tripura.

About 40 per cent of the agricultural land in Mainama was under plantation crops, primarily rubber. Thirty per cent of the remaining land was put to lowland paddy and vegetable cultivation. Irrigation was restricted to only 48 per cent of the village, with the Manu river being the primary source.

Mainama was largely a village of marginal cultivators, with 46 per cent of households operating less than 1 hectare of land. Around 33 per cent of households did not operate any land. An active tenancy market in the village assured access to lowlands to residents of remote hamlets, which was otherwise not available to them. Thirty per cent of the total operational land was under various forms of tenancy contracts and most tenant cultivators belonged to the "cultivator: sub-marginal" class with operational holdings of less than 1 acre.

The prevalence of homestead cultivation was a distinct feature of Mainama, where 92 per cent of households owned their house sites. The size of the homestead differed across the village, depending on the location of the household.

Paddy was the most important seasonal crop in the village, grown in both the pre-kharif and kharif seasons. Vegetable cultivation was undertaken in the kharif and rabi seasons on the river bed. Rubber being the most important annual crop, rubber plantations occupied around 50.8 per cent of the total gross cropped area.

There was wide variation in net incomes from crop production across different socio-economic classes. Average annual income from crop production was the highest for "cultivator: medium" households (operating more than 5 acres), at Rs 42,570. Machine use in agriculture in

Mainama was restricted to low-lying cropland. In recent years, the State government had started schemes to promote greater use of machinery in agriculture. In Mainama, cultivation was mainly undertaken by family labour.

Appendix 1

Definition of Land Use Categories

- *Cultivated plain land.* It is used for the cultivation of seasonal crops, like paddy and vegetables. This land is a distinct technical unit of cultivation separate from the homestead, and therefore does not include kitchen garden cultivation practised on the homestead.
- *Plantation land.* Land devoted to the cultivation of plantation crops, such as rubber, areca nut, pineapple, and banana.
- *Orchard land.* Land under fruit trees and other trees not classified as plantation crops, such as bamboo, jackfruit, teak, etc.
- *"Jhum" land.* This land was used for shifting or *jhum* cultivation (slash-and-burn method). It forms part of slopes or uplands.
- *Forest land.* This includes all area under forest cover or land so classed under any legal enactment or administered as forest, whether state-owned or private. This was not under any cultivation.
- *"Tila" land.* This is slope land, not included in any of the above classifications, and is kept fallow.

Reference

Government of Tripura (2015), *Basic Statistics: Area, Production and Yield,* Department of Agriculture and Farmers Welfare, Government of Tripura, available at: http.// agri.tripura.gov.in/basic_statistics

8

Agrarian Structure, Production and Agrarian Relations in Muhuripur

Tapas Singh Modak, Ritam Dutta, Subhajit Patra,
and Arindam Das[1]

Located in Jolaibari Block of the South district of Tripura, Muhuripur is primarily an immigrant village. Its population mainly comprises Bengali speakers who came in the 1970s as part of the influx of migrants from Bangladesh. The village is about 18 km from the district headquarters at Belonia, connected by an all-weather *pucca* road. Of a total of 1,054 households in the village in 2016, 628 were Other Caste Hindu households, 272 were Other Backward Class (OBC) households, and 154 were Scheduled Caste (SC) households. There was not a single Scheduled Tribe (ST) household in the village.

In this chapter, we discuss Muhuripur's agrarian structure, production and agrarian relations. The first section of the chapter presents features of land tenure structure and land use in the village, including the distribution of land, inequality in ownership of land, and the forms of tenancy and land markets in the village. The second section focuses on the nature of irrigation, cropping patterns, and estimation of incomes from crop production across socio-economic classes. The third section briefly discusses the extent of machine use in agriculture. The fourth section explores the forms of labour absorption in agriculture.

---

[1] Ritam Dutta authored the section on "Land Tenure and Land Use." Tapas Singh Modak wrote the sections on "Irrigation," "Cropping Pattern and Crop Incomes," and "Machine Use in Agriculture." Subhajit Patra and Arindam Das jointly wrote the section on "Labour Use in Crop Production." Tapas Singh Modak was the lead author of the overall chapter.

Land Tenure and Land Use

Muhuripur village has predominantly lowland areas with no forest land, unlike the other two study villages. The river Muhuri that flows next to the village is the major source of irrigation for the lowlands. In our sample, a total of 214 households collectively possessing 178 acres of land were surveyed. In the following analysis, we have used the results of sample-based estimated value to provide a picture of the entire village.

Plain land is classified as lowland, and undulating or sloped land is termed as upland. About two-thirds of the total agricultural area in this village were lowlands and the remaining uplands. The lowlands were primarily used to cultivate paddy and a wide variety of vegetables. Of the upland area, 75 per cent was covered with rubber plantations.

Land Tenure

We classified the land possessed by the households of Muhuripur into the following three categories.

Owned land: Land over which the household has complete ownership rights, including the right to sell.

Assigned land: Land received by a household under title deeds or *pattas* from the government. The household has "use rights" over the holding, but does not hold "right to sale." Assigned lands transferred by inheritance to a household have been considered as its *patta* holdings.

Occupied or encroached land: The National Sample Survey Organisation (NSSO) defines this type of land as "otherwise possessed land." This type of land is under possession of the household through encroachment. The

Table 1 *Distribution of land under possession of households, by tenure, Muhuripur, 2016,* in numbers, acres, and per cent

Type of tenure	Households		Extent		Average size (acres)
	Number	Per cent	Acreage	Per cent	
Assigned	24	2.3	15	1.7	0.63
Occupied	44	5.6	41	4.7	0.93
Owned	722	92.1	814	93.6	1.13
Total	790	100.0	870	100.0	0.82

Note: *Households owned multiple plots across different types of tenure. Percentages have been calculated on total number of households in the village.
Source: Survey data.

household does not have any ownership and sale rights over this land.

The distribution of land owned by households by form of tenure shows that 93.6 per cent of the total land was under complete ownership of the households (Table 1). The extent of assigned land received through *pattas* from the government was very low in Muhuripur, and constituted only 1.7 per cent of the total land in the survey year. The remaining 4.7 per cent of total land under possession, mostly uplands, was encroached land.

Land Use

As Table 2 shows, about 63 per cent of total agricultural land was cultivated plain land, predominantly sown with seasonal crops like paddy and vegetables. Upland has been broadly classified into four categories, i.e. plantation land, forest land, orchard land, and *tila* land. (See Appendix 1 for the list of land use categories.) Plantation land was mostly covered by rubber trees, and constituted the second highest share of agricultural land in the village (25.2 per cent). Forest and orchard lands were insignificant in Muhuripur, unlike in the other two study villages. About 2.6 per cent of the total land was sloped *tila* land, which was mostly left fallow. Water bodies (ponds) were significant in Muhuripur, and constituted 9 per cent of all land. About one-fourth of all households received incomes from fisheries in the survey year.

Table 2 *Distribution of land according to land use, Muhuripur, 2016,* in per cent

Type of land	Proportion
Cultivated plain land	62.9
Forest land	0.2
Orchard land	0.1
Plantation land	25.2
Tila land	2.6
Water bodies	9.0
All	100.0

Source: Survey data.

Size of Landholding and Landlessness

Possession of landholding refers to all the land owned, assigned or occupied by households. It includes lands bearing crops, plantations, orchards, and water bodies, and also current fallow land. The average size of landholdings in Muhuripur was 0.82 acre, and the coefficient of variation was 1.45 (Table 3). The largest landholding household owned over 8.3 acres of land. This was a peasant household, and income from crop production was its major source of annual household income. The household cultivated paddy and vegetable in the lowlands, owned 2 acres of rubber plantation, and cultivated fish in the two ponds it owned. The household had also leased out 2 acres of lowland on a share-rent basis for a year.

The average size of operational holding in the village was 0.79 acre, and the coefficient of variation was 1.33. Operational holding refers to total extent of agricultural land available for cultivation during the reference period. The largest operational holding in the village measured 5.6 acres: this was of the same household that possessed the largest landholding. It is important to note that both in terms of possession and operation, the average size of holding of a household in Muhuripur was substantially lower than the national average size of ownership holding (1.57 acre) and operational holding (2.12 acres) in 2013 (NSSO 2015).

Table 4 shows the size-class distribution of operational holdings in Muhuripur. The size-classes are primarily those used by the National Sample

Table 3 *Distribution of land according to land use, Muhuripur, 2016,* in acres

Tenure	Average size	Largest landholding	Coefficient of variation
Possession	0.82	8.3	1.45
Operational	0.79	5.6	1.33

Source: Survey data.

Table 4 *Size-class distribution of operational holdings,* in per cent

Size-class	Proportion of households	Proportion of area
Landless (0 hectare)	34	0
Marginal (<1 hectare)	59	65
Small (1 to 2 hectares)	2	13
Semi-medium (>2 to 4 hectares)	6	22
Medium (>4 to 10 hectares)	0	0
Large (>10 hectares)	0	0
All	100	100

Source: Survey data.

Surveys of Land and Livestock Holdings.[2] In Muhuripur, landlessness with respect to operational holding was significant. Approximately 34 per cent of all households did not operate any agricultural land in the reference year. Among these landless households, about three-fourths were primarily dependent on agricultural and non-agricultural wages, and self-employed non-farm activities such as petty businesses. The remaining 25 per cent of households were those whose major source of income was government salaries, businesses, pensions, and remittances.

Households operating on marginal holdings (less than 1 hectare of land) constituted the largest category in the village, both as a share of household population and as a share of total operational land. They constituted 59 per cent of the total population and accounted for 65 per cent of total operational land. However, small cultivators (1 to 2 hectares of land) and semi-medium cultivators (less than 2 to 4 hectares of land) together constituted only 8 per cent of total village population and accounted for 35 per cent of total operated land.

From the data it emerges, therefore, that Muhuripur is a village of households with marginal and small holdings. In the survey year, it had a substantial landless population, the majority of whom were dependent on agricultural and non-agricultural wages, and petty businesses.

Inequality

Table 5 presents the Gini coefficient of ownership and operational holdings in Muhuripur village. At around 0.6 the coefficient was high for both ownership and operational landholdings. However, the inequality in land operated by households in Muhuripur does not directly imply an inequality in household incomes. The share of incomes from agriculture was not the major constituent of household incomes, not even for cultivator households. Households across the various socio-economic classes had diverse sources of non-farm incomes, ranging from government jobs and petty businesses to non-agricultural labouring out.

Inequality can also be measured by comparing the extent of land possessed and operated by the bottom 50 per cent and top 5 per cent of all households in the village. The top 5 per cent of households owned 27 per cent of the total land, and 26 per cent of land operated in the village (Table

---

[2] The NSSO records up to three decimal points but we have considered only up to two decimal points. The "landless" size-class used here refers only to households whose extent of operational holding was zero.

Table 5 *Gini coefficient of household ownership and operational holdings*

Village	Ownership holding	Operational holding
Muhuripur	0.64	0.62

Source: Survey data.

Table 6 *Share of total extent of possession and operational holdings held for bottom 50 and top 5 per cent of households in the village*

Tenure	Top 5 percentile	Bottom 50 percentile
Ownership	27	6
Operation	26	13

Source: Survey data.

6). In contrast, the bottom 50 per cent owned only 6 per cent of total land and 13 per cent of operational land. It is important to note that the bottom 50 per cent of all households operated land on a far greater scale than the total extent of land they possessed.

Tenancy

Tenancy was widely prevalent in the agricultural production system in Muhuripur. The tenancy market operated largely in respect of lowlands (cultivated plain lands) that accounted for over 95 per cent of total leased land and all the leased-out land in the reference period. Hence, the following analysis of the tenancy market is specifically focused on cultivated lowlands. Table 7 shows that about 33 per cent of all households leased in land and about 24 per cent of all households leased out land under different arrangements. The total leased-in land comprised 43 per cent of all operated land and leased-out land, around 42 per cent of all owned land (Table 7). The average size of leased-out land, at 0.92 acre, was substantially greater than the average extent of land leased in, at 0.73 acre.

Sharecropping was the most prominent form of tenancy in Muhuripur (Table 8). About two-thirds of the total leased-in area was under sharecropping leases and the remaining one-third was given to tenants under fixed rent arrangements. However, with respect to leased-out land, sharecropping was more significant, and constituted 84 per cent of total leased-out land. An annual form of tenancy contract was more prevalent in the village as compared to a seasonal contract (Table 9). The sharing arrangement was predominantly a 50:50 division of the produce. Some

Table 7 *Incidence of tenancy, households and area, Muhuripur, 2016,* in per cent

Village	Leased in		Leased out	
	Households as percentage of population	Land as percentage of total operated crop land	Households as percentage of population	Land as percentage percentage of total crop land owned
Muhuripur	32.6	43.3	23.8	42.3

Source: Survey data.

Table 8 *Distribution of area under tenancy according to type of tenancy, Muhuripur, 2016,* in acres and percentage

	Fixed rent		Share rent		Total	
	Acreage	Proportion	Acreage	Proportion	Acreage	Proportion
Leased-in land	85.1	34	165.8	66	250.8	100
Leased-out land	36.5	16	193.0	84	229.5	100

Source: Survey data.

Table 9 *Distribution of leased land under different types of tenancy, by length of contract, Muhuripur, 2016,* in per cent

	Fixed rent		Share rent	
	Annual	Seasonal	Annual	Seasonal
Leased-in land	94	6	70	30
Leased-out land	100	0	89	11

Source: Survey data.

landowners shared the cost of machine use and irrigation charges, which were not very significant in Muhuripur. In sharecropping, all payments were made in kind, whereas payment in cash was more prevalent for households that leased on a fixed rent basis. Paddy was grown on 89 per cent of the gross cropped area under tenancy, and the remaining 11 per cent was under mostly different types of vegetables.

Table 10 presents the distribution of tenancy across socio-economic classes in Muhuripur. Interestingly, the ratio between extent of leased-in land and extent of land under operational holdings was almost equal for all socio-economic classes, at more than 40 per cent of total operated land. However, the largest number of tenant households (218 out of 344) belonged to the lowest agrarian class of "cultivator: sub-marginal" (those operating

Table 10 *Distribution of tenancy by socio-economic class, Muhuripur,* in acres

Socio-economic class	Extent leased in (number of lessee households)	Extent leased out (number of lessor households)
Manual worker	0	8.93 (10)
Manual worker with diversified income	0	37.34 (52)
Cultivator: sub-marginal	103.27 (218)	66.39 (95)
Cultivator: marginal	95.42 (95)	31.97 (28)
Cultivator: small	52.15 (31)	19.65 (13)
Salaried, business and others	0	65.26 (53)

Source: Survey data.

less than 1 acre). The average extent of land leased in by households belonging to this agrarian class was 0.47 acre. The largest number of lessor households (95 out of 251) was also from the class of "Cultivators: sub-marginal". However, the numbers were far less than tenant households belonging to this category, and the extent of leased-out land (66.39 acres) was less than the extent of land leased in by them (103.27 acres).

In terms of extent of land leased out, the next significant class was the "salaried, business and other" category, followed by "manual worker with diversified income" households, those who had zero operational holdings and significant non-labour incomes. These households possessed land but did not engage in agricultural production as they had diversified to other non-farm activities. Therefore, the tenancy market in Muhuripur largely acted in favour of the poorest agrarian class of cultivators by enabling them access to agricultural land, which otherwise was unavailable to them.

Homestead Farming

Homestead farming is an important feature of the study villages in Tripura. However, the extent of homestead farming in Muhuripur was low as compared to the other two study villages. Our definition of homestead land is the same as used by National Sample Surveys of Household Ownership and Operational Holdings in India.[3] Table 11 shows

---

[3] NSSO (2015) defines homestead as the dwelling house of the household together with the courtyard, compound, garden, out-house, place of worship, family graveyard, guest house, shop, workshop and offices for running household enterprises, tanks, wells, latrines, drains, and boundary walls annexed to the dwelling house.

Table 11 *Distribution of homestead land according to tenure, Muhuripur, 2016,* in per cent

Tenure	Number of households	Proportion of households
Assigned	26	2.5
Occupied	19	1.8
Owned	1009	95.7
All	1054	100.0

Note: *Some households possessed multiple homestead plots across different types of tenure. Percentages have been calculated on total number of households in the village.
Source: Survey data.

that 95.7 per cent of all households in Muhuripur had full ownership rights over their homestead. Only 2.5 per cent of all households received homestead land as *pattas* from government, and the remaining 1.8 per cent households had occupied homestead land over which they had no ownership or sale rights. The average extent of homestead land was 0.22 acre, with the largest extent for a single household being 1.6 acres. The extent of homestead land in Muhuripur was smaller than in the other two study villages.

In the survey year, 245 households out of 1,054 households were carrying out homestead farming. The extent of land was tiny and many households were not able to report the extent precisely. Different kinds of vegetables for household consumption were grown, acting as an important supplementary source of household nutrition. Twenty-nine households sold some of their homestead production and received additional income.

The Land Market

Pressure from immigrants in the early 1970s led to the growth of an agricultural land market in Muhuripur, which continued in subsequent decades. The major land-type purchased for cultivation was lowland. Since 2006, however, purchase of plantation land has increased. One household in the village purchased 6 acres of plantation land in 2001 but started rubber production only in 2007. Thirty-nine per cent of the total operational crop land and 53 per cent of the total available plantation land in Muhuripur were acquired by households through sale over the years, mostly from people residing in and around Muhuripur.

Cropping Pattern, Yields, and Crop Incomes

Irrigation and Cropping Pattern

Crop lands were primarily irrigated by water from the Muhuri river in Muhuripur. The State government established nine river lift irrigation (RLI) schemes on the river at different points of time. These RLI schemes formed the main source of irrigation in the survey year. Almost all lowlands had irrigation facilities. However, access to irrigation was restricted on sloped lands due to the difficulties posed by topography, and also because such land was under rubber plantation.

Table 12 shows that about 85 per cent of total net sown area in lowlands received water from RLI schemes. Ponds, artesian wells, and other sources irrigated about 5 per cent of lowland net sown area, and the remaining 9 per cent was rainfed.[4] Water from artesian wells usually flowed throughout the year. In addition, a few cultivators used their diesel pumps to lift water from the river, primarily for vegetable cultivation on the river bed during rabi season. They also sold water to other cultivators.

Table 13 presents a summary of RLI schemes in Muhuripur village. In 1998, the first two RLI schemes were introduced in South Muhuripur hamlet and Banabihari hamlet. These were followed by two schemes in 1999, one in 2000, one in 2001, two in 2003, and the last one in 2008.

Table 12 *Distribution of lowland net sown area by source of irrigation, Muhuripur, 2015–16, in acres and per cent*

Source of irrigation	Extent (acre)	Share (in per cent)
River lift irrigation (RLI)	471	85
Pond	13	2
Artesian well	11	2
Multi-source	7	1
Tubewell/open well	2	0
Rainfed	49	9
Total	553	100

Source: Survey data.

---

[4] An artesian well does not require any pump to lift the water from ground. It is situated upon a confined aquifer containing groundwater under pressure. Hence, water comes out automatically to the surface due to the pressure.

Table 13 *Description of river lift irrigation (RLI) schemes in Muhuripur, by hamlet, 2016,* in numbers

No. of scheme	*Para* name (number)	Year of installation	No. of pumps installed	No. of working pumps	Outlet points
1	South Muhuripur (5)	1998	3	3	10
2	Banabihari (6)	1998	3	2	26
3	South Muhuripur (5)	1999	2	1	25
4	East Majhumdar (3)	1999	3	1	31
5	South Muhuripur (5)	2000	2	1	20
6	Latuatilla (1)	2001	2	2	29
7	West Majhumdar (7)	2003	2	1	25
8	East Majhumdar (3)	2003	2	1	60
9	Banabihari (6)	2008	2	1	15
	Total		21	13	241

Source: Survey data.

In aggregate, there were a total of twenty-one pumps installed under RLI schemes, though only thirteen pumps were in functional condition in 2016. Each RLI scheme had a different number of outlet points for conveying irrigation water to the fields. An interview with a pump operator of an RLI scheme revealed that all the outlet points were not in working condition due to lack of maintenance.

A committee was formed by the panchayat to operate each RLI scheme. Every year, members of the committee were selected in the presence of elected panchayat members. The committee members are responsible for repair, maintenance of pump machines, and clearing the channels. They are also responsible for collecting revenue from the cultivators. The annual repair and maintenance costs are paid from the revenue, and the rest handed over to the panchayat. However, in case the cost of repairs is much higher, the panchayat takes care of the expenditure. A monthly salaried pump operator was appointed to each RLI machine to operate it on time basis.

On account of public intervention in irrigation, a substantial proportion of crop land was cultivated more than once in the reference year. Cropping intensity for lowlands was 164 (and it was 141 for all agricultural land).

Table 14 presents the cropping pattern in the survey year. The major crops grown in the lowlands were paddy and a wide variety of vegetables, while the hillocks or sloping lands (*tila*) were primarily under natural

Table 14 *Proportion of different crops in gross cropped area (GCA), Muhuripur, 2015–16,* in acres and per cent

Crop season	Crops	Area (acres)	As proportion of GCA (per cent)
Kharif	Paddy	478.2	40.5
Kharif	Vegetables and others	24.0	2.0
Kharif	All kharif crops	502.2	42.5
Rabi	Paddy	356.3	30.2
Rabi	Vegetables including potato and others	81.9	6.9
Rabi	All rabi crops	438.2	37.1
Annual	Betel leaf	5.6	0.5
Annual	Mulberry	5.6	0.5
Annual	Rubber	229.1	19.4
Annual	All annual crops	240.3	20.4
All	Gross cropped area	1180.6	100.0

Source: Survey data.

rubber plantations. About 29 per cent of operational holdings were under annual crops, and the remaining operational holdings were available for seasonal crops. Paddy, sown on 71 per cent of the gross cropped area (GCA), was the most important seasonal crop in both the kharif and rabi seasons in the reference year. It was followed by natural rubber plantations (20 per cent), vegetables (7 per cent), betel leaves (0.5 per cent), and mulberry (0.5 per cent). Vegetables were grown mostly as intercrops and involved commercial production. The main vegetables were gourd, bitter gourd, ridge gourd, pumpkin, snake gourd, chilli, brinjal, and potato. Betel leaf was an important commercial crop in the village but the extent of cultivation was small. Mulberry cultivation and sericulture had been introduced recently, with substantial support from the State government.

The most important lowland crop cycle, of crops grown in different seasons, was paddy cultivation in both kharif and rabi seasons. The second most important crop cycle was paddy cultivation in the kharif season and intercropped vegetables including potato in the rabi season. The third crop cycle was paddy in the kharif season and land kept fallow in the rabi season. Mulberry and betel leaves, both annual crops, were grown on a small extent of lowland throughout the year. On sloped land, the primary crop was rubber. Orchards were absent in Muhuripur.

The following sections discuss the yield, cost of cultivation, and incomes from production of selected crops in Muhuripur village – paddy, rubber, vegetables, and betel leaf.

Cost of Cultivation and Farm Business Incomes

Productivity of paddy

Paddy was the most important agricultural crop in both the kharif and rabi seasons in Muhuripur in 2015–16. The common seed varieties used were Sona Masuri for kharif and Nabin for rabi in the survey year. Table 15 shows the average yield of paddy in Muhuripur in 2015–16, and the official yield data for South Tripura district and Tripura State. In both seasons, the average yield of paddy in Muhuripur was higher than the district and State averages. However, there was variation within the village in yield of paddy in both crop seasons, which ranged from 500 kg per acre to 2,640 kg per acre. The average yield of kharif paddy (1,508 kg per acre) was higher than rabi paddy (1,351 kg per acre). Cultivators reported that there was shortage in the supply of irrigation water from RLI schemes in the summer season in the reference period. This could have been one of the main reasons for the low yields for paddy in the rabi season. However, in comparison to other paddy-growing States, Tripura lagged behind in productivity. To take an example, in Amarsinghi, a groundwater-irrigated village in Malda district of West Bengal, a survey by FAS showed the average yield of paddy to be 1,943 kg per acre during the kharif season and 2,511 kg per acre during the rabi season in 2014–15 (Sarkar 2015).

The State government promoted the rice intensification (SRI) technique to increase productivity in rice cultivation through Block Agricultural Offices and *gram panchayats*. Substantial government support, in terms of seed, fertilizer, weeder, sprayer, and cash for labour use, was provided to the cultivators. However, our survey data suggest that the SRI technique was adopted by only a few cultivators in Muhuripur. We did not find any difference in the average yield of paddy between those who used SRI and those who did not (Table 16). We found that the SRI paddy cultivators did not follow the basic principles of the SRI technique. This may be the reason for the gap between potential yield and actual yield in paddy cultivated with SRI technique. It was also observed that sometimes farmers identified themselves as cultivators following the SRI method to avail the benefits of the government scheme even without putting the technique into practice. Hence, our main takeaway from this is that there

Table 15 *Average yield of paddy, Muhuripur, South Tripura district, Tripura, 2015–16 and 2014–15, in kg per acre*

Crop	Muhuripur village	South Tripura district	Tripura
Paddy (kharif)	1508	1243	1253
Paddy (rabi)	1351	1226	1250

Source: Survey data. Figures on yield of pre-kharif and kharif paddy for Dhalai district and Tripura state for 2014–15 are from Government of Tripura (2015).

Table 16 *Average yields of paddy, SRI and non-SRI methods, Muhuripur, 2015–16, in kg per acre*

Crop	SRI	Non-SRI	t value	p value
Paddy (kharif)	1563	1488	−1.135	0.262*
Paddy (rabi)	1302	1368	0.697	0.489*

Note: *Refers to statistically not significant at 5 per cent level of confidence.
Source: Survey data.

remains substantial potential for extending the productivity of paddy in Muhuripur.

Farm Business Income

Table 17 shows the estimated average per acre gross value of output (GVO), paid-out cost and imputed value of family labour (A2+FL), and net farm business income (FBI) incurred from paddy cultivation in Muhuripur in 2015–16. The results suggest that paddy cultivation was non-remunerative for cultivators in the survey year. The average GVO of kharif paddy for all cultivators was Rs 20,781 per acre, and for paddy sown in the rabi season it was Rs 17,156 per acre. The average cost of A2+FL was much higher than the average GVO in both the seasons: Rs 25,059 per acre in kharif and Rs 24,963 per acre in rabi. This resulted in significant losses in paddy production for cultivating households in both seasons.

Table 18 presents the average per acre GVO, paid-out cost and imputed value of family labour (A2 +FL), and net farm business income (FBI) for kharif and rabi paddy cultivation across socio-economic classes. The figures show that paddy cultivator households across socio-economic classes incurred losses in both seasons, on account of low crop yields and low GVO. However, in terms of proportion of households with losses in paddy cultivation, the proportion was much higher among the "cultivator: sub-marginal" class (with operational holdings of less than

Table 17 *Average gross value of output (GVO), paid-out cost plus imputed value of family labour (A2+FL), and farm business income (FBI), paddy, Muhuripur, 2015–16, in Rs per acre*

Crop season	Crop	GVO	A2+FL	FBI
Kharif	Paddy	20781	25059	−4279
Rabi	Paddy	17156	24963	−7807

Source: Survey data.

Table 18 *Average gross value of output (GVO), paid-out cost plus imputed value of family labour (A2+FL), and farm business income (FBI), paddy, socio-economic class, Muhuripur, 2015–16, in Rs per acre*

Crop	Cultivator: sub-marginal			Cultivator: marginal			Cultivator: small		
	GVO	A2+FL	FBI	GVO	A2+FL	FBI	GVO	A2+FL	FBI
Paddy (kharif)	19770	26738	−6967	22229	23093	−865	20571	23058	−2487
Paddy (rabi)	16509	27272	−10763	18017	22010	−3994	17702	22433	−4731

Source: Survey data.

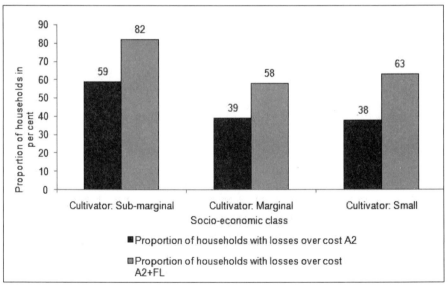

Figure 1 *Proportion of households with negative income from paddy cultivation, by socio-economic class, Muhuripur*

1 acre) in comparison to "cultivator: marginal" and "cultivator: small" classes (Figure 1).

Cost of Production

On account of the differences in cost of cultivation across socio-economic classes, this section examines item-wise costs of production for paddy cultivation (Table 19). First, the average costs of hired labour, machine labour, and rent were the three largest cost components of cost A2 for all socio-economic classes, and together constituted more than 80 per cent of cost A2. Average per acre costs of seed, manure, fertilizer, plant protection, and irrigation were low. This was mainly because cultivators received significant assistance for seed, fertilizer, and irrigation at subsidised

Table 19 *Average expenditure on different cost items in paddy cultivation, by socio-economic class, Muhuripur*, in Rs per acre

Cost Items	Cultivator: sub-marginal		Cultivator: marginal		Cultivator: small	
	Paddy (kharif)	Paddy (rabi)	Paddy (kharif)	Paddy (rabi)	Paddy (kharif)	Paddy (rabi)
Seed	259	304	175	237	355	427
Manure	410	431	342	474	62	302
Fertilizer	962	1087	828	1095	1122	1738
Plant protection	505	631	666	794	329	392
Irrigation	96	123	258	334	116	126
Casual labour	8223	8694	6771	6773	10853	8533
Animal labour	98	136	0	0	229	0
Machine labour	4625	4070	4415	3753	3258	3329
Rent	4036	3658	3707	2975	2592	2673
Other costs	537	484	849	791	910	658
Cost A2	19750	19617	18011	17227	19827	18176
Imputed family labour (FL)	6987	7655	5082	4784	3231	4256
Cost A2+FL	26738	27272	23093	22010	23058	22433

Source: Survey data.

rates or free of cost under the different State government programmes. For instance, the water rate for irrigation from RLI schemes was only Rs 250 per acre for the whole year or Rs 125 for each season in the survey year. Irrigation cost constituted only 1 per cent of total paid-out cost (cost A2) in paddy cultivation across socio-economic classes.[6]

Secondly, households in the "cultivator: sub-marginal" class incurred higher aggregate cost A2+FL as compared to the other two bigger agrarian classes. This was on account of costs for machine labour, rental payment on leased-in land, and imputed value of family labour. As discussed in the section on tenancy, there was widespread leasing-in of land for cultivation by the "cultivator: sub-marginal" class. Machine use in different operations of cultivation by rental was more prevalent among these households.

Rubber

A detailed study of rubber cultivation in the survey villages is in chapter 13. Here, we provide a summary of the features and significance of rubber cultivation in the economy of Muhuripur village. The extent of sloped land suitable for plantations was less in Muhuripur as compared to the other villages. Hence the average extent of rubber plantation per household was low, about 0.9 acre. About 36 per cent of total cultivator households owned rubber plantations, and of them, 62 per cent received income from rubber in the survey year. Income from rubber cultivation was very crucial for these households as a large proportion of cultivators in the village incurred losses in lowland cultivation in the survey year. These households were able to tide over their losses by means of the supplementary income from rubber cultivation. For example, in aggregate, income from rubber cultivation constituted about 88 per cent of total income from crop production for rubber cultivator households during the survey year. The average income from rubber cultivation was Rs 36,744 per household in 2015–16.

Vegetables

Vegetable cultivation was mainly for the market in Muhuripur. Vegetables were cultivated in both seasons, though largely in the rabi season. We

---

[6] By contrast, in Amarsinghi, a groundwater-irrigated village in Malda district, West Bengal, the average irrigation cost per acre for households that purchased water from private electric tubewells was Rs 4,000 in the cultivation of *boro* rice, a water-intensive summer crop (Modak and Bakshi 2017).

Table 20 *Average gross value of output (GVO), paid-out cost plus imputed value of family labour (A2+FL), and farm business income (FBI), vegetables, Muhuripur, 2015–16, in Rs per acre*

Crop	Number of cultivators	GVO	Cost A2+FL	Farm business income
Vegetables	255	83846	69246	14600

Source: Survey data.

have not estimated yields for intercropped vegetables, as it is difficult to measure area for individual crops in the intercropping system. The cultivators received substantial returns from vegetable cultivation in the survey year. The estimated mean of farm business incomes from vegetable cultivation was Rs 14,600 per acre (Table 20). However, significant variation was found in average income from vegetable cultivation across households, depending on the kind of vegetables grown. In addition, the average extent of crop land under vegetables was extremely low and only 34 per cent of total cultivators were involved in vegetable cultivation during the survey year. The main reason for this may have been the higher cost of cultivation (A2+FL) of vegetables.

Betel leaf
Betel leaf was the most important annual cash crop in Muhuripur. Once mature, it is productive for a period of twelve to thirteen years, and offers incomes throughout the year to cultivators. However, only twenty-seven cultivators were engaged in betel leaf cultivation and the average extent of land under betel leaf was only 0.2 acre per household in the survey year. The initial investment involved in betel leaf cultivation is high, including the construction of rectangular bamboo structure known as *baraj*. It also requires regular and rigorous monitoring and intensive labour. Table 21 shows that the average GVO in betel leaf cultivation was Rs 3,80,650 per acre, and the cost of cultivation and imputed family labour value (A2+FL)

Table 21 *Average gross value of output (GVO), paid-out cost plus imputed value of family labour (A2+FL), and farm business income (FBI), betel leaf, Muhuripur, 2015–16, in Rs per acre*

Crop	Number of cultivators	GVO	Cost A2+FL	Farm business income
Betel leaf	27	380650	349941	37364

Source: Survey data.

was Rs 3,49,941 per acre during the survey year. The estimated annual mean farm business income (FBI) per acre, at Rs 37,364 in 2015–16, was the highest for betel leaf among all crops. This is one of the potential areas for increasing incomes of cultivator households in Muhuripur. It requires government or bank support for the initial capital cost.

Farm Business Incomes from Operational Holdings

In this section, we estimate the average GVO, cost A2, cost FL, combined cost A2+FL, and farm business income (FBI) per acre of operational holding, counting all the crops across all three seasons together, for the survey year in Muhuripur (Table 22). On an aggregate level, cultivator households in Muhuripur received negative income from crop production in 2015–16. The average GVO per acre was Rs 42,510 and cost A2+FL per acre was Rs 43,079, implying a loss in net return from crop production of Rs 569 per acre in Muhuripur.

There were variations in the mean FBI across socio-economic classes. Households in the "cultivator: small" class (operating more than 2.5 acres) obtained the highest income per acre of operated land. Importantly, the average GVO per acre was slightly higher for the class of "cultivator: sub-marginal" who operated on less than 1 acre, as compared to the other two agrarian classes. This was because nine households belonging to the "cultivator: sub-marginal" class cultivated betel leaf and obtained a high GVO. But this agrarian class had a much higher A2+FL cost per acre than other classes, which resulted in losses in crop production (Rs 2,466 per acre). This class also had the highest imputed cost of family labour (Rs 13,066). The differences in GVO, cost A2+FL, and FBI across socio-

Table 22 *Average gross value of output (GVO), paid-out cost and imputed value of family labour (A2+FL), and farm business income (FBI) by operational holding and socio-economic class, Muhuripur, 2015–16, in Rs per acre*

Socio-economic class	GVO	Cost A2	Cost FL	Cost A2+FL	FBI on cost A2+FL
Cultivator: sub-marginal	44253	33653	13066	46719	−2466
Cultivator: marginal	39024	29039	8353	37392	1632
Cultivator: small	40717	26616	6871	33487	7230
All	42510	31815	11264	43079	−569

Source: Survey data.

Table 23 *Proportion of different crops in total gross cropped area, by socio-economic class, Muhuripur, in 2015–16, in per cent*

Socio-economic class	Number of households	Paddy	Rubber	Vegetables and others	Total
Cultivator: sub-marginal	469	73	18	10	100
Cultivator: marginal	182	74	16	11	100
Cultivator: small	49	62	29	9	100

Source: Survey data.

Table 24 *Average annual income from crop production, by socio-economic class, Muhuripur, 2015–16, in Rs per household*

Socio-economic class	Number of households	Average annual income from crop production (over cost A2+FL)
Cultivator: sub-marginal	414	−772
Cultivator: marginal	182	5602
Cultivator: small	49	32745
All	645	3592

Source: Survey data.

economic classes can be explained by the different cropping patterns practised by each class. As shown in Table 23, "cultivator: small" households devoted a higher share of cultivated land to rubber cultivation in their total gross cropped area (29 per cent) as compared to the other two agrarian classes. The annual operational cost of cultivation for rubber plantations was the lowest among all crops. Income from rubber contributed to higher farm business incomes for the class of "cultivator: small".

It is noteworthy that income per household from crop production for the "cultivator: small" class (operating more than 2.5 acres of land) was almost ten times higher than the average income of all cultivating households (Table 24). Income from crop production per household declined proportionally with the size of operational landholding. For example, income from crop production per household was Rs 32,745 for the "cultivator: small" class, while it was only Rs 5,602 for the "cultivator: marginal" class, and households in the "cultivator: sub-marginal" class received negative incomes in 2015–16.

Use of Machines in Agriculture

Unlike the other two study villages, in Muhuripur, low-lying agricultural land provided opportunities for the use of machines in agriculture. The State government provided assistance under different programmes to purchase agricultural machinery. Ploughing was largely done by diesel-operated power tillers. Tractors were not introduced in the village till 2015–16. Machines were deployed on a large scale for irrigation, weeding, spraying, plant protection, and threshing. Notably, small harvesting machines were introduced and used for paddy harvesting in the survey year.

Table 25 shows the distribution of agricultural machinery by year of purchase. It shows that higher numbers of agricultural machineries were purchased after 2010 in the village, particularly power tillers, sprayers, weeders, and harvesters. The number of individual pumps for irrigation was low in the village, as we have discussed above, due to the presence of public RLI schemes that covered a large extent of cultivated land. There were 67 hand power tillers, 14 thresher machines and 19 harvesting machines in the village in 2015–16.

Importantly, village data show that substantial state support was provided with the aim of expanding the level of mechanisation in agriculture, particularly after 2005. Under different programmes, cultivators either received agricultural machinery free of cost or subsidies to purchase machines. For instance, use of machines for weeding was introduced under SRI cultivation. All paddy cultivators who enrolled for SRI cultivation received weeding machines free of cost. Table 26 shows the distribution of agricultural machinery acquired by households either with subsidy or free of cost. More than 50 per cent of the total number of diesel pumps, power tillers, sprayers, and harvesting machines in the village were purchased either on subsidised rates or were distributed free of cost.

To get an idea of the level of mechanisation in cultivation, we examined the use of machines in different operations (ploughing, harvesting, threshing) of paddy cultivation. Table 27 shows that machine use was higher for ploughing and threshing, comprising about 92 and 96 per cent of the total land under paddy cultivation respectively. In comparison, use of machines for harvesting was low, at about 38 per cent of total land under paddy. This was because the use of harvesting machines left the cultivators with no straw, which is an important source of fodder.

Table 25 *Distribution of agricultural machinery by year of purchase, Muhuripur, in 2015–16, in per cent*

Year	Diesel pump	Power tiller	Sprayer	Weeder machine	Harvester machine	Thresher
Before 2005	36	15	6	–	–	29
2005 to 2010	38	37	19	37	21	43
After 2010	26	48	76	63	79	29
Total	100	100	100	100	100	100

Source: Survey data.

Table 26 *Distribution of subsidised agricultural machinery by year of purchase, Muhuripur, 2015–16, in per cent*

Year	Power tiller	Diesel pump	Sprayer	Weeder machine	Harvesting Machine
Before 2005	27	24	7	0	0
2005 to 2010	41	52	14	38	44
After 2010	32	24	79	62	56
All	100	100	100	100	100
Proportion of subsidised machines in total machines	55	50	56	100	47

Source: Survey data.

Table 27 *Spread of mechanisation and proportion of work done by rented machines in different operations of paddy cultivation, Muhuripur, 2015–16, in per cent*

Operations	Spread of mechanisation	Work done by rental machine
Proportion of land ploughed with tractor	96	81
Proportion of land harvested with harvester machine	38	87
Proportion of land output threshed with thresher	92	95

Source: Survey data.

Table 27 shows that more than 80 per cent of machine labour was done through hired machines for ploughing, harvesting, and threshing operations in paddy cultivation. The rent contract for land preparation of fields was time-rated. The average rate was Rs 250 to Rs 300 per hour for ploughing operation by power tiller. For harvesting, acreage contract prevailed and the rate was Rs 1,000 per acre. For threshing, both time-rated and acreage contracts existed in the survey year. The average rate was Rs 250 per hour and Rs 1,000 per acre, respectively.

Labour Use in Agriculture

In this section, we examine the structure and pattern of labour use in cultivation in Muhuripur. The section discusses features of labour use in agriculture. In terms of aggregate volume of labour use in agriculture, Muhuripur had higher labour use than the other two study villages. This derived from intensive cultivation due to a higher extent of lowlands and access to irrigation.

Features of Labour Use

In Muhuripur, labour use in crop production was high during the rabi season. Production of rabi crops absorbed 41 per cent of the total labour use, while it accounted for 37 per cent of total gross cropped area (GCA). This was mainly due to the large area under vegetable cultivation during the rabi season. Kharif crops absorbed about 38 per cent of total labour use in agriculture. Annual crops comprised rubber, mulberry, and betel leaf, which together absorbed 21 per cent of total labour use.

Family and Hired Labour Use

In Muhuripur, the proportion of hired labour use was higher than family labour use in agriculture. This indicates the existence of an active labour market in agriculture and dependence on hired workers to perform different agricultural tasks. About 55 per cent of total labour demand was

Table 28 *Distribution of labour use across seasons, 2016,* in per cent

Village	Kharif	Rabi	Annual crop	Total
Muhuripur	38	41	21	100

Source: Survey data.

Table 29 *Composition of total labour use, 2015–16,* in per cent

Village	Family labour	Hired labour	Exchange labour	All
Muhuripur	43.9	55.2	0.9	100

Source: Survey data.

Table 30 *Composition of total labour use across socio-economic classes, 2015–16,* in per cent

Socio-economic class	Family labour	Hired labour	Exchange labour	All
Cultivator: sub-marginal	52	47	1	100
Cultivator: marginal	51	47	2	100
Cultivator: small	47	53	0	100

Source: Survey data.

met by hired labour and 44 per cent by family labour. The ratio of family labour to hired labour use was less than one (Table 29). Exchange labour was not very significant and contributed to only 1 per cent of total labour use in the village. The cultivation of betel leaf and vegetables increased the demand for hired labour, along with transplantation, harvesting, and post-harvest operations in paddy. In addition, along with family labour a significant proportion of daily hired labour was used in rubber tapping in Muhuripur, while it was mostly done by family labour in Mainama.

Table 30 presents the pattern of labour use across socio-economic classes. The pattern was almost uniform across all agrarian classes in Muhuripur. Households belonging to the "cultivator: sub-marginal" and "cultivator: marginal" classes utilised more family labour, 51 per cent and 52 per cent respectively, than hired labour. Households in the "cultivator: small" class (operating more than 2.5 acres) absorbed more hired labour, at 53 per cent of total labour demand, than family labour in their crop production.

Gender Composition

Striking levels of gender disparity prevailed in family and hired labour use in agriculture in Muhuripur. Table 31 presents the sex-wise distribution of family labour and hired labour use in agriculture. Female participation in agriculture, in the form of both family labour and hired labour, was low in Muhuripur. Only about 15 per cent of labour use (family or hired) in agriculture was contributed by female labourers, whereas male workers provided about 85 per cent of total labour use in agriculture. Female labourers participated in transplantation, weeding, and harvesting operations in paddy and vegetable cultivation. The pattern of gender composition in labour use was similar across all socio-economic classes. One important pattern that emerged from the data was the low participation of female family labour in the "cultivator: small" class of households (operating more than 2.5 acres). Female hired labour increased as the size of operated holding increased.

Table 31 *Distribution of family and hired labour, by sex and socio-economic class, Muhuripur, 2016,* in per cent

Socio-economic class	Family labour		Hired labour	
	Male	Female	Male	Female
Cultivator: sub-marginal	86.2	13.8	84.9	15.1
Cultivator: marginal	83.9	16.1	81.9	18.1
Cultivator: small	91.2	8.8	81	19
All	86.3	13.7	83	17

Source: Survey data.

Table 32 *Distribution of family and hired labour, by crop and sex, Muhuripur, 2016,* in per cent

Crop	Family labour		Hired labour	
	Male	Female	Male	Female
Paddy	89.4	10.6	80.0	20.0
Rubber	97.7	2.3	100.0	0.0
Vegetable	76.0	24.0	62.5	37.5

Source: Survey data.

Table 32 presents sex-wise distribution of family and hired labour in three main crops cultivated in the village. The participation of female labour was substantially higher in vegetable cultivation than in paddy and rubber cultivation. This was mainly because vegetables required frequent monitoring through different operations spanning a few hours a day. Hence, the share of family labour in total labour use was high in the case of vegetable cultivation. In contrast, paddy was primarily cultivated using hired labour. About 63 per cent of total labour use in paddy cultivation was hired labour, and the remaining 37 per cent was family labour. In rubber cultivation, the two major operations of tapping and weeding, which take place during the mature stage of rubber trees, were mostly male-dominated, and the share of hired labour was higher than family labour.

Types of Wage Contracts

Two types of wage contracts prevailed in Muhuripur, namely daily and piece-rated. Table 33 shows the total hired labour-days deployed under different wage contracts. Daily wage contracts were most common in

Table 33 *Distribution of hired labour, Muhuripur, 2016,* in per cent

Village	Daily-rated	Piece-rated	Total
Muhuripur	76.8	23.2	100

Source: Survey data.

Muhuripur. Of the total hired labour-days, 77 per cent was under daily-wage contracts and the remaining 23 per cent was based on piece-rated wage contracts.

The payment made in piece-rated contracts was mainly according to acreage. Piece-rated contracts were prevalent in transplanting and harvesting of paddy. In the kharif season, harvesting of paddy was done manually, and was partially contracted out on piece-rated basis. However, in the rabi season, paddy was harvested using machines. Seasonal cross-border migration was an important feature in Muhuripur. During the peak season, especially during transplanting and harvesting, groups of labourers came from Bangladesh to participate in the labour process, and they stayed in the village for the length of the period of their work. They mainly worked on piece-rated contracts.

Summary

In this chapter, we examined features of the agrarian structure, production and agrarian relations in Muhuripur village, South district of Tripura. The village is primarily an immigrant village, predominantly inhabited by Bengali speakers. Two-thirds of the total agricultural land in the village were lowlands and the remaining were uplands.

Owned land was the most important form of possession in Muhuripur, accounting for over 93 per cent of total agricultural land. Marginal holdings dominated, constituting 59 per cent of the total population and 65 per cent of total operational land. The village had high levels of inequality in both ownership and operational holdings. However, this inequality did not directly imply inequality in household incomes, as households across socio-economic classes had diversified sources of income. In addition, tenancy was significant with respect to lowland cultivation, particularly in the form of sharecropping on an annual contract.

Since public irrigation was available, cultivation was intensive, with a substantial proportion of lowlands being cultivated more than once. Income net of cost A2 and imputed value of family labour was calculated for the main crops, namely, paddy, rubber, vegetable, and betel leaf, across socio-economic classes. Paddy cultivation was non-remunerative across agrarian classes in the survey year on account of low crop yields and low gross value of output. Costs incurred on hired labour, machine labour, and rent were the major items of cost for paddy cultivation. Average per acre costs for seed, manure, fertilizer, plant protection, and irrigation were low, as the cultivators received significant assistance for seed, fertilizer, and irrigation. Though the extent of rubber plantation per household was low in Muhuripur, income from rubber plantation was crucial for households to tide over the losses in lowland cultivation. The average income from rubber cultivation was Rs 36,744 per household in 2015–16. Although vegetable cultivation had significant commercial value, the extent of crop land under vegetables was extremely low. Betel leaf was the most important annual cash crop in Muhuripur. Among all crops, average net income per acre was the highest for betel leaf cultivation, at Rs 37,364, in 2015–16.

We also estimated the farm business income (FBI) from operational holdings in the reference period. The data show that in aggregate, a majority of the cultivator households received negative income from crop production in Muhuripur in the survey year. However, there were variations in the mean FBI across socio-economic classes. The class of "cultivator: small" that operated more than 2.5 acres had the highest income per acre of operated land (Rs 7,230), and the income declined sharply with declining operational holdings. Households of the "cultivator: sub-marginal" class had negative income per acre of operated land in the survey year (Rs 2,466).

Machine use in agriculture was significant in Muhuripur, particularly for ploughing, irrigation, weeding, spraying, plant protection, and threshing operations. The State government provided substantial assistance to purchase agricultural machinery. In crop production labour use was highest during the rabi season (41 per cent), followed by the kharif season (38 per cent) and annual crops (21 per cent). An active labour market in agriculture existed in Muhuripur. The composition of family and hired labour use in agriculture was uniform across socio-economic classes. However, female participation in agriculture, either in the form of family labour or hired labour, was low.

APPENDIX 1

Definition of Land Use Categories

- *Cultivated plain land.* It is used for the cultivation of seasonal crops like paddy and vegetables. This land is a distinct technical unit of cultivation separate from the homestead, and therefore does not include kitchen garden cultivation practised on the homestead.
- *Plantation land.* Land devoted to the cultivation of plantation crops, such as, rubber, areca nut, pineapple, and banana.
- *Orchard land.* Land under fruit trees and other trees not classified as plantation crops, such as bamboo, jackfruit, teak, etc.
- *Jhum land.* This land was used for shifting or *jhum* cultivation (slash-and-burn method). It forms a part of slope land or upland.
- *Forest land.* This includes all the area under forest cover or land so classed under any legal enactment or administered as forest, whether state-owned or private. It was not under any cultivation.
- *Tila land.* This is slope land, not included in any of the above classifications, and kept fallow.

References

Government of Tripura (2015), *Basic Statistics: Area, Production and Yield,* Department of Agriculture and Farmers Welfare, Government of Tripura, available at: http.//agri.tripura.gov.in/basic_statistics

Modak, Tapas Singh, and Bakshi, Aparajita (2017), "Changes in Groundwater Markets: A Case Study of Amarsinghi Village, 2005 to 2015," *Review of Agrarian Studies,* vol. 7, no. 2, available at http://ras.org.in/599ee0d68d0c6ca20dc6db5649b7ea4d

National Sample Survey Office (NSSO) (2015), *Report No. 501: Household Ownership and Operational Holdings in India , NSS 70th Round,* available at: http://mospi.nic.in/sites/default/files/publication_reports/Report_571_15dec15_2.pdf

Sarkar, Biplab (2015), "Cropping Pattern, Yields, and Farm Business Incomes: Some Findings from Surveys of Three Study Villages in West Bengal," presented at the Symposium on Results from Village Surveys, organised by the Foundation for Agrarian Studies, Durgapur, 11–13 September.

9

Employment and Wages of Manual Workers

Arindam Das and Subhajit Patra

This chapter deals with the number of days of employment and wages obtained by manual workers across socio-economic classes in Tripura. Overall, Tripura is characterised by limited employment opportunities in agriculture and in the non-agricultural sector. The agricultural sector is characterised by a single crop in a year, and traditional *jhum* or shifting cultivation is the dominant practice. Wage labour is the primary source of employment for the majority of households in Tripura. Village survey data show that all sections of households directly participated in rural wage employment under the Mahatma Gandhi National Rural Employment Guarantee Scheme (MGNREGS). The scheme has played an important role in contributing to cash earnings and meeting basic needs of the population. To put it differently, given the low level of employment generation in agriculture, non-agricultural work, especially through the MGNREGS, played a very significant role in increasing employment among manual workers across all sections of households in the three study villages. The objective of this chapter, therefore, is to study employment, wage rates, wage earnings by gender, social group and sector, and by socio-economic class, in the three study villages surveyed by the team for the Project on Agrarian Relations in India (PARI).

Workers

This section discusses the worker population ratio in the three study villages, and compares it with official data on Tripura and India. A worker is defined as an individual above the age of 15 years who undertakes any economic activity, either directly as part of the production process, or

Table 1 *Workers as percentage of population for age-group 15 and above, by sex, 2015–16,* in per cent

Gender	Mainama	Muhuripur	Khakchang	Tripura*	India*
Male	81	82	81	78	76
Female	59	48	76	51	30

Note: *Labour Bureau (EUS, 2015–16): UPS+UPSS.
Source: Survey data.

under supervision, in the reference year. Animal husbandry performed by any individual is considered as an economic activity irrespective of the time spent on it. Our definition, however, excludes household work performed by any household member.

According to the Labour Bureau (EUS, 2015–16), the work particpation rate (WPR) was 78 per cent for males and 51 per cent for females in rural Tripura. The male WPR for rural Tripura was slightly higher than for all-India (rural) males. However, the worker population ratio for female workers was higher than for all-India (rural) females. The survey data show that the highest WPR was in Khakchang, a less agriculturally developed village of North district, and the lowest was in Muhiripur of South district, which was the most agriculturally developed village of the three. This was because female participation in MGNREGS and other farming activity increased the WPR. The female WPR in Khakchang was 76 per cent, in Mainama 59 per cent, and in Muhuripur 48 per cent, as compared to the all-India (rural) figure of 30 per cent. While participation in *jhum* cultivation and MGNREGS was high in the case of female workers in Khakchang, female WPR in salaried households was low. In Muhuripur, female WPR was low among peasant, salaried, and business households.

Male WPR was the highest in Muhuripur at 82 per cent, followed by 81 per cent in both Mainama and Khakchang. This was slightly higher than for Tripura (rural) at 78 per cent and all-India (rural) at 76 per cent.

Occupational Structure

The major occupations with which the survey respondents identified were as follows: cultivator, animal husbandry worker (self-employed), agricultural labourer, construction worker, brick kiln worker (in Mainama), carpenter, driver, tuition teacher, small or petty businessman, and salaried employee (government and private).

Table 2 *Occupational distribution of workers, by industry, male, 2015–16, in percentages*

Village	Cultivation	AH	AL	CL	MGNREGS	Manufacture	Business	Service	Transport	Other	Total
Khakchang	61	0	3	2	14	0.0	3	7	4	6.0	100
Mainama	29	2	7	6	8	15.0	3	18	5	7.0	100
Muhuripur	43	1	2	5	9	0.5	19	11	2	7.5	100

Note: AH=animal husbandry, AL=agricultural labour, CL=construction labour.
Source: Survey data 2015–16.

Table 3 *Occupational distribution of workers by industry, female, 2015–16, in percentages*

Village	Cultivation	AH	AL	CL	MGNREGS	Manufacture	Business	Service	Transport	Other	Total
Khakchang	57	8	2	0	19	0	2	12	0	3	100
Mainama	34	16	9	1	21	7	1	9	0	1	100
Muhuripur	20	42	4	0	25	0	2	6	0	0	100

Note: AH=animal husbandry, AL=agricultural labour, CL=construction labour.
Source: Survey data 2015–16.

Tables 2 and 3 give the distribution of male and female workers by occupational category in the three study villages. Self-employed in cultivation was the single largest occupation among all workers in the study villages. In Khakchang, the main self-reported occupation of 61 per cent of male workers and 57 per cent of female workers was cultivation. This was due to extensive *jhum* cultivation by the family. In Mainama, 29 per cent of male workers and 57 per cent of female workers who participated in the survey reported cultivation as their primary activity. Male participation in cultivation was the lowest in Mainama. A major reason for this was employment in the government sector and in government-supported brick kiln factories (manufacture). Wage labour, especially MGNREGS work, was reported as "secondary occupation" in the study villages. Work under MGNREGS provided a major source of cash earnings in Khakchang.

Wage Labour Market

Participation in the wage labour market, especially for agricultural work and MGNREGS, was an important source of employment and cash earnings across all households in Tripura. Other than manual worker households, all strata of peasant classes participated in the wage market. The participation of farmer households along with manual worker households in manual work was significantly high in the study villages.

Table 4 shows the number and proportion of workers in the wage labour force in Mainama across different socio-economic classes. It shows that persons from all sections of socio-economic classes were engaged in manual work in the village. In Mainama, 97 per cent of all workers participated in wage labour in our reference year. In all classes except "cultivator: sub-marginal," the proportion of female workers in total workers was slightly lower than that of male workers. Among all the cultivating households, a significant proportion of labourers were engaged in wage work.

In Muhuripur, 89 per cent of all workers from the hired manual worker class participated in the wage labour market (Table 5). Workers from more than 50 per cent of cultivating households obtained at least one day of employment from the wage labour market. The participation of female workers in the wage labour market was lowest in Muhiripur among the three study villages. The proportion of female labourers from cultivator households in the wage labour market was between 9 and 37 per cent.

Table 4 *Number of wage workers and proportion of wage workers to total workers, by socio-economic class and sex, Mainama, 2015–16,* in numbers and percentages

Size-class	Males		Females		All	
	No. of wage workers	% of all workers	No. wage workers	% of all workers	No. of wage workers	% of all workers
Cultivator: medium	45	51	21	37	65	45
Cultivator: small	104	42	74	35	178	38
Cultivator: marginal	266	54	181	51	447	53
Cultivator: sub-marginal	347	54	263	58	610	56
Manual worker with diversified income	101	80	61	64	162	73
Manual worker	206	100	123	89	330	97

Source: Survey data 2015–16.

Table 5 *Number of wage workers and proportion of wage workers to total workers, by socio-economic class and sex, Muhuripur, 2015–16,* in numbers and percentages

Size-class	Males		Females		All	
	No. of wage workers	% of all workers	No. wage workers	% of all workers	No. of wage workers	% of all workers
Cultivator: small	103	73	5	9	108	54
Cultivator: marginal	229	73	46	24	276	54
Cultivator: sub-marginal	516	85	121	37	637	68
Manual worker with diversified income	134	80	47	37	181	61
Manual worker	118	89	76	89	194	89

Source: Survey data 2015–16.

In Khakchang, more than 70 per cent of all workers belonging to different classes received employment in the wage labour market (Table 6). Wage employment was a major source of employment and income among cultivating households in Tripura. Participation of workers from peasant households was as high as that of manual worker households in the wage labour market.

Table 7 shows that a large number of workers belonging to cultivator: marginal and cultivator: sub-marginal households worked as wage

Table 6 *Number of wage workers and proportion of wage workers to total workers, by socio-economic class and sex, Khakchang, 2015–16,* in numbers and percentages

Size-class	Males		Females		All	
	No. of wage workers	% of all workers	No. wage workers	% of all workers	No. of wage workers	% of all workers
Cultivator: mixed	100	100	62	78	162	91
Cultivator: *jhum*	256	88	259	82	515	85
Cultivator: lowland	116	81	114	77	230	79
Manual worker with diversified income	32	75	43	67	75	70
Manual worker	54	100	19	54	73	82
Cultivator: non-*jhum* upland	27	45	46	74	73	61
All	585	85	542	78	1127	81

Source: Survey data 2015–16.

labourers. Such households contributed 55 per cent of total labour-days of employment generated in wage employment in Mainama. Non-agricultural work provided more days of employment to cultivating households than agricultural work. Cultivating households laboured out mainly in MGNREGS work, in brick kilns, and in the construction sector.

In Muhuripur, cultivator: marginal and cultivator: sub-marginal households participated as manual workers in the wage labour market. Non-agricultural employment was a major source of wage employment for farming households in this village.

In Khakchang, wage employment was high among all sections of households. The majority of households practised *jhum* cultivation for their household consumption. The demand for hired labour was low in Khakchang. The proportion of hired labour use in total labour use in crop production was 15 per cent (see chapter 6). Therefore, the availability of employment in agriculture was limited in Khakchang, and non-agricultural work was the mainstay. Work under MGNREGS was the main source of cash employment for all sections of households in Khakchang.

Manual Worker Households

This section deals with the size, composition and days of employment received by manual worker households in our three study villages. The

Table 7 *Total, proportion, and average number of days of employment obtained by workers in agriculture and non-agriculture, by socio-economic class, Mainama, 2015–16, in 8-hour days*

Class	Agriculture			Non-agriculture			All		
	Total labour-days	Proportion	Average	Total labour-days	Proportion	Average	Total labour-days	Proportion	Average
Cultivator: medium	146	1	7	4608	4	54	4754	3	73
Cultivator: small	1906	8	12	10279	8	60	12184	8	68
Cultivator: marginal	5870	24	16	26314	21	57	32184	21	72
Cultivator: sub-marginal	7438	31	11	42988	34	61	50426	34	83
Manual worker with diversified income	1777	7	8	8203	7	52	10009	7	62
Manual worker	6945	29	15	33577	27	74	40522	27	123
All	24082	100	13	125969	100	62	150079	100	84

Source: Survey data 2015–16.

Table 8 *Total, proportion, and average number of days of employment obtained by workers in agriculture and non-agriculture, by socio-economic class, Muhuripur, 2015–16, in 8-hour days*

Class	Agriculture			Non-agriculture			All		
	Total labour-days	Proportion	Average	Total labour-days	Proportion	Average	Total labour-days	Proportion	Average
Cultivator: small	570	3	6	7537	6	61	8107	6	75
Cultivator: marginal	2691	16	8	20478	17	70	24453	18	89
Cultivator: sub-marginal	7617	46	11	57144	47	78	64760	47	102
Manual worker with diversified income	4491	27	16	20620	17	87	25111	18	139
Manual worker	1352	8	12	15367	13	73	16719	12	86
All	16721	100	11	121146	100	76	139150	100	100

Source: Survey data 2015–16.

Table 9 *Total, proportion, and average number of days of employment obtained by workers in agriculture and non-agriculture, by socio-economic class, Khakchang, 2015–16, in 8-hour days*

Class	Agriculture			Non-agriculture			All		
	Total labour-days	Proportion	Average	Total labour-days	Proportion	Average	Total labour-days	Proportion	Average
Cultivator: mix	5304	35	46	5564	9	33	10868	14	68
Cultivator: *jhum*	3418	22	12	25325	40	44	28742	36	56
Cultivator: lowland	2053	13	16	12364	19	53	14417	18	63
Manual worker with diversified income	2239	15	21	5447	9	73	7686	10	102
Manual worker	1793	12	23	10735	17	102	12528	16	172
Other	449	3	21	4144	7	62	4593	6	64
All	15256	100	21	63579	100	52	78834	100	70

Source: Survey data 2015–16.

Table 10 *Number of households and workers in hired manual worker households, study villages, Tripura, 2016,* in number and percentage

Village	Households		Number of workers			No of workers per household
	Number	As % of all	Female	Male	All workers	
Mainama	271	19	190	269	459	2
Muhuripur	262	25	144	267	411	2
Khakchang	102	17	70	94	164	2

Source: Survey data 2015–16.

manual worker household is defined as a household whose major income comes from paid manual work outside the house, although they can have other sources of income. The number of labour-days of monthly paid workers and long-term workers is excluded from the calculation of total number of days of employment. The actual work-hours are converted into standard eight-hour labour-days.

The class of hired manual workers was relatively small in the three villages. In Muhuripur, 25 per cent of households constituted the class of manual workers, the highest among the study villages. The class of manual workers was the smallest, and constituted 17 per cent of all households in Khakchang. In Mainama, 19 per cent of all households were hired manual worker households. In the three villages, on average, two workers from each manual worker household were engaged in manual work. Female participation in manual work was the lowest in Muhuripur; female participation in manual work was high in Mainama and Khakchang.

Caste Composition of Manual Worker Households

In Mainama, the class of hired manual workers was largely from Scheduled Caste (SC) and Scheduled Tribe (ST) households. In fact, 70 per cent of wage workers belonged to the SC and ST categories. In Khakchang, all manual worker households belonged to the STs. In Muhuripur, other caste households were the largest constituent of the class of manual workers.

Number of Days of Employment

Hired manual worker households participated in both agricultural and non-agricultural work. Agriculture was a low employment-

Table 11 *Proportion of households from different social groups in all households and hired manual worker households, Mainama, Tripura, 2015–16,* in per cent

Village	Caste	As proportion of all households	As proportion of hired manual worker households
Mainama	Non-Scheduled Tribe	33	38
Mainama	Scheduled Tribe	67	62
Mainama	All	100	100

Source: Survey data 2015–16.

Table 12 *Proportion of households from different social groups in all households and hired manual worker households, Muhuripur, Tripura, 2015–16,* in per cent

Village	Caste	As proportion of all households	As proportion of hired manual worker households
Muhuripur	Scheduled Caste	15	22
Muhuripur	Other Backward Caste	26	34
Muhuripur	Others	60	44
Muhuripur	All	100	100

Source: Survey data 2015–16.

generating activity in the study villages. Non-agricultural sectors such as construction and MGNREGS provided the major days of employment for manual worker households. However, female labourers worked only in agriculture and MGNREGS. Female participation in non-agricultural activities like construction work was absent in the three study villages.

Table 13 shows the average days of employment received by manual workers in Khakchang. Agriculture provided 11 days and 34 days of employment for male and female workers respectively. In *jhum* cultivation, the practice of exchange labour was common in cultivation. Due to this the average number of days of employment was quite low in Khakchang. In the agricultural sector, female workers were involved mainly in weeding and harvesting operations in *jhum* and paddy cultivation. MGNREGS played an important role in Khakchang, providing 59 days and 66 days of employment for female and male labourers respectively. Except work under MGNREGS, women did not participate in non-agricultural tasks. In the non-agricultural sector, male workers received 62 days of employment on average from construction and other non-agricultural tasks.

In Mainama, agriculture provided around 20 to 22 days of employment

Table 13 *Average number of days of wage employment obtained by hired manual workers in agricultural and non-agricultural sectors, by sex, Khakchang, 2015–16, in numbers*

Village	Sex	Agriculture	MGNREGS	Non-agriculture	All
Khakchang	Female	11	59	0	70
Khakchang	Male	34	66	62	162
Khakchang	All workers	25	63	33	123

Source: Survey data 2015–16.

Table 14 *Average number of days of wage employment obtained by hired manual workers in agricultural and non-agricultural sectors, by sex, Mainama, 2015–16, in numbers*

Village	Sex	Agriculture	MGNREGS	Non-agriculture	All
Mainama	Female	22	39	8	69
Mainama	Male	20	28	81	129
Mainama	All workers	21	33	51	104

Source: Survey data 2015–16.

Table 15 *Average number of days of wage employment obtained by hired manual workers in agricultural and non-agricultural sectors, by sex, Muhuripur, 2015–16, in numbers*

Village	Sex	Agriculture	MGNREGS	Non-agriculture	All
Muhuripur	Female	27	52	0	79
Muhuripur	Male	7	51	52	110
Muhuripur	All workers	14	50	34	98

Source: Survey data 2015–16.

for male and female workers. Female workers participated most in MGNREGS and received 39 days of employment, whereas male manual labourers worked for 28 days. In the non-agricultural sector, male participation was very high and workers received, on average, 81 days of employment.

In Muhuripur, on average, agriculture and MGNREGS provided more days of employment for female workers than male manual workers. Female workers received, on average, 27 days of employment in agriculture and 52 days of employment in MGNREGS work. Male workers were generally engaged in non-agricultural activity with MGNREGS, so they received 103 days of employment. A majority of male wage workers were engaged in construction work and MGNREGS (details are discussed in Table 19).

Distribution of Days of Employment

This section discusses levels of underemployment of manual worker households. Tables 16, 17, and 18 show the persistent underemployment among workers belonging to manual worker households.

Table 16 shows that 28 per cent of male workers from manual worker households received employment for over six months, whereas 85 per cent of female workers received employment of 120 days or less. The number of days of employment in Khakchang included 150 days generated under the MGNREGS and the Forest Rights Act, 2006. In Khakchang, on average, 109 days of employment came from MGNREGS for manual worker households.

Table 17 depicts the number of days of employment by size-class category in Mainama. In this village, more than half of all male workers

Table 16 *Distribution of hired manual workers by size-class of number of days of employment, Khakchang, Tripura, 2015–16, in per cent*

Village	Size-class of number of days of employment	As per cent of all workers		
		Female	Male	All Workers
Khakchang	1 to 60 days	39	23	30
Khakchang	61 to 120 days	46	11	26
Khakchang	121 to 180 days	15	37	28
Khakchang	Above 180 days	0	28	10
Khakchang	All	100	100	100

Source: Survey data 2015–16.

Table 17 *Distribution of hired manual workers by size-class of number of days of employment, Mainama, Tripura, 2015–16, in per cent*

Village	Size-class of number of days of employment	As per cent of all workers		
		Female	Male	All Workers
Mainama	1 to 60 days	61	34	45
Mainama	61 to 120 days	23	20	21
Mainama	121 to 180 days	8	7	7
Mainama	Above 180 days	8	39	26
Mainama	All	100	100	100

Source: Survey data 2015–16.

Table 18 *Distribution of hired manual workers, by size- class of number of days of employment, Muhuripur, Tripura, 2015–16,* in per cent

Village	Size-class of number of days of employment	As per cent of all workers		
		Female	Male	All workers
Muhuripur	1 to 60 days	35	34	34
Muhuripur	61 to 120 days	50	41	44
Muhuripur	121 to 180 days	11	4	6
Muhuripur	Above 180 days	4	21	15
Muhuripur	All	100	100	100

Source: Survey data 2015–16.

(61 per cent) received employment for less than six months. More than two-thirds of all female workers received employment for less than four months.

In Muhuripur, 85 per cent of all workers received employment for under six months (Table 18). Of all male workers, 75 per cent received employment for less than four months. Only 4 per cent of all female workers received employment for more than 180 days in Muhuripur.

Access to Non-agricultural Employment

Non-agricultural activity was an important source of employment for manual worker households. However, non-agricultural work available to workers was not diversified. Employment opportunities were limited to female workers in the non-agricultural sector.

Table 19 describes the non-agricultural employment by activity type, excluding MGNREGS. In Mainama, masonry, construction work, and brick kiln work were the major sources of non-agricultural employment. In Khakchang, major non-agricultural occupations available to wage workers were construction, headload work and labouring-out in carpentry. In Muhuripur, construction-related work was a major source of employment for manual worker households.

Wage Rates

This section examines wage rates for agriculture and non-agricultural work of hired manual worker households in the study villages. As

Table 19 *Distribution of days for non-agricultural employment by type of activity, study villages, Tripura, 2015–16,* in per cent

Type of activity	Khakchang	Mainama	Muhuripur
Brick kiln works	0.0	18.7	5.3
Carpenter	18.4	8.0	7.7
Cleaning and fencing	18.0	7.0	–
Construction-related work	29.4	46.0	30.5
Other work*	34.2	20.0	46.4
Total days	100.0	100.0	100.0

Note: *Other work: loading unloading, driver, electrical wiring, etc.
Source: Survey data 2015–16.

discussed, between 10 to 15 per cent of households in the study villages are classified as "manual worker households" as they derived more than 50 per cent of their income from manual work. The proportion goes beyond 70 per cent if we consider aggregate income and work participation in manual work. Therefore, a majority of workers depended on unskilled and semi-skilled wage employment. The rural wage rate is thus a critical indicator of the well-being of workers and their households. The section focuses on wage rates for major operations in crop production, and wage rates for non-agricultural occupations by sex and type of wage contract in the three study villages.

Wage Rates in Agriculture

The agriculture wage rates varied on the basis of crop operations, type of wage contract, and gender. In Mainama and Muhuripur, the daily wage rates were Rs 250 to 300 for a male labourer, and Rs 200 for a female labourer. Cooked food was provided along with cash in these two villages. In Mainama, only male labourers received cooked food, but in Muhuripur, cooked food was provided irrespective of gender. In both villages, wage rates were higher than the statutory minimum wage rates for operations performed by men. However, female wage rates were below the statutory wage rates. Among the three study villages, daily wage rates were the lowest in Khakchang: between Rs 150 and Rs 200 for male and female labourers. Cooked food was not an integral part of the daily wage contract in Khakchang.

In Mainama and Muhuripur, transplanting, weeding, and harvesting operations were done on the basis of piece-rated contracts in paddy

Table 20 *Daily wage rate of agricultural operations, by gender, study villages, 2015–16,* in Rs

Village	Male		Female	
	Cash	Kind	Cash	Kind
Mainama	250–300	Meal	200	
Muhuripur	300	Meal	200	Meal
Khakchang	150–200		150–200	

Source: Survey data 2015–16.

Table 21 *Piece rates for male and female workers by crop operations for paddy, Mainama and Muhuripur, 2015–16,* in Rs

Operations	Cash	Kind
Sowing/transplanting	3750/acre	–
Weeding	3000–3750/acre	–
Harvesting and post-harvest operations	3750–5000/acre	–

Source: Survey data 2015–16.

cultivation, and payments were made on a per acre basis. The payment varied from Rs 3,000 to Rs 5,000 per acre, based on the type of operation. The most remunerative piece-rated wage was observed for paddy harvesting and post-harvest operations.

Wage Rates in Non-Agricultural Activities

Non-agricultural work was an important occupation for labouring households. The main non-agricultural work was in MGNREGS, construction work, and masonry. The daily wage rates for masons was Rs 350–400 in Mainama, and Rs 300 in Muhuripur, for male workers. The wage rates for construction work were Rs 200 to Rs 250 in Mainama and Muhuripur. In Khakchang, the wage rate was Rs 200, lower than in the other two study villages. Except for MGNREGS work, female participation in non-agricultural activities was low. MGNREGS wage rates were lower than for other operations, as these were piece-rated contracts tied to the number of hours of work. We observed that most of the MGNREGS work was done for four hours in a day. The wage rate for MGNREGS was Rs 150 in Mainama and Rs 145–181 in Khakchang for male and female workers. In Muhuripur, however, the wage rate for MGNREGS was reported as Rs 160–165 for male and female workers.

Table 22 *Daily wage rates in non-agricultural activity by gender, study villages, 2015–16, in Rs*

Village	MGNREGS		Mason		Construction work	
	Male	Female	Male	Female	Male	Female
Mainama	150	150	350–400	–	250	–
Muhuripur	160–165	160–165	300	–	200–250	–
Khakchang	145–181	145–181	–	–	200	–

Source: Survey data 2015–16.

Wage Earnings

In this section, we calculate the wage earnings of rural manual workers in the three study villages. Average earnings are calculated as total wages from daily and piece-rated work divided by total number of days of work. We have converted wage payments that were received in kind into cash and added it to total earnings.

The average daily wage of male workers from manual worker households in crop production was Rs 177 in Khakchang, Rs 229 in Mainama and Rs 288 in Muhuripur. As we have seen, Muhuripur was the largest paddy-growing village among the three study villages. For this reason, male workers were employed overwhelmingly in harvesting work in paddy. Female wages were highest in Mainama of the three villages, at Rs 172.

In the case of MGNREGS earnings, there was not much difference among the three villages. The wages here depended on the nature of the work. Average daily wage earnings among female workers was Rs 170 in Khakchang, which was the highest wage rate for MGNREGS work in the three villages.

In the non-agricultural sector, male workers from manual worker households received Rs 337 in Mainama, the highest in the three villages.

Table 23 *Average wage earnings of manual workers in agricultural and non-agricultural wage work, study villages, Tripura, 2015–16, in Rs/day*

Village	Agriculture		MGNREGS		Non-agriculture	
	Female	Male	Female	Male	Female	Male
Khakchang	153	177	170	149	–	215
Mainama	172	229	147	148	224	337
Muhuripur	161	288	161	165	150	219

Source: Survey data 2015–16.

As noted earlier, male workers participated in non-agricultural operations far more than in the other two villages.

Conclusion

This chapter examined days of employment, wage rates and wage earnings of manual workers, and employment patterns of male and female manual workers. The conclusions are outlined below.

Our study found certain striking features related to work participation rates in the three survey villages. First, the work participation rates in all three villages (81–82 per cent for males and 48–76 per cent for women) were higher than the figures for Tripura and the country as a whole. This could be attributed to definitional differences between the official data sources and the PARI methodology. (The concept of 'worker' is much wider in our definition as compared to the Labour Bureau's EUS data.)

While the work participation rate of males was more or less uniform across the three villages, the female work participation rate was both markedly less than the male and showed far greater variation across villages and classes. It was the lowest in Muhuripur (48 per cent), the most agriculturally prosperous village, and the highest in Khakchang (76 per cent), the most agriculturally backward of the three villages; and can be explained by the higher income and employment opportunities for males in a prosperous village, which result in women not being present in the work force. On the other hand, the fact that the female work participation rate is *higher* than the State and national figures can be attributed to the three pull factors of family farming, animal husbandry, and MGNREGS. The successful role of MGNREGS in creating employment for women workers cannot be emphasised enough.

What is the most common occupation of persons of the age of 15 and above in the three villages? Our survey found that self-employment in cultivation and animal husbandry were the main occupations for more than 50 per cent of all workers. The remaining work force is scattered across a range of non-agricultural occupations.

Thirdly, given the limited employment opportunities in formal sector employment, manual work is a major source of employment in semi-skilled and unskilled work in the study villages for more than 40 per cent of the work force. Despite this, manual worker households comprised but a small proportion (17 to 25 per cent) of total households. This apparent contradiction can be explained by the fact that the remaining households had other sources of income. Manual worker households in Khakchang and Mainama were overwhelmingly from the Scheduled Tribes, whereas in Muhuripur manual workers came from a broader mix of castes.

Fourthly, agriculture provided limited employment opportunities for manual worker households. Agriculture in Tripura is characterised by a single crop in a year, and *jhum* or shifting cultivation in some regions. It generated only 26, 25, and 20 days of employment annually in Muhuripur, Khakchang, and Mainama, respectively. On an average, non-agricultural activities provided more days of employment than agricultural activities. The major contributors to household income were MGNREGS, construction work, carpentry, driving, and masonry. A female worker typically obtained employment from MGNREGS and from labouring out in crop production. Except MGNREGS, employment in non-farm activity was virtually absent for female workers. Indeed, in Khakchang, with its difficult terrain and seasonality of agriculture, more than 90 per cent of cash earnings of manual worker households came from MGNREGS.

Underemployment was a major feature of manual work. In the three study villages, a majority of the workers received less than 180 days of employment in the reference year. The average days of employment (from all sources) for manual workers varied between 98 days (Muhuripur) to 123 days (Khakchang) in the reference year. As male workers received more days of employment than female workers across all three study villages, underemployment was more severe for the latter with two-thirds of female workers receiving less than 90 days of employment in the study villages.

Given the high rate of underemployment, wage rate was an extremely important determinant of the well-being of manual worker households in Tripura. Wage rates were low in the three study villages (even though they were higher than rates in West Bengal, Assam, and the national average.) In Mainama and Muhuripur, the daily wage rates were Rs 250 to 300 for a male labourer, and Rs 200 for a female labourer. Daily-rated wages were the norm for crop operations in all the study villages. Piece-rated wages covered crop operations such as transplantation, weeding, and harvesting for paddy in Mainama and Muhuripur.

APPENDIX 1

A Note on MGNREGS in Tripura

Arindam Das and Yoshifumi Usami

This note presents a statistical profile of the implementation of the Mahatma Gandhi National Rural Employment Guarantee Scheme (MGNREGS) in Tripura. The performance of MGNREGS has been generally good in the North-Eastern States of India, particularly in Tripura, Mizoram, and Nagaland. For six consecutive years, Tripura was ranked the best in terms of implementation of MGNREGS. Given the limited employment opportunities in the State, MGNREGS played an important role in contributing to cash earnings and meeting the basic needs of the population. Official statistics and village survey data show that all sections of households directly participated in and benefited from MGNREGS. The following section examines the performance of MGNREGS in Tripura using official data.

Job Card Registration

Appendix Table 1 indicates the number of households registered for job cards from 2012–13 to 2015–16. According to the Management Information System (MIS) report, Tripura accounts for about 0.5 per cent of total job cards issued in India under MGNREGS. The total number of job cards issued in Tripura was 612,398 in 2015–16 and 641,573 in 2012–13. The total number of job cards has declined since 2013–14 in Tripura. Since 2014–15 MIS started reporting the number of deleted job cards, and the number of registered households and persons fell. As per the MIS report, the proportion of people registered under MGNREGS was the highest in Mizoram, followed by Madhya Pradesh, Chhattisgarh, Nagaland, Rajasthan, Tripura, Andhra Pradesh, Manipur, and Odisha.

Appendix Table 1 *Number of registered job card households reported by MIS, Tripura and all India*

State	2012–13	2013–14	2014–15	2015–16
Tripura	641,573	629,089	629,902	612,398
India	124,723,100	122,008,872	129,463,210	131,759,002

Source: Management Information System of MGNREGS.

Haryana and Punjab, on the other hand, were among the states with the least proportion of people registered under MGNREGS.

Provision of Employment

Table 2 shows the proportion of registered households that were provided employment in 2015–16, that is, the proportion of households that demanded manual work and were provided employment under MGNREGS.

In 2015–16, in Tripura, 93 per cent of registered households received employment under MGNREGS, as compared to 36.6 per cent at the all-India level. It is noticed that the North-Eastern States generally showed very good performance (Arunachal Pradesh, 87 per cent; Manipur, 87 per cent; Mizoram, 102 per cent; and Nagaland, 98 per cent). This indicates that most of the registered households received employment in these States. Even households that were not registered under MGNREGS were provided employment in Mizoram. In most other States, less than half of the registered households were provided employment. The percentage of

Appendix Table 2 *Proportion of registered households that received employment under MGNREGS, based on MIS data, 2015–16*

State	2015–16	State	2015–16
Andhra Pradesh	43.0	Meghalaya	74.8
Arunachal Pradesh	86.9	Mizoram	102.1
Assam	31.2	Nagaland	98.1
Bihar	10.7	Orisha	29.9
Chhattisgarh	54.7	Pujab	39.4
Gujarat	15.9	Rajasthan	42.1
Haryana	22.1	Sikkim	76.6
Himachal Pradesh	35.8	Tamil Nadu	70.5
Jammu & Kashmir	49.2	Tripura	93.1
Jharkhand	29.9	Uttar Pradesh	32.6
Karnataka	22.1	Uttarakhand	47.0
Kerala	46.9	West Bengal	27.8
Madhya Pradesh	33.5	Others	49.0
Maharashtra	15.9	All India	46.6
Manipur	87.2		

Source: Management Information System of MGNREGS.

registered households which received employment in Andhra Pradesh, Madhya Pradesh, and Rajasthan, for example, were 43, 33, and 42 per cent, respectively. Eastern Indian states such as West Bengal and Bihar performed poorly (27.8 and 10.7 per cent of the total registered households respectively in these two States received employment in 2015–16).

Days of Employment

Figure 1 indicates the number of person-days of employment provided per household. Tripura has been the best performing state with respect to this indicator from 2011–12 to 2015–16. From 2008–09 to 2015–16, there has been a big increase in the average days of employment in Tripura. The average number of days of employment was 50 in 2008–09. This figure rose to 88 days during 2011–12 and 2014–15. The number of workdays in Tripura was exceptionally high in 2015–16. A total of 94.5 days of employment per household were provided during this year. Thus it can be seen that in Tripura, most of the households were registered in MGNREGS and they were provided employment for 94.5 days on average. During 2011–12 to 2014–15, the average days of employment per household fluctuated between 40 to 50 days at the all-India level.

The state-level comparison of performance of MGNREGS in 2015–16 is summarised in Figure 2. The horizontal axis shows the proportion of

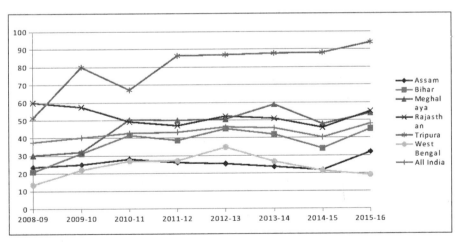

Appendix Figure 1 *Average person-days of employment per household generated through MGNREGS for the selected state, 2008–16*

Source: Management Information System of MGNREGS.

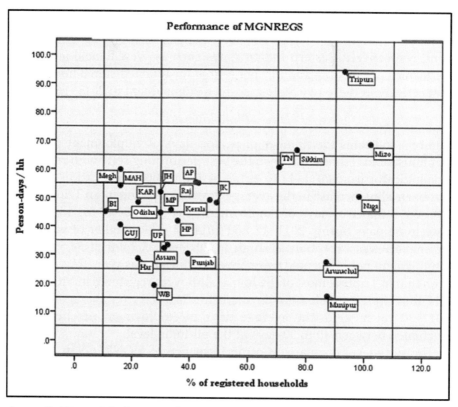

Appendix Figure 2 *Performance of MGNREGS*

households that were provided employment to total registered households. The vertical axis shows the average person-days of work per household. Figure 2 shows that the performance of MGNREGS in North-Eastern states except Arunachal Pradesh and Manipur was exceptionally good. The best performing in terms of participation and number of days of work per household were Tripura (94.5 days), Mizoram (69 days), Sikkim (67 days), Meghalaya (54.2 days), and Nagaland (50.8 days).

Regional Variation in Performance of MGNREGS in Tripura

Tables 3 and 4 summarise district and block-wise data showing the performance of MGNREGA for 2014–15 and 2015–16.

Note that the regional variation in performance of MGNREGS in Tripura is small. The district-wise statistics show that more than 90 per cent of registered households received employment in all districts. The average number of days of employment ranged from 72 days to 99 days in 2014–15. However, except in North Tripura, in 2015–16, 90 days of employment were generated on an average. The average days of employment generated per household through MGNREGS in Tripura were the highest in Dhalai, Gomati, and South Tripura district with 99 days of employment in 2015–16. Average days of work per household were the lowest in North Tripura. The data also show that the proportion of registered households that received 100 or more days of employment was highest in Gomati with 68 per cent, followed by South Tripura with 67 per cent.

The block-level data, on the other hand, showed wide variation of implementation and performance of MGNREGS. The average number of days of employment ranged from 78 days to 118 days across 58 blocks in 2015–16.

Table 4 shows the performance of MGNREGS in selected blocks. According to the MIS, more than 85 per cent of registered households received employment in the blocks of the three study villages in 2015–16. The average days of employment per household generated through MGNREGS were highest in Joliabari with 98 days of employment. Average days of work per household were lowest in Dasda block of the North district.

District- and block-wise performance show that North Tripura was the least performing district in terms of implementation and days of employment. However, panchayat-level statistics show that Khakchang *para* of the North district provided the highest number of days of employment (109) per household. This was because an additional 50 days of employment were provided under the Forest Rights Act in this panchayat. Primary data confirm this observation.

Wage Rates

Wages were paid for MGNREGS work according to the statutory fixed State minimum wage rate until 2008–09. Since 2009–10 the wage rate for MGNREGS work has been fixed and notified by the Ministry of Rural Development (MGNREGA Section 6 (1)).

The average wage paid was the same as the notified wage rate until 2012–13, but it has been slightly below the notified wage rate since 2013–14. However, since 2014–15, the average wage rates were much below the notified wage rate in Tripura. In 2013–14, the wage rate notified was Rs 135 and the average wage paid in the year was Rs 132.80. In 2014–15, the corresponding figures were Rs 155 and Rs 150.20, and in 2015–16,

Appendix Table 3 *Regional variations in performance of MGNREGS in Tripura, by district, 2014–15 to 2015–16*

District	2014–15			2015–16		
	% of registered households that received employment	Average days of employment per household	% of households that received employment of 100 days	% of registered households that received employment	Average days of employment per households	% of households that received employment of 100 days
Dhalai	96	99	62	96	99	56
Gomati	93	96	64	93	99	68
Khowai	95	88	31	93	95	51
North Tripura	91	81	33	91	86	41
Sepahijala	90	72	22	92	91	49
South Tripura	93	92	56	93	99	67
Unakoti	89	85	34	90	92	44
West Tripura	91	89	37	97	93	45

Source: Management Information System of MGNREGS.

Appendix Table 4 *Performance of MGNREGS in Tripura, by block, 2014–15 to 2015–16*

District	Block	2014–15			2015–16		
		% registered household received employment	Average days of employment per households	% of household received employment of 100 days	% registered household received employment	Average days of employment per households	% of household received employment of 100 days
Dhalai	Manu	97	95	55	95	94	43
North Tripura	Dasda	91	90	47	87	84	37
South Tripura	Jolaibari	94	82	27	91	98	53

Note: The three survey villages belong to these blocks.
Source: Management Information System of MGNREGS.

Appendix Table 5 *Performance of MGNREGS in Tripura, by panchayat, 2014–15 to 2015–16*

District	Block	Panchayat	2014–15			2015–16		
			% registered household received employment	Average days of employment per household	% of household received employment of 100 days	% registered household received employment	Average days of employment per household	% of household received employment of 100 days
Dhalai	Manu	Mainama	100	72	17	98	82	27
North Tripura	Dasda	Khakchang	91	117	75	94	109	68
South Tripura	Jolaibari	Muhuripur	97	68	5	93	93	19

Note: The survey villages belong to these panchayats.
Source: Management Information System of MGNREGS.

Appendix Table 6 *Notified wage rates and average wage rates in MGNREGS, Tripura, 2010–11 to 2015–16, in Rs per day*

Year	Notified wage rate	Average wage paid in MGNREGS
2010–11	100	102
2011–12	118	118
2012–13	124	124
2013–14	135	133
2014–15	155	150
2015–16	167	158

Source: Management Information System of MGNREGS.

Rs 167 and Rs 158.60, respectively. This could be on account of piece-rate payments: the female wage rate was lower than that of males.

Results from Village Surveys

The average number of days of employment was highest in Khakchang in Dasda block of North Tripura, followed by Muhuripur in Julaibari block, and Mainama in Manu block. In Khakchang, on average, 109 days of employment were generated per household under MGNREGS in 2015–16. An additional 50 days of employment were provided under the Forest Rights Act in this village. In Muhuripur, on average, 90 days

Appendix Table 7 *Performance of MGNREGS, by socio-economic class, Khakchang, 2016*

Class	% household received employment	Average days of employment per household	% of household received 100 days of employment
Cultivator: *jhum*	92.9	99.1	40.6
Cultivator: mix	100.0	81.2	14.2
Cultivator: lowland	82.0	104.7	59.8
Manual worker	89.0	114.2	87.7
Manual worker with diversified income	100.0	102.2	40.0
Salaried business and others	79.1	102.9	60.3
All	88.4	100.0	46.5

Source: Survey data.

Appendix Table 8 *Performance of MGNREGS by socio-economic class, Mainama, 2016*

Class	% household received employment	Average days of employment per household	% of household received 100 days of employment
Cultivator: medium	32.8	81.0	28.4
Cultivator: small	60.0	69.6	22.4
Cultivator: marginal	65.1	72.9	18.2
Cultivator: sub-marginal	72.6	75.4	35.7
Manual worker	69.8	75.9	18.3
Manual worker with diversified income	71.9	63.9	25.6
All	58.9	73.3	26.1

Source: Survey data.

Appendix Table 9 *Performance of MGNREGS by socio-economic class, Muhuripur, 2016*

Class	% household received employment	Average days of employment per household	% of household received 100 days of employment
Cultivator: Small	88.7	119.5	54.6
Cultivator: Marginal	92.4	88.6	32.0
Cultivator: Sub-marginal	84.2	91.0	26.4
Manual workers	80.9	89.0	30.3
Manual worker with diversified income	100.0	81.2	9.5
All	80.9	90.0	26.2

Source: Survey data.

of employment were provided per household, and in Mainama, it was 73 days. All socio-economic classes in the study villages participated in MGNREGS work. Our estimate is that about 10 per cent of household income was generated from MGNREGS work in Khakchang.

Conclusion

This note examined the performance of the Mahatma Gandhi National Rural Employment Guarantee Scheme (MGNREGS) in Tripura. Tripura ranked at the top of all the States in the country in terms of performance and implementation of MGNREGS. With limited employment opportunities in rural areas, the MGNREGS played an important role in contributing to the cash earnings and livelihoods of rural households. According to official data, 93 per cent of registered households received employment in Tripura. Further, households registered under MGNREGS received, on average, employment of 94.5 days, as compared to 40–50 days at the all-India level. The official data show that 50 per cent of registered households received 100 days of employment in Tripura as compared to 4 per cent nationally.

District-level statistics on MGNREGS show that more than 80 per cent of registered households received employment across all blocks of Tripura. The average days of employment ranged from 78 days to 118 days. Of 58 blocks in Tripura, 12 blocks received more than 100 days of employment through MGNREGS.

In our three study villages, the best performance was in Khakchang village, where 109 days of employment were generated per household under MGNREGS in 2015–16. MGNREGS made a significant contribution to household incomes in Khakchang.

Reference

Labour Bureau (2015–16), "Employment–Unemployment Scenario, 2015–16," 5th annual round, Ministry of Labour and Employment, Government of India, New Delhi.

10

Status and Determinants of Banking in the North-Eastern Region: The Case of Tripura

Pallavi Chavan[*]

Among the geographical regions in India, the North-Eastern region is considered to be the most underbanked. Historically, the spread of the three major formal institutions of rural credit, namely, commercial banks, regional rural banks (RRBs), and cooperatives, has been considerably limited in this region, as highlighted in the literature. Interestingly, however, even a cursory look at household data in the All-India Debt and Investment Survey (AIDIS) suggests that formal institutions are a more dominant source of credit in the region than the literature suggests. Moneylending appears to be weak, although studies have generally shown informal sources to be more active in underbanked regions. Features of the credit system in the North-East such as these are not adequately explored in the literature. Even within the North-Eastern region, a discussion on many of the smaller States is practically missing, given the bias in the literature towards the larger and more populous States.[1] In this

[*] The author thanks T. Sivamurugan for research assistance for this chapter. She also thanks Madhura Swaminathan, Ranjini Basu, Arindam Das, Anwesha Das, Aparajita Bakshi, Parvathi Menon, and an anonymous referee for useful comments and suggestions. The views expressed in the chapter are the personal views of the author and do not reflect the views of the organisation to which she is affiliated.

[1] See Mohan (2003) and Mohanty (2011) for a discussion on the limited spread of various formal financial institutions in the North-Eastern region. See Chavan (2012b) for a discussion on the general dominance of informal sources in areas where the formal financial system is observed to be relatively underdeveloped, using illustrations of village studies from Bihar, Orissa, and Uttar Pradesh. Moreover, she also illustrates that (a) periods of expansion in formal credit are associated with a retreat of the informal sources, and (b) segments of the population that are deprived of formal credit tend to rely more on informal sources. Furthermore, there is a

chapter, we make a limited attempt at addressing these gaps by analysing the present status of banking in Tripura, the second-smallest State in the North-Eastern region in terms of geographical area.

The development of banking or, more broadly speaking, of formal credit in Tripura is presented here in comparison with the North-Eastern region as a whole and India. The development of banking in Tripura is discussed in light of the major changes in banking policy over time. The major determinants of bank credit growth in the State are also analysed. To provide further insights into the status of rural credit in the State, data on the credit systems in the three villages, namely, Mainama, Muhuripur, and Khakchang, surveyed by the Foundation for Agrarian Studies (FAS) as part of its Project on Agrarian Relations in India (PARI), are used.[2] As a background to the village-level discussion, a brief analysis is provided of the status of banking in the three districts of Dhalai, (combined) North Tripura and (combined) South Tripura, to which the surveyed villages belong.[3]

The focus in this chapter is on commercial banks (including RRBs). It provides only limited insights into cooperative credit in the State, given the limitations of data with regard to cooperatives for the North-Eastern region (Chavan 2012). However, the chapter need not be seen as a partial analysis of the State's credit system. This is because banks are the main institutions of formal credit in the State, as will be shown later.

The chapter is divided into six sections. Section 2 provides a brief discussion of the changes in banking policy in India since the nationalisation of banks with a focus on policies that are directly relevant for the presence of banking in the North-Eastern region. Section 3 provides an analysis of basic indicators of development of banking in Tripura and

---

perceptible bias in the literature involving State-level studies on banking to focus on Assam as a representative State from the North-Eastern region without alluding to the other smaller States from the region.

[2] These three villages were originally surveyed as part of the *Tripura Human Development Report*, 2007. They were purposively selected for resurvey as part of PARI in 2016. A sample of 271 households from Mainama village belonging to Dhalai district were surveyed as part of PARI. A sample of 214 households were canvassed from Muhuripur village in South Tripura district. Finally, 86 households from Khakchang in North Tripura district were surveyed.

[3] The districts of Unakoti and Gomati were carved out from North Tripura and South Tripura in 2012. For the sake of comparability of data over time, I have considered them as part of North Tripura and South Tripura, respectively. Hence the analysis relates to the "combined" districts.

the three study districts. I use the *Basic Statistical Returns of Scheduled Commercial Banks in India* (BSR), an annual data source on commercial banks (including RRBs), and the AIDIS, a decennial survey of the National Sample Survey Organisation (NSSO), for this analysis. Section 4 analyses the determinants of bank credit growth in Tripura. Section 5 presents the status of formal credit in general, and banking in particular, as borne out by the village surveys. Finally, Section 6 summarises the major conclusions from the chapter.

Banking Policy in India with Special Reference to the North-Eastern Region

Banking policy in India can be classified into three broad phases: the phase of social banking following nationalisation of banks in 1969; the phase of financial liberalisation with the onset of economic reforms in 1991; and the phase of financial inclusion from 2005 onwards (Chavan 2017). Given that commercial banks have a pan-Indian presence, banking policy designed by the Reserve Bank of India (RBI) is implemented on a nation-wide basis.[4] However, while designing policy, there has often been a differential or preferential treatment accorded to the North-Eastern region. This difference in treatment has been to address the underbanked nature of the North-East. In this section, we focus on policy changes during the three phases with special reference to the North-Eastern region.[5]

With their nationalisation in 1969, banks in India which were predominantly private in nature earlier assumed a public character.[6] Several policy measures were introduced during this phase with the objective of redistribution of banking services. First, this phase witnessed the introduction of the branch licensing policy to ensure that (both public and private sector) banks opened at least four branches in unbanked rural

---

[4] This is in contrast to some of the State-specific policies implemented by State governments relating to rural credit cooperatives, as cooperatives is a State subject.

[5] Thus, we deal with only the policies that have a direct bearing on the availability of banking services in underbanked regions. These phases have also witnessed a number of other changes dealing with, *inter alia*, statutory pre-emptions, income recognition, and capital positions, which are not covered here. For a discussion of these policies, see Chavan (2017).

[6] The Imperial Bank was nationalised to become the State Bank of India (SBI) in 1955, marking the beginning of public banking in India. However, the nationalisation of 14 major commercial banks in 1969, and then six more banks in 1980, completely altered the character of Indian banking.

areas for every branch opened in metropolitan or port areas (1:4 rule) (Copestake 1985). Branch licensing, thus, became a tool to reduce not just the rural–urban divide, but also the inter-regional divide in banking services (RBI 2008). Evidently, this policy had direct implications for banking in the North-Eastern region. There were measures taken also to step up the flow of bank credit to underbanked areas. Rural and semi-urban bank branches were directed to maintain a credit–deposit ratio of at least 60 per cent (*ibid.*). The credit–deposit ratio in the North-Eastern States and other underbanked States too had to be specifically monitored.

Secondly, the lead bank scheme was introduced to address credit gaps at the district level. Specific (mostly public sector) banks were assigned the lead bank responsibility in each district. They had to design development strategies for credit deployment in a coordinated manner with other banks and credit agencies (RBI 2009).[7] Thirdly, the priority sector lending (PSL) programme was introduced to direct bank credit towards certain sectors of national priority (RBI 2015). These included agriculture, small-scale industries (SSIs), small transport operators, low-cost housing, education, and individual loans to socially and economically backward sections of the population. This scheme had direct implications for the rural areas and underbanked regions in India. Moreover, as part of PSL, higher working capital limits were sanctioned to the SSIs in the North-Eastern region to enable them to maintain higher levels of inventory (RBI 2008). Fourthly, regional rural banks (RRBs) were created as another public banking institution in 1974 to give dedicated attention to the banking needs of the rural poor, including small and marginal farmers.

As discussed in the literature, this phase witnessed a striking increase in branch presence in the rural areas and also in the North-Eastern region (Shetty 2005; Chavan 2005a). Also, there was a perceptible increase in the share of formal sources in rural debt in the 1970s and 1980s, attributable to the rise in the share of commercial banks, as borne out by data from successive rounds of the AIDIS (Chavan 2005b; Hoda and Terway 2015).

The second phase after 1991 brought about a sea-change in banking policy. The objective of banking policy changed from redistribution to financial soundness and commercial viability of banks.[8] During this phase,

---

[7] The scheme was originally limited to districts other than the metropolitan districts. The 16 metropolitan districts including Greater Mumbai were brought under its ambit in 2013.

[8] See RBI (1991), which argued that the objectives of redistribution had to be pursued not as part of monetary policy but fiscal policy.

the 1:4 norm under the branch licensing policy was done away with (RBI 2008). The PSL programme was not phased out, as recommended by the Committee on Financial Systems (CFS), but the definitions of priority sectors, particularly of agriculture, were altered significantly. These definitional changes brought large agriculturists, including corporates involved in agricultural production and processing, into the fold of PSL, and hence raised questions about the intended focus of this programme on poorer sections, including small farmers.[9] Lending rates were gradually deregulated and banks were given complete freedom to price their loans (RBI 2008).

Studies have discussed the contraction in branch networks in the North-Eastern and other underbanked regions during this phase (Shetty 2005; Chavan 2005a). Moreover, the sharp fall in the growth and share of credit to agriculture, SSIs, and socio-economically weaker sections is also brought out by these studies (*ibid.*; Chavan, 2016). There was an unprecedented fall in the share of formal sources in the debt of rural households, driven by a fall in the share of commercial banks, between the 1991 and 2002 rounds of the AIDIS (Hoda and Terway 2015).

Most of these trends, however, reversed after 2005. The period after 2005 can be regarded as a continuation of the policy of financial liberalisation, but was also marked by a change with a renewed commitment to "financial inclusion."[10] Though the objective of the financial inclusion policy (FIP) was similar to the one pursued during the phase of social banking, it was to be pursued in the broader context of financial liberalisation. In order to protect the "business considerations"of banks, the process of financial inclusion was thus premised on greater operational autonomy to banks in the form of interest rate deregulation and widening of the definition of priority sectors (RBI 2008, p. 304).

This phase witnessed the return of some policy mandates that were implemented during the phase of social banking. Illustratively, the branch authorisation policy was introduced, giving freedom to banks to open branches through an annual authorisation by the RBI. They could open

---

[9] The exact definitional changes under PSL, particularly agriculture, are discussed in Ramakumar and Chavan (2014).

[10] Financial inclusion was defined as "the process of ensuring access to appropriate financial products and services needed by all sections of the society in general, and vulnerable groups such as low income groups in particular, at an affordable cost in a fair and transparent manner by regulated mainstream institutional players" (Chakrabarty 2011).

a branch at any centre without prior permission from the RBI, provided that at least 25 per cent of the total branches to be opened during a year were located in unbanked rural centres (serving less than 10,000 persons). It was also stipulated that the total number of branches opened in urban and metropolitan centres (serving a population of 100,000 and above) during a financial year could not exceed the total number of branches opened in rural and semi-urban centres (serving a population of up to 100,000 persons) and all centres in the North-Eastern States including Sikkim.[11]

Banks were also allowed to employ the services of agents or business correspondents (BCs) and mobile vans as non-branch means for delivering banking services to customers. The list of eligible BCs was expanded over the years to include not just not-for-profit but also for-profit entities (including telecom companies and non-banking financial companies [NBFCs]) to enhance the commercial viability of the process of financial inclusion (Chavan 2017).

The financial inclusion objective of reaching banking services either through brick-and-mortar branches or non-branch means was further formalised through the financial inclusion plans adopted by banks from 2010 onwards. The targets under these plans were aligned with the targets set under the Pradhan Mantri Jan Dhan Yojana (PMJDY), announced in 2014, to provide small deposit, micro insurance and debit card facilities to unbanked sections of the population (ibid.).

This phase also saw the adoption of the Comprehensive Credit Policy in 2004–05, to double the total flow of bank credit to agriculture. However, the mandate of agricultural credit expansion was accompanied by a continued widening of the definition of agriculture under the PSL programme (Ramakumar and Chavan 2014).

Studies have shown a striking revival in the spread of bank branches in rural areas and in underbanked regions, including the North-Eastern region, after 2005 (Ramakumar and Chavan 2011). As part of the targets set under FIP, banks managed to cover all villages (74,414) with a population of more than 2,000 persons through either branch or non-branch means, and have been in the process of reaching out to villages (4,90,298) with a population of less than 2,000 persons (RBI 2016a and 2016b). The share of formal sources in the debt of rural households continued to fall between the 2002 and 2012 rounds of the AIDIS, but within formal sources, there

[11] See "Master Circular on Branch Authorisation," July 2014, RBI, at www.rbi.org.in.

was a welcome, though marginal recovery in the share of commercial banks (Hoda and Terway 2015).

Further, there was an increase in the growth and share of agricultural credit after 2005 (Ramakumar and Chavan 2014; RBI 2015). However, the question about the effective reach of agricultural credit to underprivileged sections, such as small farmers, remained (*ibid.*).

More recently, in 2017, the definition of branch has been replaced by "banking outlet".[12] A banking outlet is defined as a fixed point service delivery unit manned by either the bank's staff or its BC, where banking services of acceptance of deposits, encashment of cheques/cash withdrawal, and lending of money are provided for a minimum of four hours a day for at least five days a week.[13] To encourage banks to open branches in the North-Eastern States, it has been specified that a banking outlet at any *rural or semi-urban* centre in these States would qualify for the 25 per cent requirement for opening banking outlets at unbanked *rural* centres.

The change in the definition of banking outlet has marked a distinct break from the conventional brick-and-mortar perception of branches. It is premature to decide whether this change in policy will strengthen or weaken the availability of banking services in underbanked regions. It may, on the one hand, be cost-effective for banks to open such outlets instead of fully manned branches. Such outlets may also help in making an entry into underbanked regions faster than setting up brick-and-mortar branches.

On the other hand, however, the need for such a change in policy can itself be questioned when (a) banks were being encouraged to reach out to unbanked rural areas either through brick-and-mortar branches or non-branch means (connected to brick-and-mortar branches). The definition of branches, however, was kept limited to brick-and-mortar branches, and targets were laid down for opening such branches. Moreover, banks were fairly successful in meeting these targets till now, as discussed earlier. (b) There are lingering concerns about BCs with regard to their mobile/telecom connectivity, safety and viability (Kishore 2012; Bansal and Srinivasan 2009). Therefore, this recent change may be regarded as an alteration in policy to possibly facilitate banks' achievement of the branch target of 25 per cent.

---

[12] See RBI, "Rationalisation of Branch Authorisation Policy – Revision of Guidelines," 2017, at www.rbi.org.in.

[13] *Ibid.*

The licensing of payments banks and ‘small finance banks (SFBs) is another recent policy measure that can have direct implications for banking in the North-Eastern region in the future. SFBs are banks (most of these were earlier operating as microfinance institutions) with a focus on small borrowers with a higher PSL portfolio, while payments banks facilitate small payments/remittances and deposits.[14] By virtue of their small capital base, it is expected that the operations of SFBs may be limited to a specific region. The North-Eastern SFB with a focus on the North-Eastern region and West Bengal commenced its operations in 2017.

Basic Indicators of Banking Development in the North-Eastern Region with Special Reference to Tripura

Household Indebtedness to Formal Sources

Formal sources had a share of about 88 per cent in total household debt of Tripura in 2012. This share was comparable with the average 84 per cent for the North-Eastern region as a whole, comprising eight States/Union Territories including Tripura (Table 1). However, it was significantly higher than the national average of about 73 per cent for this year.

The share of formal sources in total debt of *rural* households in Tripura of about 77 per cent too was significantly higher than the national average of about 56 per cent in 2012 (Table 2). Interestingly, in terms of the share of formal sources for rural households, Tripura was in the same league as Maharashtra and Kerala, the two States known for a well-developed formal sector of credit (Figure 1).

Notwithstanding the seemingly important role played by formal sources in Tripura, only about 5 per cent of its rural households reported having taken a loan from the formal sector (or incidence of formal debt) in 2012 (Figure 1). The AIDIS is generally criticised for an underestimation of the incidence of debt (Chavan 2012a). Hence, the number of 5 per cent by itself may not offer us much insight. However, we can compare this number with other States assuming the possibility of a uniform underestimation

---

[14] SFBs are mandated to have at least up to 50 per cent of their loan portfolio constituting loans of up to Rs 25 lakh, and 75 per cent of their loan portfolio as PSL (as against the norm of 40 per cent applicable to commercial banks). Payments banks cannot lend and can only accept deposits of up to Rs 1 lakh. See RBI, "Guidelines for Licensing of Small Finance Banks in the Private Sector" and "Guidelines for Licensing of Payments Banks", November 27, 2014, at www.rbi.org.in.

Table 1 *Distribution of debt of all households, Tripura, North-Eastern region and India, 2012, in per cent*

Source	Tripura	North-Eastern region	India
Commercial banks (including RRBs)	44.5	38.5	43.7
Credit cooperatives	31.5	20.2	20.8
Government	2.8	10.0	1.5
Other formal sources	8.7	15.4	6.5
Formal sources	**87.5**	**84.1**	**72.6**
Moneylenders	2.0	7.1	20.0
Relatives and friends	3.2	6.5	5.8
Other informal sources	7.2	2.3	1.6
Informal sources	**12.5**	**15.9**	**27.4**
All	**100.0**	**100.0**	**100.0**

Source: NSSO (2017).

Table 2 *Distribution of debt of all and rural households, Tripura, 1991–2012, in per cent*

Sources	1991		2012	
Commercial banks	48.1	(49.9)	44.5	(46.0)
Credit cooperatives	12.1	(12.8)	31.5	(16.5)
Government	26.4	(26.5)	2.8	(2.8)
Other formal sources	3.5	(0.2)	8.7	(8.7)
Formal sources	**90.1**	**(89.4)**	**87.5**	**(76.9)**
Moneylenders	1.8	(1.9)	2.0	(3.8)
Traders	2.2	(2.4)	–	–
Relatives and friends	5.7	(6.1)	3.2	(7.3)
Other informal sources	0.2	(0.2)	7.2	(12.0)
Informal sources	**9.9**	**(10.6)**	**12.5**	**(23.1)**

Note: Figures in brackets indicate share in total debt of rural households.
Source: NSSO (1998 and 2017).

of incidence across all States. Such a comparison suggested that Tripura ranked much lower than the averages for most Indian States and the national average. Figures 1 and 2 show the comparative position of Tripura with respect to the national average, and the averages for Maharashtra and Kerala, the two States on one end with high shares of formal sector

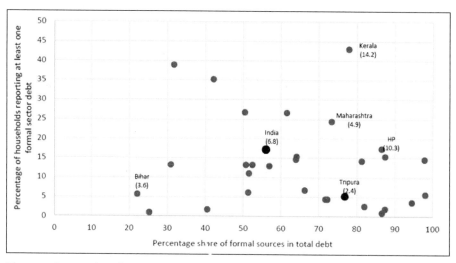

Figure 1 *Scatter plot of percentage share of formal sector debt and incidence of formal sector debt for rural households, States, 2012*, in per cent

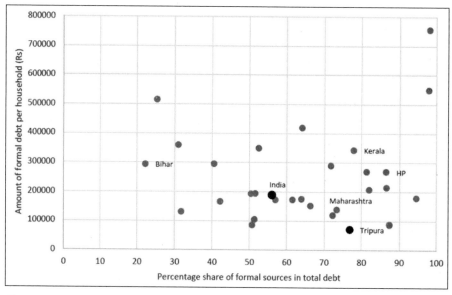

Figure 2 *Scatter plot of amount of debt per rural household and share of formal sector debt for rural households, States, 2012*, in Rs and per cent

Note: Figures in brackets in Figure 1 indicate the percentage of households reporting at least one loan outstanding from commercial banks in 2012.
Source: NSSO (2017).

debt, and Bihar, the State at the other end with the lowest share of formal sector debt.

Commercial banks (including RRBs) constituted the foremost source of formal credit in Tripura. Commercial banks accounted for close to half of the total household debt owed to formal sources in 2012 (Table 1). Credit cooperatives were the second important source accounting for about 32 per cent of the total household debt. Interestingly, urban households relied more on cooperatives for their credit needs than rural households. For rural households, commercial banks constituted the single largest source of formal credit in 2012 (Table 2).

There was practically no moneylending in Tripura or even in its villages in 2012. Sundry and occasional lenders operated as part of the informal system. This was similar to the situation in the North-Eastern region as a whole, but quite contrary to the rest of the country (Table 1). Tripura showed a low incidence of both formal and informal sources among the Indian States (Figure 3). It was situated almost on the 45^0 line (plotted assuming a positive linear relation between the incidence of formal and

Table 3 *Distribution of debt of rural households by interest rates, Tripura and India, 2012, in per cent*

Interest rate class	Tripura	India
0	9.4	8.5
*Rates less than 10 per cent**	25.3	19.7
0< rate ≤ 6	5.3	5.0
6 < rate ≤ 10	20.0	14.7
Rates more than 10 per cent	65.3	71.8
10 < rate ≤ 12	17.9	7.5
12 < rate ≤ 15	35.2	25.7
15 < rate ≤ 20	4.4	6.6
20 < rate ≤ 25	7.8	16.1
25 < rate ≤ 30	–	0.3
>=30	–	15.6
Total	**100.0**	**100.0**

Note: * The cut off of 10 per cent is taken as an indicative formal rate of interest based on the average lending rate of the top five banks in 2012 as reported in the RBI's *Handbook of Statistics on Indian Economy*.
Source: NSSO (2017).

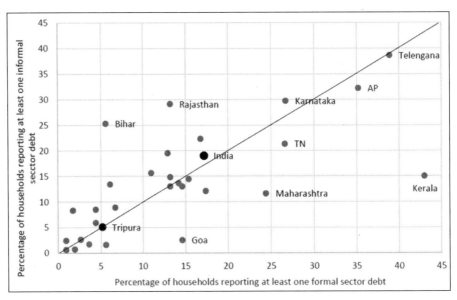

Figure 3 *Incidence of formal and informal sector debt, rural households, States, 2012*

Source: NSSO (2017).

informal debt) and close to the origin unlike most underbanked States that were located above the line.[15]

Given the dominance of formal sources, the concentration of debt was expectedly larger in the lower interest rate brackets (below 10 per cent per annum) in Tripura (Table 3). The complete absence of debt at rates above 25 per cent was not so surprising given the low incidence of debt taken from moneylenders or traders in the State. With regard to the distribution of debt by interest rates, rural Tripura was thus strikingly different from the picture at the all-India level.

The share of formal sources in Tripura showed only a moderate fall between the 1991 and 2012 rounds of AIDIS for all households (The 2002 round did not canvas information on the State) (Table 2). The fall, however, was perceptible for rural Tripura. This was also a period, as discussed in the first section of this chapter, when the share of formal sources in rural India fell for the first time since 1952.

[15] The caveat relating to the figures on incidence of debt from the AIDIS, which was noted while discussing Figure 1, also applies here.

Availability of Banking Services

Bank branch intensity

Basic availability of banking services can be discerned from the demographic intensity of branches or population per bank branch. In terms of branch intensity, Tripura was comparable with the all-India average in 2016 (Figure 4). Given that the North-Eastern region is hilly terrain that is sparsely populated, I also worked out the measure of branches per square mile to understand the physical availability of bank branches. The ratio of branches per square mile for Tripura was closely

Table 4 *Number of branches per square mile, Tripura, North-East, and India, 2016*

State/region	No. of branches	No. of branches per square mile
Tripura	379	0.09
North-East	3,345	0.03
India	1,30,482	0.10

Source: Calculated from *Basic Statistical Returns on Scheduled Commercial Banks in India*, various issues and censusindia.gov.in.

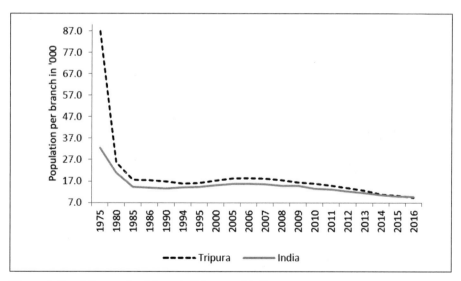

Figure 4 *Population per bank branch, Tripura and India*

Source: Calculated from *Basic Statistical Returns on Scheduled Commercial Banks in India*, various issues, and censusindia.gov.in.

comparable with that for India, and was significantly higher than for the North-Eastern region (Table 4).

It was possible to discern distinct changes in the demographic intensity of branches during the three phases of banking policy discussed earlier. Tripura, like the rest of India, showed a steep increase in branch intensity (decline in population per branch) in the phase of social banking. This was followed by a trend of decline from 1994 onwards till 2006, and a rise thereafter with the adoption of the policy on financial inclusion.

Table 5 *Number of branches per square mile, Tripura and the three study districts, 2016*

District/State	No. of branches	No of branches per square mile
Dhalai	34	0.04
North Tripura	61	0.08
South Tripura	84	0.07
Tripura	**379**	**0.09**

Source: Calculated from *Basic Statistical Returns on Scheduled Commercial Banks in India*, various issues, and censusindia.gov.in.

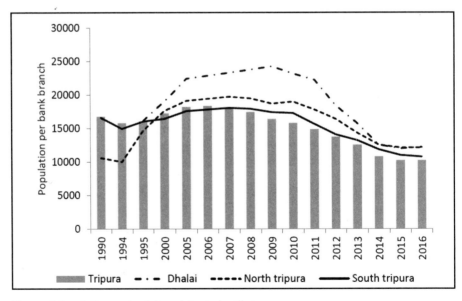

Figure 5 *Population per bank branch in study villages*

Source: Calculated from *Basic Statistical Returns on Scheduled Commercial Banks in India*, various issues; GoI (1991 and 2001); and censusindia.gov.in.

Branch intensity in the three study districts of Dhalai, North Tripura, and South Tripura also showed a broadly similar trend of decline till the first half of the 2000s, followed by a rise in the subsequent period (Figure 5). Although the gap in branch intensity between the three districts had narrowed considerably over time, the availability of branches was poorer in Dhalai and North Tripura. Dhalai also ranked the lowest in terms of the ratio of branches per square mile in 2016 (Table 5).

Bank deposit services
Tripura was one of the few States where the penetration of deposit accounts was remarkably higher than in most Indian States, including even the well-banked ones (Table 6). In 2012, about 93 per cent and 88 per cent of the rural and urban households, respectively, had access to bank deposit accounts, as per the AIDIS. The national averages for this year were only about 69 per cent and 80 per cent, respectively. One of the reasons for such high penetration of deposit accounts was the routing of pension and other welfare scheme payments by the State government through deposit accounts. It is interesting to note that while India continues to pursue the target of providing universal access to bank accounts under financial inclusion, Tripura, particularly rural Tripura, was close to achieving this target as early as 2012.[16]

Bank credit facilities
In terms of branch intensity and access to deposit accounts, Tripura was significantly above the national average and the averages for many

Table 6 *Percentage of households having access to deposit accounts, Tripura and select States, 2012*

Indicator	Tripura	All-India	Maharashtra	Andhra Pradesh	Tamil Nadu	Karnataka
Rural households having a deposit account	92.9	68.8	76.3	75.1	77.1	73.1
Urban households having a deposit account	88.2	79.5	87.7	81.8	79.4	82.8

Source: NSSO (2017).

---

[16] It is difficult to ascertain the changes in access to deposit accounts over time, as data on this head are not available from the rounds preceding 2012.

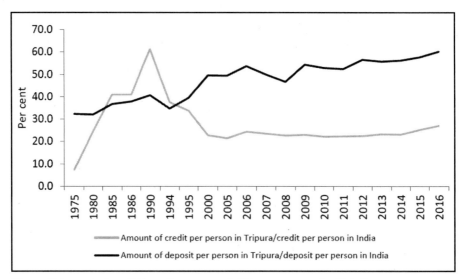

Figure 6 *Amount of credit/deposit per person in Tripura compared with India*

Source: Calculated from *Basic Statistical Returns on Scheduled Commercial Banks in India*, various issues; GoI (1991 and 2001); and censusindia.gov.in.

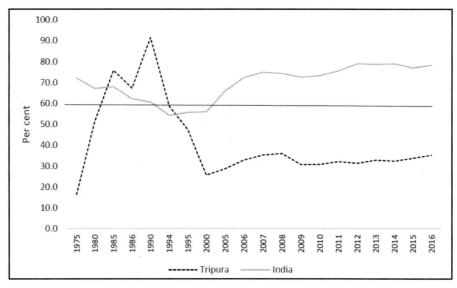

Figure 7 *Credit-to-deposit ratio, Tripura and India*

Source: Calculated from *Basic Statistical Returns on Scheduled Commercial Banks in India*, various issues.

well-banked States. However, it was below these averages with regard to supply of bank credit. Credit per capita in Tripura was only about 27 per cent of the credit per capita in India. This ratio showed a steep fall over the 1990s, and then remained by and large stagnant over the 2000s and 2010s (Figure 6). However, deposits per capita in Tripura were about 60 per cent of the deposits per capita in India.

The gap between credit and deposits was wide and remained largely unchanged over the years, suggesting the possibility of funds mobilised from the State being diverted elsewhere as credit by banks. This observation could be corroborated by the credit-to-deposit ratio in the State remaining stagnant, much below the 60 per cent norm set for rural and semi-urban branches, as discussed earlier (Figure 7).

When the amount of bank credit per capita and SDP per capita was plotted, a broadly positive association between these two variables could be seen across most States. This was evident from a clustering of most States near the 45⁰ line (Figure 8). The only outlying States which were away from the line were Goa and Delhi. Tripura was fairly close to the origin, suggesting a low level of bank credit and SDP per capita. Like all other States, it was above the 45⁰ line, signifying the provision of a lower amount of bank credit per capita for every one unit of SDP per capita generated in the State. This was also borne out from a simple ratio of bank credit per capita to SDP per capita in the State. The ratio was only 19 per cent for Tripura, when the regional average for the North-East and the national average was 27 and 66 per cent, respectively (Table 7). The low access to bank credit could also be seen from the AIDIS data discussed earlier, which showed that only about 2 per cent of the State's population in 2012 reported a loan outstanding from commercial banks (read Figure 1).

Table 7 *Ratio of bank credit per capita to per capita income, 2000–2014*, per cent

Region	2000	2010	2014
Tripura	6.9	17.2	18.5
North-Eastern region	6.8	26.3	27.0
All-India	26.8	61.6	65.7

Source: Calculated from *Basic Statistical Returns on Scheduled Commercial Banks in India*, various issues, and *Handbook of Statistics on Indian Economy*, various issues.

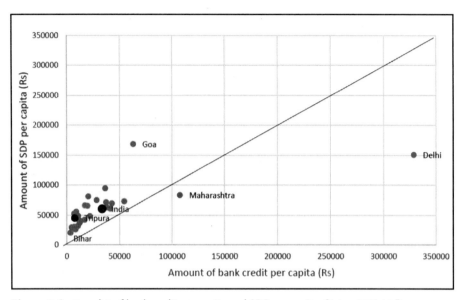

Figure 8 *Scatter plot of bank credit per capita and SDP per capita, States, 2011,* in Rs

Source: Calculated from *Basic Statistical Returns on Scheduled Commercial Banks in India,* various issues, and *Handbook of Statistics on Indian Economy,* various issues.

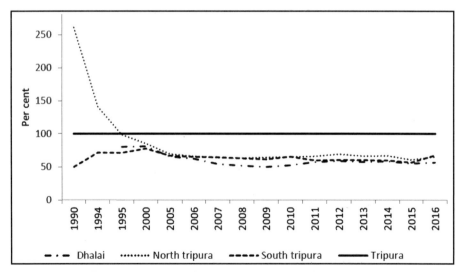

Figure 9 *Ratio of credit per person in three study districts to credit per person in Tripura*

Source: Calculated from *Basic Statistical Returns on Scheduled Commercial Banks in India,* various issues.

Tripura not only had low access to credit, but was also marked by considerable inter-district disparity in the distribution of credit despite being a small State. This could be seen from the ratio of credit per capita for each district compared with the State average (Figure 9). The ratio was close to 60 per cent for all three study districts: Dhalai, North Tripura, and South Tripura. The fourth district of West Tripura (not shown in the figure) obviously had the highest credit per capita and pulled up the State average. Also, there was hardly any change in the ratio for the three districts since the early 2000s.

The analysis in this section suggests that the major reason for considering Tripura to be an underbanked State was the low availability of bank credit. The spread of branch network in the State was comparable with the national average, and was, in fact, much better than in most States from the North-Eastern region. However, despite such a branch network and the resources mobilised through it in the form of deposits, Tripura did not get its due share in total bank credit in the country.

Yet, informal sources of credit were not as active in Tripura as in most other States. The literature on rural credit has generally shown that wherever and whenever the formal sector is weak, the informal sector consolidates itself to meet unmet credit needs (Chavan 2012b).[17] However, Tripura appeared to be an exception to this observation.

To understand the credit system in Tripura, we need to analyse the low levels of activity of not just formal but also informal sources of credit. A part of this question is answered in the next section, where an analysis of the determinants of bank credit growth in the State is attempted. As regards informal sources of credit, some insights are provided in a later section where the data from village surveys are analysed.

Determinants of Bank Credit Growth in Tripura

The discussion in the earlier section suggested that the main reason why Tripura comes across as an underbanked State was not because of the lack of branch coverage or of access to deposit accounts, but due to poor supply of bank credit. In order to understand the factors affecting bank credit growth, an econometric exercise is attempted in this section. Taking time-series data for the State from 1994 to 2014, we trace the relation between bank credit growth ((ΔlogBankCredit) and a number of other

---

[17] This can also be discerned from the successive rounds of the AIDIS.

economic indicators. This is a preliminary analysis given the small size of the sample with 20 annual observations, owing to constraints in the availability of data.

The following indicators are selected: (a) basic economic indicators: growth in real State net domestic product per capita ((ΔSNDPpc); (b) basic banking indicators: population per bank branch (branch intensity); (c) indicators of alternative sources of private and public funds: growth in total cooperative credit ((ΔlogCoopCredit) and growth in revenue expenditure on agriculture, irrigation, and rural development ((ΔlogAgriExpenditure); (d) physical infrastructure indicators: number of telephone connections per capita (TeleDensity) and total road length per 100 square kilometres (RoadConnectivity).

These variables were selected based on (a) the literature on finance and growth in the context of developing economies, and (b) the specific insights gained from village surveys in the State. First, the literature is replete with studies that analyse the relation between economic growth and finance/banking development.[18] In the context of developing economies, the literature also discusses the role of physical infrastructure to understand why some regions remain underserved by the banking system.[19] In the context of the hilly North-Eastern region, underdeveloped physical infrastructure is often cited as an impediment to the flow and "absorptive capacity" of credit (RBI 2006; Mohanty 2011, p. 7).

As borne out by the village surveys, the Tripura government supports agriculture (the largest employer and second largest sector of economic activity) through subsidies (for fertilizers, seeds, irrigation, and mechanisation/tillers). After accounting for these subsidies, the cost of cultivation on all purchased inputs (except labour) turns out to be very low for most crops grown in the State, including rubber and paddy (Sivamurugan 2017). Given that subsidies bring down the cost of cultivation, they are expected to affect the demand for agricultural credit in the State. In the regression, the revenue expenditure on agriculture

---

[18] For an excellent review of literature on finance and growth, see Hermes (1994). Also see the set of papers from the International Monetary Fund and World Bank, which uses panels of country-level data to estimate the relation between finance and growth. Illustratively, see Levine *et al.* (2000) for an analysis of the causal impact of finance on growth.

[19] See the review of literature on the linkages between physical infrastructure and financial access in the context of developing economies in Rajeev and Vani (2017). Illustratively, see the cross-country analysis in Sarma and Pais (2010) on the role of road and telecommunications connectivity in furthering financial inclusion.

(including rural development and irrigation) is used as a proxy for subsidies to agriculture and rural areas.

Given the problem of unit root that afflicts any time-series data, the non-stationarity in the data series was first checked and corrected for.[20] Also, any analysis of economic growth and bank credit is expected to be beset with endogeneity concerns, with the independent variables in the model being correlated with the error terms. The endogeneity was controlled using an auto-regressive term in the model.[21]

The results from the baseline model suggested a positive and significant coefficient of the lagged credit growth (column I in Table 8). A positive impact of economic growth could be seen on bank credit growth in the State. Incidentally, the causality between bank credit per capita and real SDP per capita was also analysed; there was bi-directional Granger causality between these two variables during the study period (Appendix 3).[22]

The coefficient of branch intensity, the basic banking indicator which facilitates bank credit, had the expected negative sign but was not statistically significant. The growth in alternative sources of funds had the expected negative impact on bank credit growth, suggesting a possible substitution effect.

In the second model, controls for road and telephone connectivity were introduced to test the hypothesis of whether physical infrastructure had any impact on bank credit growth in the State (column II in Table 8). While roads, a basic means for physical connectivity, had a significant but negligible impact on bank credit growth, telephone connectivity did not show any significant impact.

---

[20] This was done with the help of the commonly used Augmented Dickey Fuller (ADF) test. The series with unit roots, namely, TeleDensity and RoadConnectivity, were found to be difference stationary integrated of order "2," and branch intensity of order "1." The pair-wise correlation coefficients were also worked out to check for multi-collinearity. It was expected to be minimal given the weak degree of correlation (less than (+/−) 0.3) between the variables used in the model. For descriptive statistics of the variables, see Appendix 1.

[21] The literature on finance and growth, which was discussed earlier, has rich cross-country or panel data studies. Generally, in the literature, the issue of endogeneity is taken care of through the instrumental variables. However, given the constraints in terms of data availability, there were a limited number of observations across only the time dimension. Hence I resorted to the Ordinary Least Square (OLS) framework with an autoregressive term. For an illustration of the model used for this regression, see Appendix 2.

[22] For the estimation of Granger causality, I checked and corrected for unit roots in these series.

Table 8 *Determinants of bank credit growth, Tripura*

Explanatory variable	Dependent variable: ΔlogBankCredit$_t$	
	Baseline model	Model II (controls for physical infrastructure)
	(I)	(II)
ΔlogBankCredit$_{t-1}$	0.831***	0.784***
	(0.163)	(0.149)
ΔSNDPpc$_t$	0.443**	0.477***
	(0.177)	(0.152)
BranchIntensity$_t$	−0.003	−0.009
	(0.060)	(0.054)
ΔlogCoopCredit$_t$	−0.055***	−0.055***
	(0.016)	(0.013)
ΔlogAgriExpenditure$_t$	−0.230	−0.354*
	(0.225)	(0.205)
TeleDensity$_t$		−0.0003
		(0.005)
Road Connectivity$_t$		0.002**
		(0.0007)
Observations	20	20
Adjusted R-squared	0.44	0.61
DW Statistic	2.25	1.90

Notes: Figures in parentheses are standard errors.
***p<0.01; **p<0.05; *p<0.1
Source: Estimated from GoT (2014); *Basic Statistical Returns of Scheduled Commercial Banks in India,* Mumbai, various issues.

Major Features of the Credit Systems in the Three Surveyed Villages of Tripura

High Proportion of Formal Debt

In all three villages, the proportion of total debt taken from formal sources was remarkably high, ranging above 80 per cent at the time of the survey in 2015–16 (Table 9). It was the highest in Khakchang, where nearly the entire amount of debt outstanding was owed to formal sources. The village data thus corroborated the State-level AIDIS data discussed earlier. It is possible that the high share of formal sources in outstanding debts was a result of old accumulated debts. However, formal sources accounted for

Table 9 *Amount of debt outstanding, three study villages, Tripura, 2015–16*, in Rs

Source	Khakchang	Mainama	Muhuripur
Formal sources	**5,804,298**	**94,054,333**	**48,148,712**
	(99.0)	(98.8)	(81.4)
Commercial banks	2,268,682	27,725,272	18,414,778
	(38.7)	(29.1)	(31.1)
Credit cooperatives	442,603	6,289,532	314,990
	(7.5)	(6.6)	(0.5)
Regional rural banks	2,685,711	59,982,963	28,917,883
	(45.8)	(63.0)	(48.9)
Other formal sources	407,301	56,565	501,061
	(6.9)	(0.1)	(0.8)
Informal sources	**60,965**	**1,150,091**	**10,985,730**
Friends and relatives	–	779,208	880,852
	–	(0.8)	(1.5)
Moneylenders	60,965	–	2,398,906
	(1.0)	–	(4.1)
Self-help groups	–	–	6,068,889
	–	–	(10.3)
Trader/ other service providers	–	194,238	273,508
	–	(0.2)	(0.5)
Other informal sources	–	176,645	1,363,575
	–	(0.2)	(2.3)
All sources	**5,865,263**	**95,204,424**	**59,134,441**
	(100.0)	(100.0)	(100.0)

Note: Figures in brackets indicate percentage share in total.
Source: Survey data.

an equally high share also in the amount of borrowings during the survey year (Table 10).

Striking Differences across Villages in Level of Credit Activity

Going by the share of formal sources in total debt/borrowings, it appeared that all three villages had a well-developed formal system of credit. However, this impression is somewhat misleading. There was a striking differential in the levels of credit activity in general, and formal credit activity in particular, across the three villages.

First, there was little activity in the credit system in Khakchang, which belonged to North Tripura district, a relatively backward district in the

Table 10 *Amount borrowed during the survey year, three study villages, Tripura, 2015–16,* in Rs

Source	Khakchang	Mainama	Muhuripur
Formal sources	**2,505,100**	**46,167,160**	**25,872,755**
	(97.6)	**(97.9)**	**(88.8)**
Commercial banks	2,132,000	16,277,320	9,424,127
	(83.1)	(34.5)	(32.3)
Credit cooperatives	–	3,805,950	–
	–	(8.1)	–
Regional rural banks	373,100	26,021,040	16,448,628
	(14.5)	(55.2)	(56.4)
Other formal sources	–	62,850	–
	–	(0.1)	–
Informal sources	**61,590**	**1,001,928**	**3,272,945**
	(2.4)	**(2.1)**	**(11.2)**
Friends and relatives	–	636,996	600,320
	–	(1.4)	(2.1)
Moneylenders	61,590	–	529,281
	(2.4)	–	(1.8)
Self-help groups	–	–	1,394,300
	–	–	(4.8)
Traders/other service providers	–	264,870	292,188
	–	(0.6)	(1)
Other informal sources	–	100,062	456,856
	–	(0.2)	(1.6)
All sources	**2,566,690**	**47,169,088**	**29,145,700**
	(100.0)	**(100.0)**	**(100.0)**

Note: Figures in brackets indicate percentage shares.
Source: Survey data.

State in terms of banking development, as discussed earlier. This was a tribal village with a predominance of community farming. There was subsistence farming in the village with households producing primarily for self-consumption. As a result, the use of inputs in crop production and, consequently, the demand for crop credit were relatively low. Furthermore, the cash nexus in economic transactions was less in Khakchang than in the other two villages.[23] Owing to a combination of these factors, credit

---

[23] The only major source of cash was the wage payments made under the Mahatma Gandhi National Rural Employment Guarantee Act (MGNREGA).

Table 11 *Incidence of debt/borrowing, three study villages, Tripura, 2015–16*

Source	Debt outstanding at the time of the survey			Borrowing during the survey year		
	Khakchang	Mainama	Muhuripur	Khakchang	Mainama	Muhuripur
Formal sources	**64**	**565**	**536**	**21**	**399**	**412**
	(11.0)	**(39.0)**	**(51.0)**	**(7.4)**	**(27.5)**	**(39.1)**
Commercial banks	19	332	255	5	267	194
	(3.2)	(23.0)	(24.2)	(1.8)	(18.4)	(18.5)
Credit cooperatives	5	39	5	–	17	–
	(0.9)	(3.0)	(0.5)	–	(1.1)	–
Regional rural banks	40	241	361	16	109	218
	(6.8)	(17.0)	(34.3)	(5.5)	(7.5)	(20.7)
Other formal sources	5	6	10	–	6	–
	(0.9)	(0.4)	(0.9)	–	(0.4)	–
Informal sources	**14**	**39**	**259**	**14**	**23**	**148**
	(2.3)	**(2.6)**	**(24.5)**	**(4.7)**	**(1.6)**	**(14.0)**
Friends and relatives	–	22	25	–	11	10
	–	(2)	(2.4)	–	(0.8)	(1.0)
Moneylenders	14	–	54	14	–	29
	(2.3)	–	(5.2)	(4.7)	–	(2.8)
Self-help groups	–	–	139	–	–	65
	–	–	(13.2)	–	–	(6.1)
Traders/other service providers	–	6	40	–	6	25
	–	(0.4)	(3.8)	–	(0.4)	(2.4)
Others	–	11	40	–	6	19
	–	(1)	(3.8)	–	(0.4)	(1.8)
All	**72**	**583**	**675**	**35**	**412**	**520**
	(12.0)	**(40.0)**	**(64.0)**	**(5.9)**	**(28.4)**	**(49.4)**

Note: Figures in brackets indicate percentages of total number of households in the villages.
Source: Survey data.

transactions in the village, both with formal and informal sources, were very few in number. At the time of the survey, only about 11 per cent of the households in the village reported outstanding debts (Table 11).

When the window was narrowed to the survey year, the extent of credit transactions came down even further. During the survey year, only about 7 per cent of the households reported fresh loans in Khakchang (Table 11).

The credit system in Mainama – the second village located in Dhalai, another underbanked district in the State – was relatively more active than Khakchang. At the time of the survey, about 39 per cent of the households reported debts outstanding (Table 11). During the survey year, the percentage was about 28 per cent, again significantly higher than Khakchang (Table 11).

The credit market in Muhuripur, in South Tripura, was the most active. About 51 per cent of the households reported debts outstanding at the time of the survey; the incidence was about 39 per cent during the survey year. Hence, a much larger proportion of the village population approached both formal and informal sources for credit. It is noteworthy that the incidence of debt in both Mainama and Muhuripur compared very closely with the incidence of debt observed in other PARI villages from Andhra Pradesh, Maharashtra, Karnataka and Punjab (Chavan and Das 2015).

Notwithstanding the differences in survey years, if we resort to a broad comparison of the village data with the AIDIS data, the picture is completely different. The average incidence of debt of about 5 per cent for Tripura in 2012 was far lower than the incidence shown by all three study villages, particularly Mainama and Muhuripur. This again raises concerns about the possibility of underestimation of incidence by the AIDIS, as discussed earlier.

Banks: The Main Source of Formal Credit

Notwithstanding the differences in levels of credit activity, the major source of formal credit in all three villages was banks, particularly RRBs (Tables 9 to 11). In both Mainama and Muhuripur, the RRB Tripura Grameen Bank had a bank branch either in the village or in the close vicinity. Khakchang was served by a commercial bank branch. Another major (private) commercial bank that was found to be active in Mainama and Muhuripur was Bandhan Bank. This was originally a microfinance institution regulated by the RBI. It was granted a commercial banking license in 2015 and at the time of the survey, it was operating as a bank. Notwithstanding this shift, Bandhan had continued with many of its old lending and recovery practices even as a bank. A brief discussion on some of these practices based on the evidence collected during the village surveys is provided in Box 1.

Cooperatives constituted a relatively weak source of credit for households in all three villages. Interestingly, Muhuripur had a credit cooperative (primary agricultural credit society). However, households

> # Box 1
> ## The Operating Practices of Bandhan in the Surveyed Villages in Tripura
>
> Till the time it obtained a banking license in 2015, Bandhan operated as an MFI regulated by the RBI. Following the crisis in the microfinance sector in 2010, the RBI introduced a new category of non-banking financial companies (NBFC)–MFIs, and stipulated stricter regulations for these institutions with regard to interest rates, annual margins, size of lending, etc. (RBI 2011). Bandhan belonged to this category of NBFC–MFI.
>
> Bandhan originated in West Bengal and later spread to other eastern and North-Eastern States, including Tripura. Possibly, the low penetration of banking in most of these States provided a fertile ground for the spread of MFIs like Bandhan.
>
> At the time of the survey, Bandhan was active in Muhuripur and Mainama. As will be discussed later, there was very low incidence of moneylending or other forms of informal lending in these villages. Informal credit was often easily accessible, which explains its persistence even if it came at higher rates of interest. Bandhan's spread in Tripura despite some onerous operating practices can also be seen in light of the relative ease in access that it provided to borrowers, and the near-absence of moneylending/informal lending in the State.
>
> The details on the operating practices of Bandhan collected during the surveys of Mainama and Muhuripur suggested the following:
>
> 1. Loans were generally group loans with a weekly instalment. Every member of the group was expected to contribute towards repayment.
> 2. Loans were generally given for production-related activities, including agriculture and small enterprise/business.
> 3. The amount varied by purpose. However, it did not exceed Rs 1 lakh. Loans for agriculture, including crop loans, generally had an informal ceiling of Rs 25,000.
> 4. The rates of interest varied from 16 to 18.5 per cent per annum. There was an additional charge of 5.25 per cent collected annually towards insurance.
> 5. The recovery was done by collection agents specially appointed and trained by Bandhan.
> 6. Group loans were all un-collateralised. Group monitoring and peer pressure acted as securities for these loans. Loans to individuals, which were rare, were against personal guarantee and required the borrower to furnish income tax returns to prove a regular source of income.
> 7. There was hardly any default reported during the surveys. Hence, there was little clarity about the penalty for defaults. However, a similar survey of Bandhan

in West Bengal villages (Bhavani 2015) suggested that there was considerable fear among borrowers with regard to defaults. Defaulters were made to sit in the collection office till they settled the dues or were made to sell off personal belongings. It was also reported that defaulters who fled the village were tracked down by the collection agents (Chavan, with Sivamurugan 2017).

in the village did not report any cooperative loan during the survey year (Table 11).

Low Incidence of Moneylending

Moneylenders, generally an important source of informal credit in the Indian countryside, were not very active in the villages of Tripura. In this regard, the village data resembled the AIDIS data for the State. Some transactions involving moneylenders were reported in Khakchang and Muhuripur (Tables 9 to 11). However, there were no moneylenders in Mainama. In Mainama, the informal sector was a mix of sundry lenders, including friends and relatives, traders/other service providers.

In Muhuripur, the village with the most active credit system, moneylending was present. However, even in this village, the incidence of moneylending was significantly less as compared to other villages surveyed by PARI from Andhra Pradesh, Karnataka, Maharashtra and Bihar (Chavan and Das 2015).

Interestingly, moneylending had a taken a new group form (Shivashakti groups) in Muhuripur. It was akin to a group of savers who contributed a certain amount of money every month to the group's saving pool.[24] At the end of the year, the money was either lent out to one of the members (resembling an SHG) or to a non-member (similar to a moneylending group). The rate of interest charged to non-members was higher than that charged to members.[25] At the time of the survey, Muhuripur had about 10–15 groups of this kind. The prevalence of such groups was a reflection of the stronger cash nexus in Muhuripur's economy as compared to that in the other villages. These groups are classified under self-help groups (SHGs) in Tables 9, 10, and 11.

---

[24] It was an informal group of 10 to 12 men who contributed a sum of Rs 50–200 per month.
[25] The money thus collected was lent out at a monthly rate of interest of two per cent to members or three per cent to non-members at the end of the year.

Apart from these groups, SHGs also included groups formed under the Tripura Rural Livelihood Mission (TRLM) programme, which had credit linkages with banks. Contrary to the Shivashakti groups, all the groups formed under TRLM had female members and some established linkages with banks for savings. However, despite banking linkages, all SHGs are considered as informal entities in this chapter, given the complete absence of any regulation for these groups at present.[26]

Mainama and Muhuripur also showed the presence of traders/input dealers (fertilizer shops), giving credit to village households. However, there was no interest charge, not even implicit, associated with these loans, unlike in the villages from West Bengal (Bhavani 2015).

Low Average Rates of Interest

In all three study villages, the weighted average rates of interest were low, ranging between 13 and 15 per cent per annum (Table 12). The average rates in all three villages were comparable with the rates observed in the PARI villages of Maharashtra – the State with a well-developed formal system of credit, and significantly lower than the rates seen in Bihar and Madhya Pradesh – States with an underdeveloped formal system (Chavan and Das 2015).

Taking the same size-classes as in the AIDIS, there was concentration of both the amount and incidence of debt at interest rates less than 15 per cent per annum. Thus, interest rate distribution was broadly in line with the high share of the formal sector in all three villages, as discussed earlier.

In Muhuripur, where informal sources were relatively more active, the concentration of debt at rates ranging above 20 per cent was higher than in Khakchang and Mainama. This was also true of the prevalence of moneylending groups in the village, as noted earlier. Yet, even informal sources in Muhuripur did not charge rates as high as those usually seen in the villages from other States surveyed by PARI, particularly the underbanked ones (Chavan and Das 2015).[27] There were no interlinked credit transaction involving implicit interest charge in any of these villages, unlike what was observed in other PARI villages (Chavan and Das 2015).

---

[26] See Chavan and Das (2015) for the reasons why several players in the microfinance sector, including SHGs, should be considered as informal players.

[27] Illustratively, in the village from Bihar, 53 per cent of the loans were contracted at rates above 50 per cent per annum (*ibid.*).

Table 12 *Distribution of debt outstanding by interest rate size-classes, three study villages, 2015–16, in per cent*

Interest rate (per annum) class	Khakchang	Mainama	Muhuripur
Debt outstanding			
0	1.4	1.3	2.3
0< rate ≤ 6	–	0.7	2.4
6 < rate ≤ 10	8.6	8.9	14.7
10 < rate ≤ 12	22.2	16.0	39.9
12 < rate ≤ 15	58.8	68.1	22.9
15 < rate ≤ 20	1.0	1.8	0.3
20 < rate ≤ 25	–	0.1	11.4
Above 25	8.0	3.1	6.0
Total	**100.0**	**100.0**	**100.0**
Incidence of debt			
0	1.4	3.9	8.0
0< rate ≤ 6	–	0.7	6.2
6 < rate ≤ 10	2.3	8.3	17.1
10 < rate ≤ 12	0.9	14.0	18.2
12 < rate ≤ 15	4.5	16.7	16.8
15 < rate ≤ 20	0.9	1.1	1.4
20 < rate ≤ 25	–	0.3	11.8
Above 25	2.3	7.0	11.8
Average incidence	**12.0**	**40.0**	**64.0**
Weighted average rate of interest	15.08	12.05	13.59
Modal rate of interest	14.00	14.00	7.00

Source: Survey data.

Greater Reliance on Credit for Meeting Consumption-related Needs

In all three study villages, households relied on credit more for meeting various consumption-related needs, albeit in varying degrees (Table 13).[28] Credit was thus primarily used to make up for shortfalls in household budgets towards meeting health, education, repayment of old debts, and

---

[28] In PARI surveys, like in other village surveys, the purpose of borrowing is the "stated" and not the "actual" purpose. Hence, some diversion of borrowed funds given their fungibility cannot be entirely ruled out.

Table 13 *Distribution of amount borrowed and incidence of borrowing during the survey year by purpose, three study villages, Tripura, 2015–16,* in per cent

Purpose	Khakchang	Mainama	Muhuripur
Amount borrowed			
1 Directly income-generating activities	**2.1**	**49.5**	**40.4**
1.1 Agriculture	2.1	1.0	16.0
1.2 Allied activities	–	1.4	0.9
1.3 Non-agricultural activities	–	47.1	23.5
2 Not directly income-generating activities	**97.9**	**50.5**	**59.6**
2.1 Housing	–	20.2	26.4
2.2 Others	97.9	30.3	33.2
Incidence of borrowing			
1 Directly income-generating activities	**0.9**	**11.4**	**18.7**
	(0.9)	*(11.0)*	*(15.8)*
1.1 Agriculture	0.9	2.3	10.1
	(0.9)	*(2.3)*	*(8.7)*
1.2 Allied activities	–	1.6	0.5
	(–)	*(1.6)*	*(–)*
1.3 Non-agricultural activities	–	7.5	8.1
	(–)	*(7.1)*	*(7.1)*
2 Not directly income-generating activities	**5.0**	**17.0**	**29.0**
	(2.7)	*(15.8)*	*(22.0)*
2.1 Housing	–	7.6	9.7
	(–)	*(7.2)*	*(7.8)*
2.2 Others	5.0	9.4	20.7
	(2.7)	*(8.6)*	*(14.2)*

Notes: Agricultural loans referred to crop loans. There were no borrowings for meeting investment needs in agriculture.
Figures in brackets indicate the incidence of borrowing from the formal sector.
Source: Survey data.

other forms of expenditure. As needs such as health and education are not purely consumption needs but also have intrinsic value in enhancing the income-generating capacity of a household, these activities have been referred to as "not directly income-generating" activities in Table 13.

In Khakchang, the village with a less active credit market, borrowing for any kind of activity was, of course, muted (Table 13). The incidence of borrowing for production activities was relatively higher in Mainama and was the highest in Muhuripur. Households in Mainama borrowed more for non-agricultural activities, including purchase of commercial vehicles for transport.

In both Mainama and Muhuripur, households met their production credit needs, including in agriculture, mainly from formal sources. As discussed earlier, agricultural production in Tripura, including high-cost commercial crops like rubber, is subsidised by the State government. As a result, the effective cost incurred by cultivators on purchased inputs was estimated to be very low.[29] We also observed a negative impact of the proxy for subsidies to agriculture and rural areas on bank credit growth. This possibly points to demand-side constraints on bank credit growth in the State.

Village-level data also corroborated the demand-side constraints, at least in the context of agricultural credit. Not only was there less demand for agricultural credit in these villages, but the demand was being met by formal sources. However, that is not to say that there were no constraints in the supply of bank credit. These constraints could be seen when the access to formal credit was modelled, pooling data from all three villages.

Determinants of Household Access to Formal Credit: A Mix of Demand- and Supply-side Factors

I attempted a logistic regression to model the access to formal sector with the following dependent variable:

FormalSectorAccess = {1 if a household reported at least one formal sector loan at the time of the survey (commercial bank/credit cooperative/RRB/any other formal source); 0 otherwise}.

Various household-level characteristics as given below were used as explanatory variables:

(a) Basic socio-economic characteristics: (a.1) Land Operated – land operated during the survey year by household 'i'; (a.2) Social Group – social group of household (if SC/ST/Muslim = 1; otherwise = 0); (a.3) Year of Schooling – average years of schooling of all members (above 16 years of age).

(b) Income profile of a household: (b.1) salaried – the presence of salaried members in a household (if any member employed in a salaried job = 1; otherwise = 0); (b.3) Labour Income Share – the share of income

---

[29] Even as regards labour, the cost was less in villages like Khakchang that relied on exchange labour.

received from manual labour as a proportion of total household income during the survey year.

(c) Alternative sources of funds: (c.1) Informal Sector Borrowing Share – the proportion of debt outstanding from informal sector in total debt of a household; (c.2) Cash Subsidy – cash subsidy received from the government as a proportion of total household income during the survey year.[30]

Table 14 *Modelling the access to formal credit, three study villages, Tripura, 2015–16*

Explanatory variable	Dependent variable: FormalSectorAccess (access to formal credit at the time of the survey – 1 if access; 0 if no access)		
	(1)	*(2)*	*(3)*
	Baseline model	Model II: Control for income profiles of households	Model III: Control for alternative sources of funds
LandOperated	0.129***	0.147**	0.148***
	(0.048)	(0.049)	(0.049)
SocialGroup	0.162	−0.023	−0.018
	(0.291)	(0.307)	(0.307)
YearsofSchooling	0.157***	0.117***	0.117***
	(0.040)	(0.045)	(0.045)
Salaried		1.204***	1.206***
		(0.298)	(0.302)
LabourIncomeShare		0.621	0.624
		(0.441)	(0.441)
CashSubsidy			−3.196
			(4.741)
InformalSectorBorrowingShare			−0.527
			(0.860)
Village dummies	Yes	Yes	Yes
Constant	Yes	Yes	Yes
No of observations	357	357	357
P-value (Hosmer-Lemeshowc²)^	0.66	0.73	0.72

Notes: Figures in parentheses are robust standard errors.
***p <0.01, **p<0.05, *p<0.1.
^ gives the p-value for the null hypothesis that the specified model fits the data.
Source: Estimated from village survey data.

---

[30] Salaried jobs included all government and private sector services jobs.

The village-specific factors were controlled through village dummies.[31]

The results showed that land and the presence of salaried jobs were significant determinants of household access to formal credit (Table 14). Given the role of security in obtaining formal sector credit, these could be broadly regarded as supply-side factors in ensuring access. Average years of schooling had a positive and significant impact on access to formal credit, possibly suggesting the role of education in enhancing financial literacy/ awareness in a household. The share of manual labour income also had a positive impact on access to formal credit. This was perhaps owing to the ability of households to raise credit from banks against their MGNREGA job cards. Interestingly, the probability of a household gaining access to formal credit under the baseline model increased if it belonged to backward social groups; the impact, however, was not statistically significant.

Alternate sources of funds involving cash subsidy and informal credit dampened the access to formal credit. These could be broadly regarded as the demand-side factors to access. However, it could, of course, be argued that the presence of informal sources was by itself a reflection of gaps in the supply of formal credit. The impact of these two factors, however, was not found to be statistically significant.[32]

Concluding Observations

Tripura belongs to the underbanked North-Eastern region of India. Given its regional identity and that it is one of the smallest States in the region, the fact that it has an underdeveloped banking system need not come as a surprise. Using secondary and primary village-level data, this chapter analyses the nature and extent of underdevelopment of banking in Tripura, while making an attempt to analyse why banking in the State remains underdeveloped. It also provides certain insights into the State's banking system and, broadly speaking, the banking system in the North-Eastern region as a whole, which have not been explored till now in the literature.

The major conclusions of the chapter are as follows. First, the average

[31] Two dummies for Khakchang and Muhuripur were introduced in the model. The presence of multi-collinearity was expected to be minimal given the moderate to weak degree (less than (+/−) 0.5) of pair-wise correlation between the variables used in the model. For descriptive statistics of the variables used, see Appendix 5.

[32] However, here only the cash component of subsidies was considered. The kind component of subsidies (including price subsidies) could not be evaluated, and hence, was not factored in the analysis.

branch outreach in Tripura, measured with the help of both demographic and geographical intensity of bank branches, compared favourably with the national average. There were, of course, district-wise variations within the State. Illustratively, the outreach was generally lower in Dhalai (to which Mainama belongs) and North Tripura (to which Khakchang belongs) than in South Tripura (to which Muhuripur village belongs). Also, it could be inferred that the fourth district of West Tripura, although not covered separately in the chapter, was the most well-banked. There were distinct changes in the branch outreach in the State during the three phases of banking policy discussed earlier. It was evident that branch outreach in Tripura improved significantly in the last phase of financial inclusion.

Secondly, the average access to deposit accounts for households in the State was remarkably higher than the national average. This could be attributed to the provision of various welfare scheme payments by the State government through bank accounts of beneficiaries.

Thirdly, notwithstanding the access to bank branches and deposit accounts, the State did not get its due as far as the supply of bank credit was concerned. On average, for every one unit of domestic product generated in the State, the supply of bank credit to the State was much smaller than the national average or even the average for the North-Eastern region. The supply of bank credit was also less than the deposit mobilisation from the State, as evident from its persistently low credit-to-deposit ratio. The average incidence of households reporting a loan from the formal sector in general, and the banking sector in particular, was also minuscule in the State, as shown by the AIDIS data, suggesting low availability of bank credit.

Fourthly, as banks (including RRBs) were the key source of formal credit in the State, low availability of bank credit implied limited supply of formal credit to the State. Although cooperatives were an alternative source of formal credit in other Indian States, their role in credit provision in Tripura, particularly rural Tripura, was relatively small.

Fifthly, the credit system in a State as underserved by banks as Tripura was expected to be under the control of informal sources but the reality appeared to be somewhat different. The average incidence of debt in the State was low for both formal and informal sources. In this regard, Tripura appeared different from other underbanked States such as Bihar. Moneylending was less widespread in the State. This was, in fact, a unique feature of the North-Eastern region as a whole. It distinguished the region from most Indian States (well-banked and underbanked) where moneylending is still widely prevalent. An enquiry into why the incidence of both bank and informal credit was low brought out several interesting facts about the credit system, particularly the rural credit system, of Tripura.

The low availability of bank credit could partly be attributed to a lack of demand for credit from households. This point was well-illustrated by the credit system in Khakchang. In this village, tribal households practised community farming primarily for subsistence on the *patta* forest land allotted to them. The weak nexus of economic activities with cash partly explained why moneylending was less prevalent. Also, the subsidies for health and education provided by the State government illustrated why households sought less credit for needs other than production.

The low availability of bank credit was possibly also a result of supply-side factors. These factors could be discerned in the credit systems of the other two villages, particularly Muhuripur. Households in Muhuripur sought credit from both formal and informal sources for meeting their credit needs. They relied on formal sources to meet their production credit needs, including agriculture. However, for their other needs, they relied heavily on informal sources. While traditional moneylending was less prevalent in Muhuripur, the village witnessed the rise of a new kind of group moneylending at fairly high rates of interest. The thriving informal sector in the village was a reflection of gaps in the supply of formal credit.

The logistic model taking data from all three villages showed availability of land and salaried employment as important determinants of access to formal credit. Given the thrust of conventional banking on securities, these factors could be regarded as supply-side constraints to bank credit in the study villages. The model also showed a negative impact of the proportion of cash subsidy received by a household on its access to formal credit, indicating a role for demand-side factors as well.

In sum, the chapter illustrated the features of underdevelopment of banking in Tripura. It underlined the need for continued efforts to strengthen the outreach of banking in the State, particularly in its underbanked/unbanked pockets. Notwithstanding some demand-side constraints, as a policy measure, steps are also necessary to address the supply-side bottlenecks in the flow of bank credit to the State and the North-Eastern region as a whole. Apart from countervailing the informal sources in whichever guise they operate, the availability of bank credit will also support higher economic growth in the region.

Appendices

Appendix 1 *Descriptive statistics of variables used in the State-level model*

Variable	Mean	SD	Maximum	Minimum
ΔlogBankCredit$_t$	0.131	0.090	0.382	0.022
ΔSNDPpc$_t$	0.085	0.064	0.289	−0.025
BranchIntensity$_t$	16.597	1.500	18.333	12.548
ΔlogCoopCredit$_t$	−0.066	2.525	−3.241	1.020
ΔlogAgriExpenditure$_t$	0.102	0.073	0.220	−0.017
TeleDensity$_t$	15.576	8.629	25.478	2.623
RoadConnectivity$_t$	118.398	56.372	198.577	54.000

Source: Village survey data.

Appendix 2 *Illustration of the State-level model for determining bank credit growth*

ΔlogBankCredit$_t$ =

$\beta_1\Delta$logBankCredit$_{t-1}$ + β_2SNDPpc$_t$ + β_2BranchIntensity$_t$ + $\beta_4\Delta$logCoopCredit$_t$ +

$\beta_1\Delta$logAgriExpenditure$_t$ + β_6Teledensity$_t$ + β_7RoadConnectivity$_t$ + E_t

Appendix 3 *Granger causality between bank credit per capita and SDP per capita, Tripura*

Null hypothesis	F statistic
Bank credit per capita does not Granger cause SDP per capita	3.133[*]
SDP per capita does not Granger cause bank credit per capita	2.846[*]
No. of observations	20
No. of lags	2

Note: [***]$p<0.01$, [**]$p<0.05$, [*]$p<0.1$
Source: Estimated from GoT (2014); *Basic Statistical Returns of Scheduled Commercial Banks in India,* various issues.

Appendix 4 *Illustration of the village-level model for determining access to formal credit*

$FormalSectorAccess_i =$

$C + \beta_1 LandOperated_i + \beta_2 SocialGroup_i + \beta_3 YearofSchooling_i + \beta_4 Salaried_i +$
$\beta_5 LabourIncomeShare_i + \beta_6 CashSabsidy_i + \beta_7 InformalSectorBorrowingShare_i + \eta_i$

where,

β_i = household-specific effect for idiosyncratic characteristics of household 'i'.

Appendix 5 *Descriptive statistics of variables used in the village-level model*

Variable	Mean	SD	Maximum	Minimum
LandOperated	2.07	2.87	18.6	0
YearsofSchooling	6.67	3.30	16	0
CashSubsidy	0.0067	0.045	0.603	−0.105
InformalSectorBorrowingShare	0.07	0.242	1	0
LabourIncomeShare	0.33	0.69	13.89	−3.92

Note: The minimum LabourIncomeShare and CashSubsidy are negative given that the total income of the household itself was negative owing to a crop failure during the survey year. The maximum LabourIncomeShare is more than 1 as the household reported negative crop income in the survey year, which pulled down the total income significantly.
Source: Village survey data.

References

Bansal, Yeshu, and Srinivasan, N. (2009), "Business Correspondents and Facilitators: The Story So Far", *CAB Calling*, no. 33, April–June.

Bhavani, R. V. (2015), "Indebtedness in the West Bengal Study Villages," presentation at the Symposium on Results from Village Surveys, Durgapur.

Chakrabarty, K. C. (2011), "Financial Inclusion and Banks: Issues and Perspectives," Speech at the FICCI UNDP Seminar, New Delhi, October 14.

Chavan, Pallavi (2005a), "Banking Sector Reforms and Growth and Distribution of Rural Banking in India," in V. K. Ramachandran and Madhura Swaminathan (eds.), *Financial Liberalisation and Rural Credit*, Tulika Books, New Delhi.

Chavan, Pallavi (2005b), "How Inclusive are Banks under Financial Liberalisation," *Economic and Political Weekly*, vol. 40, no. 43, October 22–28.

Chavan, Pallavi (2012a), "Debt of Rural Households in India: A Note on the All-India Debt and Investment Survey," *Review of Agrarian Studies*, vol. 2, no. 1.

Chavan, Pallavi (2012b), "A Study of Rural Credit in Maharashtra: The Resurvey of a Village from Western Maharashtra," Ph.D. thesis submitted to the University of Calcutta, Kolkata.

Chavan, Pallavi (2016), "Inclusion of Small Borrowers by Indian Banks: An Analysis Based on Supply and Demand-Side Indicators," RBI Occasional Papers, vols. 35 and 36, nos. 1 and 2, Mumbai.

Chavan, Pallavi (2017), "Public Banks and Financial Intermediation in India: The Phases of Nationalisation, Liberalisation, and Inclusion," in Christoph Scherrer (ed.), *Public Banks in the Age of Financialisation: A Comparative Perspective*, Edward Elgar Publishing Limited, Gloucestershire.

Chavan, Pallavi, and Das, Amalendu (2015), "Contemporary Rural Credit System in India: Some Insights from Village Surveys," paper presented at FAS conference, Kochi.

Chavan, Pallavi, with Sivamurugan, T. (2017), "Formal Credit and Small Farmers in India," in Madhura Swaminathan and Sandipan Baksi (eds.), *How Do Small Farmers Fare? Evidence from Village Studies*, Tulika Books, New Delhi.

Copestake, James (1985), "The Transition to Social Banking in India: Promises and Pitfalls," *Development Policy Review*, no. 6.

Government of India (GoI) (1991), *Final Population Totals – Series 1*, New Delhi.

Government of India (GoI) (2001), *Provisional Population Totals: Rural and Urban Distribution for India and States/Union Territories*, New Delhi.

Government of Tripura (GoT) (2014), *Statistical Abstract – 2014*, Agartala.

Hermes, Niels (1994), "Financial Growth and Economic Development: A Review of Literature," *International Journal of Development Banking*, vol. 12, no. 1.

Hoda, Anwarul, and Terway, Prerna (2015), "Credit Policy for Agriculture in India: An Evaluation," ICRIER Working Paper No. 302, New Delhi.

Kishore, A. (2012), "Business Correspondent Model boosts Financial Inclusion in India," https://www.minneapolisfed.org/publications/community-dividend/business-correspondent-model-boosts-financial-inclusion-in-india.

Levine, Ross, Loayza, Norman, and Beck, Thorsten (2000), "Financial Intermediation and Growth: Causality and Causes," *Journal of Monetary Economics*, vol. 46.

Mohan, Rakesh (2003), "Economic Development of the North East Region: Some Reflections," *RBI Bulletin*, December.

Mohanty, Deepak (2011), "Economic and Financial Developments in the North-Eastern States," www.rbi.org.in.

National Sample Survey Organisation (NSSO) (1998), *Indebtedness of Rural Households as on 30-6-91 – Report no. 420*, New Delhi.

National Sample Survey Organisation (NSSO) (2017), *Households' Indebtedness in India – Report no. 577*, New Delhi.

Rajeev, Meenakshi, and Vani, B.P. (2017), *Financial Access of the Urban Poor in India: A Story of Exclusion*, Springer.

Ramakumar, R., and Chavan, Pallavi (2011), "Changes in the Number of Rural Bank Branches in India, 1991 to 2008," *Review of Agrarian Studies*, vol. 1, no. 1, January–June, pp. 141–48.

Ramakumar, R., and Chavan, Pallavi (2014), "Agricultural Credit in the 2000s: Dissecting the Revival," *Review of Agrarian Studies*, vol. 4, no. 1, February–June.

Reserve Bank of India (RBI) (1991), *Report of the Committee on the Financial System*, Mumbai.

Reserve Bank of India (RBI) (2006), *Report of the Committee on Financial Sector Plan for North Eastern Region*, www.rbi.org.in.

Reserve Bank of India (RBI) (2008), *Report on Currency and Finance – 2006–08*, Mumbai.

Reserve Bank of India (RBI) (2009), *Report of the High Level Committee to Review the Lead Bank Scheme*, Mumbai.

Reserve Bank of India (RBI) (2011), "Bank Loans to MFIs: Priority Sector Status – May 3," www.rbi.org.in.

Reserve Bank of India (RBI) (2015), *Report of the Internal Working Group to Revisit the Existing Priority Sector Lending Guidelines*, Mumbai.

Reserve Bank of India (RBI) (2016a), *RBI Annual Report – 2015–16*, Mumbai.

Reserve Bank of India (RBI) (2016b), *Financial Stability Report – December 2016*, Mumbai.

Sarma, Mandira, and Pais, Jesim (2010), "Financial Inclusion and Development," *Journal of International Development*, vol. 23.

Shetty, S. L. (2005), "Regional, Sectoral and Functional Distribution of Bank Credit," in V. K. Ramachandran and Madhura Swaminathan (eds.), *Financial Liberalisation and Rural Credit*, Tulika Books, New Delhi.

Sivamurugan, T. (2017), "Agricultural Subsidy in Tripura," www.fas.org.

SECTION III

Aspects of Income Generation

11

Income Levels and Variations in Three Villages of Tripura

Tapas Singh Modak and Madhura Swaminathan

Annual income or current income is an important indicator of economic status. However, household income is rarely studied in India because of a lack of data. This chapter draws on estimates of incomes based on three village surveys.

Over the years, the Foundation for Agrarian Studies (FAS), as part of the Project on Agrarian Relation in India (PARI), has developed a detailed methodology for the calculation of incomes. An essential component of this methodology is the collection of detailed and disaggregated data on all sources of income, as the calculation is based on the understanding that income is a derived variable (Bakshi 2017).[1] Specifically, data are collected for twelve main sources of income from each household (Appendix 3). The estimates of income in the PARI village surveys include all cash incomes and incomes in kind (including cash transfers). All incomes are net of costs incurred by the households in the process of production or income generation. Estimates of household income for the three villages of Tripura refer to the agricultural year 2015–16.

A word of caution is in order here. Current income, the subject of this chapter, is likely to have a large transitory component, especially in rural areas where earnings are largely generated in the informal sector. The discussion in this chapter should thus be read alongside chapters 14 and 15 on assets and amenities, to get a picture of long-term economic status.

We begin with some estimates of absolute current income in the three villages, and then examine the composition and distribution of incomes within each village separately (in the second, third and fourth sections).

---

[1] For further details of the methodology, see Bakshi (2010).

The fifth section discusses emerging sources of income and the sixth section is a brief summary.

Levels of Household Incomes and Incidence of Poverty in the Three Villages

We begin with descriptive statistics on annual and per capita household incomes in the three villages (Tables 1 and 2).

Households in Khakchang, a resettled and relatively small tribal village and economy largely dependent on traditional *jhum* cultivation, had the lowest absolute level of incomes among the three villages in the survey year. The mean household income was just over Rs 1 lakh, ranging from Rs 22,000 to Rs 5.29 lakhs. There was one household (an elderly couple) with no reported income.

Annual household incomes were on average higher in Muhuripur (Rs 1.46 lakhs) in South Tripura and Mainama (Rs 1.81 lakhs) in Dhalai. As we show, household incomes were also more diversified in these two villages compared to Khakchang. Mainama was the largest village in terms of population and this was reflected in the aggregate incomes of all residents of the village (Rs 26 crores). Mean incomes can be misleading, and in all three villages the median income was lower than the mean.

Muhuripur was the only village where 11 households (or 1 per cent of total households) incurred negative incomes in the reference year. The negative annual income or deficit was primarily on account of losses incurred in crop cultivation. As discussed in chapter 8, around 35 per cent of cultivator households in Muhuripur made losses in crop production during the survey year on account of low yield and output prices. There were households that made losses in crop production in Khakchang (3 per cent of cultivator households) and Mainama (6 per cent of cultivator households), but income from other sources made up for the losses in crop production in these two villages.

Khakchang was a village with relatively low incomes and also low differentiation. The range of household income here was around Rs 5 lakhs. The range was highest in Muhuripur at around Rs 20 lakhs. In comparison to villages surveyed by PARI in other parts of India, the income range is extremely low. For example, the range of household income was around Rs 64 lakhs in 25 F Gulabewala, Rajasthan, in 2007 and around Rs 17.5 lakhs in Alabujanahalli, Karnataka, in 2009 (see Swaminathan and Rawal 2015; Bakshi and Das 2017).

Table 1 *Descriptive statistics of annual household income, three villages, Tripura, 2015–16, in Rs*

Description	Khakchang	Mainama	Muhuripur
Mean	1,14,434	1,81,113	1,46,489
Median	83,010	1,07,883	93,725
Minimum	22,363*	6,491	−13,781
Maximum	5,29,008	19,23,338	21,14,623
Aggregate for village	6,73,58,235	26,27,81,019	15,43,63,012
Number of households with negative income	0	0	11
Total number of households	589	1451	1054

Note: *Excludes one elderly couple who reported no income, and were dependent on the PDS and handouts from others.
Source: Survey data.

Table 2 *Descriptive statistics of per capita household income, study villages, Tripura, 2015–16, in Rs*

Description	Khakchang	Mainama	Muhuripur
Mean	30,451	50,788	42,281
Median	20,301	26,129	25,572
Minimum	3,727*	2,164	−4,594
Maximum	2,15,400	6,41,113	5,70,497
Coefficient of variation	1.09	1.50	1.39

Note: *One sample elderly couple household with no income and they depended on handouts in the survey year.
Source: Survey data.

Per capita household income was estimated to be Rs 30,886 in Khakchang, Rs 42,281 in Muhuripur, and Rs 50,788 in Mainama in the survey year. Again, median incomes were lower than the mean in each village, and of the order of Rs 20,000 to Rs 25,000. By way of comparison, in Alabujanahalli, the rice-growing village of Karnataka, mean household incomes were Rs 89,968 in 2008–09 and around Rs 1,82,288 in 2015–16.[2]

Another way to make sense of absolute income figures is in relation to poverty. As estimates of poverty in India are based on monthly per capita expenditure, not income, we use a minimum wage-based income

[2] In 2015–16, the national per capita income was Rs 92,293 at current prices (CSO 2016).

Table 3 *Percentage of households in poverty, using minimum wage-based poverty line, study villages, Tripura, 2015–16*

Village	Minimum income (Minimum wage x 300 days)
Khakchang	17.3
Mainama	18.3
Muhuripur	16.0

Source: Survey data.

as a measure of poverty (following Bakshi 2017). A household's minimum income requirement is calculated as the income received from 300 days of employment at the minimum agricultural wage (Rs 150 a day).[3] For 2015–16, this amounts to Rs 45,000 for Tripura. Table 3 shows that the proportion of households with income below this minimum income was 17.3 per cent in Khakchang, 18.3 per cent in Mainama, and 16 per cent in Muhuripur.

These estimates are actually close to the official estimate of rural poverty for Tripura (16.5 per cent in 2011–12) made by the Planning Commission.

Diversification of Household Incomes in the Study Villages

An interesting feature of household incomes in the three villages was the diversification of income sources. To measure income diversification, we have used a ten-fold classification of source of income.

  (i) Crop production (includes income from trees and sericulture)
  (ii) Animal husbandry (includes income from fish cultivation)
  (iii) Agricultural wages
  (iv) Non-agricultural wages
  (v) Salaries
  (vi) Non-agricultural self-employment (business and trade)
  (vii) Rent from agricultural land
(viii) Rent from machinery and other assets
  (ix) Pensions, remittances and transfers
  (x) Other sources.

---

[3] The minimum wage of an agricultural worker was Rs 150 per day in Tripura State as on April 2016.

Table 4 *Distribution of households by number of sources, study villages, 2015–16, in per cent*

Number of sources of income	Khakchang	Mainama	Muhuripur
1 to 2	2	13	4
3 to 4	36	48	41
5 to 6	59	36	50
More than 6	3	3	5
Total	100	100	100
Mean	4.8	4.1	4.6
Maximum	9	7	8

Source: Survey data.

Table 4 shows the distribution of households by number of income sources, and the average and maximum number of income sources per household. In all three villages, on average, a household received incomes from more than four sources. About 90 per cent of the households received income from three to six income sources in the study year.

The high level of income diversification in the study villages indicates that no single source provided adequate income. For example, while 70 per cent of households in the study villages were dependent on crop production, returns from agriculture were not high. The geographical isolation of the State has implications for markets as well as employment in non-agricultural sectors. In this context, as will become clear with our data, it is the State government that has initiated several activities through village panchayats, ranging from implementation of MGNREGS works to public sector employment, and the introduction of new avenues of income generation such as rubber cultivation.

Khakchang, North District

Sources and Composition of Household Incomes

Khakchang is near Jampuii Hills and has a predominantly hilly terrain. The village economy was largely dependent on the primary sector and government-generated non-agricultural wage employment. No household relied on a single source of income. Table 5 shows that about 98 per cent of households in the village received incomes from primary as well as secondary and tertiary sectors. The primary sector – comprising crop

Table 5 *Sources and composition of household incomes, Khakchang, in per cent*

Income source	Per cent of households that received income from specific source	Share of specific source in aggregate household income of residents
Crop production	82.0	18.7
Animal resources	79.0	5.1
Agricultural labour	37.0	3.9
Trees	78.0	3.6
Fisheries	24.0	3.5
Minor forest produce	51.0	5.3
Rental income from agricultural land	2.0	0.1
Primary sector	**99.0**	**40.3**
Non-agricultural casual labour earnings	92.0	15.6
Government salaries	20.0	19.9
Private salaries	6.0	2.7
Business and trade	30.0	11.3
Rental income	2.0	0.9
Secondary and tertiary sectors	**98.0**	**50.5**
Transfer and remittances	61.0	6.2
Any other sources	10.0	3.0
All other source	**67.0**	**9.2**
All households	100.0	100.0

Source: Survey data.

cultivation, animal husbandry, agricultural wages, income from trees, fish cultivation, and collection of minor forest produce – was the major source of income and contributed 40 per cent of aggregate income of all residents of the village. The practice of agriculture in this village was primarily of the traditional *jhum* type, though there was some settled lowland cultivation of rice and vegetables. Income from crop production constituted 18.7 per cent of aggregate household income in the survey year, and animal husbandry contributed another 5 per cent. Pig farming was the principal livestock activity and a regular supplementary source of income for tribal households. The residents of Khakchang went to the nearby forests on a regular basis to collect minor forest produce, such as bamboo shoot, mushroom, vegetables, firewood, and to catch fish from the streams. The collected produce was used for household consumption as well as for sale in a nearby market at Anandabazar in Dasda block. Income from trees, fish cultivation, and collection of minor forest produce provided an income floor to households in Khakchang. The contribution of earnings from agriculture wage to total household income was low (3.9 per cent), as major agricultural operations in *jhum* cultivation were done by family and exchange labour.

The major components of non-agricultural income were non-agricultural wages, government salaries and incomes from petty business. An overwhelming majority of households, 92 per cent, received incomes from non-agricultural wages in the survey year, on account of participation in MGNREGS employment. In addition to the 100 days assured under the regular programme, residents of Khakchang obtained an additional 50 days of MGNREGS employment through the Forest Department, since the population of the village had land under the Forest Rights Act. Earnings from non-agricultural wages constituted 15.6 per cent of total household income.

One-fifth of the households received income from salaried government jobs and this source contributed about 20 per cent of aggregate household incomes. Employment in government included jobs as ICDS workers, school teachers, and in the Tripura Police Service. Around 30 per cent of households were engaged in non-agricultural self-employment activities such as sale of traditional alcohol, handloom (Pachra) weaving and sale, sale of bamboo baskets, running small tea shops, grocery shops, and other petty businesses. These activities contributed about 11 per cent of aggregate income.

Last but not least, more than 60 per cent of households received incomes from social security schemes including old age pensions, widow pensions, scholarships, and remittances. These transfer incomes, however, constituted only 6 per cent of aggregate household incomes.

Distribution of Household Income across Socio-Economic Classes

Table 6 shows the distribution of total household incomes in Khakchang village. A distinctive aspect of this tribal village is that unlike villages surveyed by PARI in other parts of India, the share of income here of the lowest quintile was not minuscule (Bakshi, Das, and Swaminathan 2014). The poorest 20 per cent received 7 per cent of aggregate household incomes, and the next 20 per cent received 11 per cent of aggregate incomes. The poorest quintile had a mean income of Rs 37,955 and that of the richest quintile was Rs 2,53,917, or a ratio of 1:7. The Gini coefficient of per capita

Table 6 *Distribution of annual household income by income quintile, Khakchang, 2015–16, in per cent and Rs*

Income quintile	Share in annual household income	Mean household income
Poorest	7	37,955
2	11	69,623
3	17	91,856
4	23	127,969
Richest	42	253,917
Total	100	114,434

Source: Survey data.

household income in Khakchang village was 0.489, which is not low but not as high as in other PARI villages (Swaminathan and Rawal 2011).[4]

The data in Tables 7 and 8 show a clear variation in incomes across different socio-economic classes. Annual household incomes were lowest for manual worker households, followed by cultivator households dependent on *jhum* cultivation. Next in the income and socio-economic class hierarchy were households falling under cultivator: mixed and cultivator: lowland categories. Incomes were on average highest for those belonging to the class of salaried and business persons, followed by manual workers with diversified income.

Manual worker households were the poorest class in the village. They comprised 8 per cent of all households but received only 5 per cent of household incomes. For households in this class, incomes from agricultural and non-agricultural wage employment constituted as much as 74 per cent of household incomes (Table 9). Earnings from employment through MGNREGS were the primary source of non-agricultural employment in Khakchang. The location of the village, and its hilly terrain and difficult access offered very few opportunities for other forms of employment.

Among the agrarian classes, households relying on only *jhum* cultivation were the worst-off in terms of income. Their share in the population was 41 per cent in the village, while they received only 28 per cent of total household incomes. The average income of *jhum*-dependent households was Rs 79,559, only marginally higher than that of manual

[4] In eight villages of Andhra Pradesh, Uttar Pradesh, Maharashtra, and Rajasthan studied by Swaminathan and Rawal, the Gini coefficient of per capita income was less than 0.5 in only one village.

worker households. The composition of income shows that households engaged in *jhum* derived a large part of their income from activities in the primary sector (67 per cent of total household income). Earnings from non-agricultural wage labour, in particular MGNREGS, contributed 20 per cent of their household income.

Table 7 *Number of households and mean annual income by socio-economic class, Khakchang, 2015–16, in Rs*

Socio-economic class	Number of households	Mean annual income
Manual worker	49	64,459
Cultivator: *jhum*	240	79,559
Cultivator: mixed	60	112,349
Cultivator: lowland	122	103,243
Manual worker with diversified income	53	174,511
Salaried, business, and others	56	292,681
Total	580	116,069

Note: The socio-economic class, cultivator: plantation is combined with Salaried, business, and others as the income from plantation had not yet started in the survey year, and government salary and business were the primary income source of these households.
Source: Survey data.

Table 8 *Distribution of annual household income by socio-economic class, Khakchang, 2015–16, in number and per cent*

Socio economic class	Number of households	Share in total households	Share in total household income
Manual worker	49	8	5
Cultivator: *jhum*	240	41	28
Cultivator: mixed	60	10	10
Cultivator: lowland	122	21	19
Manual worker with diversified income	53	9	14
Salaried, business, and others	56	10	24
Total	580	100	100

Note: The socio-economic class, cultivator: plantation is combined with Salaried, business, and others as the income from plantation had not yet started in the survey year, and government salary and business were the primary income source of these households.
Source: Survey data.

Table 9 *Composition of income by socio-economic class, Khakchang, 2016, in per cent*

Income source	Manual worker	Cultivator: *jhum*	Cultivator: mixed	Cultivator: lowland	Manual worker with diversified income	Salaried, business, and others
Crop production	2	42	45	10	1	1
Animal resources	2	8	7	6	3	3
Agricultural labour	10	3	12	4	4	1
Trees	3	2	3	5	7	2
Fisheries	4	6	2	4	0	4
Minor forest produce	8	6	9	6	5	2
Rental income from agricultural land	0	0	0	0	1	0
Primary sector	**29**	**67**	**78**	**33**	**20**	**12**
Non-agricultural casual labour earnings	64	20	12	19	11	4
Government salaries	0	2	2	12	18	58
Private salaries	0	0	0	5	9	2
Business and trade	5	3	1	16	19	18
Rental income	0	0	6	0	0	1
Secondary and tertiary sectors	**69**	**25**	**21**	**52**	**57**	**84**
Transfer and remittances	2	4	0	8	19	3
Any other sources	0	3	0	7	4	1
All other sources	**2**	**8**	**0**	**14**	**23**	**4**
All households	**100**	**100**	**100**	**100**	**100**	**100**

Note: The socio-economic class, cultivator: plantation is combined with Salaried, business, and others as the income from plantation had not yet started in the survey year, and government salary and business were the primary income source of these households.
Source: Survey data.

The next two agrarian classes in the socio-economic class hierarchy were cultivator: mixed (engaged in both *jhum* and lowland cultivation) and cultivator: lowland (engaged solely in lowland cultivation). Households in these two classes were similar in terms of income, with the population share of each class corresponding roughly to its income share (Table 8). However, there were significant differences in composition of income between the two classes. Cultivator: mixed households obtained their income mainly from the primary sector (78 per cent of total household incomes) (see Table 9). Cultivator: lowland households, however, had diversified their income base, and obtained income from agriculture as well as non-agricultural activities including wages, government salaries, and incomes from business and trades. One reason for this diversification was the easier access to non-agricultural employment opportunities, as the majority of households in this class lived near the main road.

Manual worker households with diversified income were relatively better off than cultivators in income terms with an average annual income of Rs 1,74,511 in 2015–16. Income from activities in the secondary and tertiary sectors accounted for 57 per cent of their total household income. In addition, remittances contributed around one-fifth of aggregate household income.

The socio-economic category comprising households dependent on salaries and incomes from business reported the highest incomes: this class accounted for 10 per cent of total population while it received 24 per cent of aggregate household income of all residents of the village. The mean annual household income for members of this class was Rs 2,92,681. Government salaries contributed 58 per cent of total incomes. Interestingly, almost all households in this socio-economic class had invested in plantations including of rubber, banana, and pineapple. These were new investments and had not started yielding incomes yet. However, they indicate that in the future, this class would not only receive substantially higher incomes but participate in agriculture and primary sector activities as well.

Distribution of Household Incomes across Hamlets ('Para')

A prominent feature of the settlement pattern in Khakchang is the remoteness of certain hamlets or *para*s on account of the geographical terrain. The terrain in Khakchang ranged from sloping hill or *tila* land to central lowlands. To examine the relationship between remoteness and income levels, we classified all hamlets into remote and central hamlets based on the distance from the main road that cut through the village, and characteristics of the terrain of the hamlet. Our data show a significant association between income and remoteness (Table 10). The mean annual income of households in remote hamlets was Rs 83,595, as compared to Rs 1,67,779 among households in central hamlets.

The composition of income also differed across households in central and remote hamlets (Table 11). Households in remote neighbourhoods derived income mainly from agricultural and allied activities, accounting for 66 per cent of aggregate household income. Crop production constituted about 38 per cent, and the rest was from livestock rearing, agricultural wages, trees, fishery, and minor forest collection. The share of government salaries and income from business in aggregate household incomes was very low, at only 4.5 per cent. Non-agricultural wages (from MGNREGS) accounted for 16 per cent of aggregate income.

By contrast, households residing in central hamlets had diversified to non-agricultural activities. Incomes from crop production for these households accounted on average for only 3 per cent of household incomes. Incomes from salaries were one-third of aggregate incomes, and incomes from petty business and non-agricultural wages contributed another 15 and 17 per cent respectively.

We also find that households from two agrarian classes, namely, cultivator: *jhum* and cultivator: mixed, were those living in relatively remote hamlets (Table 12). Households from these two agrarian classes that depended on income from the primary sector and lived in remote locations received lower incomes than households living in more central hamlets.

The latter were able to diversify into non-agricultural activities and obtain higher aggregate incomes.

Table 10 *Average values of annual household income and t test for difference of means, by hamlet, Khakchang, Tripura, 2015–16*

Hamlet	Number of households	Annual income (in Rs)			t value	p value
		Mean	Minimum	Maximum		
Remote	356	83,595	22,363	2,42,160	4.07	0.00016*
Central	224	1,67,779	35,264	5,29,008		

Note: *Refers to statistically significant at 1 per cent level of confidence.
Source: Survey data.

Table 11 *Composition of household income by hamlet, Khakchang, 2016,* in per cent

Income source	Remote	Central
Crop production	38.4	3.1
Animal resources	7.5	3.2
Agricultural labour	5.1	3.0
Sericulture	0.0	0.0
Trees	2.8	4.2
Fisheries	5.4	2.0
Minor forest produce	6.6	4.2
Rental income from agricultural land	0.0	0.2
Primary sector	65.8	20.0
Non-agricultural casual labour earnings	16.8	14.7
Government salaries	4.5	32.2
Private salaries	0.0	4.8
Business and trade	4.0	17.2
Rental income	1.3	0.6
Secondary and tertiary sectors	26.6	69.4
Transfer and remittances	5.0	7.3
Any other sources	2.6	3.3
All other source	**7.6**	**10.5**
All households	100.0	100.0

Source: Survey data.

Table 12 *Distribution and share of households by socio-economic class and hamlet, Khakchang, 2015–16*

Socio-economic class	Central		Remote	
	Number	Share	Number	Share
Manual worker	53	100	0	0
Cultivator: *jhum*	16	7	224	93
Cultivator: mixed	11	18	50	82
Cultivator: lowland	64	52	58	48
Manual worker with diversified income	32	65	17	35
Salaried, business, and others	48	86	8	14

Source: Survey data.

Mainama, Dhalai District

Sources and Composition of Household Incomes

Households in Mainama had diversified sources of income as reflected in the fact that 95 per cent of households received incomes from primary sector activities, and 93 per cent received incomes from activities in the secondary and tertiary sectors (Table 13). Within the primary sector, crop production, animal rearing, and tree produce were three important sources of income. The primary sector, however, contributed only 22 per cent of aggregate income.

In Mainama, agriculture itself is diverse, from cultivation of rubber and banana on upland or *tila* land to rice cultivation on lowlands and vegetable cultivation on the river bed. There was a substantial sector of homestead cultivation as well. An important characteristic of this village is that rubber has been planted on a relatively large extent of *tila* land but has not matured yet. These rubber trees will attain maturity within the next few years, providing an important additional source of income (see the last section of this chapter).

In the primary sector, allied activities included animal rearing and fishing. These were important sources of income, activities that were supported by government intervention. The panchayat in Mainama, for example, distributed crossbred cows, pigs, and chicks to several households, and arranged for free vaccinations from the nearby veterinary hospital. The Fisheries Department and panchayat provided fingerlings, lime, oilcake, and paddy husk to households to encourage fish cultivation. Ponds for fish cultivation were dug under the Mahatma Gandhi National Rural Employment Guarantee Scheme (MGNREGS).

The contribution of non-agricultural sources of income was vital for the household economy of Mainama in the reference year. The secondary and tertiary sectors contributed 71.5 per cent of aggregate household incomes in the survey year, of which the single largest contribution came from government salaries. One-fourth of the households receive income from government jobs, and these salaries constituted 41 per cent of aggregate household income. The share of salaries, government salaries in particular, in aggregate incomes is much higher in Mainama than in any of the other villages surveyed by PARI; this clearly reflects provision of government employment along with progressive implementation of a reservation policy for public sector jobs.

In Mainama too there was high participation in non-agricultural wage labour, mainly MGNREGA, with 68 per cent of households engaged in non-agricultural labour wage employment, and earnings from such labour contributing around 11 per cent of aggregate household incomes. Non-agricultural employment other than under MGNREGS was limited. Households were engaged in varied petty businesses and trades such as handloom weaving, sale of areca nut, wood trading, transport (autorickshaws), carpentry, electrical work, sale of alcohol, etc. Around 30 per cent of households reported some business or trade activity and these incomes accounted for 8 per cent of aggregate household income. Transfers and remittances contributed another 6 per cent of aggregate income in the survey year.

Table 13 *Sources and composition of household incomes, Mainama*

Income source	Per cent of households receiving incomes from specific sources	Share of specific sources in aggregate village income
Crop production	67	7.3
Animal resources	69	4.5
Agricultural labour	34	2.2
Trees	73	2.6
Fisheries	18	3.9
Minor forest produce	8	0.2
Rental income from agricultural land	13	1.4
Primary sector	**95**	**22.1**
Non-agricultural casual labour earnings	68	11.4
Government salaries	25	40.8
Private salaries	3	1.1
Business and trade	30	17.6
Rental income	7	0.6
Secondary and tertiary sectors	**93**	**71.5**
Transfer and remittances	52	6.1
Any other sources	10	0.4
All other sources	**56**	**6.5**
Total	**100**	**100**

Source: Survey data.

Distribution of Household Income across Socio-Economic Classes

Income inequality in Mainama was, of course, more pronounced than in Khakchang. The richest quintile accounted for 50 per cent of total household incomes (Table 14), whereas the poorest quintile accounted for only 4 per cent of total household incomes. The Gini coefficient of per capita household income in Mainama village was 0.563.

As the data in Tables 15 and 16 show, there is a clear relation between location in the socio-economic class hierarchy and level of income.

At the bottom of the hierarchy are manual worker households, followed by those in the category cultivator: sub-marginal. For households in these two classes, mean incomes were around Rs 70,000 and Rs 1.1 lakhs respectively. Manual worker households accounted for 13 per cent of all households but their share of household incomes was only 5 per cent. Similarly, cultivator: sub-marginal households accounted for 30 per cent of households but only 19 per cent of total household incomes. The main source of income for Manual labour households was wage earnings, accounting for 90 per cent of household incomes (Table 17). Further, non-agricultural earnings from casual labour were the predominant source of wage earnings, contributing around 77 per cent of household incomes. In the case of cultivator: sub-marginal households, there were multiple sources of income, with income from crop production accounting for less than 10 per cent of aggregate income. These households too were largely dependent on non-agricultural sources of income, including non-agricultural wages, salaries, and income from petty businesses.

As Table 16 indicates, for the three lowest classes in the socio-economic hierarchy, the share of income was lower than the share of population.

Table 14 *Distribution of annual household income and per capita household income, by income quintile, Mainama, 2015–16,* in per cent

Income quintile	Share in annual household income	Mean annual income
Poorest	4	37,594
2	9	81,302
3	12	116,587
4	25	197,414
Richest	50	497,205
Total	100	181,113

Source: Survey data.

Table 15 *Mean annual household income by socio-economic class, Mainama, 2015–16*

Socio-economic class	Number of households	Mean annual income
Manual worker	187	75,888
Manual worker with diversified income	110	164,186
Cultivator: sub-marginal	438	111,712
Cultivator: marginal	321	204,278
Cultivator: small	162	246,000
Cultivator: medium	63	283,457
Salaried, business, and others	169	344,084
All	1450	181,119

Source: Survey data.

Table 16 *Distribution of annual household income by socio-economic class, Mainama, 2015–16*

Socio-economic class	Number of households	Share in total households	Share in total income
Manual worker	187	13	5
Manual worker with diversified income	110	8	7
Cultivator: sub-marginal	438	30	19
Cultivator: marginal	321	22	25
Cultivator: small	162	11	15
Cultivator: medium	63	4	7
Salaried, business, and others	169	12	22
Total	1450	100	100

Source: Survey data.

The situation was the opposite for the remaining classes, for whom the income share was higher than the population share. Among households with operational holdings, cultivator: sub-marginal households were distinctly similar to wage labour households.

In terms of absolute incomes, mean incomes were of the same order of magnitude for the next two agrarian classes (that is, cultivator: marginal and cultivator: small households). However, income from crop production accounted for only one-third of household incomes for households in these two classes, with the rest coming from secondary and tertiary sector activities. The average picture hides some important variations.

Table 17 *Composition of income by socio-economic class, Mainama, 2015–16, in per cent*

Income source	Manual worker	Manual worker with diversified income	Cultivator: sub-marginal	Cultivator: marginal	Cultivator: small	Cultivator: medium	Salaried, business, and others
Crop production	0.1	0.2	7.6	9.3	16.9	13.4	0.1
Animal resources	2.8	3.4	8.0	5.8	5.4	2.4	0.7
Agricultural labour	10.4	2.7	3.9	2.2	1.2	0.2	0.0
Sericulture	0.0	0.0	0.0	0.0	0.0	0.0	0.0
Trees	2.3	2.4	3.4	2.1	3.0	3.5	1.8
Fisheries	0.5	0.1	0.9	12.3	2.0	2.9	0.7
Minor forest produce	0.2	0.1	0.3	0.1	0.0	0.2	0.3
Rental income from agricultural land	1.0	0.0	0.6	1.4	0.7	6.0	1.6
Primary sector	**17.2**	**9.0**	**24.8**	**33.2**	**29.3**	**28.7**	**5.1**
Non-agricultural casual labour earnings	77.4	12.3	19.2	6.9	4.3	6.1	0.0
Government salaries	0.0	27.6	31.8	35.7	29.9	42.6	75.3
Private salaries	0.0	0.0	2.3	1.1	2.7	0.3	0.0
Business and trade	2.1	36.5	13.2	15.4	30.4	15.7	13.4
Rental income	0.0	0.2	0.3	1.4	0.9	0.0	0.2
Secondary and tertiary sectors	**79.5**	**76.7**	**66.7**	**60.4**	**68.2**	**64.7**	**88.9**
Transfer and remittances	3.1	14.0	7.9	6.0	2.3	6.6	5.5
Any other sources	0.1	0.3	0.6	0.3	0.2	0.0	0.5
All other sources	**3.2**	**14.3**	**8.5**	**6.3**	**2.5**	**6.6**	**6.0**
All households	**100.0**	**100.0**	**100.0**	**100.0**	**100.0**	**100.0**	**100.0**

Source: Survey data

The household with the highest estimated income in the survey year belonged to the class of cultivator: small. Its main source of income was from fisheries, which brought in about Rs 14 lakhs during the survey year. This household owned three big-size ponds, engaged in scientific fish cultivation, and sold fingerlings to government agencies and individual pond owners.

Thirdly, the two distinctly better-off socio-economic classes comprised cultivator: medium households, and households dependent on salaried employment and business. The latter accounted for 12 per cent of all households and 22 per cent of aggregate income. Salaries from government jobs contributed as much as 75 per cent of household incomes. To put it differently, access to good public sector jobs made a huge difference to the level (and stability) of household incomes.

Another feature of households belonging to these two classes is their expansion into rubber plantations, an activity that has not yet yielded incomes but is likely to make a significant contribution in the coming years (see below).

Incomes of Rubber Cultivators

At the time of our survey, incomes from crop production in Mainama, as discussed above, constituted a small share of total incomes. This is likely to change in the future. New or young rubber plantations occupied about two-thirds of the total operated land in the village. These plantation lands have not yet begun to yield an income. In the future, as these trees mature, income from rubber will contribute significantly to household income. To get an idea of these future incomes, we report here the extent of land under rubber trees across socio-economic classes.

First, in our survey data, we find no significant difference in mean household incomes as between cultivator households with incomes from rubber and those yet to receive incomes from rubber trees (Table 18). We argue, however, that disparities are likely to grow, based on the current composition of household incomes (Table 19). For households that received income from rubber trees in the survey year, these incomes accounted for a major (55 per cent) share of household income. A majority (75 per cent) of these households had received plantation land and rubber trees under various State government initiatives. By contrast, households with rubber cultivation but no income yet depended on salaries and other incomes. These households had invested in rubber trees out of their own savings. To put it differently, as discussed in chapter 13, households with

Table 18 *Mean household income, rubber cultivator households, Mainama*

Size category of household operational landholdings	Households that received income from rubber cultivation in the survey year		Households that owned rubber plantation, but production had not started in the survey year		t test	p value
	Number of households	Mean household income	Number of households	Mean household income		
>0<=1	18	88,542	33	147,351	0.856	0.427
>1<=5	63	175,531	186	191,076	0.306	0.763
>5	7	268,596	44	283,498	–	–

Note: The t test showed no difference in mean incomes between households that had received income from rubber and those that had not yet received income from rubber.
Source: Survey data.

Table 19 *Composition of incomes, rubber cultivators, Mainama,* in per cent

Income source	>0<=1		>1 <=5		>5	
	Received income	Production yet not started	Received income	Production yet not started	Received income	Production yet not started
Crop production	55	6	24	6	89	7
Income from rubber trees	55	0	21	0	88	0
Other primary sector incomes	24	14	10	12	2	22
Salary	0	47	24	54	0	39
Other secondary and tertiary sector incomes	12	24	7	24	0	25
All other sources	9	10	15	3	9	8
Total	100	100	100	100	100	100

Source: Survey data.

good salaried employment had begun to invest in rubber plantations a few years ago, and this will become a new source of income in future. The socio-economic class with salaried employment will not only remain the group with highest incomes but move ahead of other classes in absolute terms as well.

Distribution of Household Incomes across Hamlets ('Para')

Mainama is a village with a significant Scheduled Tribe (ST) population and one that is spread across several hamlets. Unlike Khakchang, in Mainama, we did not find any significant difference in income as between

Table 20 *Average value of annual household income by hamlet, Mainama, Tripura, 2015–16*

Hamlet	Number of households	Annual household income (in Rs)			t value	p value
		Mean	Minimum	Maximum		
Remote	630	173852	8397	1009327	0.646	0.5185
Central	821	186697	6491	1923338		

Source: Survey data.

Table 21 *Composition of household income by hamlet, Mainama, 2016,* in per cent

Income source	Remote	Central
Crop production	10.2	5.2
Animal resources	5.1	4.0
Agricultural labour	2.9	1.7
Trees	2.5	2.6
Fisheries	2.1	5.2
Minor forest produce	0.2	0.2
Rental income from agricultural land	1.3	1.4
Primary sector	**24.4**	**20.3**
Non-agricultural casual labour earnings	10.3	12.2
Government salaries	42.9	39.3
Private salaries	2.0	0.5
Business and trade	16.6	18.3
Rental income	0.4	0.7
Secondary and tertiary sectors	**72.2**	**71.0**
Transfer and remittances	3.0	8.3
Any other sources	0.3	0.4
All other sources	**3.4**	**8.7**
All households	**100.0**	**100.0**

Source: Survey data.

households residing in remote and central hamlets (Table 20). What is interesting is the similarity in composition of income for households across hamlets, and we argue that State intervention has played a role in providing opportunities for households in remote hamlets, thus bridging the gap between central and remote hamlets. To take an example, households in remote hamlets mostly occupy and operate *tila* and forest land, which is not as productive as lowland for crop cultivation. The State government undertook a massive plantation drive of rubber trees on government *tila* and forest land through the Tripura Rehabilitation and Plantation Corporation (TRPC), and distributed this land to households in the village. Subsequently, as observed in our survey, many households that had obtained such land began to receive regular incomes from the rubber trees. As the trees attain maturity, incomes will rise further for households in the remote hamlets.

Secondly, Table 21 shows that the contribution of government salaries to household incomes was higher for households residing in remote hamlets (43 per cent) than those residing in central hamlets (39 per cent). There is reservation for ST persons in public sector employment, and as the proportion of ST persons is higher in remote hamlets than in central hamlets, this may reflect better access to government jobs.

Muhuripur, South Tripura District

Sources and Composition of Household Incomes

At our first visit, Muhuripur appeared to be a largely agriculture-dependent economy. A detailed analysis of incomes, however, indicates diversification of incomes.

Almost all households (98 per cent) in Muhuripur obtained some income from the primary sector, which accounted for 21 per cent of aggregate income (Table 22). Agricultural incomes included income from crop production, animal rearing, agricultural labour, fish cultivation, trees, and rental incomes from agricultural land. Agriculture in this village comprised primarily lowland paddy and vegetable cultivation. Rubber trees were planted in a scattered way on *tila* land (which was limited in extent). Income from crop production, however, accounted for only 6.3 per cent of total household incomes in the survey year. Low returns from crop cultivation, and the fact that a large section of cultivator households incurred losses in crop production due to lack of irrigation water in the

Table 22 *Sources and composition of household incomes, Muhuripur, 2015–16*

Income source	Per cent of households that received incomes from specific sources	Share of specific sources in aggregate village income
Crop production	69	6.3
Animal resources	83	3.3
Agricultural labour	28	3
Sericulture	2	0.1
Trees	73	3.5
Fisheries	25	2.7
Minor forest produce	1	0.1
Rental income from agricultural land	23	1.8
Primary sector	**98**	**20.8**
Non-agricultural casual labour earnings	83	16.2
Government salaries	15	22.4
Private salaries	3	1.3
Business and trade	36	21.4
Rental income	3	0.5
Secondary and tertiary sectors	**96**	**61.8**
Transfer and remittances	63	16.2
Any other sources	27	1.2
All other sources	**71**	**17.4**
All households	**100**	**100.0**

Source: Survey data.

reference period, is an important reason for this. Earnings from animal rearing, agricultural labour, trees, and fish cultivation each contributed about 3 per cent of aggregate household income.

At the same time, almost all (96 per cent) households also received incomes from secondary and tertiary sector activities in the survey year (Table 22), which together accounted for 62 per cent of aggregate household income. Participation in non-agricultural wage employment was high in Muhuripur: 83 per cent of households worked at non-agricultural labour, and these earnings contributed 16 per cent of household incomes. In addition to MGNREGS work, there were workers in construction and in other sectors like transport (auto drivers). Around 15 per cent of households received incomes from government salaried jobs; this constituted more than one-fifth of aggregate income (22 per cent). Specifically, residents of Muhuripur were employed as schoolteachers, in the Tripura police service, in administration (as group D employees), in health centres (as ASHA workers), etc. Income from business and trade was another important source of non-agricultural incomes. There was a small daily market in the village, and many households were engaged in petty businesses such as grocery stores, tea shops, and vegetable-vending. About 36 per cent of households were engaged in such activities, and incomes from petty business contributed 21 per cent of household incomes.

Lastly, 63 per cent of households received income from transfers and remittances, and this constituted 16 per cent of aggregate household incomes.[5] This included government pensions, as well as monetary assistance under different social security schemes such as old age pensions, widow pensions, and scholarships for students.

Distribution of Household Incomes across Socio-Economic Classes

The distribution of household incomes in Muhuripur shows that the richest 20 per cent of households received 51 per cent of total household income. The mean household income of the top quintile, however, was only Rs 3,76,264 in 2015–16 (which is low compared to the other villages we have studied). The poorest quintile accounted for only 5 per cent of total household income with a mean annual household income of Rs 36,279. The Gini coefficient of per capita household income in Muhuripur was 0.506.

The story of income distribution becomes clearer when we group households by socio-economic class (Tables 24 and 25).

Manual worker households were the poorest income group in terms of average household income (Rs 63,775 in 2015–16). The class of manual workers constituted 10 per cent of all households and received only 4 per cent of total village income. The major sources of income for members of this class were non-agricultural wages (71 per cent of total income) and agricultural wages (14 per cent of total income) (Table 24). In a year with a good agricultural harvest, this ratio may be different.

Secondly, the average income was similar for two socio-economic classes, manual worker with diversified income and cultivator: sub-marginal households. The share of income accruing to these two classes

---

[5] In one household, a member employed by the Indian Navy remitted around Rs 18.5 lakh during the survey year. This figure has pushed up the share of transfer and remittances in total household income in Muhuripur.

Table 23 *Distribution of annual household income and per capita household income, by income quintile, Muhuripur, 2015–16, in per cent*

Income quintile	Share in annual household income	Mean household income
Poorest	5	36,279
2	11	76,820
3	13	95,531
4	21	149,799
Richest	51	376,264
Total	100	146,489

Source: Survey data.

Table 24 *Mean and median annual household income by socio-economic class, Muhuripur, 2015–16*

Socio-economic class	Number of households	Mean household income
Manual worker	108	63775
Manual worker with diversified income	159	109238
Cultivator: sub-marginal	469	102287
Cultivator: marginal	182	174565
Cultivator: small	49	273122
Salaried, business, and others	87	423448
Total	1054	146489

Source: Survey data.

Table 25 *Distribution of total household income by socio-economic class, Muhuripur, 2015–16*

Socio-economic class	Number of households	Share in total household	Share in annual income
Manual worker	108	10	4
Manual worker with diversified income	159	15	11
Cultivator: Sub-marginal	469	44	31
Cultivator: Marginal	182	17	21
Cultivator: Small	49	5	9
Salaried, business, and others	87	8	24
Total	1054	100	100

Source: Survey data.

Table 26 *Composition of income by socio-economic class, Muhuripur, 2016, in per cent*

Income source	Manual worker	Manual worker with diversified income	Cultivator: sub-marginal	Cultivator: marginal	Cultivator: small	Salaried, business, and others
Crop production	0.1	0.4	6.3	11.4	22.8	0.0
Animal resources	2.9	2.9	5.0	3.8	4.1	0.5
Agricultural labour	14.2	1.5	4.8	3.1	1.3	0.0
Sericulture	0.0	0.0	0.1	0.2	0.0	0.0
Trees	1.9	2.3	4.1	4.6	6.9	1.5
Fisheries	1.0	1.1	3.1	2.5	9.7	1.0
Minor forest produce	0.6	0.0	0.0	0.0	0.4	0.0
Rental income from agricultural land	0.2	2.1	1.9	1.0	1.1	2.6
Primary sector	**21.0**	**10.3**	**25.3**	**26.6**	**46.3**	**5.6**
Non-agricultural casual labour earnings	71.2	16.1	23.5	14.1	11.1	0.0
Government salaries	2.0	4.1	21.2	18.5	3.8	46.5
Private salaries	0.0	0.3	0.5	0.7	0.7	3.8
Business and trade	2.9	38.8	14.6	32.1	30.7	13.1
Rental income	0.0	0.5	0.2	0.0	0.0	1.7
Secondary and tertiary sectors	**76.1**	**59.7**	**60.0**	**65.5**	**46.3**	**65.0**
Transfer and remittances	2.8	28.1	12.6	7.1	7.2	29.0
Any other sources	0.2	1.9	2.1	0.9	0.3	0.4
All other sources	**3.0**	**30.0**	**14.7**	**8.0**	**7.4**	**29.4**
All households	**100.0**	**100.0**	**100.0**	**100.0**	**100.0**	**100.0**

Source: Survey data.

was less than their population share. For the former, a major source of incomes was petty business (38.8 per cent), followed by pensions and remittances (28.1 per cent), and non-agricultural wages (16.1 per cent). For the latter, the category cultivator: sub-marginal, only 6 per cent of incomes came from crop production. Two-fifths of households in this class made losses from agriculture in the survey year. Incomes were diversified and included non-agricultural wages, government salaries, income from petty businesses, and pension and remittances.

Thirdly, the mean household income for the agrarian class cultivator: marginal was Rs 1,74,565 in 2015–16. The contribution of crop production was 11.4 per cent and aggregate incomes from the primary sector were 26.6 per cent of household incomes. Other sources of income were petty business (32.1 per cent), government salaries (18.5 per cent), and non-agricultural wages (18.1 per cent).

Fourthly, the largest landholding class in the village, cultivator: small households, received the highest incomes among all agrarian classes in the reference year. A substantial share of incomes was from the primary sector (46.3 per cent), including 22.8 per cent from crop production. These households received incomes from rubber, vegetable cultivation, fisheries (9.7 per cent), trees (6.9 per cent), and animal resources (4.1 per cent).

Fifthly, households falling under the socio-economic class of salaried, business, and others had the highest levels of household income in the village (Rs 4,23,448). Salaries from government jobs (46.5 per cent of aggregate incomes) were an important reason for the relatively high incomes. Other sources of income were pensions and remittances (29 per cent), and businesses (13.1 per cent).

Although the economy of Muhuripur village is largely agrarian, the low returns and even losses from crop production in the survey year reduced the share of crop incomes in total incomes. All cultivator households had diversified into other activities. Access to non-agricultural employment, MGNREGA work in particular, along with access to government jobs and a local market, helped cultivator households.

Some Emerging Sources of Income in the Study Villages

As already mentioned, households in all three villages, Mainama and Muhuripur in particular, had diversified their income base, and the policies of the State government facilitated this process of diversification. Below, we briefly discuss some of the new and emerging sources of income.

Rubber Cultivation on Upland

In Mainama, an initiative to convert *tila* land to commercially viable rubber plantations was undertaken by the State government. Though the first rubber trees were planted in 1988, the total extent of rubber plantations was low till 2005. After 2005, the Tripura Rehabilitation and Plantation Corporation (TRPC) facilitated the growth of rubber plantations in the village. Ninety-five per cent of existing rubber plantations were planted after 2005. At present, rubber plantations occupy about 55 per cent of total net sown area in the village. Institutional support from TRPC includes the provision of rubber saplings, fertilizers, plant protection, and labour charges for clearing the land till the rubber trees attain maturity. A TRPC latex collection centre was established in the village in 2007 to collect latex directly from the cultivators.

The composition of household income of households cultivating rubber shows that income from rubber accounted for a significant proportion of total household income. The average annual income from rubber was Rs 65,000, constituting about 53.5 per cent of total household income for these households. Rubber cultivation has also increased family labour use, employment in harvesting operations, and processing units. Over the next few years, a significant proportion of rubber plantations will start production and more households are expected to receive income from this sector. This will substantially increase household incomes in future.

Rubber cultivation in South district began in 1990 and in Muhuripur in 1994, but gathered pace from 2007. At present, small and medium farmers in Muhuripur are engaged in rubber cultivation, which provides regular income to farming households. Thirty per cent of households in the village have planted rubber over the years. In Muhuripur, the highest income drawn by a household from rubber cultivation was Rs 2,50,000, which comprised 45 per cent of total household income. Income from rubber constituted 10 per cent of the total household income of rubber-cultivating households. This proportion is expected to substantially increase in the future. New cultivators have planted rubber on *tila* land, in expectation of higher profits.

Vegetable Cultivation

The lowlands in the study villages are under paddy and vegetables. Vegetables are mostly grown in the river bed and involve commercial production. Several households cultivated vegetables on homestead land.

Some of the commercially important vegetable crops are chilli, spine gourd, pointed gourd, brinjal, radish, bottle gourd, snake gourd, broad beans, tomato, and pumpkin. Cultivators received institutional support from the State in the form of subsidised seeds and fertilizers for vegetable cultivation. If transport facilities are developed (and this, of course, requires large-scale public investment to connect with the "mainland"), Tripura can become a major centre for fresh vegetable production.

Potato

About 20 per cent of farmers in Muhuripur cultivated potato. Cultivators used True Potato Seed (TPS), as well as Jyoti and Chandramukhi varieties. TPS was commercially cultivated in Muhuripur and Mainama as its production cost was low and it gave higher returns. Government support was available in the form of inputs at subsided rates and extension services. The government also procured potato directly from farmers. Jyoti and Chandramukhi were mainly cultivated for household consumption.

Sericulture

Sericulture involves the cultivation of mulberry and silkworm-rearing for the production of silk. This was a new source of income for 10 households in Muhuripur and was undertaken by households with less than 2.5 acres of land. The practice of sericulture started in 2013–14 and is fully supported by the State government. The production cycle is 60 days and harvesting is carried out four times a year.

Fishery

The fisheries sector is an important source of income for about 25 per cent of households in the study villages. The composition of primary sector income shows that income from fish cultivation constituted about 15 per cent of total primary sector income in the study villages. It provides a regular source of income and nutrition for cultivating households. Households engaged in fisheries use fish for their own consumption as well as for sale. Ponds are dug either on plain land or on homestead land. Several households reported that ponds were dug under MGNREGS. The total area under ponds was 42 hectares in Muhuripur. The average annual income from fish cultivation was about Rs 13,800. The highest income was Rs 2,00,000 for one household in Muhuripur. Income from fish cultivation constituted about 18 per cent of total primary sector income in Mainama. The panchayat provided support for fish cultivation in the form of fingerlings, feed, and lime, all free of cost. In addition, some households received high incomes from commercial cultivation of fingerlings. For example, the highest income from fingerling cultivation by a household was approximately Rs 14,00,000 – comprising 72 per cent of its total annual household income. Fish cultivation can be an emerging source of income for households if extension and marketing services are improved.

Poultry

Poultry farming is an emerging source of income for many households in Muhuripur and especially Mainama. The initial investment is partially or fully supported by the State government. Poultry farming involves six cycles annually, with a growing cycle of 40 days. Broiler units provide regular income to households. The size of the units varies between 200 and 800 chicks. The selling price of a unit is Rs 100. Each chick costs Rs 35. At the end of the growth period of 40 days, a chick weighs around 2 kilograms. Net income from poultry ranges between Rs 40,000 and Rs 1,00,000, depending on the size of the unit. Households are increasing the size of farms in expectation of greater profitability and regular income.

Government Salaried Jobs

The sources and composition of household income in Mainama show that about 25 per cent of households receive incomes from government jobs. The contribution of government salary to annual household income was the highest in Mainama, at about 40 per cent. The types of government salaried jobs included teaching in primary and higher secondary schools, group D employment in government offices, Integrated Child Development Scheme (ICDS) workers, nursing staff, and employment in the Tripura police force. The progressive implementation of a reservation policy for government salaried jobs has substantially increased household incomes in Mainama.

Three Villages: A Summary

Households in Khakchang, a remote tribal village, had the lowest mean incomes (Rs 1,14,434) among the three villages. In Khakchang, households that depended primarily on *jhum* cultivation had less income than others. In 2015–16, the mean annual income of *jhum*-dependent households was Rs 79,559. There was also a clear geographical factor, with households in remote hamlets reporting significantly lower incomes than those in more central hamlets, closer to the main road. For example, the mean annual income of households in remote hamlets was Rs 83,595, while it was Rs 1,67,779 among households in central hamlets.

Mainama is a large village, and households here had higher and more diversified incomes than in the other two villages. Cultivation was of different types, including on lowland and upland. There was clearer socio-economic differentiation in this village. Households with access to government salaries had the highest incomes, followed by cultivators with more than 5 acres of operational land. Inequality in incomes across households was higher than in Khakchang. The value of Gini coefficient, a commonly used indicator of inequality, of the distribution of per capita income in Mainama village was 0.563, and in Khakchang it was 0.483. There are new sources of future incomes including from rubber.

Our third village, Muhuripur, is a lowland village practising paddy and vegetable cultivation. Paddy cultivation, however, was not very remunerative, and as a result, incomes from crop production were modest. About 35 per cent of cultivator households incurred negative incomes from crop production during the survey year on account of low yields and output prices. Salaries and returns from a range of petty businesses were important sources of income. In all villages, access to non-agricultural employment through MGNREGS made a difference to aggregate incomes.

It is evident that there is substantial government support for income-generating activities such as provision of agricultural inputs and extension, besides proper implementation of central government schemes such as MGNREGS, old age and widow pensions.

APPENDIX 1

Definition of Household Income

Incomes of households in the survey villages were estimated separately for the following sources. The survey used detailed modules on incomes from each of the following sources.

1. Crop production
2. Animal resources
3. Wage labour
    (i) Agricultural labour (casual)
    (ii) Agricultural labour (long-term)
    (iii) Non-agricultural labour (casual)
    (iv) Non-agricultural labour (monthly/long term)
4. Salaried jobs
    (i) Government salaried jobs
    (ii) Other salaried jobs
5. Business and trade
6. Moneylending
7. Income from savings in financial institutions and equity
8. Pensions and scholarships
9. Remittances and gifts
10. Rental income
    (i) Rental income from agricultural land
    (ii) Rental income from machinery
    (iii) Rental income from other assets
11. Artisanal work and work at traditional caste calling
12. Any other sources

The definition of "costs of cultivation" closely followed the definition of the "Cost A2" category used under the Comprehensive Scheme for Studying Cost of Cultivation/Production of Principal Crops (CCPC), of the Commission of Agricultural Cost and Prices (CACP), India. It includes the cost of all material inputs (purchased and home-produced), the cost of hired labour, rental payments, the imputed value of interest on working capital, and depreciation of owned fixed capital other than land. It excludes cost of family labour and rental value of owned land.

Data are collected at various levels of disaggregation to assist in more accurate reporting and better recall from respondents. For example, crop incomes and costs of production are reported and calculated for each crop and crop-mix during the agricultural year. Livestock incomes are calculated for each type of livestock. Similarly, for wage labour income in agriculture, each worker was asked questions on the number of days of employment and on earnings (in cash, kind, or both) for each season, crop, and crop operation.

References

Bakshi, Aparajita (2010), "Rural Household Incomes," PhD thesis submitted to the Department of Economics, University of Calcutta, Kolkata.

Bakshi, Aparajita, and Das, Arindam (2017), "Household Incomes in the Three Study Villages," in Madhura Swaminathan and Arindam Das (eds.), *Socio-Economic Surveys of Three Villages in Karnataka: A Study of Agrarian Relations*, Tulika Books, New Delhi

Bakshi, Aparajita, Das, Arindam, and Swaminathan, Madhura (2014), "Household Incomes in Rural India: Results from PARI Village Studies," paper presented at the Tenth Annual Conference, Foundation for Agrarian Studies, Kochi, January 9–12, 2014.

Bakshi, Aparajita, with Modak, Tapas Singh (2017), "Incomes of Small Farmer Households," in Madhura Swaminathan and Sandipan Baksi (eds.), *How Do Small Farmers Fare? Evidence from Village Studies*, Tulika Books, New Delhi.

Swaminathan, Madhura, and Rawal, Vikas (2011), "Is India Really a Country of Low Income-Inequality? Observations from Eight Villages," *Review of Agrarian Studies*, vol. 1, no. 1, available at http://www.ras.org.in/is_india_really_a_country_of_low_income_inequality_observations_from_eight_villages

Swaminathan, Madhura, and Rawal, Vikas (eds.) (2015), *Socio-Economic Surveys of Two Villages in Rajasthan: A Study of Agrarian Relations*, Tulika Books, New Delhi.

12

Homestead Economy of Tripura[*]

Surjit Vikraman

The State of Tripura is primarily an agrarian economy with more than 33 per cent of GDP coming from agriculture and nearly 75 per cent of the population dependent on agriculture for their livelihood. Being a landlocked State with highly undulating topography and a very small share of the geographical area that can be used for cultivation (27 per cent of net sown area), the agricultural production units are predominantly small and marginal holdings with high cropping intensity and diversity. The geographical and agro-ecological specificities and demographic characteristics of the State have resulted in a predominance of homestead farming systems, which play a major role in ensuring food and nutritional security of households in Tripura.

This chapter on the nature and characteristics of homestead production systems and their contribution to household economies is based on a detailed study of three villages representing three distinct agricultural production systems in three different districts of the State of Tripura. Mainama village, in Manu block of Chailengta tehsil in Dhalai district, is situated on the banks of the Manu river, and has a mix of lowland and (*tila*) upland. Paddy is grown on the lowlands, rubber on the hill slopes, and vegetables on the river bank. Homestead cultivation is prominent in this village. Agriculture in Khakchang, which is in Dasda block of Anand Bazar tehsil in North district, is characterised by diverse forms of production systems, ranging from slash-and-burn shifting cultivation, varied forms of plantation agriculture, lowland rice cultivation, and homestead cultivation. It also has the most diverse cropping pattern of the three villages, with

[*] The author thanks Ritam Dutta for providing research assistance and inputs for this chapter.

more than 30 crops grown together in *jhum* fields. Muhuripur belongs to Muhuripur tehsil of Julaibari block in South district. It is a predominantly rice-growing lowland village, but a wide variety of vegetables are also grown. Mulberry is cultivated here to support sericulture. Rubber is grown on the slopes. Our discussion focuses on the cropping patterns adopted in homesteads, the input use pattern, contribution to the household economy (both in terms of consumption and value of production), and variations in homestead production across districts.

Homestead Land in the Study Villages

Only a few studies have identified and analysed the structure, composition, and role of homestead land in agricultural production systems in India. A few scientific studies focusing on technical aspects of homestead land (crop diversity and components that support agro-forestry systems) were carried out in the 1980s (studies under the USAID project, cited in John 2014). Most of these studies fall short of providing a socio-economic assessment of homestead production systems, particularly its contribution to household food and nutritional security. Among the noted scholarly attempts to understand and analyse the socio-economic importance of homestead land are John and Nair (1999), Ramakumar (2004), and John (2014).

In this study, the definition of homestead land we have adopted is in line with the definition adopted by the NSSO. A homestead is the dwelling house of a household, together with the courtyard, compound, garden, out-house, place of worship, family graveyard, guest house, shop, workshop and offices for running household enterprises, tanks, wells, latrines, drains, and boundary walls annexed to the dwelling house. All land coming under homestead is defined as homestead land. Homestead may constitute only a part of a plot. Sometimes gardens, orchards or plantations, though adjacent to the homestead and lying within the boundary walls, may be located on a separate piece of land. In such cases, land under gardens, orchards or plantations is *not* considered as homestead land. Homestead land in Tripura assumes significance in the light of the diverse crops cultivated on it, and their contribution to household consumption. While adding to household income, homestead produce contributes substantially to the food and nutritional security of the household.[1]

---

[1] The work by John (2014), based on a review of studies on homestead farming systems in India, brings out their role in supporting farmers to tackle risk and price fluctuations. Ramakumar

In the study villages, homestead land accounts for nearly 20 per cent to 28 per cent of the operational holdings of a household. It varies from 18.9 per cent in Khakchang to 27.4 per cent in Muhuripur (Table 1).

The average size of homestead land per household varied from 0.22 acre in Muhuripur to 0.41 acre in Mainama and 0.71 acre in Khakchang. A comparison with an earlier study on these villages carried out during 2005 reveals that there has been an increase in the average size of homestead land in all three villages (Table 2). The largest increase is in Khakchang village, where the average size of homestead land increased from 0.07 acre during 2005 to 0.71 acre in 2016 (GoT 2007). The 2005 study noted that the homestead plots in Khakchang, which is a resettled village, were then in the process of development.[2] The change reflects the progress in resettlement and provision of livelihood security to households.

The most notable feature of the homestead with respect to agricultural

Table 1 *Share and extent of average homestead land of households in study villages in Tripura, 2015–16, in per cent and acres*

Village	Average homestead land per household (acres)	Share of homestead land in total operational holding (per cent)
Mainama	0.41	23.8
Muhuripur	0.22	27.4
Khakchang	0.71	18.9

Source: Survey data, 2016.

Table 2 *Average size of household homestead holding in West Muhuripur, Mainama, and Khakchang villages, 2005, in acres*

Village	Size of homestead land
West Muhuripur	0.33
Mainama	0.2
Khakchang	0.07

Source: Government of Tripura (2007).

(2004), whose work is based on a study of socio-economic characteristics of agricultural workers in Kerala, estimates that the average net income from homesteads in Kerala accounts for 6–10 per cent of the amount considered as poverty line.

[2] A resettled village refers to inhabitation and settlement by people in a particular area that was traditionally not a village, in the recent past. Khakchang is a resettled village formed in 2003, primarily on forest land.

Table 3 *Average extent and composition of homestead land in study villages, 2015–16*, in acres and per cent

Category	Study villages					
	Khakchang		Mainama		Muhuripur	
	Area	Share	Area	Share	Area	Share
Area of the house	3.0	5.1	10.4	9.2	4.0	8.3
Other buildings	0.01	0.0	0.9	0.8	0.4	0.9
Open space	1.0	1.6	9.8	8.7	4.7	10.0
Animal shed	0.01	0.0	0.7	0.7	0.2	0.4
Land available for cultivation/fallow land	54.7	92.3	81.3	72.0	32.6	68.6
Lawn	0.0001	0.0	3.9	3.5	1.1	2.3
Water bodies	0.6	1.0	5.9	5.3	4.4	9.2
Total homestead land	**59.2**	100.0	**112.9**	100.0	**47.3**	100.0

Source: Survey data, 2016.

production is the rich diversity of crops grown. The composition of homestead lands in study villages is presented in Table 3.

Typically, nearly 70 to 90 per cent of the homestead land is either used or available for cultivation. The ratio varies with the specificities of the agricultural production system. For example, in Muhuripur, which is predominantly lowland with intensive commercial vegetable cultivation, the share of homestead land available for cultivation is the lowest (68.6 per cent) compared to other villages. This is because intensive commercial cultivation is organised in low-lying plains. Crop land in the slopes and homestead land is generally used for other purposes. In the case of Khakchang, which is a resettled village, the share available for cultivation is 92.3 per cent, and in Mainama village it is 72 per cent of homestead land. These two villages have an undulating topography interlaced with hills and forest areas. A major chunk of the homestead plot, apart from the house area, constituted the area available for cultivation, or at times was kept fallow.

Cropping Pattern in Homestead Land

The average cropping pattern of homestead land in the study villages is presented in Tables 4, 5 and 6.

There are three important features of the cropping pattern of the homestead land in the study villages in Tripura. The first feature is that nearly 60–90 per cent of the homestead land is cultivated with intercrops.

Table 4 *Average cropping pattern of homestead land in Khakchang village, 2015–16,* in acres and per cent

Crop category	Extent (acres)	Share (%)
Intercrop	15.7	90.4
Radish	1.7	9.6
All crops	17.4	100.0

Source: Survey data, 2016.

Table 5 *Average cropping pattern of homestead land in Mainama village,* in acres and per cent

Crop category	Extent (acres)	Share (%)
Intercrop	59.2	77.5
Ash gourd	0.2	0.2
Bitter gourd	0.5	0.7
Broad bean	0.1	0.1
Chilli	0.8	1.1
Leafy vegetable	0.2	0.2
Elephant ear	0.6	0.8
Ginger	0.1	0.1
Green pigeon peas	0.2	0.2
Lady's finger	0.6	0.8
Mixed vegetable	0.5	0.7
Paddy	3.0	4.0
Pineapple	3.8	5.0
Potato	2.2	2.9
Pumpkin	0.2	0.2
Ridge gourd	1.0	1.3
Spiny gourd	0.7	0.9
Sweet potato	1.9	2.5
Yam	0.5	0.7
All crops	76.4	100.0

Source: Survey data, 2016.

Table 6 *Average cropping pattern of homestead land in Muhuripur village*, in acres and per cent

Crop category	Extent (acres)	Share (%)
Intercrop	3.9	62.1
Arecanut saplings	0.05	0.8
Bitter gourd	0.3	4.2
Chilli	0.1	1.6
Rubber	2.0	31.3
All	6.3	100.0

Source: Survey data, 2016.

Intercrop is defined as a cropping pattern in which more than one crop is cultivated on the same plot of land, and the crops are grown in a mixed pattern with no definite planting arrangement to distinguish areas under individual crops. In Mainama village, the major crops grown as intercrops are sweet potato, chilli, and potato. In Muhuripur, the major crops grown together are potato, ridge gourd, and pumpkin. In Khakchang, which, as mentioned earlier, is a resettled village with households practising shifting cultivation and largely for their own consumption, more than 30 types of crops are grown in intercropping and shifting cultivation fields. The major crops are paddy, pumpkin, sesame, chilli, maize, ridge gourd, brinjal, ash gourd, and coriander. The second feature of homestead cultivation here is that the presence of a wide variety of crops which includes a large number of vegetables provides the household an assured source of nutritionally diverse and rich food, ensuring their food and nutritional security. The third feature of homestead cultivation is that many high-value vegetable crops contribute to household income through sale in markets after household consumption needs are met. In the case of Muhuripur village, uplands are under rubber cultivation, which earns them higher incomes from the sale of latex.

Input use Pattern in Homestead Land

The average input use pattern in homestead agriculture is given in Tables 7, 8, and 9. As indicated in Table 7, the use of farmyard manure per acre of homestead land is higher in Khakchang and Muhuripur, and marginally lower than that used for agricultural land in Mainama village. Khakchang, with its practice of shifting cultivation, uses more farmyard manure than chemical fertilizers. On homestead land too, village residents do not use chemical fertilizers for growing crops. If we look at the use of chemical fertilizers in the study villages, the per acre use is higher in

Table 7 *Average farm yard manure use pattern in homestead and agricultural land in study villages*, in kg per acre

Village	Agriculture land	Homestead land
Khakchang	201	450
Mainama	3541	2538
Muhuripur	3564	4380

Source: Survey data, 2016.

Table 8 *Average fertilizer use pattern in homestead and agricultural land in study villages*, in kg per acre

Village	Agriculture land	Homestead land
Khakchang	18	0
Mainama	189	151
Muhuripur	127	98

Source: Survey data, 2016.

Table 9 *Average use of plant protection in homestead and agricultural land in study villages*, in kg per acre

Village	Agriculture land	Homestead land
Khakchang	384	175
Mainama	2683	1723
Muhuripur	6331	5500

Source: Survey data, 2016.

Table 10 *Average expenditure on irrigation in homestead and agricultural land in study villages*, in Rs per acre

Village	Agriculture land	Homestead land
Khakchang	NA	NA
Mainama	3742	3025
Muhuripur	1057	500

Source: Survey data, 2016.

agricultural fields, where cultivation is largely for the market rather than in the homestead (Table 8). The pattern of input use on agricultural and homestead land is shown in Table 9. The same is the case with irrigation expenses, where expenditure is greater on agricultural land than on homestead land (Table 10).

Value of Production and Consumption from Homestead Land

The average gross value of output from agricultural production on homestead land and agricultural land, and the value of home consumption, are given in Tables 11 and 12. This gives an estimate of the contribution of agricultural production from homestead land to the food and nutritional security of households in the study villages. The value of production from homestead land is specific to the nature and characteristics of the agricultural production systems in the three study villages.

The estimate of average gross value of output from homestead land and agricultural land in the study villages brings out three important features. The first is that Muhuripur village, with its intensive commercial vegetable cultivation, had the highest value of production (Rs 54,661 per household). This is followed by Mainama (Rs 45,251 per household), which had a mixed production system consisting of lowland and upland. Khakchang village, with its traditional shifting cultivation production system, had the lowest value of output per household. Households here largely produce for their own consumption.

The second feature is that with respect to value of agricultural production from homesteads, Khakchang village had the highest value (Rs 7,161 per household), followed by Mainama village (Rs 3,965 per

Table 11 *Average gross value of output (GVO) from homestead and agricultural land in the study villages*, in Rs per household and Rs per capita

Village	GVO per household			GVO per capita		
	Homestead land	Agriculture land	Total	Homestead land	Agriculture land	Total
Khakchang	7161 (18)	33103 (82)	40264	1397 (15)	7756 (85)	9153
Mainama	3965 (8)	45251 (92)	49216	1093 (9)	11545 (91)	12638
Muhuripur	1634 (3)	53027 (97)	54661	379 (3)	12077 (97)	12456

Note: Figures in parentheses are shares of GVO from each category.
Source: Survey data, 2016.

Table 12 *Average gross value of quantity kept for consumption from homestead and agricultural land in the study villages*, in Rs per household

Village	Household consumption			Share in per cent	
	From homestead land	From agricultural land	Total	Homestead land	Agricultural land
Khakchang	1858	21946	23804	8	92
Mainama	2821	17858	20679	15	85
Muhuripur	503	13218	13721	3	97

Source: Survey data, 2016.

household) and Muhuripur village (Rs 1,634 per household). Among the study villages, Khakchang had the highest extent of homestead land per household (0.71 acre), constituting 18 per cent of the gross value of output from agriculture. Mainama had 0.41 acre and Muhuripur 0.22 acre, constituting 8 per cent and 3 per cent respectively, of the total value of agricultural production.

The third significant feature is that the two study villages of Khakchang and Mainama, with their undulating topography and diverse land utilisation pattern, had the highest contribution of homestead land to total value of production. Muhuripur, located as it is in low-lying plains, has less area under homestead cultivation as the larger share of agricultural land is cultivated with high-value vegetable crops and rubber plantations on the slopes. Though the total value of production is high in this village, the contribution of homestead land to total value of production is comparatively lower than in the other two study villages.

The average gross value of produce kept for consumption contributed by homesteads and agricultural land is given in Table 12. The share of homestead consumption depends on the nature and characteristics of agricultural production. This assumes great significance in a state like Tripura where agriculture is the major source of livelihood.

In Mainama village, homestead land contributed 15 per cent of the per capita household consumption, whereas in Khakchang village with its traditional production system, homestead land production contributed 8 per cent of the total consumption of the household from its own production. This share was lower for Muhuripur village where the extent of commercialisation is higher with high-value vegetable crops grown for the markets.

Two Illustrative Cases of Homestead Farming from Khakchang and Mainama Villages

Khakchang

Pusporam Reang resides in Horsing Para I, a hamlet that is part of Khakchang. The Government of Tripura assigned him 1.6 acres of land and 1.6 acres of water bodies. The homestead land of 0.8 acre he resides on with his family is occupied. This plot of land is not legally under the ownership of the household. They needed a place to stay after settling in this village, so this plot, which was vacant in the remote areas of Khakchang, was taken by them to reside. The terrain of the homestead is primarily sloped land.

Mr Reang and his family cultivated horticultural crops like pineapple, mango, guava, jackfruit, areca nut, and coconut on the homestead. Of these, he sold pineapples and guava in the market. The mango, coconut, and jackfruit trees have not yet started fruiting.

An interesting feature of Khakchang that emerged from the primary data was that while crops under *jhum* comprised vegetables along with paddy, cultivation on the homestead was more of horticulture crops along with a few vegetables, like drumstick. The homestead land in Khakchang is rich in terms of crop diversity as compared to that in the other study villages.

Of the household income, 74 per cent was from crops grown on the homestead. Pineapple cultivation was a major contributor to income ensuring a steady cash flow.

Mainama

Santosh Debbarma resides in Bhuban Das Para, a remote para of Mainama. He owns 0.8 acre of cropland and has possession of 5.6 acres of plantation land. He owns 1.6 acres of homestead land, of which 0.5 acre is under cultivation.

In Mainama, most homestead cultivation was of vegetables. This household had diversified its cropping pattern on its homestead land, and grew crops like ridge gourd, bitter gourd, lady's finger, chilli, bamboo, banana, areca nut, drumstick, and berry.

Almost 60 per cent of the gross value of output of homestead cultivation came from vegetables. It is to be noted here that latex was also produced by this household, and was a constituent of the total value of output. Of the total vegetable production 45 per cent was sold in the market, thereby ensuring a steady source of income for the household. Family labour was used in the cultivation of vegetables on the homestead.

Conclusions

A major characteristic of the agricultural production system in the State is the presence of homestead land and its considerable contribution to the total agricultural production of households. In the study villages, homestead land accounted for 20 to 28 per cent of the operational holdings of a household. The share of homestead land ranged from 18.9 per cent in Khakchang to 27.4 per cent in Muhuripur. The most notable feature of the homestead land was the rich diversity of crops grown. The share and composition of homestead land in the three study villages varied depending on the agro-ecological features of the production landscape. Nearly 60 to 90 per cent of the homestead land was under intercrop cultivation.

The value of production from homestead land was determined by the agricultural production systems in the three study villages. Khakchang had the highest extent of homestead land per household (0.71 acre), constituting 18 per cent of the total value of production. Mainama had 0.41 acre and Muhuripur 0.22 acre, which constituted 8 per cent and 3 per cent respectively of the total value of agricultural production. Consumption from homestead land production played a significant role in providing food and nutritional security for the households. In Khakchang village with its traditional production system, 86 per cent of the homestead land production was kept for home consumption. This share was low for Mainama and Muhuripur villages where the extent of commercialisation was higher, with high-value vegetable crops being grown for the market. The significance of homestead land lies in the fact that it not only contributes to agricultural production, but also plays a major role in contributing to the food and nutritional security of a household. Homestead production systems can support crop diversity that promotes household nutrition.

Besides this, homestead land has immense potential to improve household incomes, especially in villages like Khakchang and Mainama, as unused land available for cultivation is high (Table 3). There is a preference for crops and vegetables cultivated by the slash-and-burn method with no use of chemical inputs, which fetches a higher market price in the market.

References

Government of Tripura (GoT) (2007), *Tripura Human Development Report 2007,* Agartala.

John, J. (2014), "Homestead Farming in Kerala: A Multi-Faceted Land-Use System," *Review of Agrarian Studies,* vol. 4, no. 1. February–June.

John. J., and Nair, M. A. (1999), "Socio-economic Characteristics of Homestead Farming in South Kerala," *Journal of Tropical Agriculture,* vol. 37, no. 1/2, pp. 107–09.

Ramakumar, R. (2004), "Socio-Economic Characteristics of Agricultural Workers: A Case Study of a Village in the Malabar Region of Kerala," Ph.D. thesis submitted to the Indian Statistical Institute, Kolkata.

13

Natural Rubber in Tripura: A Harbinger of Change

D. Narayana with Tapas Singh Modak

Introduction

Natural rubber is one of the most strategic agricultural products to be used as an industrial raw material. It has very wide industrial applications – from simple cycle tyres to advanced sealants in aerospace and defence. Unlike field crops that are sown and harvested within a year, natural rubber is the produce of a tree that has one of the longest gestation periods, about seven years, and also a long life, of over 25 years. As the produce is available throughout the year and remains productive for a long period, it is an investment that yields employment and income throughout its life and through the year – almost like a capital asset in manufacturing.

In India, Kerala has been home to natural rubber cultivation for over a century. Till recently, almost 90 per cent of the area under natural rubber and its production was contributed by the State. But recent decades have seen the crop spreading to Tamil Nadu, Karnataka, and the North-East. Tripura has emerged as the second largest producer of natural rubber in India, accounting for about 10 per cent of the total area under the crop, and about 5 per cent of total production in the country. In Kerala, the crop has brought about some remarkable socio-economic changes. Regular income from natural rubber saw household income and consumption rise for a large cross-section of small holders. Income from natural rubber production financed education in a big way in Kerala, especially professional education. It also saw the State emerge as home to a large number of non-tyre rubber products industries. Of about 6,000 non-tyre rubber products manufacturing units in India, around 850 are in Kerala.

The issue taken up for study in this chapter is the state of natural rubber cultivation in Tripura, and its impact on incomes, consumption, and human resource development in the state.

The economy and society of Tripura are marked by diversity – with the hilly, largely forested North and Dhalai districts inhabited predominantly by Scheduled Tribes who are poor and with uncertain incomes. The districts of the west and south grow rice. They are also more urbanised, have diversified non-agricultural activities, and report higher incomes. Natural rubber was introduced in Dhalai more than a quarter of a century back, initially in estates by the government and the Rubber Board, but more recently by private individuals. Has natural rubber made a change to the incomes and seasonality of income flow in the poorer and largely forested regions of Tripura?

We answer this question using village survey data from three different physical and agricultural typologies of Tripura, as represented in three villages from three districts. Khakchang in North Tripura district is a newly resettled forest village. This village represents traditional as well as more settled forms of *jhum* (slash-and-burn) cultivation, and also some lowland rice and vegetable cultivation.

Mainama in Dhalai district represents a mixed agricultural terrain. On the slopes or *tila* land, as well as on forest land, there are plantations/orchards of rubber, banana, and pineapple. The households of these hamlets were mostly relocated from hamlets even more removed and inaccessible in the years of extremist violence. Rubber plantation land was assigned to them under the Tripura Rehabilitation and Plantation Corporation (TRPC) programme. In the central hamlets (near the village market), paddy and vegetables are grown on lowlands. Vegetables are grown commercially on the river bed, and homestead cultivation is also significant.

Muhuripur village in South district represents a third agrarian typography, namely that of settled agriculture, characteristic of the plains region. The agricultural pattern is mostly cultivation of lowland paddy and vegetables. Less *tila* and forest land for plantations is available here than in the other two villages, and therefore the average extent of rubber plantations is low.

Tripura: The Diverse Regions and Economic Activity

Tripura is characterised by hill ranges interspersed by small isolated hillocks, locally known as *tilas*, in the north and east, and alluvial plains in the west and south. The State was originally divided into the four districts of North, South, West, and Dhalai (that were more recently subdivided into eight districts), and is characterised by low levels of urbanisation. Close to half the population of Tripura resides in the West district where the density of population is about 60 per cent higher than the State average (Table 1). Another quarter of the population resides in South district, and the rest of the population is distributed between North and Dhalai.

Almost 50 per cent of the population of the State comprises Scheduled Castes (SCs) and Scheduled Tribes (STs). While the proportion of SCs does not show much variation across the districts, the proportion of STs is highest (55 per cent) in Dhalai. West district reports the lowest proportion of STs in the total population of the district, but it has the largest ST population in numbers, accounting for over one-third of the total ST population of the State.

Out of the geographical area of 10,49,169 hectares, a vast area (57.8 per cent) is under forests in Tripura (Table 2). The inter-district variation in the area under forests is also high. While in Dhalai and North districts, 80.6 per cent and 61.3 per cent respectively of the geographical area are under forests, the proportions are lower in West (31.6 per cent) and South (45.8 per cent) districts. The high proportion of area under forests is partly responsible for the relatively low net sown area as a proportion of geographical area in the State – 26.7 per cent with considerable inter-district variation. It is fairly low in Dhalai at 11.3 per cent and high in West district at 40.5 per cent.

In respect of urbanisation and distribution of non-agricultural enterprises too there is considerable variation among the districts of Tripura. As per Census 2011, the level of urbanisation in the State was

Table 1 *Area, population – composition and density, by district, Tripura, 2011*

District	Area (sq. km)	Share (%)	Population	Share (%)	Scheduled Caste (%)	Scheduled Tribe (%)	Population density
West	2996.8	28.6	17,25,739	46.98	19.6	25.0	576
South	3051.5	29.1	8,76,001	23.84	16.0	39.4	287
Dhalai	2348.1	22.4	3,78,230	10.29	16.3	55.7	161
North	2095.3	19.9	6,93,947	18.89	16.6	25.9	331
Tripura	10491.7	100.0	36,73,917	100.00	17.8	31.8	350

Source: Directorate of Census Operations Tripura (2011).

Table 2 *Land-use classification in Tripura, by district, 2004–05*

District	Net sown area as % of geographical area	Forest area as % of geographical area	Cropping intensity
West	40.5	31.6	176
South	28.9	45.8	191
Dhalai	11.3	80.6	158
North	32.9	61.3	157
Tripura	26.7	57.8	176

Source: Government of Tripura (2007).

Table 3 *Urbanisation and distribution of enterprises in Tripura, 2013*

District	Urbanisation (in %)	Rural		Urban	
		Establishments (no.)	Share (%)	Establishments (no.)	Share (%)
West	39.3	53940	37.3	60637	65.0
South	14.1	46199	31.9	14841	15.9
Dhalai	10.7	28365	19.6	13491	14.5
North	17.3	16170	11.2	4259	4.6
Tripura	26.2	144674	100.0	93228	100.0

Source: Directorate of Census Operations Tripura (2011); Government of Tripura (2013).

26.2 per cent (Table 3). West Tripura district was highly urbanised at 39.3 per cent, but South and Dhalai reported low levels of urbanisation at 14.1 per cent and 10.7 per cent respectively. As regards the distribution of enterprises too, Dhalai reported but a few. Low levels of urbanisation and a lower number of non-agricultural establishments has meant higher dependence on the primary sector in Dhalai. The share of the primary sector in district domestic product too was one of the highest in Dhalai.

The relatively low proportion of area under crops, lower number of establishments, and low levels of urbanisation in Dhalai relative to the other districts gets reflected in lower levels of per capita district domestic product (Table 4). While per capita district domestic products were comparable in West, South and North districts, it was about 9 per cent lower in Dhalai than the State average in 1993–94. The distance between the three districts and Dhalai has widened since then.

Table 4 *Per capita gross State/district product at factor cost, Tripura and districts, at constant 1993–94 prices, in Rs*

Year	Tripura	West	South	Dhalai	North
1993–94	6073.9	6215.2	6232.4	5534.6	6097.9
1999–00	8671.0	9183.1	8448.0	7263.3	8519.0
2000–01	10216.6	10677.8	10221.5	8124.7	10242.5
2001–02	10479.5	10937.3	10925.7	8608.8	10722.6

Source: Government of Tripura (2007).

Rehabilitation of *Jhumias* and Rubber Cultivation in Tripura

Traditionally, most of the tribal population in forest-rich Tripura practised *jhum* (slash-and-burn) cultivation, and were termed *jhumias*. In 1961, about 25,000 families were dependent on *jhum* cultivation for their livelihood. By 1978 their number had increased to 46,854 families, and by 1999 the number had grown to 51,265. The largest concentrations of *jhumias* were in Dhalai and South districts. *Jhum* is a high-risk system of cultivation, and cannot provide an adequate and steady means of livelihood. The dependence of tribal families on *jhum* for their livelihood, with all its uncertainties and its adverse impact on the environment, has long been a matter of public and official concern.

The first major attempt on the part of the government to resettle *jhumias* was made in 1931 with the establishment of the Kalyanpur Reserve in Khowai sub-division, located in Khowai district at present. This met with limited success, and there have been numerous attempts since then. By the 1980s, nearly 1.2 lakh acres were occupied by tribals in reserved, to be reserved, and protected forest areas. Various horticulture crops were tried. While rubber was introduced into Tripura by the Forest Department for soil and moisture conservation in 1963, one of the oldest rubber plantation projects was started as a tribal resettlement initiative in 1985 in Ambassa, the headquarters of Dhalai district. Although it was completely destroyed by a cyclone in 2002, the plantation was later revived.

The Tripura Forest Development and Plantation Corporation (TFDPC), formed in 1976–77, implemented a rubber-based rehabilitation package for landless shifting cultivators at Warrangbari, near Bisramgunj, West Tripura. The Corporation also had the mandate for management and operation of all plantations raised earlier by the Forest Department commercially. The establishment of a regional office of the Rubber Board in 1979 at Agartala, and of the Nucleus Rubber Estate and Training Centre in 1984, accelerated the expansion of natural rubber in Tripura. The extension activities of the Rubber Board, comprising free distribution of planting materials (i.e. polybag and budded stumps), provisions for maintenance cost, fencing materials, and technical advice resulted in expansion of plantations under private ownership also. The scheme of financial subsidy and the potential of the crop for creating economic opportunities led to the formation of the Tripura Rehabilitation and Plantation Corporation (TRPC) Limited in 1983 with the specific objective of settlement of landless tribal people for reclamation of land under *jhum* cultivation.

The TRPC played a significant role in expanding plantation area in subsequent years, including the rubber-based rehabilitation of surrendered extremists in accordance with the terms of the peace accord between the State government and the Tribal National Volunteers (TNV) in 1988–89. The much-acclaimed 'Tripura Block Plantation Project' was initiated by the Rubber Board in collaboration with the Department of Tribal Welfare, Government of Tripura, with sponsorship from the World Bank, in 1992–93. The Rubber Board expanded its operations with the establishment of regional offices at Udaipur (in South Tripura district) and Dharmanagar (in North Tripura district) in 1988 and 1994, respectively.

The resettlement schemes for tribals generally provide land occupancy rights over 1 hectare for a family, with income accruing to the recipient, as the trees mature and reach tapping stage, from the sale of latex and ribbed smoked sheets. Natural rubber is a long-duration crop with a seven-year gestation period. During the immature stage, the individual is engaged as a labourer in his own field for land development and production-augmenting activities on daily wages by the rehabilitating agency. Moreover, intercropping of banana, pineapple, and other crops are encouraged for ancillary income. The beneficiary is entitled to various financial subsidies given by the Rubber Board, and is provided technical support and training by the implementing agencies in association with the Rubber Board. The resettlement programmes bring together the beneficiaries of an area as a unit at the processing stage to reap economies of scale. In most cases, the beneficiaries tap their trees and bring the latex to the processing centre, where it is coagulated, laid, smoked, and dried as sheets. The beneficiary is paid according to the quantity of latex and its dry rubber content. This rehabilitation model was utilised *mutatis mutandis* by other rehabilitating agencies like the Department of Tribal Welfare and the Tripura Tribal Areas Autonomous District Council (TTAADC).

The total plantation area for resettlement promoted by the three major rubber-promoting agencies, namely the Rubber Board, TFDPC and TRPC, accounts for almost 20,000 hectares (Viswanathan and Bhowmik 2014).

Over a period of half a century, the crop has become firmly established in the State. The mature area under rubber increased year-on-year from 11,000 hectares in 2000–01 to 37,346 hectares in 2014–15. The period from 2004–05 to 2014–15 saw an annual increase in area under natural rubber of over 3000 hectares, a boom period in which prices rose and more and more people shifted to natural rubber cultivation. Not only poor tribals, but also tribal elites, government servants residing in Agartala, and non-tribals bought land to set up rubber plantations. The setting up of the Tripura Rubber Mission in 2006 has also helped in spreading the advantages of rubber.

The concentration of natural rubber cultivation has increasingly shifted to the West and South districts with increased activity by individual cultivators. It may be seen that only 20 per cent of the total area under rubber is accounted for by Dhalai and North districts; the bulk of the area is concentrated in West and South districts (Table 5). Especially high is the concentration of natural rubber area in the developed West district.

Recent growth in the area under rubber and its distribution across the districts of the State suggest that the focus of development of rubber cultivation has shifted away from rehabilitation of *jhumias*. The districts with a higher proportion of forest area, such as North and Dhalai – where rubber was first encouraged to provide job opportunities with high incomes to *jhumias* – have lost out to the commercial interests driving rubber cultivation in the West district. It has increasingly become a commercial crop with private investment of the salaried and other larger landholding groups flowing into it.

Table 5 *Distribution of natural rubber area by district, Tripura, 2012–13*, in hectares

District	Immature area	Mature area	Total area
West	15677	13392	29060
South	7185	12795	19980
North	3517	3925	7442
Dhalai	3736	1004	4740
Total	30115	31116	61231

Source: Government of Tripura (2014).

Population and Land in the Three Survey Villages

The three survey villages show distinct population composition and landholding patterns. As may be seen from Table 6, Khakchang is an entirely tribal village and Muhuripur is entirely non-tribal. Mainama is a mix of tribal and others. Land ownership bears a close relationship to the caste/tribe composition of population. Khakchang has a large extent of assigned and occupied land, Muhuripur reports almost entirely owned land, and Mainama has a combination of owned and assigned land.

Land types are very different in the three villages. Khakchang has very little lowland (only 10 per cent), the rest of the land being *jhum* or non-*jhum* upland (Table 7). Mainama has over 30 per cent of all land falling in the lowland category, the rest being non-*jhum* upland. Muhuripur has over 60 per cent of the total land classified as lowland, most of it irrigated. In Mainama, 48 per cent of crop net sown area was irrigated. In Khakchang, irrigation was totally absent. The cropping pattern in the villages is conditioned by land type and availability of irrigation.

Paddy and vegetables are the main crops grown in all three villages. These accounted for over three-fourths the gross cropped area in Khakchang and Muhuripur (Table 8). Of upland (non-*jhum* land), a sizeable proportion was under plantations in Mainama and Muhuripur villages. Natural rubber seems to occupy a prime place among plantation crops.

Table 6 *Population composition and ownership of land in the three villages, Tripura, 2015–16*

Village	Number of households	Population	Percentage share of			Percentage share of land owned		
			SC	ST	Others	Assigned	Occupied	Owned
Khakchang	589	2884	0	100	0	74	8	18
Mainama	1451	6693	1	67	32	14	12	74
Muhuripur	1054	4404	15	0	85	2	4	94

Notes: Assigned land: This includes agricultural land allotted to households by the government through *patta* (title deed). We have considered all land as assigned that has been inherited from the previous generation, who in turn received it as *patta* from the government. For this type of land, the household has the "right to use" but does not have any "right of sale". Occupied land: This includes the agricultural land of households which has been reported as encroached land. For this type of land, the household does not have any ownership or sale rights. Owned land: This includes agricultural land over which the households have complete ownership rights.
Source: PARI survey, 2015–16.

Table 7 *Ownership of land by type in the three survey villages, Tripura, 2015–16, in per cent*

Village	Percentage share of				Total	% irrigated of crop net sown area
	Lowland	*Jhum* land	Non-*jhum* upland	Water body		
Khakchang	11	14	71	4	100	0
Mainama	31	Neg.	62	7	100	48
Muhuripur	63	0	28	9	100	91

Source: PARI survey, 2015–16.

Table 8 *Cropping pattern in the three survey villages, Tripura, 2015–16, in per cent*

Village	Percentage share of land in gross cropped area					Total
	Jhum	Paddy	Vegetables	Plantation	Other	
Khakchang	52	22	4	19	3	100
Mainama	0	41	6	51	3	100
Muhuripur	0	71	9	19	1	100

Source: PARI survey, 2015–16.

Natural Rubber Cultivation in the Three Villages

Rubber plantations were introduced for the first time in the forest and upland in Khakchang village as recently as 2008, with the support of the Tripura Tribal Areas Autonomous District Council (TTAADC). The TTAADC provided all the inputs and labour costs for the plantations. However, the extent of rubber plantation land was very low till the survey year (2016). Rubber tapping had not started as the trees had not matured yet. Hence, the rest of this section will focus only on Mainama and Muhuripur. Sharply contrasting pictures emerge from these two villages.

Natural rubber trees were planted for the first time in Mainama in 1988 under the initiative of the Tripura Rehabilitation and Plantation Corporation (TRPC). However, the area planted was very low till 2005. A latex collection centre set up by the TRPC is situated next to the Anganwadi Centre in Arjun *para* (a remote hamlet) of Mainama village. It is spread over 0.6 acre of government land and became functional in 2007. About 95 per cent of the area under rubber was planted after 2005, and TRPC played a key role in it (Table 9). But individual planters too have

Table 9 *Extent of rubber plantation by year of planting and by institution, Mainama, in acres*

Year of planting	TRPC	Panchayat	Individual	Unspecified	All	Share in total rubber plantation land (%)
Before 2005	51	0	0	0	51	5.2
Between 2005 and 2010	184	12	209	0	405	41.2
After 2010	189	28	218	0	435	44.2
Unspecified	29	5	36	23	93	9.5
All	453	45	463	23	984	100.0
Share in total rubber plantation land (%)	46.0	4.6	47.1	2.3	100	

Source: PARI survey, 2015–16.

come in large numbers. Today, close to 47 per cent of the total area under natural rubber has been planted with individual effort.

A study of the beneficiaries of the TRPC shows that it facilitated rubber cultivation by landless households in Mainama village that had relocated from inaccessible *paras* in the years of extremist violence in the mid-2000s. TRPC first gave Rs 2,000–3,000 to beneficiary households to construct houses. It then asked the households to identify 1 hectare each of forest *tila* land to establish a rubber plantation. Groups of villagers were formed for planting rubber trees. The family members of beneficiary households together did the forest cleaning and sowing operations. For these operations labourers were paid Rs 70 per day. They cleared the plantation land twice or thrice a year, for 15–20 days each time. All agricultural operations on this plantation land were done collectively for the initial six years. Once the trees attained maturity, the land was divided among the households.

The TRPC provided rubber planting material, fertilizer, plant protection, and labour costs for clearing the forest land till the rubber trees attained maturity. It then allocated 2.47 acres or 1 hectare of plantation land with between 250 to 300 rubber trees to each member of the group. The land was under occupied or assigned or *patta* category. The TRPC also employed a person to guard the plantation land from cattle in the years between 2007 and 2014. However, there is a clause that binds the registered beneficiaries to sell the entire latex production to the TRPC throughout the productive life of the rubber trees. It provided the first batch of cups, hangers, spouts, and *jabongs* (hand implement used to tap latex) to the

beneficiary households. After latex production began, the beneficiary had
to bear the cost of cleaning the plantation on his own.

As already mentioned, the trend of private individuals investing in
rubber plantations grew, particularly after 2006. A majority of them
came from the category of salaried employees. In our survey, out of 162
individual planters, 79 reported salaried employment, and the average
extent of rubber plantation for this category was about 2.9 acres of
plantation land (Table 10). While small cultivators, agricultural and non-
agricultural labourers, and petty businessmen also invested individually,
the extent was comparatively less than that of the salaried group (1.3
acres of plantation land).

The TRPC was also indirectly responsible for spurring private rubber
cultivation. Take the case of Tantu Chakma, a respondent in the PARI
survey. He owned 25 acres of forest land. In 2004, he planted his first
batch of rubber stumps received from the TRPC on about 10 acres of this
land. The first batch of trees did not achieve the desired growth, however.
Tantu Chakma therefore started his own nursery for preparing rubber
saplings. At present, he has 18 acres of rubber plantation. Of the 4,000
trees he originally had, 3,000 survived. In 2015, 600 trees were destroyed
due to a cyclone. In 2016, the survey year, he produced latex from 1,500
trees, and he planned to produce latex from another 1,430 trees the
following year. He has his own processing unit to make rubber sheets. He

Table 10 *Rubber plantation by institution and primary occupation, Mainama, 2015–16*

Plantation institution	Big rubber cultivator		Small peasant, agricultural, and non-agricultural labour		Salaried job	
	Number of house-holds	Average size of rubber holding (in acres)	Number of house-holds	Average size of rubber holding (in acres)	Number of house-holds	Average size of rubber holding (in acres)
TRPC	5	2.5	147	2.4	21	4.1
Individual	12	11.9	71	1.3	79	2.9
Support from panchayat	0		32	1.4	0	
Unspecified	0		5	4.8	0	0.0
All	17	9.08	255	2.0	100	3.2

Source: PARI survey, 2015–16.

earned the highest income (about Rs 2,40,000) in the village from rubber plantation in the survey year.

In our survey we found that a few households – those that had been allocated rubber plantation by TRPC in 2005, and that had started getting incomes from the sale of rubber latex and sheets – reinvested their surplus in new rubber plantations. For example, Anil Debbarma received 2.5 acres of rubber plantation land from TRPC in 2006, and earned a net income of about Rs 1 lakh in our survey year from rubber plantations. He planted another 700 trees on 4 acres of occupied land financed by his own earnings in 2013.

Unlike in Mainama and Khakchang, there was no evidence of the intervention of TRPC in Muhuripur. A few rubber cultivators reported that they received monetary support ranging from Rs 5,000 to Rs 10,000 for rubber plantation from the Rubber Board. One rubber cultivator, D. Debnath, reported that he received Rs 3,000 from the Board. Generally, the Rubber Board offered subsidy thrice to rubber cultivators in Muhruipur – during the initial plantation period, after two years of planting, and once the trees became mature. However, this household received subsidy only twice. Debnath said that for ST and priority groups, the Rubber Board does much more than for others. It may be noted that Muhuripur is a village where the Bengali-speaking population is predominant.

Whether through the active involvement of government departments in rehabilitation programmes or otherwise, the popularity of rubber cultivation has spread far and wide in Tripura. Small holders too saw an opportunity in rubber cultivation, as is evident from our survey data of the three study villages (Table 11). The large concentration of rubber cultivators suggests that rehabilitation initiatives in the districts have taken the message far beyond the beneficiaries of schemes. Large holders are also taking up rubber cultivation in a big way. Most striking has been the experience of Muhuripur where a large proportion of small holders have taken up rubber cultivation in the absence of any rehabilitation programme or major government programme of rubber cultivation. Thus, rubber has come to stay as the main cash crop of the State.

As regards labour employed in rubber cultivation in Mainama, all operations, particularly rubber tapping, were undertaken solely by household members. Latex collection was done on alternate days, i.e. for 15 days in a month. The tapping period was usually eight to 10 months in a year. The family members left the house early morning for tapping and by 8 a.m. their work was over. There was no female participation

Table 11 *Distribution of rubber cultivators by size of rubber holding, study villages, Tripura, 2015–16*

Size of landholding (acres)	Khakchang		Mainama		Muhuripur	
	Number	Share (%)	Number	Share (%)	Number	Share (%)
<=1	21	44	72	21	183	72
1–2.5	27	56	156	45	65	26
2.5–5	0	0	78	23	5	2
>5	0	0	39	11	0	0
Total	48	100	345	100	253	100

Source: PARI survey, 2015–16.

Table 12 *Income from rubber plantation, 2015–16*, in Rs

Village	Average net income per 100 trees in a year
Mainama, Dhalai district	18,480
Muhuripur, South Tripura	18,823

Source: PARI survey, 2015–16.

in rubber tapping in Mainama. However, two households that had significant earnings from rubber cultivation kept long-term labourers for rubber operations, from tapping to preparing the rubber sheets. In Muhuripur village, along with family labour, there was a significant proportion of daily hired labour used for rubber tapping. Here we noted female participation in rubber cultivation (unlike in Mainama), although their presence was low. Four households reported that all work related to rubber cultivation, from tapping to preparing sheets, was done by permanent workers.

Turning to yields, the average latex yield per tree varied between 35 and 60 ml per day in Mainama, and between 50 and 70 ml per day in Muhuripur. It was seen that cultivation practices varied between the two villages. In Muhuripur there was higher use of manure and chemical fertilizers in rubber cultivation across all size-classes, and higher use of wage labour. These two factors led to higher costs. In Mainama, in contrast, these factors did not operate. Thus, average net incomes from rubber cultivation were comparable as between Mainama and Muhuripur.

In computing incomes from rubber holdings, care has been taken to consider only mature trees. Hence, we have taken the average income per

100 trees during the survey year. Profitability in rubber cultivation was significant, since the input cost was very low. The average income per 100 matured trees in a year was equal in Mainama and Muhuripur (Table 12). While the average latex collection per tree in a day in Muhuripur village was higher compared to Mainama village, higher use of paid labour and material inputs here led to the net incomes being equal in both study villages – Rs 18,480 in Mainama and Rs 18,823 in Muhuripur.

Impact of Natural Rubber Cultivation on Earnings and Well-being

The foremost result of the growth of natural rubber in Tripura has been the improved living conditions of landless shifting cultivators (Joseph *et al.* 2010; Viswanathan 2005; Viswanathan and Bhowmik 2014). The annual income of the tribal (resettled) beneficiaries has increased more than tenfold owing to a regular flow of income from the plantations. Previously, as *jhumia* households moved from one place to another in search of newer lands for cultivation, health and education facilities were mostly beyond their reach. Rubber plantations have provided regular employment, and while settling them in one place, have also facilitated institutional benefits on a much larger scale, leading to measurable improvements in the development status of these households. The children in these families are not illiterate like their parents and grandparents; rather, many of them have obtained their education in various parts of the country and even abroad, and are well settled in other vocations. The asset base of the grower households has widened along with improved housing conditions, possession of consumer goods, and better nutrition (Kuki and Bhowmik 2013). The Kerala experience appears to be repeating itself in Tripura. Non-tribal rubber growers have also reaped similar benefits due to consistent returns from the sector (Bhowmik and Chouhan 2013).

Survey data from the villages confirm these findings. As the tapping of rubber from trees had not started in the study villages during the survey period, incomes were projected for rubber cultivators. Average net income from 100 rubber trees village-wise was taken as the standard to project income from rubber. The projected rubber income was added to total crop income when household incomes were computed. It is evident from Table 13 that as the rubber income was fully realised by the households, the total income went up by close to 50 per cent in Mainama, 32 per cent in Muhuripur, and close to 20 per cent in Khakchang. The percentage

Table 13 *Projected mean crop and household income of rubber cultivators in the survey villages, Tripura, 2015–16*

Primary occupation	Number of households	Crop income (Rs)			Household income (Rs)		
		Actual	Projected*	Increase in per cent	Actual	Projected*	Increase in per cent
Khakchang							
All	48	6352	61792	873	287686	343126	19
Mainama							
Peasant, agricultural, and non-agricultural labour	109	11801	81369	590	86461	156028	80
Salaried jobs	60	7690	102785	1237	308029	403124	31
All	169	10337	88994	761	165352	244009	48
Muhuripur							
Peasant, agricultural, and non-agricultural labour, and petty business	95	10138	46761	361	96651	133274	38
Salaried jobs	19	3287	51431	1465	230645	278789	21
All	114	9001	47536	428	118893	157428	32

Note: *Projected refers to the income after including the potential income from natural rubber trees yet to be tapped. Peasant here refers to all cultivator categories.

Source: PARI survey, 2015–16.

increase in incomes for the category of "peasants, agricultural, and non-agricultural labourers" is particularly sharp.

Turning to the impact of rubber cultivation on household health and education, it needs to be noted that most of the households in remote *para*s in Mainama, and all households in Khakchang, were resettled or relocated during the period of extremist violence (mid-2000s). In addition to introducing such households to settled agriculture, the shift has facilitated institutional interventions in schooling and health, which can be seen in the establishment of primary and secondary schools, hostels for ST students, and health centres, especially in remote *paras*.

The PARI survey data on literacy, schooling, and education for 2015–16 compared with that for 2005 shows that significant gains have been made (see chapter 16). For example, literacy levels increased between 2005 and 2015, and there was a closing of the gender gap in literacy levels. Of course, these improvements were not due to just the introduction of rubber cultivation, as income from rubber had not started accruing to many households because the trees had not reached maturity. It can be argued, however, that settled agriculture through the establishment of rubber cultivation has helped in better access to education and health.

It is well known that the value of household assets increase as incomes go up. It has already been observed that there is a correlation between higher income and higher asset holding (see chapter 14). Table 14 presents the asset values for different income classes in the survey villages. It may

Table 14 *Average value of consumer assets according to income groups, study villages, Tripura, 2015–16* , n Rs and per cent

Annual income class (Rs)	Khakchang		Mainama		Muhuripur	
	% of households	Average asset value (Rs)	% of households	Average asset value (Rs)	% of households	Average asset value (Rs)
<50,000	24	13441	20	24283	20	42614
50,000–1 lakh	36	16273	27	36249	34	39828
1–2 lakhs	27	23756	25	44424	28	76836
2–5 lakhs	13	221450	22	105516	15	96283
5 lakhs+	–		6	560586	3	345396
All classes	100		100		100	

Source: PARI survey, 2015–16, drawn from chapter 14.

be inferred that as the income from rubber increases in the future, the household asset holding will go up, especially for households classified as small peasant, agricultural, and non-agricultural labour, and petty businesses.

Overall, the data from the village surveys confirm many of the findings of earlier studies. Income from rubber cultivation has raised the incomes of rural households. With rising incomes, consumption, access to education, and value of asset holdings of households have gone up.

Conclusions

Tripura, a small Indian state with a large proportion of its geographical area under forests, was characterised by 'slash-and-burn' cultivation (*jhum*) with uncertain incomes for the tribal population. Resettlement of the *jhumias* is a very old story full of failures. The introduction of natural rubber brought a new dimension to the resettlement. It was instrumental in settling the tribal households in select locations with better access to health and education services. Rubber cultivation began in a small way, but in course of time brought together government departments and the Rubber Board. Subsidies, better planting material, other inputs, and extension services were made available primarily to tribal families. The shift to settled agriculture improved their regular income flow, and extremist activity came down.

The period after 2005 witnessed rubber prices rising in tandem with international crude oil prices. By then many of the new rubber plantations had reached maturity, and the economic benefits that accrued attracted other classes of people living in areas close to the rehabilitation sites as well as elsewhere in the State towards rubber cultivation. Private savings started flowing as investment into rubber cultivation; the already built public infrastructure for extension and collection of rubber helped.

Even in other districts of the State, the process of shifting to rubber had begun; Kerala had already demonstrated that the crop was a harbinger of change. In Tripura, in a span of about ten years, the area under the crop as a proportion of net sown area increased from close to zero to 30 per cent. It is bound to go up further whether government support is available or not.

In Kerala, in due course, the availability of rubber as a raw material led to the emergence of a sizeable rubber products industry. In Tripura too, the industry offers a possibility for many to enter the manufacture of rubber products. The Department of Industry of the State can play a role here.

References

Bhowmik, Indraneel, and Chouhan, Pradip (2013), "An Inquiry into the Employment Status, Income and Assets of Rubber Tappers Working in the Large Estates of Tripura," *Labour and Development*, 20, pp. 104–29.

Directorate of Census Operations Tripura (2011), *District Census Handbooks: Tripura (Dhalai, North Tripura, South Tripura, West Tripura)*, Office of the Registrar General and Census Commissioner, Ministry of Home Affairs, Government of India.

Government of Tripura (GoT) (2007), *Tripura Human Development Report*, available at http://planningcommission.nic.in/plans/stateplan/sdr_pdf/tripura%20hdr.pdf, viewed on October 30, 2018.

Government of Tripura (GoT) (2013), "6th Economic Census, 2013," Directorate of Economics and Statistics Planning (Statistics) Department, Government of Tripura, Agartala.

Government of Tripura (GoT) (2014), *Economic Review of Tripura, 2013–14*, Directorate of Economics and Statistics Planning (Statistics) Department, Government of Tripura, Agartala.

Joseph, Joby, George, K., Tharian, and Dey, S. K. (2010), *Report on the Socio-Economic Impact of Natural Rubber Cultivation under the Block Planting scheme in Tripura* available at https://mpra.ub.uni-muenchen.de/52370/

Kuki, Vanlalrema, and Bhowmik, Indraneel (2013), "Empowerment of Scheduled Tribes through Natural Rubber Plantations in Tripura: A Case Study of Dhuptali Village," paper presented at the 15th Annual NEEA Conference, organised by Department of Economics, Mizoram University.

Viswanathan, P. K. (2005), "Emerging Small Holder Rubber Farming System in India and Thailand: A Comparative Economic Analysis," *Asian Journal of Agriculture and Development*, vol. 5, no. 2, pp. 1–20.

Viswanathan, P. K., and Bhowmik, Indraneel (2014), "Compatibility of Institutional Architecture for Rubber Plantation Development in North East India from a Comparative Perspective of Kerala," Discussion Paper No. 35, National Research Programme on Plantation Development (NRPPD), Centre for Development Studies, Thiruvanthapuram.

SECTION IV

Standard of Living

14

Features of Asset Ownership in the Three Study Villages

Ranjini Basu

Asset holdings are an important indicator of the economic security of a household, as they provide a buffer to the family in times of economic uncertainty. Studying patterns of asset ownership also tells us about overall levels of wealth in a village. In recent times, asset poverty has been recognised as an important variable in measuring poverty.

This chapter discusses the ownership of assets among households in the three study villages of Tripura chosen as part of the Project on Agrarian Relations in India (PARI). The first section discusses some unique features of landholding in rural Tripura, which makes it difficult to compare the State to other States in the country. The second section discusses the asset composition of households in the three study villages. The third section is about the low levels of asset ownership in the villages of Tripura. The fourth section deals with ownership of modern assets in our study villages. The fifth section tries to understand the impact of remoteness on the asset composition of rural households in Tripura, using Khakchang and Mainama villages as case studies. The last section presents some conclusions.

Asset Holdings in Rural Tripura: Evidence from NSSO

The National Sample Survey Organisation (NSSO) carried out its 70th Round of sample household surveys in 2013 to study the status of debt and investment in the country (All India Debt and Investment Survey [AIDIS]). This survey provides data on asset holdings and levels of indebtedness among both urban and rural households. The value of land, buildings, livestock, farm business equipment, non-farm business

Table 1 *Average asset holdings of cultivator and rural households, India and Tripura, 2012–13, in Rs*

	India		Tripura	
	Current prices	Constant prices*	Current prices	Constant prices*
Cultivator households	13,85,632	17,04,327	3,97,903	5,17,274
Rural households	10,06,985	12,38,592	2,78,635	3,62,226

Note: *Values adjusted to 2015–16 price levels using CPI-RL.
Source: NSSO 2016.

equipment, means of transport, and financial assets in the form of shares, deposits, and receivables were included in the definition of assets.

Table 1 shows the average value of asset holdings of cultivator and rural households in India and Tripura, as estimated in the NSSO survey data, at current prices and also after adjusting prices to the 2015–16 level using the consumer price index for rural labourers (CPI-RL). The data show a wide gap between the national average and that of Tripura. For both cultivator and rural households, the average value of asset holdings at the national level was 3.5 times higher than the Tripura average at both current and constant prices.

While this suggests lower levels of asset ownership in rural Tripura, the difference could also partly be on account of the valuation of land. A disaggregated analysis of all the components of household asset ownership shows that the highest contributor to the asset basket of a household was the value of owned agricultural land. The 70th Round of the NSSO survey defined ownership of landholding as "permanent heritable possession, with or without the right to transfer the title, which is vested in a member or members of the household. Land held in owner-like possession under long term lease or assignment is also considered as land owned." However, there is lack of clarity regarding how value is assigned to land in different States. In a country like India, having a great variation in topography and soil fertility, and the presence of an active land market, it is but natural that the price of land as an asset will vary greatly. In the largely hilly, forested, and remote State of Tripura, this factor can become significant while determining the value of agricultural land owned by households, and hence influence the overall value of assets held by them.

Table 2 shows the average value of assets of cultivator and rural households in Tripura and India, calculated from NSSO data after excluding the value of agricultural land. It can be observed that by

Table 2 *Average asset holdings excluding value of agricultural land of cultivator and rural households, India and Tripura, 2012–13*, in Rs

	India		Tripura	
	Current prices	Constant prices*	Current prices	Constant prices*
Cultivator households	1,94,075	2,38,712	1,10,696	1,43,905
Rural households	2,75,937	3,39,403	1,19,574	1,55,446

Note: *Values adjusted to 2015–16 price levels using CPI-RL.
Source: NSSO (2016).

excluding the value of agricultural land, although the gap between State and national averages remain, it is reduced. This suggests a possibility of undervaluation of agricultural land in Tripura as compared to other States of the country. This creates problems in comparing the asset ownership of rural households across States using NSSO data.

A second problem relates to the types of land included in the asset basket. Agricultural land is usually the most important component of the total assets of a rural household. In Panahar, a West Bengal village surveyed in 2010 and 2015, for example, agricultural land constituted 59 per cent of total assets in 2015.

A specific feature of Tripura is successful land reforms. It is one of the few States where thorough land reforms were implemented, and in more recent times, it featured amongst the best performers in the implementation of the Forest Rights Act (FRA). As a result, there are a significant number and proportion of households in the State who were either beneficiaries of land reforms or the FRA, and have received *pattas* or assigned land. The share of assigned land in total land possessed by households in our study villages varied between 80.8 per cent in Khakchang to 13.5 per cent in Mainama and 1.7 per cent in Muhuripur. In Khakchang, 76 per cent of the households were beneficiaries of land reforms, while in Mainama and Muhuripur, the figures were 12.2 per cent and 2.3 per cent respectively. Beneficiary households enjoy "use rights" over assigned land but have no rights of sale. Therefore, we have not included assigned land as ownership holding of a household. In addition, households had possession of "occupied" or encroached land. The share of occupied land in all land possessed by households in the study villages varied between 3.9 per cent in Khakchang, 11.6 per cent in Mainama, and 4.7 per cent in Muhuripur. Households had no legal rights over these lands, therefore these too were not considered as part of the assets they owned. To put it differently, only land owned by households over which they had sale rights were included in household assets. Due to the success of land reforms in Tripura many households gained user rights over land, but this is not reflected in the assets they own.

Due to this unique success of land reforms in Tripura, land as an asset held by a household in the State is not comparable to the majority of other States in India which have seen no significant state-led land reforms.

Levels and Composition of Assets in the Three Study Villages

We now turn to the village survey data. Information on assets in the surveys included the following items:

- Agricultural land
- Homestead, other land, and buildings
- Consumer durable goods
- Electrical equipment
- Inventory of agricultural produce
- Inventory of commercial and non-agricultural goods
- Means of transport
- Means of production
- Livestock
- Trees.

Financial assets and jewellery were excluded as it was observed that there are cases of gross misreporting of these values, especially by richer households.

On average, the value of all assets owned by a household in 2016 was Rs 12.6 lakhs in Muhuripur, Rs 10.1 lakhs in Mainama, and Rs 3.6 lakhs in Khakchang at current prices.

Table 4 shows the proportion of households owning assets and the average value by each type of asset category. The first striking result is the difference in value of agricultural land across the three villages. In Muhuripur and Mainama, the majority of households (62 and 56 per cent respectively) owned agricultural land, and the value of such land accounted for one-half or more of total assets. In absolute terms, an average household owned agricultural land valued at around Rs 6,00,000 in both villages. Unlike these two villages, where households had full ownership rights over the agricultural land under their possession, in Khakchang, the majority of households were beneficiaries of the Forests Rights Act. As such, land was not in their possession nor was

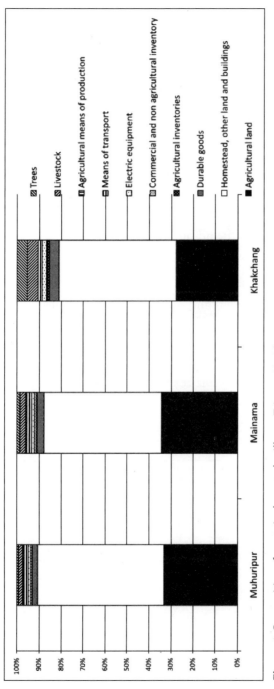

Figure 1 *Composition of assets in three study villages, Tripura, 2016*, in per cent

Source: Survey data.

it heritable, and therefore was not valued under household assets. The category of "agricultural land" refers to the value of all land over which a household held exclusive ownership rights. While 94 per cent of the total land possessed by households in Muhuripur was under full ownership rights, in Mainama and Khakchang the proportion was 75 and 15 per cent respectively. Thus, the share of agricultural land in total value of assets was the lowest in Khakchang at 27 per cent, as 85 per cent of the land possessed by households was either assigned or occupied land, for which a value was not imputed. Further, there was variation in land prices across the villages with a higher price for irrigated lowlands of Muhuripur and Mainama, than for the largely undulated rainfed land of Khakchang.

Figure 1 shows the composition of assets in the three study villages. Across the villages, the value of "homestead land, other land, and buildings" accounted for a big share of total assets, close to the value of agricultural land. Table 3 provides the average value of assets for all households in the villages, which were lower than the figures projected in Table 4. In Table 4, the averages were calculated only for those households that owned the different assets.

In Khakchang, the value of trees and livestock were more important in total assets than in the other two villages. The share of livestock in the total asset holdings of Khakchang was 4.9 per cent, while it was 1.8 per cent and 2.5 per cent respectively in Muhuripur and Mainama.

Table 3 *Average value of different assets, Tripura, 2016, in Rs*

Asset category	Muhuripur	Mainama	Khakchang
Agricultural land	4,18,248	3,50,159	1,01,212
Homestead, other land, and buildings	7,26,057	5,46,923	1,94,813
Durable goods	29,103	30,457	15,782
Agricultural inventories	3,125	3,858	3,270
Commercial and non-agricultural inventory	7,735	9,217	1,383
Electrical equipment	11,618	12,639	6,867
Means of transport	27,474	22,691	6,985
Agricultural means of production	6,103	6,162	20
Livestock	22,519	25,417	17,826
Trees	10,392	14,628	16,803
All	12,62,373	10,15,990	3,64,961

Source: Survey data.

Table 4 *Proportion of households owning assets and their average value, by asset category, Tripura, 2016, in per cent and Rs*

Asset category	Muhuripur		Mainama		Khakchang	
	Proportion of households	Average value of assets	Proportion of households	Average value of assets	Proportion of households	Average value of assets
Agricultural land	62	6,75,580	56	6,21,905	34	2,96,255
Homestead, other land, and buildings	99	7,31,819	99	5,52,824	99	1,96,562
Durable goods	100	29,103	100	30,457	100	15,782
Agricultural inventories	90	3,489	87	4,412	96	3,391
Commercial and non-agricultural inventory	13	57,361	13	70,137	15	9,476
Electrical equipment	98	11,899	97	12,968	87	7,909
Means of transport	86	31,792	63	35,918	31	22,304
Agricultural means of production	30	20,463	38	36,670	4	570
Livestock	83	27,173	69	19,370	77	22,978
Trees	87	11,890	76	16,204	84	20,050
All	100	12,62,373	100	10,15,990	100	3,64,961

Source: Survey data.

Similarly, the proportion of value of trees to total assets was 4.6 per cent in Khakchang, as compared to 0.8 per cent in Muhuripur and 1.4 per cent in Mainama. Khakchang being a heavily forested village, the access to wooded trees bearing higher value was greater.

One of the remarkable features of the three villages was the near-complete ownership of dwelling sites and houses by households. However, the quality of housing differed across the villages, which was reflected in the average value of buildings. Fewer households in Khakchang – only about 5 per cent – had fully *pucca* houses, as compared to 33 per cent in Muhuripur and 21 per cent in Mainama. The lower share of *pucca* houses in Khakchang as compared to the other two villages was reflected in the low value of buildings (see chapter 15).

The biggest difference between Khakchang on the one hand, and Mainama and Muhuripur on the other, was in respect of agricultural means of production. All three villages were characterised by low levels of mechanisation: only 30 per cent of households in Muhuripur, 38 per cent in Mainama, and 4 per cent in Khakchang owned agricultural implements of any value. The average value of agricultural means of production in Muhuripur and Mainama was around Rs 6,000, whereas in Khakchang it was merely Rs 570 (see Table 4). This was due to the fact that in Khakchang, cultivation was in the form of *jhum*, which depended entirely on hand implements. In contrast, there was lowland cultivation in both Muhuripur and Mainama, where agricultural implements such as power tillers were used.

Ownership of livestock is an important source of income for rural households, especially for landless and near-landless households. As Table 4 shows, 83 per cent of households in Muhuripur, 69 per cent in Mainama, and 77 per cent in Khakchang reported ownership of livestock.

Table 5 *Number of animals of different types per 100 households, Tripura, 2016*, in numbers

	Muhuripur	Mainama	Khakchang
Milch cattle	71	48	17
Adult male cattle	4	29	19
Calves	77	44	19
Goats	40	76	142
Pigs	2	39	180
Poultry	528	466	549

Source: Survey data.

When disaggregated (Table 5), we find that the number of milch cattle was the highest in Muhuripur and the lowest in Khakchang. In Khakchang, ownership of pigs was widespread (58 per cent of the households in the village owned pigs), and their value ranged from Rs 1,000 to Rs 20,000, depending on the age of the animal. Households in Mainama had the largest number of draught animals due to the still-prevalent use of animal labour in agricultural operations in the village. In Mainama, 42.4 per cent of all lowland under paddy was ploughed using draught animals, as compared to 4 per cent in Muhuripur.

Consumer Durables

Another notable feature of asset ownership in the villages of Tripura is the low level of consumer durables. This category includes durable goods such as electrical equipment and means of transport or vehicles.

Table 6 *Average consumer asset value according to income groups in the study villages, Tripura, in Rs and per cent*

Village	Income category	Average consumer asset value	Proportion of households
Muhuripur	<=50 K	42,614	21
	>50 K <= 1 lakh	39,828	34
	>1 lakh <= 2 lakhs	76,836	28
	>2 lakhs <= 5 lakhs	96,283	15
	>5 lakhs	3,45,396	3
Mainama	<=50 K	24,283	20
	>50 K <= 1 lakh	36,249	27
	>1 lakh <=2 lakhs	44,424	25
	>2 lakhs <= 5 lakhs	1,05,516	22
	>5 lakhs <= 9 lakhs	2,53,195	4
	>9 lakhs	3,07,391	2
Khakchang	<=50 K	13,441	24
	>50 K <= 1 lakh	16,273	36
	>1 lakh <=2 lakhs	23,756	27
	>2 lakhs <= 3 lakhs	58,257	7
	>3 lakhs	1,63,193	6

Source: Survey data.

Table 7 *Asset composition of richest asset holding households, Tripura, 2016,* in Rs

Village	Category of asset	Description	Value
Muhuripur	Agricultural land	4.8 acres lowland	33,00,000
	Homestead land, other land, and buildings	0.4 acre homestead land, house, land in Kolkata and Udaipur	1,08,90,000
	Trees	Jackfruit, mango	2,500
	Livestock	1 female calf, 4 ducks	11,800
	Durable goods	Furniture, kitchen appliances, other durable goods	55,775
	Electrical equipment	4 mobile phones	48,150
	Inventories	100 kg rice, 200 kg paddy	4,900
	Means of transport	1 bicycle, 1 scooter/motorcycle, 1 car	5,23,000
	Non-agricultural inventory	2 fishing nets	5,000
	All		1,48,41,125
Mainama	Agricultural land	29.6 acres of lowland, 4.8 acres plantation land, 4 acres orchard land	1,55,00,000
	Homestead land, other land, and buildings	4 acres homestead land, 0.09 acre other land, 3 shops, 1 rice mill, 1 house, 2 acres pond	44,00,000
	Trees		71,000
	Livestock	2 goats, 7 chicken	7,500
	Durable goods	Furniture, kitchen appliances, other durable goods	72,600
	Electrical equipment	Iron, mixer, 2 mobile phones, 1 refrigerator, 1 table fan, 2 colour TVs, 6 ceiling fans, 2 computers, electric heater	60,400
	Means of transport	2 cars, 1 scooter/motorcycle	3,90,000
	Non-agricultural inventory	Inventory in commercial establishments	1,68,000
	Inventories	2000 kg of paddy, 50 kg of rice	21,350
	Agricultural means of production	1 power tiller, 1 diesel pump	45,000
	All		2,07,35,850
Khakchang	Agricultural land	3.6 acres lowland, 1.2 acres rubber plantation	25,50,000
	Homestead land, other land, and buildings	0.74 acres Homestead land, 0.006 acre Pond, 1 House, 1 Shop	13,69,000

(continued)

Table 7 *(continued)*

Village	Category of asset	Description	Value
	Durable goods	Furniture, kitchen appliances, other durable goods	23,800
	Electrical equipment	3 ceiling fans, 2 mobile phones, 2 refrigerators, 1 table fan, 2 colour TVs, 1 inverter, 1 iron	38,300
	Non-agricultural inventory	Commercial inventories in shop	90,000
	Means of transport	2 bicycles, 1 car	1,53,000
	Trees		20,250
	Livestock	2 pigs, 2 goats	45,000
	All		42,89,350

Source: Survey data.

Table 6 shows the average consumer asset holding of households across the different income categories. While absolute levels of ownership were low, consumer assets rose with level of income across the villages. In Muhuripur, the average consumer asset holding of the highest income group was eight times that of the lowest income group. In the case of Mainama, the ratio of assets owned by the lowest income group to the highest income group was 1:1.3. Note, however, that there were only a few households in each village in the highest income group.

To get an insight into the kind of assets owned by village households, in Table 7 we have listed all the assets reported by the richest household in each village. It should be noted that most of these households were not rich in an absolute sense relative to the wealth of households in other parts of the country. For example, the richest household in Panahar, a village in Bankura district of West Bengal surveyed in 2015, was worth over Rs 3 crore (30 million). Of the three villages studied in Tripura, the wealthiest or richest household was in Mainama, with assets worth Rs 20 million. The differences arose in this case on account of ownership of means of production, agricultural machinery in particular. The richest household of Mainama owned one power tiller and a diesel pump worth Rs 45,000, whereas the richest household of Panahar owned agricultural machinery worth Rs 4,30,380, which included a tractor, tractor trolley, a rotavator, electric pump, thresher, and sprayer.

Access to Modern Assets

Next, we turn to ownership of items that can be categorised as "modern assets" in our study villages. These modern assets, we argue, are in today's world not luxury items but essential for service delivery and enhancing communication. The items include television, computer, car, scooter/motorcycle, mobile phone, and radio/transistor. The Census of India collects data on ownership of these assets. Table 8 provides the proportion of households that reported owning any one of the modern assets, along with the Census 2011 figures for rural Tripura and rural India.

Although not strictly comparable in terms of the geographical unit, there appears to have been substantial expansion in the spread of certain modern assets like televisions and mobile phones in the last five years. The 2011 Census recorded that 34 per cent of rural households in Tripura owned televisions. In our village surveys, we found that 76 per cent of households in Muhuripur, 71 per cent in Mainama, and 35 per cent in Khakchang owned televisions. Ownership of mobile phones had also spread. The Census reported that 35 per cent of rural households in Tripura owned a mobile phone. The village survey results showed that there was a significant upward trend in mobile phone ownership, with 93 per cent of households in Muhuripur, 89 per cent in Mainama, and 80 per cent in Khakchang owning mobile phones.

Among the three villages, Muhuripur had the greatest spread of modern assets, followed by Mainama and Khakchang. Khakchang fell behind the other two villages in terms of ownership of modern assets by a significant degree. One reason for this could be the lower coverage of grid-based

Table 8 *Proportion of households with modern assets in the three study villages, rural Tripura and rural India, 2011–16, in per cent*

Asset item	Rural Tripura (2011)	Rural India (2011)	Muhuripur	Mainama	Khakchang
TV	34	33	76	71	35
Car	1	2	3	3	2
Computer	6	5	4	4	1
Mobile phone	35	48	93	89	80
Scooter/motorcycle	5	14	18	19	5
Transistor/radio	13	17	5	5	0

Source: Census of India 2011; survey data, 2016.

electricity in Khakchang. A government lighting scheme for utilising solar energy through solar lighting panels was used to charge mobile phones in remote *para*s, but it was inadequate to operate televisions.

Remoteness and Asset Ownership

The remote location of Tripura and its hilly forested terrain have to be taken into consideration while making an assessment of assets owned by rural households in the State. In trying to capture the effect of remoteness on a household's asset possession in this section, we use data from Khakchang and Mainama villages. In both villages, the location of a household in terms of remoteness of location (based on distance from the village centre) affected the level and composition of assets owned.

Khakchang was the remotest in terms of accessibility and the presence of a difficult terrain among the three study villages. Within the village too, some of the *para*s or hamlets were relatively more accessible than others. Table 9 shows the proportion of households located in the remote and central *para*s, and their share in the total asset value of the village. Note that 76 per cent of households in Khakchang had received forest *patta*s, for which we have given no value – so we excluded all agricultural land from the analysis. In Khakchang, 63 per cent resided in the remote *para*s, although their share in the total asset value of the village was only 33 per cent. The average asset holding of a household in a remote *para* was substantially lower (by around Rs 3 lakhs) than the average asset holding of a central *para* household.

Table 10 shows the proportion of households owning assets, the average value of different assets, and the share of each asset type in total assets for households resident in central and remote *para*s. Households residing in remote *para*s were generally poorer in terms of their asset holdings as compared to residents of central *para*s. Differences in asset ownership were very large in respect of means of transport and

Table 9 *Distribution of assets and households by "para" location, Khakchang, 2016*, in per cent

Para location	Proportion in all assets	Proportion in all households	Mean value of assets
Central *para*	67	37	4,75,230
Remote *para*	33	63	1,37,582

Source: Survey data, 2016.

Table 10 *Proportion of households owning assets, share in total value, and average value of asset, by "para" and asset category, Khakchang, 2016, in per cent and Rs*

Asset category	Central *paras*			Remote *paras*		
	Proportion of households	Proportion in total value	Average value of assets	Proportion of households	Proportion in total value	Average value of assets
Homestead, other land, and buildings	98	72	3,83,790	100	28	87,523
Durable goods	100	55	23,189	100	45	8,375
Agricultural inventories	91	18	1,713	100	82	4,297
Commercial and non-agricultural inventory	24	93	14,405	9	7	1,775
Electrical equipment	95	58	11,157	82	42	5,653
Means of transport	38	95	46,769	27	5	1,917
Agricultural means of production	9	100	570	0	0	0
Livestock	67	37	26,215	84	63	21,447
Trees	83	59	31,724	84	41	13,147

Source: Survey data.

agricultural means of production. None of the households in the remote *para*s owned any valuable agricultural means of production. The majority of these households practiced *jhum* or shifting cultivation, largely using hand implements. The roads connecting remote *para*s to the village centre were often such that they could only be travelled on foot. This was one of the chief reasons for the lack of ownership of modern means of transport. Houses were mostly built of *katcha* materials in the case of remote *para* households. As it was difficult to put a market value on homestead land, the value of land was also low in the remote *para*s. The average value of a house and homestead land owned by a remote *para* household was Rs 87,523, whereas the same for a household living in any of the central *para*s was Rs 3,83,790. There was also a big difference in the extent of ownership of electrical equipment as between central and remote *para* households. As discussed above, this may be due to the restricted availability of grid-based electricity in the remote *para*s even though efforts had been made to provide solar lighting. However, there were two asset categories where the remote *para* households fared better than their central *para* counterparts: agricultural inventories and livestock. Most of the agricultural inventory found in the remote *para* households was the produce of *jhum* that had been stored. While the frequency of livestock ownership was higher in the remote *para* households, the average value of livestock was higher among the central *para* households.

In short, remoteness and presence of a difficult terrain were factors in the pattern of asset ownership in Khakchang village.

In Mainama, the hamlets were spread out and ranged from more remote hilly slopes to accessible lowland tracts of the village. Table 11 provides the distribution of households according to the location of the *para*s and their share in the total asset value of the village. Twelve per cent of the households in Mainama reported that they were beneficiaries of land reforms, and 9 per cent of all land under the possession of households in

Table 11 *Share of assets and households, and mean value of assets, by "para" location, Mainama, 2016*, in per cent and Rs

Para location	Proportion in all assets	Proportion in all households	Mean value of assets
Central *para*	68	58	8,35,840
Remote *para*	32	42	5,09,671

Source: Survey data, 2016.

the village was encroached land. As stated above, we have not assigned a monetary value to these lands as the households do not hold sale rights over them; thus we have excluded the value of agricultural land from the analysis. It was seen that households residing in central *paras* or those hamlets that were relatively close to the village centre held a disproportionately greater share of the total value of assets, as compared to households living in remote hamlets. The average value of assets held by a central *para* resident was Rs 8,35,840, whereas the same was Rs 5,09,671 for a remote *para* household.

Table 12 shows the proportion of households owning assets, their share in the total value of assets, and the average value of the assets according to the different asset categories across *paras*.

There was a clear difference in the average value of assets held by households in remote and central *paras*. This pointed to a qualitative difference in the nature of asset ownership. While 99 and 98 per cent respectively of central and remote *para* households reported owning homestead land and houses, there was clearly a difference in the average value of homestead land and houses owned between the two groups. The average value of homestead land and house owned by a central *para* household was Rs 6,76,401, whereas the same for a remote *para* resident was Rs 3,83,505. This was on account of the quality of houses in the remote *paras* (built of temporary rather than permanent material) and the lower price of homestead land in interior parts of the village. Similar was the case with the average value of durable goods and electrical equipment: 68 per cent of central *para* households reported owning some form of transport, as against 56 per cent in the remote *paras*. Some of the remote hamlets were only accessible by foot. Households in remote *paras* tended to own more and better quality livestock. This may be because these households had easier access to the woods, and were also more likely to own rubber plantations. The value of trees owned was clearly higher for those in remote *paras*. Interestingly, the value of agricultural means of production was higher for households in remote *paras*. This may have been on account of the State government's scheme of providing subsidies for purchasing power tillers, diesel pumps, and sprayers. The residents of remote *paras* were beneficiaries of this scheme.

It can thus be said that remote *para* households fared poorly as compared to central *para* residents in terms of the quality and range of assets owned by them. State intervention in the recent past has had a role in raising the value of assets owned by the residents of remote *paras*, for

Table 12 *Proportion of households owning assets, share in total value, and average value of asset, by "para" and asset category, Mainama, 2016, in per cent and Rs*

Asset category	Central *paras*			Remote *paras*		
	Proportion of households	Proportion in total value	Average value of asset	Proportion of households	Proportion in total value	Average value of asset
Homestead, other land, and buildings	99	71	6,76,401	98	29	3,83,505
Durable goods	100	59	31,337	100	41	29,236
Agricultural inventories	85	57	4,465	90	43	4,336
Commercial and non-agricultural inventory	17	65	62,401	8	35	93,922
Electrical equipment	97	62	14,025	98	38	11,555
Means of transport	68	65	37,317	56	35	33,420
Agricultural means of production	38	44	12,448	38	56	21,271
Livestock	63	47	33,325	78	53	40,589
Trees	73	48	16,823	79	52	23,032

instance, through schemes providing subsidised agricultural machinery and promoting rubber plantations.

Conclusion

This chapter examined asset holdings of households in the three study villages of Tripura. A comparison of asset holdings of rural households in Tripura with that of households in other States or the national average, it is pointed out, was not easy on two counts. First, the remote location of the state, its highly forested terrain, and a relatively weak land market imply that land prices are not governed by the same forces that operate in other States, and the price of agricultural land is not as high as in many other States. Secondly, thorough implementation of land reforms has led to a large number and proportion of households gaining use-rights over their land as well as access to forest land through forest *pattas*. These lands cannot be termed ownership holdings and are thus typically excluded from assets. In most parts of rural India, land – particularly agricultural land – is the most valuable asset. Tripura is perhaps unique in that land is not the primary asset of many rural households.

There were clear variations across the three villages: households in Muhuripur, South Tripura, had the highest asset holdings, followed by those in Mainama, Dhalai district. Households in Khakchang, a resettled tribal village in North district, were the worst off in terms of household assets. Khakchang's remoteness and heavily forested geography were the major reasons for the low levels of asset possession by its households.

Low incomes contributed to low levels of asset holdings across the study villages. The majority of households in all three villages were estimated to have an income of less than Rs 1 lakh a year. Further, while the average household had limited assets, even the richest household did not have as many assets as found in villages in other parts of India.

In terms of access to modern assets, mobile phones and televisions were the two most frequently reported assets. It appears that there has been a big rise in ownership of these assets between 2011 and 2016. Amongst the three villages, households in Muhuripur were most likely to own these two assets, followed by Mainama. One of the reasons for low ownership of modern assets in Khakchang is likely to be the restricted reach of grid electricity. There have been government interventions to provide solar energy to remote households in Khakchang. Nevertheless, there remains scope for further extending the reach of modern assets in the village.

Remoteness or poor accessibility and the presence of difficult terrain featured as determining factors in the asset composition of households in Mainama and Khakchang. In Khakchang, asset poverty among the more remotely located households was far greater as compared to residents closer to the village centre. In Mainama, those in remote hamlets owned qualitatively poorer and fewer assets than those in less remote hamlets. State financial support through subsidies for machinery had promoted asset purchase in the remote areas of Mainama. Geography clearly poses a challenge to improved economic status in rural Tripura.

References

Census of India (2011), *H Series: Tables on Census Houses, Household Amenities and Assets*, Registrar General and Census Commissioner of India, Ministry of Home Affairs, New Delhi.

National Sample Survey Organisation (NSSO) (2016), "Household Assets and Liabilities: Report Number 570 (70/18.2/1)," New Delhi.

15

Basic Amenities and Housing in the Study Villages

Rakesh Kumar Mahato and Sandipan Baksi

Tripura is a land-locked State located in the northeast of India. With Bangladesh forming its international border on the north, south, and west, on its east Tripura shares a border with the neighbouring States of Assam, Mizoram, and West Bengal. Much like other States of the region, Tripura has limited connectivity to the rest of the country. With two-thirds of its land area classified as forested land, its natural terrain is best described as hilly and densely forested (Government of Tripura 2007, pp. 3–4).

Tripura's modern history has seen much conflict and violence. Ethnic insurgency started in the 1980s, and till the end of the first decade of the 2000s when it was brought under control, the conflict presented the greatest political and developmental challenge to the State.[1] Tripura's path to peace has been recognised as "one that was not dependent solely on security measures, but involved investment in human development and people's participation in the implementation of socio-political and economic policy as well" (Swaminathan and Ramachandran 2017, see chapter 4). The "Tripura model" – whereby civil and ethnic conflict is doused through well-planned, people-centric development efforts by the elected government – has been successful in achieving a marked upswing in levels of human development in the State (*ibid.*).

Despite the difficulties posed by its topography, by socio-economic barriers of other kinds, and a political landscape marred by ethnic violence, various development indicators of the State such as literacy, per

[1] The roots of Tripura's ethnic violence can be traced back to the Partition of India in 1947. See Government of Tripura 2007, pp. 3–5, for details on the effect of the Partition on social and economic development in the State.

capita state domestic product (SDP), employment, and increasing work participation rates, to name but a few, saw sustained improvement in the last decade. These changes translated into higher living standards for the people of Tripura, a fact corroborated by data from the Census of India and the National Family and Health Survey (NFHS), which plots the remarkable achievements of the State in terms of penetration of electricity, availability and accessibility to covered sources of drinking water, and improved levels of sanitation.

This chapter evaluates changes in the living standards of Tripura, particularly rural Tripura. While we make use of State-level indicators of welfare from the Census of India (2001, 2011) and NFHS-4, we base our study essentially on data collected by the Foundation for Agrarian Studies (FAS) through household-level surveys conducted in three villages in the State as part of the Project on Agrarian Relations in India (PARI).

The chapter builds on a framework of analysis developed by FAS (see Singh 2017, 2017a). We analyse the conditions of housing and access to basic household amenities as factors that constitute critical components of the quality of life, human development, health, and dignity. They include housing, electricity, toilets, separate kitchens, cooking fuel, and drinking water. With regard to housing, the specific indicators we have examined include ownership of dwelling, type of house structure, availability of living space measured in terms of number of rooms and persons per room, and provision of a separate kitchen. In addition, we have examined the type of fuel used for cooking.[2]

We have analysed these variables across different income levels and socio-economic categories. We have also tried to evaluate the livelihood status of different social groupings such as Muslim, Scheduled Tribe (ST), Scheduled Caste (SC), Other Backward Class (OBC), and Others. Lastly, we have studied differences across the centrally situated and more isolated forest hamlets that fall under the villages of Khakchang and Mainama. There are no remote hamlets in Muhuripur.

We begin the discussion of the three villages, each very different in terms of social and geographical indicators, with a brief, impressionistic description of the village and its living conditions. This, we hope, will provide the context for the detailed data-based description that follows.

---

[2] Unclean fuels like firewood and crop residue constitute a health hazard for all residents, particularly for persons engaged in cooking. Clean fuels like liquefied petroleum gas (LPG) and biogas are smokeless and relatively safe.

Khakchang

Impressions

A tribal settlement located in the shadow of the Jampuii hills that form the border between the States of Tripura and Mizoram, Khakchang was created by resettling families from insurgency-affected areas. The village is part of the Tripura Tribal Areas Autonomous District Council (TTAADC), and its population largely comprises persons from the Reang tribe.

The village is actually a loose cluster of seven hamlets scattered over an area of 2,395 hectares on hilly slopes that are surrounded by thick forests. The distance between the hamlets can go up to 7–8 kilometres. Ananda Bazar Para is the only hamlet out of the seven that is within easy reach of the village market and well connected by road to Dasda block. Subhas Nagar Para is another hamlet that is somewhat close to the main road, although many of its households are dispersed and at considerable distance from the main road. All the other hamlets of Khakchang are located very far from the village centre and are difficult to access.

A village in this part of Tripura, therefore, is quite different from the idea of a village that popular imagination would conceive of as a single territorial and social unit. Here several hamlets constitute a village, and each is sparsely populated with a dispersed housing pattern. The total number of households resident in Khakchang is 589, and the total population is just 2,884. The scattered nature of the hamlets and the households within the hamlets stands out as the most striking feature of the village. Most hamlets do not enjoy easy access to the village market, and are mostly connected by brick and mud roads that are often not motorable. The undulating landscape and heavy seasonal rains make accessibility even more of a problem. Indeed, a resident would have to traverse a distance of almost 10 kilometres on foot from the village market along steep paths to reach the most isolated household in the village. Despite these odds, the presence of electricity, piped drinking water, and solar panels even in the farthest hamlet is striking.

A typical house in Khakchang is a bamboo structure raised on stilts. Bamboo is used for the walls, roofs, and even floors of dwelling units.[3]

---

[3] It is important to appreciate that materials like bamboo or wood, although classified as *katcha* material by the Census and the NSSO, are qualitatively different from other *katcha* materials like mud. Bamboo or wooden flooring does not pose any health hazard and may in fact be suitable for certain types of regional and climatic conditions. It is also regarded as fashionable

Wood and mud are also commonly used for house construction. The area below the house is used for the rearing of pigs and hens, an activity seen in every household in the village. Some households also rear goats. The main house typically comprises a large room in which the whole family resides. The kitchen space is usually cut off from the main hall by a bamboo thatch or cloth curtain. A narrow sit-out often extends out from the hall.

In Khakchang, there is a striking contrast between homesteads located in hamlets near the village centre and those up in the Jampuii hills in densely forested terrain. Here, typically, homesteads are not clearly demarcated and are rarely used for kitchen cultivation. The farther inside the forest a homestead is located, the more likely it will appear as a cleared extension of the surrounding forest that is not however fenced off. A narrow pathway leads to the elevated house directly from the village road. The backyards of these houses are uncultivated, and have dense vegetation and lots of naturally growing trees. A small bamboo structure with a blue plastic cover in a corner of the homestead serves as the toilet. In the centrally located hamlets, however, homesteads are clearly demarcated and kitchen gardens are a common sight.

Survey Data

Our survey data show that in Khakchang, houses are predominantly temporary structures. The proportion of households living in fully *pucca* structures – where the walls, roof, and floor of dwellings are made up of permanent material – was in single digits.[4] In fact, it was low (29 per cent) even among the highest income group (see Table 1).

In terms of socio-economic categories, about one-third of the class of "cultivator: non-*jhum* upland" resided in fully *pucca* houses. The corresponding number is almost zero for all other classes (see Table 2). The near-absence of *pucca* housing in the village is due to the persistent use of traditional materials, particularly bamboo, for house construction.

---

in some places. The authors are grateful to Shamsher Singh for pointing this out as a comment.

[4] The Census of India and the National Sample Survey Organisation (NSSO) define a permanent (*pucca*) house as a house with both roof and walls made of *pucca* or permanent materials. If either the roof or wall of the house is made of temporary (*katcha*) material, it is termed as a semi-*pucca* or semi-permanent house, and if both are made of temporary (*katcha*) materials, it is called a *katcha* or temporary house. For our analysis we have used slightly more stringent criteria. A fully *pucca* house is defined by us as one with roof, walls and floors, all three, made up of *pucca* or permanent materials. See Shamsher, Swaminathan, and Ramachandran (2013) for a critique of the definition used by Census and NSSO.

Table 1 *Proportion of households having fully "pucca" houses, by income level, Khakchang, 2016*

Income level	Per cent
0 to 50 K	0
50 K to 1 lakh	3
1 lakh to 2 lakhs	0
2 lakhs to 5 lakhs	29
All households	6

Source: Survey data.

Table 2 *Proportion of households having fully "pucca" houses, by socio-economic class, Khakchang, 2016*

Socio-economic class	Per cent
Manual worker with diversified income	0
Manual worker	0
Cultivator: mixed	0
Cultivator: *jhum*	0
Cultivator: lowland	5
Cultivator: non-*jhum* upland	33
Salaried, business, and others*	100
All households	6

Note: *There is only one salaried household in the sample.
Source: Survey data.

Sourcing permanent material for construction in Khakchang was difficult for its residents, as not only was it a newly settled village located in hilly and forested terrain, but also because the distance from the village centre made transportation of material difficult. On the other hand, bamboo was plentiful. Therefore, *katcha* dwelling structures were the standard in six of the relatively remote hamlets of the village. However, even in the single centrally located hamlet, the proportion of surveyed households living in permanent structures was just about 10 per cent. It is indeed telling that just one of the 44 survey households located in the inaccessible hamlets of the village resided in a structure that could qualify to be called a fully *pucca* house, as per our definition.

Almost 60 per cent of the surveyed households lived in single-room structures, and in about 70 per cent of them, more than two persons were found to share one room. While the proportion of households living in single-room houses declined as incomes grew, it still remained at about 30 per cent even among the highest income group (see Table 3).

A single-room house – where the family resided together in what was actually a large hall – was the norm across socio-economic categories. It was only among the class of "cultivator: non-*jhum* upland" that a shift away from single-room housing was apparent (see Table 4).

Kitchens in Khakchang were often a part of the main hall separated by a temporary partition, although many households had opted for an adjoining but separate kitchen. Notably, about 70 per cent of surveyed households in Khakchang reported having a separate kitchen facility. The

Table 3 *Proportion of households having single-room structure and more than two persons per room, by income level, Khakchang, 2016*

Income level	Single room	>2 persons per room
0 to 50 K	83	83
50 K to 1 lakh	63	70
1 lakh to 2 lakhs	58	67
2 lakhs to 5 lakhs	29	50
All households	60	69

Source: Survey data.

Table 4 *Proportion of households having single-room structure, by socio-economic class, Khakchang, 2016*

Socio-economic class	Per cent
Manual worker with diversified income	70
Manual worker	87
Cultivator: mixed	50
Cultivator: *jhum*	70
Cultivator: lowland	53
Cultivator: non-*jhum* upland	22
Salaried, business, and others*	100
All households	60

Note: *There is only one salaried household in the sample.
Source: Survey data.

proportion was reported as more than 60 per cent even in the "remote" hamlets. It is, however, difficult to infer whether the response about a separate kitchen actually points to a physically distinct kitchen facility, or to the part of the main hall used as a kitchen but separated by bamboo thatch or cloth curtain.

The use of clean fuel was low in Khakchang, with just about 13 per cent of the 86 households surveyed reporting LPG use. There was not a single household in the annual income group of up to Rs 1 lakh that used LPG for the purpose of cooking, and the proportion remained in single digits even in the Rs 1 lakh to Rs 2 lakhs bracket. While the use of LPG tended to increase as incomes rose, it was just 64 per cent even in the highest income group (see Table 5).

Table 5 *Proportion of households using clean fuel for cooking, by income level, Khakchang, 2016*

Income level	Per cent
0 to 50 K	0
50 K to 1 lakh	0
1 lakh to 2 lakhs	8
2 lakhs to 5 lakhs	64
All households	13

Source: Survey data.

Table 6 *Proportion of households using clean fuel for cooking, by socio-economic class, Khakchang, 2016*

Socio-economic class	Per cent
Manual worker with diversified income	10
Manual worker	0
Cultivator: mixed	0
Cultivator: *jhum*	7
Cultivator: lowland	11
Cultivator: non-*jhum* upland	56
Salaried, business, and others*	100
All households	13

Note: *There is only one salaried household in the sample.
Source: Survey data.

Among the different socio-economic categories, only "cultivator: non-*jhum* upland" tended to use LPG for cooking, while for all other classes, the usage was low (see Table 6). The difficulty in delivery of LPG cylinders was one obvious reason for its low penetration in areas where firewood was both cheap and plentiful. More generally, however, this reflects the low-income levels of households. Of the 44 households surveyed in the remote areas of Khakchang, only one reported using LPG for cooking, although even in that one house, firewood remained the main source.

The penetration of electricity in Khakchang appears relatively low when seen against the context of the remarkable achievements in electrification in the State of Tripura.[5] Only 65 per cent of surveyed households in the village had electricity connections. Households with higher incomes are certainly more likely to have been electrified (see Table 7).

However, it was less a matter of a household's income and more of the geographical remoteness of hamlets that determined the penetration of grid-based electricity in Khakchang. As we can see from Table 8, more than 80 per cent of the households located in the central hamlets had

Table 7 *Proportion of households having access to electricity, by income level, Khakchang, 2016*

Income level	Per cent
0 to 50 K	61
50 K to 1 lakh	50
1 lakh to 2 lakhs	71
2 lakhs to 5 lakhs	93
All households	65

Source: Survey data.

Table 8 *Proportion of households with access to electricity and lighting (including solar), by hamlet, Khakchang, 2016*

Hamlets	Electricity	Lighting
Remote hamlets	48	68
Central hamlets	83	88

Source: Survey data.

---

[5] As per NFHS-4 (2015–16), 99 per cent of households in Tripura, and 90 per cent of households in rural Tripura were electrified.

authorised access to electricity, whereas the proportion was less than 50 per cent for those living in the six relatively inaccessible hamlets. It is revealing that of the 14 surveyed households belonging to the highest income group in Khakchang, only one household did not have access to electricity connection. This particular household was located in one of these six hamlets of the village.

Inaccessibility and the segregated nature of hamlets in Khakchang, along with the fact that the terrain is hilly and forested, is indeed a huge challenge for the delivery of grid-based electricity. There have been attempts to provide solar-based lighting in Khakchang. Under the Remote Village Electrification (RVE) Programme, panchayats made provisions for solar home lighting systems. The panchayat provided a solar plate, a battery (24 volts), and two bulbs at a subsidised price of Rs 2,000. Consequently, we see a much high proportion of the households located in these remote hamlets with access to solar lighting than to the electricity grid (see Table 8).

Solar and other non-conventional sources of energy, though important, can never substitute for grid-based electricity. The usage of consumer durables in a home, and indeed the productive capacity of the village economy as a whole, requires grid-based electricity to prosper.

Private sources of drinking water are almost absent in Khakchang, again perhaps because its hilly terrain makes pump installation a difficult and expensive proposition. The panchayat has played an important role in providing drinking water in the village: 97 per cent of households that were surveyed reported access to sources of drinking water provided by the panchayat. Village-level data shows that the panchayat has provided 43 taps, five hand pumps, one tube well, and 14 wells in Khakchang. A nearby stream is another important source of drinking water. Given the almost total preponderance of panchayat-installed sources of drinking water, it is not surprising that only 5 per cent of all surveyed households had the source of drinking water located within the homestead.

More than 40 per cent of the surveyed households in Khakchang drank water from open sources (see Table 9), which shows that public sources of drinking water are non-covered sources. This proportion goes up to 60 per cent in the more inaccessible hamlets, while the corresponding figure for the central hamlets was less than 20 per cent. This variation, once again, points to the constraints on development imposed by geography. Of the drinking water sources provided by the panchayat, the proportion of open sources – wells, for example – is much higher in the remote hamlets than

Table 9 *Proportion of households having access to open source of drinking water, by hamlet, Khakchang, 2016*

Hamlets	Per cent
Central hamlets	19
Remote hamlets	61
All households	41

Source: Survey data.

Table 10 *Proportion of households using panchayat/government-provided sources and having access to closed source of drinking water, Khakchang, 2016*

Hamlets	Closed source	Open source	Total
Central hamlets	85 (35)	15 (6)	100 (40)
Remote mamlets	40 (17)	60 (26)	100 (43)

Note: The figures in brackets are the absolute number of households.
Source: Survey data.

in the central ones. Table 10 shows that among households in the central hamlets that were dependent on panchayat-provided sources of drinking water, more than 85 per cent consumed water from covered sources. The corresponding number for inaccessible hamlets was just 40 per cent. We must make the observation here that uncovered sources of drinking water appeared to be under proper maintenance.

Despite its difficult terrain and remoteness, Khakchang has done very well in at least one area of sanitation. More than 90 per cent of its surveyed households had access to lavatories. Even in the inaccessible hamlets, this proportion was as high as 86 per cent. Notably, 48 per cent of the surveyed households, even in remote villages, reported getting institutional support for the construction of housing and/or toilets. It is only among the highest income category households that this proportion goes down to 29 per cent. Among all other income groups, we see that about half of all households received such support (see Table 11). The support was mostly in the form of cash and tin-sheets. Our data show that support under the Indira Awaas Yojana was commonly available to the households.

These findings indicate the active role of the state in ensuring high levels of sanitation even where geographical conditions pose a challenge for service delivery. However, the physical condition of toilets in the

Table 11 *Proportion of households that received institutional support for housing and/or toilets, by income level, Khakchang, 2016*

Income level	Per cent
0 to 50 K	50
50 K to 1 lakh	57
1 lakh to 2 lakhs	46
2 lakhs to 5 lakhs	29
All households	48

Source: Survey data.

village was poor. A typical toilet is a bamboo-supported structure with polythene walls and, more often than not, no roof. Sewage lines for the disposal of waste water were absent. Overall, the quality of the toilets was worse in the remote hamlets than in the central hamlets.

In conclusion it can be said that Khakchang represents a distinct typography of rural living in Tripura. Its experience illustrates both the achievements and the challenges of taking public services to a newly settled area with unfavourable physical and geographical conditions.

Mainama

Impressions

Mainama village in Dhalai district has an unusual mix of geographical and demographic features. Topographically, the village encompasses lowlands where paddy is cultivated and sloping land where rubber is cultivated. Demographically, its residents are from both tribal and non-tribal groups, the former living in the relatively isolated, hilly and forested hamlets, and the latter occupying the central lowland areas of the village. The village is part of the Tripura Tribal Areas Autonomous District Council (TTAADC). Most of the tribal families were relocated from the forests by the State government in the recent past through rubber plantation schemes.

The village and its 11 hamlets lie scattered across an area of 1,081 hectares, with distances between its sparsely populated hamlets varying from anywhere between 1 to 8 kilometres. There are about 1,451 households resident in the village, with a population of about 6,693. The hamlets are connected mostly by mud and brick roads, and in the monsoon season are accessible only on foot. Within hamlets, houses are dispersed, a feature that can be particularly noticed in the outlier hamlets rather than in the central ones. Typically, in these remote hamlets, a fairly long walk along narrow mud paths flanked by agricultural fields or natural vegetation separate clusters of two or three households each.

Houses built of concrete are a rare sight. All of Mainama's houses have tin roofs that provide effective shelter from the copious rains that are received in these parts. On the flip side, however, the permanent roofs create a deafening noise when the rain beats down on tin roofs during the monsoons. Bamboo, available locally in abundance, is also used for house construction, especially in the forest hamlets. Here, houses have large homesteads with lots of trees. The central hamlets, on the other hand, have smaller homesteads with dense kitchen gardens. Unlike Khakchang, homesteads here are fenced off and closed with bamboo or tin gates.

The cattle shed is an important part of the homestead, especially in the lowland hamlets where cattle are used for ploughing and other agricultural operations. Pigs are reared, as pork is an important part of the diet of tribal households. The pig sheds are always located at a distance from the cattle sheds. All homesteads have hens, with some households in the central hamlets rearing them commercially. Goats and ducks are reared but far less commonly.

While the practice of open defecation does not exist in the village, the lavatories are not hygienically maintained. Every household has a toilet, but with no sewage lines. In the central hamlets, toilets are concrete structures but with no roofs or doors. In the forest hamlets, toilets are constructed with bamboo, thatch or tin.

While the village is well connected by an all-weather road to the block headquarters at Manu, the roads connecting the scattered hamlets are of varying quality, ranging from tarred and motorable roads to mud passages.

Survey Data

Village-level data from Mainama indicates that while almost all the households surveyed owned their place of dwelling, the structures themselves were mostly made of non-permanent material. Only one-fifth of the households surveyed lived in permanent or fully *pucca* houses, which, by our definition, are houses with roof, walls, and floors made up of *pucca* or permanent materials.

Income of course played an important role in determining the quality of housing structure in the village. The proportion of households enjoying the safety of a permanent dwelling among those earning between Rs 1,00,000 to Rs 2,00,000 in a year was less than 15 per cent. This proportion rose sharply among the higher income households. Almost 40 per cent of those falling in the income category of Rs 2,00,000 to Rs 5,00,000 resided in permanent structures. The proportion went as high as 63 per cent among households earning more than Rs 5,00,000 (see Table 12).

Equally, a household's socio-economic class status was an important factor influencing the quality of housing structure in Mainama. About one-third of those belonging to the salaried class and 45 per cent of "cultivator: medium" households enjoyed the benefits of permanent

Table 12 *Proportion of households having fully "pucca" houses, by income level, Mainama, 2016*

Income level	Per cent
0 to 50 K	9
50 K to 1 lakh	11
1 lakh to 2 lakhs	13
2 lakhs to 5 lakhs	40
Above 5 lakhs	63
All households	20

Source: Survey data.

Table 13 *Proportion of households having fully "pucca" houses, by socio-economic class, Mainama, 2016*

Socio-economic class	Per cent
Manual worker with diversified income	9
Manual worker	9
Cultivator: sub-marginal	18
Cultivator: marginal	21
Cultivator: small	23
Cultivator: medium	45
Salaried, business, and others	33
All households	20

Source: Survey data.

Table 14 *Proportion of households having single room structure and more than two persons per room, by income level, Mainama, 2016*

Income level	Single room	>2 persons per room
0 to 50 K	62	53
50 K to 1 lakh	45	54
1 lakh to 2 lakhs	34	59
2 lakhs to 5 lakhs	28	38
Above 5 lakhs	0	6
All households	39	49

Source: Survey data.

dwelling structures. The proportion was about 20 per cent among all other socio-economic classes. The "manual worker" and "manual worker with diversified income" households seemed to fare the worst, with about 90 per cent of them residing in structures made of non-permanent material (see Table 13).

Notably, very few houses could be technically termed as temporary or fully *katcha*, as the walls and roofs of these houses were made of tin.[6] The floors, however, were invariably of mud.

With regard to availability of living space and crowdedness, the survey data reveal that about 40 per cent of surveyed households in Mainama resided in structures with just one room. In about half of all the surveyed households, more than two persons had to share a room (see Table 14).

The survey data show a clear correlation between the proportion of households living in single-room structures and income levels (see Table 14). Not a single household belonging to the highest income level group, of more than Rs 5,00,000, resided in a single-room house. A similar pattern can be observed in respect of the proportion of households with more than two persons sharing a room, which remained more than 50 per cent in households earning less than Rs 2,00,000. This proportion declined rapidly to less than 40 per cent among those falling in the income category of Rs 2,00,000 to Rs 5,00,000, and further to single-digit figures among the richest households (see Table 14).

An analysis of crowdedness across socio-economic classes in Mainama

---

[6] Though tin is classified as permanent material by the Census and NSSO due to its durability, this material has drawbacks. In summer especially, homes with tin roofs become very hot.

reveals that manual worker households fared the worst, with 60 per cent of them living in single-room structures. About the same proportion of labouring households resided in houses where more than two persons shared a room. The salaried and business class enjoyed the maximum living space in the village: about 73 per cent of such households lived in structures with more than one room. Not surprisingly, in almost 90 per cent of households belonging to this class, a room was shared by two or less than two persons. "Cultivator: medium" households constituted another class category that lived in relatively less crowded spaces (see Table 15).

A very high proportion (90 per cent) of the surveyed houses had separate kitchen facilities, and the proportion was more than 80 per cent even among the lowest income group. The socio-economic category that fared lowest on this particular criterion was that of manual worker households. More than one-third of such surveyed households reported not having a separate kitchen (see Tables 16 and 17).

Use of LPG appeared to be on the rise with 46 per cent of the surveyed households in the village using it as the primary fuel for cooking. This was much better than the figure for rural India (24 per cent), as reported by the NFHS-4 (2015–16). Surprisingly, the level of LPG use in the village, as pointed to by the survey data, was considerably higher than the figures in NFHS-4 (2015–16) for the State of Tripura as well as for Dhalai district.[7]

Table 15 *Proportion of households having single-room structure and more than two persons per room, by socio-economic class, Mainama, 2016*

Socio-economic class	Single room	>2 persons per room
Manual worker with diversified income	36	41
Manual worker	60	60
Cultivator: sub-marginal	35	59
Cultivator: marginal	47	55
Cultivator: small	33	47
Cultivator: medium	18	36
Salaried, business, and others	27	12
All households	39	49

Source: Survey data.

---

[7] NFHS-4 (2015–16) reported that 31 per cent of Tripura, and just about 16 per cent of rural Tripura, use clean fuel for cooking. The corresponding figures for Dhalai are 19 and 15 per cent respectively.

Table 16 *Proportion of households having separate kitchen,*
by income level, Mainama, 2016

Income level	Per cent
0 to 50 K	82
50 K to 1 lakh	93
1 lakh to 2 lakhs	93
2 lakhs to 5 lakhs	91
Above 5 lakhs	94
All households	90

Source: Survey data.

Table 17 *Proportion of households having separate kitchen,*
by socio-economic class, Mainama, 2016

Socio-economic class	Per cent
Manual worker with diversified income	95
Manual worker	66
Cultivator: sub-marginal	96
Cultivator: marginal	91
Cultivator: Small	97
Cultivator: Medium	82
Salaried, business, and others	94
All households	90

Source: Survey data.

This big difference in the two sets of figures can only be reconciled through an in-depth study of fuel consumption.

The use of LPG was much higher in the higher income categories, with more than 90 per cent of households with an annual income of more than Rs 5,00,000 using clean fuel for cooking. The corresponding proportion remained low at about 25 per cent among households earning less than Rs 1,00,000 (see Table 18).

In terms of socio-economic categories, use of clean fuel for cooking was most prevalent among the salaried and business classes, followed by "cultivator: medium" households. The manual worker class fared the worst, with just about a quarter of such households shifting away from firewood (see Table 19).

Only one out of four Scheduled Caste (SC) and two out of six Muslim

Table 18 *Proportion of households using clean fuel for cooking, by income level, Mainama, 2016*

Income level	Per cent
0 to 50 K	20
50 K to 1 lakh	28
1 lakh to 2 lakhs	50
2 lakhs to 5 lakhs	78
Above 5 lakhs	94
All households	46

Source: Survey data.

Table 19 *Proportion of households using clean fuel for cooking, by socio-economic class, Mainama, 2016*

Socio-economic class	Per cent
Manual worker with diversified income	59
Manual worker	29
Cultivator: sub-marginal	37
Cultivator: marginal	47
Cultivator: small	47
Cultivator: medium	64
Salaried, business, and others	76
All households	46

Source: Survey data.

households surveyed in Mainama used LPG as the primary fuel for cooking. An important determining factor for the use of clean fuel for cooking was the location of the hamlets. In the inaccessible hamlets of Mainama, clean fuel usage covered 35 per cent of the surveyed households, much lower than in the central hamlets where it was at 55 per cent (see Table 20). As we noted for Khakchang, in Mainama's remote hamlets too, the low penetration of LPG was due to the availability of wood from the forests and the problem of service delivery to these parts.

Our survey data revealed that more than 95 per cent of the households surveyed had electricity connections, a proportion that remained high even in the relatively inaccessible hamlets.

In respect of drinking water sources, the survey data show that about

Table 20 *Proportion of households using clean fuel for cooking, by hamlets, Mainama, 2016*

Hamlets	Per cent
Central hamlets	55
Remote hamlets	35
All households	46

Source: Survey data.

Table 21 *Proportion of households having source of drinking water within homestead, by income level, Mainama, 2016*

Income level	Within homestead	Outside the house <200 metres	Outside the house >200 metres
0 to 50 K	29	47	24
50 K to 1 lakh	49	33	18
1 lakh to 2 lakh	49	35	16
2 lakhs to 5 lakhs	67	26	7
Above 5 lakhs	69	25	6
All households	50	35	15

Source: Survey data.

50 per cent of surveyed households travelled outside their homestead to fetch drinking water (see Table 21). The data suggest that about half of all surveyed households depended on water sources owned by them, while the other half depended on either public sources, or on sources that were either jointly owned with another household or belonged to another household. Table 22 clearly demonstrates that while panchayat or government sources seem to provide drinking water to more than 25 per cent of the village, dependence on such sources was much higher among the lower income groups. The same was true for the socio-economic class of manual workers (see Table 23).

The figures regarding ownership of the source of drinking water were dismal for the Muslim population, with just one out of six Muslim households surveyed reporting personal ownership of the source. The poorest households – landless Muslim households – travelled longer distances than others to fetch drinking water.

About 70 per cent of the village had access to covered sources of

Table 22 *Proportion of households having personal access to drinking water, by income level, Mainama, 2016*

Income level	Personal	Joint/group/ public	Other person	Panchayat/ government
0 to 50 K	31	22	18	29
50 K to 1 lakh	46	18	9	27
1 lakh to 2 lakhs	50	12	9	29
2 lakhs to 5 lakhs	60	12	5	23
Above 5 lakhs	56	13	6	25
All households	48	15	10	27

Source: Survey data.

Table 23 *Proportion of households having personal access to drinking water, by socio-economic class, Mainama, 2016*

Socio-economic class	Personal	Joint/group/ public	Other person	Panchayat/ government
Manual worker with diversified income	45	23	0	32
Manual worker	34	9	26	31
Cultivator: sub-marginal	46	20	11	23
Cultivator: marginal	48	16	9	27
Cultivator: small	63	17	3	17
Cultivator: medium	55	18	9	18
Salaried, business, and others	48	6	6	40
All households	48	15	10	27

Source: Survey data.

drinking water, although it was only 56 per cent in the remote hamlets and 80 per cent in the central hamlets.

In keeping with the remarkable record of Tripura in fighting open defecation, almost all the surveyed households in Mainama had access to toilets. However, many of these were tin structures of poor quality that lacked proper sewerage lines. The NFHS-4 (2015–16) reported that only 15 per cent of households in the rural areas of Dhalai district had good sanitation facilities. Most village latrines had poor upkeep.

The survey data show that 44 per cent of the surveyed households in the village – the proportion was much higher among the lower income groups – received institutional support for the construction of their house and/or lavatory. Similarly, households under the categories of manual worker, cultivator: sub-marginal, and cultivator: marginal were more likely to have received institutional support for constructing toilets than households with higher operational landholdings. The proportion of households receiving monetary or other support for building toilets was also low (33 per cent) among the salaried, business, and others class (see Table 24). Much of this institutional support was under the Indira Awaas Yojana. The support for house construction was mostly in the form of cash and tin-sheets. Support was also provided in the form of materials for the construction of toilets.

Finally, the data reveal that only 11 per cent of the surveyed households in the village enjoyed living in what has been defined as "integrated housing", i.e. in permanent structures with two or more rooms, with a metred electricity connection, access to a source of drinking water within the homestead or just outside, and a closed toilet.[8] This number leaves a lot to be desired in terms of the living conditions that prevail in the village (see Appendix 1 for a picture of integrated housing across PARI villages). Noticeably, quality of housing, particularly on account of the majority of surveyed households having *katcha* floors, was the predominant factor in preventing many households from attaining the status of integrated housing, despite the availability of institutional support.

Table 24 *Proportion of households that received institutional support for housing and/or toilets, by socio-economic class, Mainama, 2016*

Socio-economic class	Per cent
Manual worker with diversified income	59
Manual worker	43
Cultivator: sub-marginal	51
Cultivator: marginal	45
Cultivator: small	27
Cultivator: medium	36
Salaried, business, and others	33
All households	44

Source: Survey data.

---

[8] See Singh, Swaminathan, and Ramachandran (2013) for details of "integrated housing."

The socio-economic classes that scored high on the quality of living indicators were the "cultivator: medium" and "salaried and business" classes. Labouring households among the landless had the lowest standards of living in the village. The inaccessible hamlets of the village were more deprived than the central hamlets, and the proportion of deprivation was much higher among lower income groups than higher income groups, particularly in terms of access to clean fuel for cooking and covered sources of drinking water.

Muhuripur

Impressions

A well-developed irrigated village, Muhuripur is primarily an immigrant village with a dominance of Bengali speakers who were part of the influx of migrants from Bangladesh in the 1970s. Agriculture here is characterised mainly by the cultivation of rice, and a wide variety vegetables and tubers including winter potato. The village has a small sericulture sector, and rubber is cultivated on slopes.

Muhuripur is much like a typical West Bengal lowland village. It gets its name from the river Muhuri, a major irrigation source. The village, spread over 551 hectares, comprised 11 densely settled hamlets, and though some of them extend to the nearby hill slopes, there was no habitation on the slopes. There was also no forest land in the village. There were 1,054 households resident in the village, and the total population was 4,404. The population was a mix of caste Hindus, Other Backward Classes (OBC), and Scheduled Caste (SC) households. There were very few Scheduled Tribe (ST) households in the village. Hamlets were more or less divided on the basis of caste.

The houses here were generally constructed of permanent materials like concrete and cement, and can be regarded as good quality housing. Despite its high population density, per capita living space was high. The houses generally had sit-outs in the front (spaces where the PARI interviews were often conducted), and were surrounded by moderately-sized homesteads ringed by bamboo fencing. A bamboo or tin gate led to the house through a courtyard filled with trees like coconut and betel-nut. A typical courtyard would, in addition to a kitchen garden, also have lots of flowering plants. Cows and bullocks were housed in the cattle shed situated on the homestead. Most households reared hens, ducks, and goats. Ponds and small water bodies, in which fish for home consumption are cultivated, lie adjacent to the homesteads.

The PARI team was struck by the overall cleanliness of the village. There was no open defecation here, and toilets, which were mostly made of permanent material, were well maintained. Gatherings around common sources of water were rarely seen, suggesting that most homes had access to private sources of drinking water. A good-quality all-weather road passes through Muhuripur to connect it with the district headquarters at Belonia.

Survey Data

Almost all the surveyed households owned their places of dwelling, and about one-third lived in fully *pucca* or permanent houses (only 6 per cent of all the surveyed households in Khakchang and 20 per cent in Mainama lived in fully *pucca* houses).[9]

There were, in fact, no fully *katcha* houses in Muhuripur, as tin was generally used for constructing roofs and walls. In semi-permanent structures, the floors were generally made of mud. The use of *katcha* material for floor construction declined with increases in income levels. This is reflected by the fact that while just 16 per cent of the households falling into the lowest income category (less than Rs 5,00,000 annually) lived in permanent structures, the proportion increased to about 70 per cent among households falling in the Rs 2,00,000–Rs 5,00,000 income group. For households with incomes over Rs 5,00,000, the proportion was 100 per cent (see Table 25).

As noted for the other villages, the extent of a household's landholding also determined the quality of housing in Muhuripur. Two-thirds of salaried and business households lived in permanent structures. Households belonging to the cultivator classes were more likely to live in permanent dwelling structures than the manual worker households (see Table 26).

Variation in the quality of housing across social groups was also observed. While 40 per cent of the 130 surveyed households belonging to the category of "Others" resided in fully *pucca* structures, the proportion

---

[9] According to the Census of India, 2011, the proportion of *pucca* or permanent houses in Tripura was 19 per cent. The corresponding figure for rural Tripura was less than 10 per cent. The corresponding figure for rural India was 47 per cent. While, of course, the figures arrived at through PARI surveys are incomparable to the Census surveys of the Government of India, this definitely hints at the fact that the proportion of people living in permanent structure dwellings in Muhuripur was unusually high for the State of Tripura.

Table 25 *Proportion of households having fully "pucca" houses, by income level, Muhuripur, 2016*

Income level	Per cent
0 to 50 K	16
50 K to 1 lakh	25
1 lakh to 2 lakhs	32
2 lakhs to 5 lakhs	68
Above 5 lakhs	100
All households	34

Source: Survey data.

Table 26 *Proportion of households having fully "pucca" houses, by socio-economic class, Muhuripur, 2016*

Socio-economic class	Per cent
Manual worker with diversified income	16
Manual worker	29
Cultivator: sub-marginal	31
Cultivator: marginal	41
Cultivator: small	60
Salaried, business, and others	65
All households	34

Source: Survey data.

came down to 30 per cent of SC households, and further down to 21 per cent of OBC households surveyed (see Table 27).

The survey data indicate a general picture of less crowded and relatively larger living space in village households, a sharp contrast to Mainama and Khakchang. More than 80 per cent of the households resided in houses that had more than one room. Moreover, the proportion of households where we saw more than two persons sharing one room was just about 25 per cent (see Table 28).

Income was certainly a deciding factor for the determination of crowdedness in village homes. Households belonging to the lowest income category lived in much more crowded conditions, with about 35 per cent of them dwelling in single-room structures. We noted that as incomes rise, living quarters expand. In Muhiripur, not even a single

Table 27 *Proportion of households having fully "pucca" houses, by caste, Muhuripur, 2016*

Caste	Per cent
Scheduled Caste (SC)	30 (9)
Other Backward Class (OBC)	21 (11)
Other	40 (52)
All households	34 (72)

Note: Absolute number of households is given in parentheses.
Source: Survey data.

Table 28 *Proportion of households having single-room structures and more than two persons per room, by income level, Muhuripur, 2016*

Income level	Single room	>2 persons per room
0 to 50 K	35	49
50 K to 1 lakh	18	27
1 lakh to 2 lakhs	7	17
2 lakhs to 5 lakhs	6	6
Above 5 lakhs	0	14
All households	16	25

Source: Survey data.

household belonging to the highest income group lived in a single-room house. (see Table 28).

A similar trend was seen in relation to households having more than two persons sharing one room (Table 28). While the proportion was about 50 per cent among the surveyed households belonging to the lowest income category, it declined as incomes increased. The data in Table 28 indicate a sudden spike in the proportion of households with more than two persons per room among the highest income group in the village. This was due to two village households with large family sizes in this income bracket. (There were a total of 16 persons in these two households who lived in six rooms.) In none of the other five surveyed households belonging to the highest income group did we see more than two persons sharing a room.

It was only in the case of manual worker households that we found relatively more crowded conditions of living. About 43 per cent of such households lived in single-room houses. Not surprisingly, our study indicates that in more than 50 per cent of households from this socio-economic class, more than two persons share a room. Conditions were much better for other classes. The class of "salaried, business, and others", and the class of "cultivator: small" lived in much less crowded conditions (see Table 29).

Across social groups, households belonging to the "Others" category lived in the least crowded conditions, followed by SC households. OBC households fared the worst (see Table 30).

A very high proportion of households, 72 per cent, claimed to use LPG as the main fuel for cooking. Even in the lowest income group (see Table 31), the figure was about 50 per cent. Of all the socio-economic categories, it was only among manual workers that we witnessed relatively low penetration of LPG (43 per cent). The penetration of clean fuels is a major achievement in this village, especially when seen in the context

Table 29 *Proportion of households having single-room structures and more than two persons per room, by socio-economic class, Muhuripur, 2016*

Socio-economic class	Single room	>2 persons per room
Manual worker with diversified income	9	16
Manual worker	43	52
Cultivator: sub-marginal	17	24
Cultivator: marginal	14	38
Cultivator: small	0	0
Salaried, business, and others	6	0
All households	16	25

Source: Survey data.

Table 30 *Proportion of households having more than two persons per room, by caste, Muhuripur, 2016*

Caste	Per cent
Scheduled Caste (SC)	30
Other Backward Class (OBC)	37
Others	19
All households	25

Source: Survey data.

Table 31 *Proportion of households using clean fuel for cooking, by income level, Muhuripur, 2016*

Income level	Per cent
0 to 50 K	47
50 K to 1 lakh	69
1 lakh to 2 lakhs	78
2 lakhs to 5 lakhs	94
Above 5 lakhs	100
All households	72

Source: Survey data.

of rural India as a whole, where, notwithstanding some improvements in the last decade, the use of clean fuels for cooking continues to be low.[10] Penetration of LPG as cooking fuel is generally low in Tripura, possibly a result of its hilly terrain and dense forest cover which can be a hindrance to delivery services. The National Family and Health Survey (2015–16) indicates that the proportion of households using clean fuel for cooking in rural Tripura, at 16 per cent, is lower that the corresponding all-India figure (24 per cent).

It is noteworthy that almost the whole village had authorised electricity connections. This is somewhat in line with the general trend of high electrification in Tripura, including rural Tripura. The survey data indicate that the proportion of households with access to electricity is unusually high in the other two surveyed villages as well. The progress of electrification in Tripura, despite geographic and economic obstacles, has been impressive. According to the *Economic Review of Tripura 2015–16* (Government of Tripura 2016), the proportion of electricity for domestic use has increased significantly – from 24 per cent in 1995–96 to 54.1 per cent in 2015–16.[11] The Census of India data also show a significant increase

[10] According to the Census of India, the proportion of households using clean fuel for cooking in India has increased from 18.1 per cent in 2001 to 29.1 per cent in 2011. In the case of rural India, the proportion has increased from 6.3 per cent in 2001 to 11.9 per cent in 2011. NFHS-4 (2015–16) data indicate that about 44 per cent of all households in India use clean fuel for cooking. The number comes down to 24 per cent for rural India.

[11] The *Economic Review of Tripura 2015–16* (Government of Tripura 2016) reveals that in 1995–95, of 223.66 million units (MU) of power sold to ultimate consumers in the State, 53.76 MU was sold for "domestic light and fan use." In 2015–16, the total units of power sold to ultimate consumers were 813.06 MU, of which 439.79 MU were sold for domestic use.

in the proportion of households with electricity connections. According to NFHS-4 (2015–16), 99 per cent of households in Tripura, and 90 per cent of those in rural Tripura, were electrified.

In terms of access to drinking water, our study shows that about 60 per cent of all surveyed households depended on sources owned by them. Panchayat and government sources were the other important sources of drinking water, with more than 25 per cent households having access to such sources (Table 32).

All households belonging to the highest income group of more than Rs 5,00,000 had personal sources of drinking water. The proportion was about 80 per cent among the "salaried, business, and others" as well as "cultivator: small" classes. For all other categories the figure was close to the village average of 60 per cent (see Table 33).

Access to drinking water, defined as the distance a household has

Table 32 *Proportion of households having personal access to drinking water, by caste, Muhuripur, 2016*

Caste	Personal	Joint/group/ public	Other person	Panchayat/ government
Scheduled Caste (SC)	70	10	3	17
Other Backward Class (OBC)	63	2	10	25
Other	59	7	4	30
All households	62	6	5	27

Source: Survey data.

Table 33 *Proportion of households having personal access to drinking water, by socio-economic class, Muhuripur, 2016*

Socio-economic class	Personal	Joint/group/ public	Other person	Panchayat/ government
Manual worker with diversified income	69	9	3	19
Manual worker	67	0	9	24
Cultivator: sub-marginal	56	6	4	34
Cultivator: marginal	57	8	11	24
Cultivator: small	80	0	0	20
Salaried, business, and others	76	6	0	18
All households	62	6	5	27

Source: Survey data.

to travel in order to get to its source, reflects very similar results to ownership of water sources. About two-thirds of the surveyed households had their source of drinking water within or just outside the homestead. A household's caste or other indicators of social status did not appear to have any impact on access to drinking water facilities in the village. Almost all sources of drinking water were covered sources.

Instances of open defecation were rare in the village. This, as we have seen, was generally true for the other two villages as well, and is indicative of the achievements of Tripura in its fight against open defecation. Data from the Census of India show that the proportion of households having access to toilets in the State went up from 81.5 per cent in 2001 to 86 per cent in 2011. Similarly, in the rural areas of Tripura, the proportion increased from 77.9 per cent in 2001 to 81.4 per cent in 2011. These numbers were much higher than the all-India figure (47 per cent) for 2011.

The quality of latrines in Muhuripur was much better than what was observed in the other two villages, and many of the households' lavatories were made of permanent material. All toilets had sewage lines. This is in line with the findings of NFHS-4 (2015–16) for South Tripura district, which show that more than 60 per cent of the households had good sanitation facilities.

It is noteworthy that about 45 per cent of surveyed households reported having received institutional support for constructing their house and/or toilet. The proportion of households receiving such support was much higher among the lower income groups (see Table 34). Indira Awaas Yojana, under which such institutional support was made available, was certainly one of the most successful schemes. Support for house

Table 34 *Proportion of households that received institutional support for housing and/or toilets, by income level, Muhuripur, 2016*

Income level	Per cent
0 to 50 K	56
50 K to 1 lakh	63
1 lakh to 2 lakhs	40
2 lakhs to 5 lakhs	6
Above 5 lakhs	14
All households	45

Source: Survey data.

Table 35 *Proportion of households that received institutional support for housing and/or toilets, by socio-economic class, Muhuripur, 2016*

Socio-economic class	Per cent
Manual worker with diversified income	53
Manual worker	71
Cultivator: sub-marginal	49
Cultivator: marginal	38
Cultivator: small	30
Salaried, business, and others	0
All households	45

Source: Survey data.

construction was mostly in the form of cash and tin-sheets. Support was also provided in the form of materials for the construction of toilets.

A majority of "manual worker" households reported receiving such institutional support. About half the households in the "cultivator: sub-marginal" class reported receiving financial support, while the number was relatively low among the higher landholding classes. None of the seventeen households in the "salaried, business, and others" class reported receiving such support (see Table 35).

It is quite clear that living standards in Muhuripur were much better than in the other two villages. A significant proportion of the village, across class and social categories, had access to basic amenities. About a quarter of the surveyed families lived in integrated housing, implying that they lived in permanent structures with two or more rooms and a metred electricity connection, with access to a source of drinking water within the homestead or just outside, and their own toilets. This number is comparable to some of the agriculturally advanced villages that PARI has surveyed (see Appendix 1).

"Salaried and business" and "cultivator: small" households undoubtedly enjoyed the highest living standards in the village, while "manual worker" households fared the worst. Income, of course, is an important determinant of living standards. Social groupings like caste and religion did not appear to be determining factors with respect to levels of well-being or a lack thereof in Muhuripur, although it was observed that OBC households generally fared worse than "Others" and SC households. Nevertheless, the numbers portray a situation of relatively less inequality in terms of quality of housing and access to amenities within Muhuripur as compared to other villages.

Conclusions

This chapter examined housing conditions and access to basic amenities in the three study villages of Tripura. It is evident that the three villages are distinct in more than one way. They differ in terms of the stage of development; they also differ starkly in geographical conditions.

The case of Khakchang is particularly striking. The village economy was marked by primitive forces of production and a near-total lack of product or labour markets. The terrain is hilly and is covered with dense forests. The hamlets were geographically segregated and houses in the hamlets were dispersed over long distances. Most of the houses in the village were difficult to physically access from the main road or the village centre. Consequently, we found the prevalence of a traditional style of housing in the village. The housing condition in Mainama was poor. Dwelling structures in this village were predominantly made of temporary materials. At least half the village lived in crowded conditions. Muhuripur outperformed the other two villages in various parameters of housing. In fact, housing conditions in this village appeared to be better than the figures for Tripura as a whole, and particularly for rural Tripura.

The study reveals relatively low levels of inequality in living standards within the villages. Nonetheless, it is clear that an increase in incomes invariably led to improved standards of living. The impact of income level, however, remained relatively subdued in the case of Khakchang, where the roots of a traditional life style are strong. At the same time, it was very clear that socio-economic classes with access to greater operational land holdings, as well as the salaried classes, had the best housing conditions and highest living standards in all the villages. Labouring households with no access to land fared the worst.

The survey data indicate the prevalence of separate kitchen facilities in houses in all the villages. Use of LPG for cooking was quite commonplace in Muhuripur and in the central hamlets of Mainama, but firewood continued to be the main energy source for cooking in the remote areas of Mainama and in Khakchang. The same held true for the penetration of electricity, which was much lower in the inaccessible areas of Mainama and Khakchang. Low usage of clean fuel and relatively poor levels of electrification in remote areas clearly pointed to the problem of access.

Service delivery of public utilities to such inaccessible regions posed a significant challenge.

The village data on lavatories clearly reflected the achievement of the State in fighting open defecation. However, the condition of the toilet structures needed considerable improvement. This was especially true for the physically remote hamlets of Mainama and in Khakchang.

In terms of access to drinking water, we found fewer personally owned and more panchayat/government drinking water sources as we moved from Muhuripur to Mainama to Khakchang. Panchayat-provided sources of drinking water were often open sources, especially in remote hamlets. Nevertheless, such sources were well maintained. In fact, the spread of panchayat-operated drinking water supply stood out as a special feature in the villages.

The three villages provided numerous examples of successful government schemes in the realm of service delivery, even in a State where the geographical terrain is sometimes difficult to access and with a limited market economy. On the other hand, the survey also revealed various limitations of the public delivery system in the State, in terms of its quality and access in remote locations.

Appendix Table 1 *Proportion of households living in houses with "pucca" roofs, walls, and floors, two rooms, a water outlet within the premises, domestic electricity connection, and a latrine, across PARI survey villages*

Village	State	Overall %
25F Gulabewala	Rajasthan	32
Nimshirgaon	Maharashtra	28
Alabujanahalli	Karnataka	28
Ananthavaram	Andhra Pradesh	25
Rewasi	Rajasthan	21
Muhuripur	Tripura	20
Gharsondi	Madhya Pradesh	14
Kothapalle	Andhra Pradesh	12
Mainama	Tripura	9
Harevli	Uttar Pradesh	8
Warwat Khanderao	Maharashtra	3
Bukkacherla	Andhra Pradesh	2
Khakchang	Tripura	2
Mahatwar	Uttar Pradesh	1
Siresandra	Karnataka	1
Zhapur	Karnataka	0
Badhar	Madhya Pradesh	0

Source: Survey data.

References

Census of India (2001), *H-Series Tables on Census Houses, Household Amenities and Assets,* Registrar General and Census Commissioner, India, Ministry of Home Affairs, New Delhi.

Census of India (2011), *H-Series Tables on Census Houses, Household Amenities and Assets,* Registrar General and Census Commissioner, India, Ministry of Home Affairs, New Delhi.

Government of Tripura (2007), *Tripura Human Development Report 2007,* Agartala.

Government of Tripura (2016), *Economic Review 2015–16,* Directorate of Economic and Statistics Planning (Statistics) Department, Agartala.

National Family and Health Survey-4: 2015–16 (NFHS-4) (2016), Ministry of Health and Family Welfare, Government of India.

Singh, Shamsher (2017), "Condition of Housing and Access to Basic Household Amenities," in Madhura Swaminathan and Arindam Das (eds), *Socio-Economic Surveys of Three Villages in Karnataka: A Study of Agrarian Relations,* Tulika Books, New Delhi.

Singh, Shamsher (2017a), "Living Standards of Small Farmers in India," in Madhura Swaminathan and Sandipan Baksi (eds), *How Do Small Farmers Fare? Evidence from Village Studies in India,* Tulika Books, New Delhi.

Singh, Shamsher, Swaminathan, Madhura, and Ramachandran, V. K. (2013), "Housing Shortages in Rural India," *Review of Agrarian Studies,* vol. 3, no. 2, available at http://ras.org.in/housing_shortages_in_rural_india

Swaminathan, Madhura, and Das, Arindam (eds) (2017), *Socio-Economic Surveys of Three Villages in Karnataka: A Study of Agrarian Relations,* Tulika Books, New Delhi.

Swaminathan, Madhura, and Ramachandran, V. K. (2017), "The Tripura Model," *The Hindu,* available at https://www.thehindu.com/todays-paper/tp-opinion/the-tripura-model/article20462435.ece, accessed on October 1, 2018.

16

Literacy and Schooling in Three Villages of Tripura

Sanjukta Chakraborty and Madhura Swaminathan

Tripura has made remarkable progress in education as well as in other indicators of human development. In this chapter, we document the progress in education both at the State level and with data from our three survey villages. We examine literacy rates, followed by years of schooling, and, lastly, school attendance and infrastructure. Overall, in terms of literacy rates and educational attainments of adults, the three villages studied in Tripura are way ahead of other PARI villages from other parts of the country.

Literacy Rates

Literacy has been described as "the basic personal skill that underlies the whole modernising sequence" (Swaminathan and Ramachandran 2017). Data from the Census of India, 2011 show that literacy rates in Tripura, for men and women, rural and urban, are distinctly higher than the corresponding all-India numbers (Table 1). For example, literacy among rural women in India was 59 per cent in 2011 and it was 80 per cent among rural women in Tripura, a gap of over 20 percentage points. The gap for rural men was smaller but notable, at 13 percentage points. Further, there has been remarkable progress in literacy in rural Tripura over the last few decades. According to the Census, the share of literate persons above the age of seven years rose from 70 to 85 per cent between 2001 and 2011 (Tables 1 and 2).

More recent evidence from the National Family Health Survey (NFHS) confirms the progress in women's literacy. Between 2005–06 and 2015–16, literacy among women in the age group 15–49 years rose from 68.5 to

Table 1 *Literate persons as a proportion of the population, sex-wise, Census of India 2011, in per cent*

Category	Proportion of literates		
	Male	Female	Person
Tripura (rural)	90	80	85
Tripura (all)	92	83	87
India (rural)	77	59	68
India (all)	81	65	73

Source: Government of India (2011).

Table 2 *Literate persons as a proportion of the population, sex-wise, Census of India 2001, in per cent*

Category	Proportion of literates		
	Male	Female	Person
Tripura (rural)	78	61	70
Tripura (all)	81	65	73
India (rural)	71	46	59
India (all)	75	54	65

Source: Government of India (2001).

80.4 per cent in Tripura. In the same period, the corresponding increase at the all-India level was from 55 to 68.4 per cent.

We now turn to the three study villages: Khakchang, a fully tribal village in the North district; Mainama, a majority Scheduled Tribe (ST) village in Dhalai district; and Muhuripur, a village in South district with no Scheduled Tribe persons. The PARI survey used the following definition of literacy. All individuals in the survey were classified into one of the following categories: (i) cannot read or write, (ii) can only sign name, (iii) can read but not write, and (iv) can read and write. Only category (iv) was marked as being literate.

Using this definition – one that is more stringent than the definition of the Census of India – the overall literacy rate for persons above seven years ranged from 77 per cent in Khakchang and Mainama, to 86 per cent in Muhuripur (Table 3). The female literacy rate ranged from 65 in Khakchang and 70 in Mainama to 81 in Muhuripur village.

Using data from the earlier survey, in 2006, of the same three villages,

Table 3 *Literate persons as a proportion of the population aged 7 and above, sex-wise, study villages, 2015–16, in per cent*

Village	Female	Male	Persons
Khakchang	65	87	77
Mainama	70	85	77
Muhuripur	81	90	86

Note: Data are for persons of the age of seven years and above.
Source: PARI survey data, 2016.

Table 4 *Gender gap in literacy, by survey village, 2005 and 2016, in percentage points*

Village	Gender gap (2016) (7–49 years)	Gender gap (2005) (Above 7 years)
Khakchang	18	29
Mainama	12	16
Muhuripur	3	13

Source: PARI survey data, 2016 and Government of Tripura (2007).

published in the *Tripura Human Development Report 2007*, we can gauge the change over the last decade. Table 4 shows that the gender gap in literacy achievement has closed over the last ten years, and was only 3 percentage points in Muhuripur village.

Median Years of Schooling

A measure of the educational achievement of the general population is the median years of schooling (that is, completed years of schooling). To exclude those currently in school, we measured the median years of schooling for all persons aged 16 years and above in each study village. If the median years of schooling for a group is, say, zero, then at least 50 per cent of all members of that group have had no schooling at all.

There are some remarkable results in Table 5. The surveys show that the median years of schooling for all persons was eight for each of the three villages. Women in Khakchang had a lower median of seven, and men in Muhuripur had a higher median of nine years. Nevertheless, these data show that for the population above the age of 16, the achievements are close to the national goal of ten years of schooling. At the all-India

Table 5 *Median number of years of completed school education for population above 16 years, sex-wise, study villages in Tripura, 2015–16, in years*

Village	Female	Male	Person
Khakchang	7	8	8
Mainama	8	8	8
Muhuripur	8	9	8

Source: PARI survey data, 2016.

Table 6 *Median number of years of completed school education for population above 16 years, sex-wise, PARI survey villages*

State	Village	Year of survey	Female	Male	Person
Andhra Pradesh	Ananthavaram	2006	5	7	6
	Bukkacherla	2006	0	7	5
	Kothapalle	2006	0	8	4
Karnataka	Alabujanahalli	2009	3	9	7
	Siresandra	2009	0	9	5
	Zhapur	2009	0	1	0
Madhya Pradesh	Gharsondi	2008	0	8	4
Maharashtra	Nimshirgaon	2007	7	9	8
	Warwat Khanderao	2007	4	9	7
Rajasthan	25F Gulabewala	2007	0	4	2
	Rewasi	2010	0	7	1
West Bengal	Amarsinghi	2010	2	5	4
	Kalmandasguri	2010	2	5	4
	Panahar	2010	0	4	3
Bihar	Katkuian	2012	0	3	0
	Nayanagar	2012	0	7	2

Source: PARI survey data.

level, for rural women, the median years of schooling was reported to be 3.1 years by the NFHS-4 in 2015–16. The achievements in Tripura are demonstrably superior.

A quick comparison with data from selected villages surveyed by PARI in different parts of the country shows that the Tripura villages stand out in terms of overall high achievement, especially among women, with respect to school education (Table 6). Although some of these surveys were done a decade ago, the results are shocking. The median year of schooling for women was zero in two villages of Andhra Pradesh (in 2006), two villages of Karnataka (in 2009), two villages of Rajasthan and one village of Madhya Pradesh (2008), one village of West Bengal (2010), and two villages of Bihar (2012). In other words, 50 per cent of women in each of these villages reported zero schooling.

School Infrastructure and Attendance

Data from DISE show the overall progress in school infrastructure in Tripura (Table 7). Not only has there been progress over the last decade

Table 7 *Performance indicators for schools, Tripura and India, 2005–06, 2015–16*, in percentages

Performance indicators	Tripura (2005–2006)	Tripura (2015–2016)	India (2015–2016)
Single-classroom schools	9.2	3.1	4.2
Single-teacher schools	1.4	0.2	7.5
Schools approachable by all-weather road		80.5	89.2
Schools with playground facility		62.0	60.6
Schools with boundary wall		19.3	63.8
Schools with girls' toilet	18.0	99.9	97.6
Schools with boys' toilet		99.7	97.1
Schools with drinking water	73.8	89.8	96.8
Schools with mid-day meal *		99.1	97.6
Schools with electricity		28.2	57.3
Schools with computers		15.6	26.0
Schools with ramp, if needed	24.0	79.4	82.6
Schools established	17.5 **	31.9 ***	29.5***
Schools with kitchen-shed *		92.3	80.0
Schools with enrolment <=50	15.5	40.5	33.4
Schools with School Management Committee *		99.9	94.0
Pupil–teacher ratio	23.0	12.0	24.0
Student–classroom ratio	38.0	23.0	27.0
Average teachers per school	8.6	9.6	5.6
Female teachers	25.6	29.2	48.0
Girls' enrolment	48.0	49.0	48.4

Notes: *Government + aided.; **since 1994; ***since 2001.
Source: DISE, 2005–06, 2015–16, cited in NUEPA (2007) and NUEPA (2016).

in respect of most indicators, but Tripura's school infrastructure is also better than the Indian average in most cases. An outstanding achievement is that only 0.2 per cent of schools in Tripura were single-teacher schools in 2015–16. The comparable figure for India was 7.5 per cent. Correspondingly, the average number of teachers per school was almost 10 in Tripura as compared to six at the national level.

In Tripura, the junior basic school is till the fifth standard, the senior basic school is till the eighth standard, the secondary school is till the 10th standard, and the higher secondary school is till the 12th standard.

Turning to the study villages, Khakchang had six schools, three of which were junior basic schools, two were senior basic schools, and one was a secondary school. All the school buildings were *pucca* (permanent)

Table 8 *Proportion of children attending school, by age group and sex, 2011,* in per cent

Category	Age group	Female	Male	Person
Tripura (rural)	6–10 years	83	84	84
	11–14 years	92	92	91
	15–16 years	76	78	77
	17–18 years	50	59	55
	All	80	82	81
Tripura	6–10 years	84	84	84
	11–14 years	92	92	92
	15–16 years	78	79	79
	17–18 years	53	61	57
	All	81	82	82
India (rural)	6–10 years	76	78	77
	11–14 years	84	87	85
	15–16 years	66	71	69
	17–18 years	46	54	50
	All	73	76	75
India	6–10 years	77	79	78
	11–14 years	85	87	86
	15–16 years	70	73	71
	17–18 years	51	57	54
	All	75	77	76

Source: Government of India (2011).

structures. All the schools and college were managed by the government.

Mainama had 12 schools: seven junior basic schools, four senior basic schools, and one higher secondary school. There was a college that offered courses at the undergraduate level. All the buildings were *pucca* structures. All schools and college were managed by the government.

Muhuripur had eight schools: two nursery schools, four junior basic schools, one secondary school, and one higher secondary school. All the buildings were *pucca* structures. Nursery schools were managed by private organisations. The remaining schools were managed by the government.

Table 8 shows data on school attendance in Tripura and at the all-India level in 2011. In every age category, the performance in Tripura was better than the national average.

The village surveys are both more recent and more likely to capture attendance accurately. During the period of fieldwork, we would leave our quarters for the survey early in the morning, and at the time of our return for breakfast at around 9 a.m., whichever location we went to, we would see children dressed neatly in their school uniforms heading to school. This was a heartening and memorable sight. The statistics confirm this picture of near-universal school attendance.

Not surprisingly, the village data also show extremely high levels of

Table 9 *Proportion of children attending school, by age group, by sex, study villages, 2015–16, in per cent*

Village	Age group	Female	Male	Person
Khakchang	6 to 10 years	100	100	100
	11 to 14 years	100	100	100
	15 to 16 years	76	83	79
	17 to 18 years	80	59	68
Mainama	6 to 10 years	97	100	98
	11 to 14 years	97	98	97
	15 to 16 years	86	83	84
	17 to 18 years	48	85	68
Muhuripur	6 to 10 years	100	100	100
	11 to 14 years	100	100	100
	15 to 16 years	82	88	87
	17 to 18 years	49	77	62

Source: PARI survey data, 2016.

school attendance (Table 9). School attendance for children in the age group of 6–14 years was 100 per cent in Khakchang and Muhuripur. For the age groups of 6–10 years and 11–14 years, school attendance in Mainama was 98 per cent and 97 per cent respectively. In other words, up to the age of 14, school attendance was universal in all three villages. In the age group of 15–16 years, attendance fell to around 80 per cent, and attendance rates were even lower for the 17–18 age group.

A large majority of school-going children in the age group 6–14 years received scholarships from the government: 68 per cent in Khakchang, 73 per cent in Mainama, and 81 per cent in Muhuripur village.

Village-specific Disparities

The big picture shows near-universal schooling up to the age of 14, relatively high levels of literacy and educational attainment, and a bridging of gaps between boys and girls, and between tribal and non-tribal persons. Nevertheless, some disparities remain.

The village survey data show that the gender gap in education has fallen but still persists. In Khakchang, people in inaccessible hamlets were educationally deprived as compared to those residing in centrally located hamlets. The proportion of literate persons aged seven years and above was 79 per cent in central hamlets and 72 per cent in remote hamlets. For the age group of 18 years and above, the proportion of persons who had completed 10 years of school education was 11 per cent in central hamlets and 4 per cent in remote hamlets. Schools in remote hamlets did not function during the years of insurgency, and while there has been notable progress in the last 10 years, more is required to ensure access to education for those in locations far removed.

In Mainama, a village with Scheduled Tribes (STs) in a majority, educational attainment was slightly lower for Scheduled Tribes in comparison with non-Scheduled Tribes. The proportion of literate persons aged seven years and above was 81 per cent for non-Scheduled Tribe persons and 72 per cent for Scheduled Tribe persons. For the age group 18 years and above, the proportion of persons who had completed 10 years of school education was 27 per cent for non-Scheduled Tribe persons and 24 per cent for Scheduled Tribes.

In Muhuripur, a multi-caste village, Scheduled Castes (SCs) were a little worse off than persons from Other Backward Classes (OBCs) in respect of educational attainment. The proportion of literate persons for those aged seven years and above was 72 per cent for SCs and 83 per cent for OBCs. For the age group 18 years and above, the proportion of persons who had completed 10 years of school education was 24 per cent for SCs and 27 per cent for OBCs.

These data thus help identify specific sectional deprivation in each of the villages surveyed, and the inequalities that still need to be addressed.

Conclusion

Tripura is one of the best performing States of India in respect of the spread of education and literacy. The data from the three villages are in line with national statistics from the Census of India (2011) and, more recently, from the NFHS survey of 2015–16. The first finding of note from primary and secondary data is that of rapid progress in school education over the last decade, reaping the benefits of peace or what can be termed the "peace dividend" (Swaminathan and Ramachandran 2017, chapter 4).

The three study villages showed an expected pattern in respect of literacy. Literacy rates were highest in Muhuripur village of South Tripura, a lowland village, and lowest in Khakchang, a forest village with several remote hamlets. The gaps between the three villages, however, were much less in respect of school attendance, suggesting that the education disparity will be less in the next generation. Another remarkable achievement is the closing of the gender gap in access to school education. Although narrow, disparities across caste and tribe do remain.

With high levels of school attendance, in future, issues of quality of education need to be addressed.[1] The State has also to prepare to meet the growing aspirations for higher education.

---

[1] This is flagged as a concern by Sen (2018).

References

Government of India (GoI) (2001), *Census of India 2001*, Registrar General and Census Commisioner of India, Ministry of Home Affairs, New Delhi.

Government of India (GoI) (2011), *Census of India 2011*, Registrar General and Census Commisioner of India, Ministry of Home Affairs, New Delhi.

Government of India (GoI) (2007), *National Family Health Survey-2, 2005–06*, International Institute for Population Sciences, Mumbai.

Government of India (GoI) (2017), *National Family Health Survey-3, 2015–16*, International Institute for Population Sciences, Mumbai.

Government of Tripura (GoT) (2007), *Tripura Human Development Report 2007*, Government of Tripura, Agartala, available at http://planningcommission.nic.in/plans/stateplan/sdr_pdf/tripura%20hdr.pdf, viewed on September 13, 2018.

Government of Tripura (GoT) (2018), *Draft Tripura Human Development Report 2018*, available at https://planning.tripura.gov.in/sites/default/files/Draft%20Tripura%20Human%20Development%20Report%20%28THDR%29%20-%20II%2010%20April%202018.compressed.pdf, viewed on September 13, 2018.

National University of Educational Planning and Administration (NUEPA) (2007), *Elementary Education in India: Where Do We Stand? State Report Cards 2005–06*, District Information System for Education (DISE), National University of Educational Planning and Administration, New Delhi.

National University of Educational Planning and Administration (NUEPA) (2016), *Elementary Education in India: Where Do We Stand? State Report Cards 2015–16*, District Information System for Education (DISE), National University of Educational Planning and Administration, New Delhi.

Sen, Amartya (2018), "Foreword," *Tripura Human Development Report 2018*, Government of Tripura, Agartala.

Swaminathan, Madhura, and V. K. Ramachandran, 2017, "The Tripura Model," *The Hindu*, November 15, available at https://www.thehindu.com/opinion/op-ed/the-tripura-model/article20461140.ece, viewed on September 13, 2018.

SECTION V

Overview

17

Three Villages of Tripura:
A Summary of Agrarian Relations

Tripura was the eleventh State chosen for village studies under the Project on Agrarian Relations in India (PARI) of the Foundation for Agrarian Studies (FAS). In May–June 2016, detailed household surveys based on a stratified sample were conducted in three villages: Mainama in Manu block of Dhalai district, Muhuripur in Julaibari block of South district, and Khakchang in Dasda block of North district. The three villages were first surveyed in 2005 for the *Tripura Human Development Report, 2007*, and resurveyed under PARI in 2016.

The villages have distinct topologies, land-use patterns and crop systems. Khakchang in the North district is a resettled forest village, characterised by slash-and-burn cultivation (*jhum*). Mainama village of Dhalai district represents settled plain and *tila* or upland cultivation. Muhuripur of South district represents settled lowland agriculture that is characteristic of the plains.

Each of these villages comes with its own unique set of agrarian production systems and relations. Here we highlight some of the major findings drawn from our surveys for each village.

Khakchang

Khakchang is illustrative of the tribal-dominated forest villages of Tripura. It is located in Dasda block, under Ananda Bazaar tehsil of North Tripura district. It is at a distance of 13 kilometres from Dasda block and 26 kilometres from Kanchanpur, the sub-divisional headquarters and nearest town, and connected to both by an all-weather road. It is close to the Jampuii Hills, which border Mizoram. The village is part of the Tripura

Tribal Areas Autonomous District Council (TTAADC). It is a newly settled or regrouped village, formed in 2003. It has seven hamlets, spread across an area of 5,919 acres. Some of the hamlets are as far as 8 kilometres from the village centre. In 2016, there were a total of 589 households in the village with a population of 2,884. About 95 per cent of the households belonged to the Reang tribe and the rest to the Tripuri tribe.

The village terrain is predominantly hilly, with 41.8 per cent of its total land under dense forests and just 11 per cent comprising lowlands. The hamlets are geographically segregated and houses in the hamlets are dispersed over long distances. Most of the houses in the village are difficult to physically access from the main road or village centre, and a traditional style of housing (made of bamboo and thatch) is still prevalent.

Implementation of the Forest Rights Act (FRA), 2006 brought tenurial security to a majority of the residents of Khakchang: 76 per cent of all households had received forest *pattas* in the village. Not surprisingly, landlessness (in terms of operational holdings) in Khakchang, at 8 per cent, was the lowest among all the villages studied thus far by PARI.

The system of *jhum* cultivation prevails in the village, and was practised on 52 per cent of gross cropped area. Lowland cultivation, including of paddy and vegetables, covered 25 per cent of the gross cropped area. Rubber plantations had been started but were not yet mature, and had not started generating incomes. In Khakchang, each of these three types of cultivation is distinct and associated with specific crops, input use, and income levels. We have therefore based our socio-economic classification of cultivators on the basis of type of land/cultivation practices, as follows:

1. Cultivator: *jhum*
2. Cultivator mixed: *jhum* and lowland cultivation
3. Cultivator: lowland cultivation
4. Cultivator: non-*jhum* upland cultivation

There are some unique features of the *jhum* economy including a system of allocation of forest land by means of a village lottery, and leasing of land on contractual basis. The system of contract leasing existed in the village before the implementation of the FRA in 2006, and gave the villagers access to land for *jhum* cultivation in the Jampuii hills. The system of allocation of forest land through a lottery system ensures that land adequate for each participant household, depending on household size and food requirement, is made available during the *jhum* cycle. This system primarily takes into consideration the fact that *jhum* cannot be performed on the same plot of land in consecutive years, and requires intensive use of family and exchange labour. Land and labour relations are interlinked in this system of *jhum* cultivation in Khakchang. All the participant households collectively perform the crop operations in each other's allotted land.

Labour supply for agriculture in Khakchang was met predominantly by family labour and exchange forms of labour, with the share of hired labour at 15 per cent. *Jhum* cultivation accounted for 54 per cent of labour use, drawing on family labour and exchange labour that spanned eight to 10 months of the year, and involved only intensive human labour. Lowland cultivation accounted for 39 per cent of labour use, and was restricted to the kharif season. There was dominance of male labour both in family labour and exchange labour. However, female participation was high in lowland cultivation, especially in transplanting and weeding operations. Indeed, women's work participation rate (76 per cent) was very high on account of participation in *jhum* cultivation as well as NREGA work.

The class of manual workers was small, constituting 17 per cent of all households in Khakchang. The MGNREGS played an important role in Khakchang, providing 59 days and 66 days of employment, respectively, for female and male labourers from manual worker households. The major non-agricultural occupations available to wage workers were construction, headload work, and labouring-out in carpentry.

Incomes from both *jhum* and lowland cultivation were low. The average yield of rough rice or paddy was 1,168 kg per hectare, but households made a profit as the expenditure on inputs was also low. There was practically no use of animal or machine labour, and there was heavy dependence on family labour and exchange labour. The low cash nexus of economic activities may explain why moneylending was not observed.

It was found that households which practised a mixed form of crop production, combining *jhum* and lowland cultivation, had the highest share of annual income from crop production. Households dependent on only *jhum* cultivation had lower incomes than other cultivator households. In 2015–16, the mean annual income of *jhum*-dependent households was Rs 79,559, as compared to the village average of Rs 1,14,434.

The geography of this village was distinct with households spread out over seven hamlets and almost 6,000 acres. We found a difference in the incomes of households across hamlets, with households in remote hamlets reporting lower incomes than those in more central hamlets, closer to the main road. The mean annual income of households in remote hamlets was

Rs 83,595, while it was Rs 1,67,779 among households in central hamlets.

Another distinctive feature of the village was the homestead economy: homestead land accounted for 19 per cent of the total operational land in the village. The average extent of homestead land per household was 0.71 acre. Khakchang had the widest range of crop varieties grown by households in both *jhum* and homesteads. A total of 63 varieties of crops were listed in the village, with a maximum of 42 crops being grown by a single household. Homestead land accounted for around 10 per cent of the total value of production. Further, 86 per cent of the produce of homestead land was kept for home consumption, a potential source of nutrition.

Lastly, the average value of assets owned by a household in Khakchang was low in absolute terms, Rs 3.6 lakhs at current prices. In most village economies, land is the most important asset. In Khakchang, the share of land in total asset values was only 27 per cent, reflecting the fact that 85 per cent of land possessed by households was either assigned or occupied land, for which a value was not imputed. In short, the low average value of wealth of village households was on account of land not having a market price.

The value of agricultural means of production was also low, as most households depended only on hand implements. Pigs were widely owned. Lastly, there was very little ownership of modern assets. One of the reasons for this could have been the low coverage of grid-based electricity in Khakchang. A government lighting scheme utilising solar energy through solar lighting panels was used to charge mobile phones in the remote hamlets, but was inadequate to operate television sets.

Mainama

Mainama is located in Manu block of Dhalai district of Tripura. It is at a distance of 3 kilometres from Manu town, the block headquarters, and is connected by an all-weather road. The village is part of the Tripura Tribal Areas Autonomous District Council (TTAADC). In 2016, there were 1,451 households in the village, spread across 11 hamlets. The Scheduled Tribe (ST) population constituted 66.2 per cent of households. Tripuris (42.6 per cent) and Chakmas (23.6 per cent) were the two major social groups within Scheduled Tribes. Of the remaining households, 26 per cent belonged to Other Backward Classes (OBCs), 4 per cent were caste Hindus, and 2 per cent were Muslims.

There were three main types of cultivation in Mainama: lowland paddy cultivation, plantation crops, and homestead cultivation. About 40 per cent of the agricultural land in the village was under plantation crops, primarily rubber. Thirty per cent of the remaining land was under lowland paddy and vegetable cultivation. Irrigation was restricted to 48 per cent of the village, with the Manu river being the primary source of irrigation.

In Mainama, we identified socio-economic categories among cultivator households on the basis of extent of land operated. Specifically, four classes were identified:

1. Cultivator: sub-marginal, with operational holdings of less than 1 acre of land
2. Cultivator: marginal, with operational holdings between 1 and 2.5 acres of land
3. Cultivator: small, with operational holdings more than 2.5 acres and less than 5 acres
4. Cultivator: medium, with operational holdings above 5 acres.

Mainama was largely a village of marginal and sub-marginal cultivators, with 46 per cent of households operating less than 1 hectare (or 2.5 acres) of land. An active tenancy market in the village assured access to lowland to residents of remote hamlets, which was otherwise not available to them. Thirty per cent of the total operational land was under various forms of tenancy contracts, and most tenant cultivators belonged to the "cultivator: sub-marginal" category with operational holdings of less than 1 acre.

Prevalence of homestead cultivation was a distinct feature of Mainama, where 92 per cent of the households owned their house site. The size of the homestead differed across the village, depending on the location of the household. Households in remote hamlets, residing on sloped terrain, tended to have larger homesteads than households residing on lowland in the central hamlets.

Paddy was the most important seasonal crop in the village, grown in both the pre-kharif and kharif seasons. Vegetable cultivation was undertaken in the kharif and rabi season on the river bed. Rubber being the most important annual crop, rubber plantations occupied around 50 per cent of the total gross cropped area.

There was wide variation in net incomes from crop production across different socio-economic classes. Average annual income from crop production was highest among cultivators from the "cultivator: medium" group of households (operating more than 5 acres), at Rs 42,570. Machine use in agriculture in Mainama was restricted to low-lying crop land. In recent years, the State government had started schemes to promote greater machine use in agriculture. In Mainama, cultivation was mainly undertaken by family labour.

There was a significant section of the village, around 33 per cent of households, which did not operate any land. We classified 19 per cent of all households as hired manual worker households, most of whom belonged to Scheduled Castes (SCs) and Scheduled Tribes (STs). Among these households, one group comprised manual workers who obtained more than 50 per cent of household income from wages of manual labour. A second group was termed manual workers with diversified income, as less than 50 per cent of their household income came from wage earnings from manual labour.

At the same time, 97 per cent of all workers in the village participated in wage labour in the survey year. Wage labour was prevalent among all classes, including cultivator households. Employment under MGNREGS was important, especially for female workers. During the reference year, women received 39 days of employment, whereas males received 28 days, from MGNREGS.

Lastly, Mainama had a non-agricultural stratum, that is, those dependent on incomes from salaries, business, and other sources. Government service (18 per cent of male workers) and employment in the government-run brick kiln (15 per cent of male workers) emerged as major employers of non-agricultural workers.

Mainama is a large village, and households here had higher and more diversified incomes than in the other two villages. There was clear socio-economic differentiation in this village. Households with access to government salaries had the highest incomes, followed by "Cultivators: medium." Inequality of incomes across households was higher in Mainama than in Khakchang. The Gini coefficient, a commonly used indicator of inequality, of the distribution of per capita income was 0.563 in Mainama and 0.483 in Khakchang.[1] Of the three villages studied, the wealthiest household was in Mainama, with assets worth Rs 20 million, though this level of wealth is much lower than that observed in other PARI survey villages.

---

[1] The Gini coefficient ranges from 0 to 1, with 0 representing no inequality.

There are new sources of future income, including from rubber. The introduction of rubber plantations in Mainama as a rehabilitation policy of the State to counter extremist violence in the mid-2000s has boosted the household incomes of those with plantations. Further maturation of more rubber trees and increased private investment in rubber production can have a far-reaching impact on the household incomes of rubber growers. We project that once all the rubber trees mature, the incomes of households with plantations will be 80 per cent higher than that recorded in 2016.

On average, the value of all assets owned by a Mainama household in 2016 was Rs 10.1 lakhs. The majority of households (56 per cent) owned agricultural land, and the value of such land accounted for one-half or more of total assets. Only 38 per cent of households in Mainama owned agricultural implements of any value. However, there were a large number of draught animals, due to the still prevalent use of animal labour in agricultural operations. In Mainama, 42.4 per cent of all lowland under paddy was ploughed using draught animals

Mainama village comprised 11 hamlets, of which eight were characterised as remote hamlets. Interestingly, while the average level of household income was similar as between households resident in remote and central hamlets, the composition of income showed that government salaries were a bigger part of total incomes in the remote hamlets. In terms of the quality and range of assets, households in the remote hamlets fared poorer than those in the central hamlets. We argue that state intervention played a role in the composition of incomes and assets of residents of the remote hamlets. Reservation for STs in government employment, for example, benefited households in remote hamlets, as did schemes for the promotion of rubber plantations. Government schemes promoting subsidised agricultural machinery also raised the value of assets held by residents of the remote hamlets.

Muhuripur

Located in Julaibari block of the South district of Tripura, Muhuripur is primarily an immigrant village. Its population mainly comprises Bengali speakers who came originally as part of the influx of migrants from Bangladesh in the 1970s. The village is about 18 kilometres from the district headquarters at Belonia, and is connected by an all-weather *pucca* road. Of the 1,054 households in the village in 2016, 628 were caste

Hindus, 272 belonged to Other Backward Classes (OBCs), and 154 were Scheduled Caste (SC) households. There was not a single Scheduled Tribe (ST) household in the village. Two-thirds of the total agricultural land was lowland and the remaining was upland.

In Muhuripur, lowland cultivation of rice and vegetables is the predominant type of cultivation, accompanied by homestead cultivation and a very small segment of upland cultivation. Our classification of cultivator households was based on extent of operational holding, and three socio-economic categories were identified:

1. Cultivators: sub-marginal, with operational holdings of less than 1 acre of land
2. Cultivators: marginal, with operational holdings between 1 and 2.5 acres of land
3. Cultivators: small, with operational holdings above 2.5 acres.

In Muhuripur village, there was no cultivator who belonged to the traditional class of landlords.

Muhuripur was a village of marginal and sub-marginal cultivator households; together, they constituted 61 per cent of the total population and accounted for 75 per cent of total operational land. Though the village had a substantial landless population (34 per cent), tenancy was widely prevalent in the survey year. The land area under lease or tenancy comprised 43 per cent of all operated land. The majority of tenant households belonged to the lowest agrarian category of "cultivator: sub-marginal." Sharecropping was the most prominent form of tenancy in Muhuripur, accounting for about two-thirds of the total leased-in area.

On account of assured public irrigation, a substantial proportion of agricultural land in the lowlands was cultivated more than once in Muhuripur. Among seasonal crops, paddy was the most important in both the kharif and rabi seasons, sown on 71 per cent of the total gross cropped area (GCA). Vegetables were grown on lowlands. Betel leaf was an important commercial crop in the village, but the extent of cultivation was very small. In addition, mulberry cultivation and sericulture were started in the village with substantial support from the State government. The uplands were primarily under natural rubber plantations, accounting for about 29 per cent of operational holdings.

Machine use in agriculture was high in Muhuripur, particularly for ploughing, irrigation, weeding, spraying, plant protection, and threshing. The State government provided substantial assistance to purchase agricultural machinery. In crop production, labour use was high during the rabi season (41 per cent), followed by the kharif season (38 per cent) and annual crops (21 per cent). An active labour market existed in Muhuripur. The composition of family labour and hired labour use in agriculture was such that about 55 per cent of total labour demand was met by hired labour and 44 per cent by family labour.

Paddy cultivation was non-remunerative for cultivators in the survey year on account of low crop yields and low gross value of output. This resulted in significant financial losses among paddy-growing households in both seasons. Further, the proportion of loss-incurring households was much higher among "cultivator: sub-marginal" households than the other two agrarian classes. To put it differently, the average income from crop production for "cultivator: small" households was almost ten times higher than the village average. The main factor for this difference was that "cultivator: small" households devoted a higher share of land to rubber cultivation in their total gross cropped area, and could tide over their losses from paddy by supplementary income from rubber cultivation, than the other two categories of cultivators.

One-third of households did not operate any land in the reference year. About 25 per cent of households were classified as hired manual worker households. As in the other two villages, two categories of manual workers were identified in Muhuripur: manual worker households who obtained more than 50 per cent of their household income from earnings of manual work, and manual worker households with diversified income (with less than 50 per cent of total household income coming from wages of manual labour).

Among the class of manual workers, 89 per cent of all workers participated in the wage labour market. The participation of female workers in the wage labour market was, however, the lowest in Muhuripur among the three study villages. Wage rates for daily-paid casual labour in crop production were in the range of Rs 250 to Rs 300 for a male, and Rs 200 for a female. MGNREGS was a source of employment for a large number of male and female workers from manual worker households. In Muhuripur, construction-related work was a major source of employment for manual worker households. Male workers were generally engaged in non-agricultural activities under NREGS, and received, on average, 103 days of employment during the survey year.

Finally, there was a non-agricultural stratum comprising households dependent on salaries, income from business, and other sources.

Muhuripur village had high levels of inequality in both ownership and operational holdings. However, this inequality did not directly imply inequality in household incomes, as households across socio-economic classes had diversified their sources of income. All cultivator households, as they obtained low returns and even losses from crop production in the survey year, had diversified into other activities. Access to non-agricultural employment, under MGNREGS in particular, helped raise the incomes of cultivator households. Among the categories identified, households in the non-agricultural stratum had the highest levels of household income, followed by "cultivator: small" households (with more than 2.5 acres of operational land) and "cultivator: marginal" households. "Manual worker" households were the poorest in terms of household income, with an average annual income of Rs 63,775 in 2015–16.

The average value of assets owned by a household in Muhuripur was Rs 12.6 lakhs at current prices, the highest among the three survey villages. In Muhuripur, a majority of households, or 62 per cent, owned agricultural land, and the value of such land accounted for one-half or more of total assets. Around 94 per cent of the total land possessed by households in Muhuripur was under full ownership rights. Among the three villages, households in Muhuripur had the highest likelihood of owning modern assets.

Muhuripur had a relatively active credit market, with 51 per cent of households reporting debt outstanding at the time of the survey, and 39 per cent reporting fresh borrowing during the survey year. Households in Muhuripur sought credit from both formal and informal sources for meeting their credit needs. Households relied on formal sources to meet their production credit needs, including agriculture. However, for their other needs, they relied heavily on informal sources. While traditional moneylending was not prevalent, there was a new kind of group moneylending at fairly high rates of interest.

18

Public Support for Rural Households

Madhura Swaminathan

This chapter brings together village-level evidence on public support for rural households in Tripura.[1] Earlier studies, in particular, the *Tripura Human Development Report 2007* (GoT 2017) and the *Draft Tripura Human Development Report 2018* (Pratichi Institute 2018), have documented in great detail the types of government support for enhancing human development. These include both income support, such as through employment guarantee programmes, and direct support, such as through provision of free school education or in-kind food rations. Not surprisingly, in his foreword to the *Tripura Human Development Report 2018*, Amartya Sen refers to Tripura as a State government that shows "benevolence."[2] The expansion of public support became easier after the Left government (1993–2018) had controlled extremist violence. As has been noted, "The progress achieved over the last ten years in several indicators of human development – especially in education, health, and employment – is the State's peace dividend, and is worthy of public attention" (Ramachandran and Swaminathan 2017, chapter 4).

In the three villages surveyed by the Foundation of Agrarian Studies (FAS) in 2016, a remarkable finding is that almost every household in the survey was in receipt of government support. The forms of support – as

---

[1] This chapter draws on material from earlier chapters, and also from Notes on the FAS website: Patra (2017) and Dutta (2017) in particular.

[2] He says, "Even as we cheer the benevolence that characterises what the state has been trying to do, with notable success, we have to point to the need to pay greater attention to the role of agency of the worse-off, especially of tribals and of women in general. Perhaps, this beautiful and dynamic state can fruitfully be a bit more dynamic in developing people's agency, going beyond the undoubtedly well-planned achievements of the benevolent state." Sen (2018).

Table 1 *Number and proportion of beneficiary households that received institutional support, by government scheme, study villages in Tripura, in numbers and per cent*

Scheme	Khakchang		Mainama		Muhuripur	
	Number of beneficiary households	Per cent of total	Number of beneficiary households	Per cent of total	Number of beneficiary households	Per cent of total
PDS	567	96	1432	98	1044	99
MGNREGS	521	88	855	59	852	81
Housing	290	49	623	43	482	46
Rubber	48	8	209	14	50	5
Cultivation (inputs, saplings, or in form of cash)	148	25	228	16	423	40
Agricultural machinery	5	1	210	14	164	16
Animal husbandry including fishery	180	31	316	22	160	15
Pond digging (under MGNREGS)	76	13	162	11	174	17
Medical support from health centres in terms of medical smart card, mosquito nets, assistance during pregnancy	387	66	140*	10*	876	83
Land assigned/FRA	448	76	177	12	24	2
Pension	95	16	284	20	292	28
Scholarships#	386	68	597	73	398	81

Notes: *It could be under-reported. Mainama was our first survey village, and initially we missed information on access to medical smart cards and mosquito nets. #Number of children between 6–14 years who received scholarships.

Source: Survey data.

has been discussed in many of the preceding chapters – were diverse and multiple. They ranged from distribution of land titles to subsidies for agriculture and rubber cultivation, and pensions for the elderly.

In this chapter, I touch upon some of the major forms of public support, drawing on earlier chapters. Let me start, however, with the big picture (Table 1). Almost all households held a ration card and benefited from subsidised food distributed through the public distribution system (PDS). The MGNREGS came second in terms of participation of households, with coverage of more than 80 per cent of households in Muhuripur and Khakchang villages, and 59 per cent in Mainama village. There were a significant number of households in each village that received government support from other programmes, be it assigned land in Khakchang or subsidies for cultivation in Muhuripur. Our data also show that a large majority of children were recipients of government scholarships. Table 1 excludes direct provisioning by the state, such as through government schools or health clinics.

Forest Rights Act[3]

Land under forest cover and the livelihood of tribal communities are interlinked in multiple ways. The dependence of tribal communities in forest-fringe villages on forest land ranges from housing to crop production to collection of natural forest produce for consumption. These factors make the successful implementation of the Scheduled Tribes and Other Traditional Forest Dwellers (Recognition of Forest Rights) Act, 2006, popularly known as the Forest Rights Act (FRA), vital for the socio-economic improvement of tribal communities. Implementation of the FRA is especially important for ensuring legal rights to land for Scheduled Tribes (STs) and forest dwellers as it positively affects their livelihood. Further, once the *"patta"* is allocated, all *patta* holders are eligible to certain economic benefits. These benefits accrue to those beneficiaries who are identified by the concerned government department, such as those of Agriculture, Animal Resources Development, Fisheries, Forest, Horticulture, Handloom, Handicrafts, Sericulture, and Tribal Welfare, in convergence with the Mahatma Gandhi National Rural Employment Guarantee Scheme (MGNREGS).

Implementation of the FRA in Tripura started in 2006. Tripura has been

---

[3] This section draws on Ritam Dutta (2017), and chapters 6 and 7.

one of the leading States of the country in respect of implementation of the FRA. According to data available till March 2017, a total of 17,91,706 titles have been distributed to forest dwellers across the country, covering 1,37,36,530 acres of forest land. In Tripura, 1,25,075 titles have been distributed, covering 4,35,817 acres of forest land.[4] The area accounts for 3.2 per cent of the national forest land distributed, but the number of *patta*s or land titles in Tripura were 6.98 per cent of the total land titles distributed in the country.

Of the three study villages surveyed in Tripura, Khakchang, situated in North district, is the most remote in terms of accessibility and has the most rugged terrain. It is located close to the Tripura–Mizoram border. This is a newly formed resettled village comprising the Reang community that shifted from the border region of Mizoram about 20 years ago. The predominant form of cultivation is *jhum* or shifting cultivation. Khakchang has received significant support through the FRA. Seventy-six per cent of total households in this village have been assigned *patta*s by the Government of Tripura (chapter 6). Of the total agricultural land of resident households in Khakchang, 81 per cent was assigned as land under the FRA. Further, 6 per cent of households were assigned homestead land.

In Khakchang village, households did not have any ownership rights over land before the implementation of the FRA. Rather, they were dependent on forest land for shifting cultivation, collection of forest produce for consumption, and for building their homes. This is why successful implementation of the FRA was important for Khakchang, as it gave the residents user rights to the forest. A major portion of *patta* land is forest land, and continues to be used for collection of forest produce and is not put to any cultivable use. However, a portion of the *patta* land is used for shifting cultivation. Here the primary produce (paddy) is entirely used for household consumption.

Mainama village in Dhalai district presents a mix in terms of land type, i.e. it has both *tila* (upland) and lowland. The FRA has been implemented in Mainama but to a lesser extent. Around 12 per cent of households had been assigned *patta*s by the government, accounting for 14 per cent of agricultural land. The average size of *patta* land per beneficiary was higher (1.98 acres) than the average size of operational holding (1.64 acres). In Mainama village, the FRA has benefited a limited number of households – around one-seventh of all households. However, the forest land assigned

---

[4] www.fra.org.in (2017).

to these households is now used primarily for rubber cultivation, a major new source of income (see chapter 13).

Muhuripur village, in South district, is a lowland village predominantly inhabited by Bengalis, most of who migrated to India from Bangladesh over a period of time. Because of its flat terrain, this village has not been a site for FRA. However, 3 per cent of households were assigned land (accounting for 1.7 per cent of total agricultural land) in the 1990s, prior to FRA.

Public Distribution System[5]

In Tripura, the National Food Security Act (NFSA), 2013 was implemented in September 2015. Following this, the State government created a special category, termed the "Priority Group," in line with the NFSA.[6] This category comprised the below poverty line (BPL) category and an ad hoc BPL category comprising those who were eligible to receive benefits under the Act. Many households that were previously categorised as above poverty line (APL) were included in the ad hoc BPL category.

As Subhajit Patra shows, 96 per cent of all households in Khakchang village in North district had ration cards. The 4 per cent without ration cards were households recently separated from their main families and newly married persons. Further, 85 per cent of the cards were Antyodaya cards (for the poorest 10 per cent of households) or Priority cards. In Mainama and Muhuripur, 99 per cent of all households had ration cards. Priority and Antyodaya cards constituted 67 per cent of all ration cards in Mainama, and 52 per cent in Muhuripur.

Thus, the overwhelming majority of households in the forest-fringe village of Khakchang were covered under NFSA, while the proportion of households covered was two-thirds in Mainama and one-half in Muhuripur. Being a paddy-growing village, Muhuripur in South Tripura, not surprisingly, received a lower supply of foodgrain from the PDS than the other villages.

The main commodities supplied through the PDS were rice, wheat, sugar, salt, and kerosene. Periodically, mustard oil (1 litre), at a subsidised rate of Rs 15 per litre, and pulses (2 kg), at Rs 20 per kg, were also distributed.

---

[5] This section is based on Patra (2017).
[6] The NFSA created two categories: Priority and Non-priority, with entitlements assured only for Priority households.

Semolina (*suji*) at Rs 13 per kg and 300 gm per card was available on special occasions. A truly remarkable finding of the village surveys is that in all three villages, all commodities were available to every category of card holder in the same quantity and at the same price as announced officially.

Additionally, card holders received Rs 35 as subsidy for purchase of 2 kg of pulses and 1 litre of oil under a scheme of the Government of Tripura. From April 2016, the subsidy (transferred directly to bank accounts) was increased to Rs 50. This scheme was in operation in Mainama village – it had not started in the other two study villages.

The village studies confirm universal access to PDS in rural Tripura, and, more importantly, bring out the fact that the quantities and prices or rations offered to households corresponded to their entitlement.

Mahatma Gandhi National Rural Employment Guarantee Scheme (MGNREGS)[7]

Tripura has been ranked first among all States in the North-East region for six consecutive years in terms of performance of the Mahatma Gandhi National Rural Employment Guarantee Scheme (MGNREGS), and fifth nationally.[8] Usami (2016) measured performance on the basis of the following indicators: coverage of job cards, percentage of registered households (with job cards) that received employment, and number of person-days of employment per household. On the first indicator, there are problems with data as the number of registered households in the MIS or Management Information System and as estimated from NSS data are very different. Nevertheless, one can conclude that around 80 per cent of households in Tripura had job cards.

In all the North-Eastern States including Tripura, a very high proportion of registered households received employment. In 2015–16, 93 per cent of registered households received employment under MGNREGS in Tripura, and the proportion was 90 per cent or more in the previous five years (Usami 2016). In most other States, less than half the registered households received employment. For example, in 2015–16, registered households that received employment in Andhra Pradesh, Madhya Pradesh, and Rajasthan, were 43, 33, and 42 per cent, respectively (*ibid.*).

Thirdly, the number of days of employment provided under MGNREGS

---

[7] This section draws on Usami (2016) and Appendix 1 to chapter 9.
[8] Report in *The Telegraph*, April 26, 2016, as cited in Usami (2016).

to registered households averaged 94.5 days in 2015–16. Further, 50 per cent of registered households received more than 100 days of employment in Tripura as compared to less than 5 per cent at the all-India level, where the norm was 45–50 days of employment per household. The number of work-days in Tripura was exceptionally high.

In short, if we combine coverage (or household reach) and employment provided, Tripura, along with Mizoram and Nagaland (and the North-East in general), is a very high performer (Usami 2016).

Wages paid for MGNREGS work are fixed and notified by the Ministry of Rural Development. The notified wage rate for Tripura was Rs 167 in 2015–16; the average reported wage rate was slightly lower at Rs 159.

The official statistics are mirrored in our three study villages, as our survey showed. The average number of days of employment was highest in Khakchang in Dasda block in North Tripura, followed by Muhuripur in Julaibari block, and Mainama in Manu block.

For "manual worker" households, the average employment generated by MGNREGS was 68 days in Khakchang, though the average was 80 for men and 32 for women. As Table 2 shows, MGNREGS accounted for half the number of days of wage employment obtained by women and 38 per cent by men.

In Mainama, female workers had received 39 days of work in the previous agricultural year through MGNREGS, while male workers received 30 days of employment. In Muhuripur, on average, MGNREGS provided 52 days of employment to female workers and 43 days to male manual workers.

Wages for MGNREGS work are based on piece-rated contracts and depend on hours of work. The survey found that the average wage rate for MGNREGS was Rs 150 in Mainama, and Rs 145 to Rs 181 in Khakchang for female and male workers respectively. However, the wage rate for

Table 2 *Average number of days of wage employment obtained by hired manual workers under MGNREGS and total days of wage employment (WE), by sex, study villages, 2015–16, in days*

Sex	Mainama (MGNREGS)	Mainama (WE)	Khakchang (MGNREGS)	Khakchang (WE)	Muhuripur (MGNREGS)	Muhuripur (WE)
Females	39	75	32	62	52	113
Males	30	164	80	211	43	150
All workers	34	127	68	172	46	140

Source: Survey data.

Table 3 *Employment under MGNREGS*, in per cent and days

Village	Block	Percentage of households that received employment	Average days of employment per household
Mainama	Manu	59	73
Muhuripur	Jolaibari	81	90
Khakchang	Dasda	88	109

Source: Survey data.

MGNREGS was reported at around Rs 160 in Muhuripur. The average daily wage of female workers was Rs 170 in Khakchang, which was the highest among the three villages.

In Tripura, MGNREGS was available to a large section of the village population (Table 3). Over 80 per cent of households reported benefits from MGNREGS in Muhuripur and Khakchang. Adding the employment under MGNREGS for men and women within a household, on average, the days of employment obtained per household were 109 in Khakchang, 90 in Muhuripur, and 73 in Mainama (Table 3).

Computing wage earnings from MGNREGS, the contribution of these earnings to household incomes ranged from 4 per cent in Mainama and 8 per cent in Muhuripur to 12 per cent in Khakchang. If we consider only landless households with a major source of income from wage labour, that is, "manual worker" households, MGNREGS wage earnings contributed around 35 per cent of total incomes in Khakchang, 22 per cent in Mainama, and 30 per cent in Muhuripur.

It is clear that at the time of our surveys in 2016, wage earnings from MGNREGS constituted an important form of income support for manual worker households, accounting for one-fifth to one-third of aggregate household incomes.

Livelihood Support

As documented in earlier chapters of this book, the Government of Tripura had several schemes for livelihood support in rural areas, especially to promote improved rice production, different forms of animal rearing, and rubber cultivation on uplands. To promote the System of Rice Intensification (SRI), the government provided a kit with 1 kg of paddy seeds, 10 kg of urea, 5 kg of superphosphate, and a cash grant of around Rs 2,000, to meet labour and other costs. Paddy cultivation was thus significantly subsidised. This scheme was operational in Mainama and Muhuripur. In addition, there were subsidies for the purchase of agricultural machinery. In Mainama, for instance, 65 per cent of diesel pumps in use, 40 per cent of power tillers, and 59 per cent of sprayers were either subsidised or given free of cost. In addition, in Muhuripur, there had been public investment in irrigation over the years, and at the time of our survey, publicly funded river lift irrigation schemes provided 85 per cent of total irrigation. There were also a range of schemes to support animal rearing and fisheries.

Last but not the least, promotion of rubber plantations was a major focus of the Government of Tripura, and has been discussed in detail in chapter 13. The introduction of rubber, as D. Narayana argues, "brought a new dimension to rehabilitation. It was instrumental in settling tribal households in a select location with better access to health and education services." Tribal households were given support of various kinds, including planting material, other inputs, extension information, subsidies, and of course market support for the purchase of rubber. Rubber cultivation is clearly a new source of income, and has even higher potential in the future.

This book has attempted to analyse economic conditions in rural Tripura in the contemporary period. The analysis in the book is based mainly on three in-depth household-level village surveys conducted in 2016. Our study shows the remarkable progress – led by State intervention – in respect of multiple indicators of well-being that was achieved in Tripura. It also deals with the challenges that remained to be addressed.

Although the Left Front was defeated in the Assembly elections of 2018 (and in the Parliamentary elections of 2019), the record is clear: whatever the tasks that remained undone, the years of Left Front government were years of a radical and progressive transformation of agrarian relations, and of improvement in the standards of living of the mass of rural people – tribal and non-tribal.

References

Dutta, Ritam (2017), "Forest Rights Act," *Notes from Socio-Economic Surveys of Three Villages in Tripura*, available at http://fas.org.in/wp-content/themes/zakat/pdf/Tripura-Notes/FRA_Tripura.pdf, viewed on October 30, 2018.

Government of Tripura (GoT) (2007), *Tripura Human Development Report 2007*, Government of Tripura, Agartala, available at http://planningcommission.nic.in/plans/stateplan/sdr_pdf/tripura%20hdr.pdf, viewed on September 13, 2018.

Government of Tripura (GoT) (2018), *Draft Tripura Human Development Report 2018*, available at https://planning.tripura.gov.in/sites/default/files/Draft%20Tripura%20Human%20Development%20Report%20%28THDR%29%20-%20II%2010%20April%202018.compressed.pdf, viewed on September 13, 2018.

Patra, Subhajit (2017), "Public Distribution System in Tripura," *Notes from Socio-Economic Surveys of Three Villages in Tripura*, available at http://fas.org.in/wp-content/themes/zakat/pdf/Tripura-Notes/PDS_Tripura.pdf, viewed on October 30, 2018.

Ramachandran, V. K., and Swaminathan, Madhura (2017), "The Tripura Model," *The Hindu*, available at https://www.thehindu.com/opinion/op-ed/the-tripura-model/article20461140.ece, viewed on September 13, 2018.

Sen, Amartya (2018), "Foreword," *Tripura Human Development Report 2018*, Government of Tripura, Agartala.

Usami, Y. (2016), "A Note on MGNREGA in Tripura," prepared for the Consultation on Three Villages, Agartala, March 18.

Contributors

SANDIPAN BAKSI, Director, Foundation for Agrarian Studies, Bengaluru.

SUMEDHA BAJAR, Assistant Professor, National Institute of Advanced Studies, Indian Institute of Science, Bengaluru.

RANJINI BASU, Research Scholar, Tata Institute of Social Sciences, Mumbai.

SANJUKTA CHAKRABORTY, Senior Data Analyst, Foundation for Agrarian Studies, Bengaluru.

PALLAVI CHAVAN, researcher on rural credit, Mumbai.

ARINDAM DAS, Joint Director, Foundation for Agrarian Studies, Bengaluru.

RITAM DUTTA, Senior Data Analyst, Foundation for Agrarian Studies, Bengaluru.

SAQIB KHAN, Research Scholar, Tata Institute of Social Sciences, Mumbai.

RAKESH MAHATO, Senior Data Analyst, Foundation for Agrarian Studies, Bengaluru.

TAPAS SINGH MODAK, Programme Manager, Foundation for Agrarian Studies, Bengaluru.

D. NARAYANA, Director, Gulati Institute of Finance and Taxation, Thiruvananthapuram.

SUBHAJIT PATRA, Senior Data Analyst, Foundation for Agrarian Studies, Bengaluru.

V. K. RAMACHANDRAN, Vice Chairman, Kerala State Planning Board, Thiruvananthapuram.

SHAMSHER SINGH, Assistant Professor, Flame University, Pune.

MADHURA SWAMINATHAN, Professor and Head, Economic Analysis Unit, Indian Statistical Institute, Bengaluru.

YOSHIFUMI USAMI, Research Fellow, University of Tokyo, Japan.

SURJIT VIKRAMAN, Associate Professor, National Institute of Rural Development and Panchayati Raj, Hyderabad.